Stories Beneath the Stones

The Hidden History of a Small Texas Town
Told Through the Lives of Those Buried in the City Cemetery

Canton, Texas

Lawrence O. Greer
Benja Pittman Mize

L&M
Greer Publishing
Canton, Texas

Stories Beneath the Stones: The Hidden History of a Small Texas Town Told Through the Lives of Those Buried in the City Cemetery.

L&M Greer Publishing. Canton, TX.

Library of Congress Control Number: 2017957156

ISBN 978-0-692-96285-5

For my wife, Mickie, who has tolerated my genealogy hobby for many years; my children, Donna and Edward; my son Justin, who passed away while serving as Van Zandt County Assistant District Attorney; and my pioneer ancestors who are buried in Hillcrest Cemetery. Peace to their bones.
Lawrence O. Greer

For Eddy, Kim, Brittany, and Taylor Mize; the two Jackie's—Jackie Mize and Jackie Pittman; and my Little Brother (Mike) for being my best buddy. I also want to recognize the dozens of people buried in Hillcrest's Unmarked Graves. We tried to tell your stories. We know you are there. A special "thank you" to Mickie Greer for letting me camp out in her favorite chair for many, many days.
Benja Pittman Mize

The authors' first intent in writing this book was to honor the individuals buried in the Hillcrest Cemetery of Canton, Texas, by telling their stories.

We reviewed thousands of newspaper articles, death notices, death certificates, courthouse records, funeral home records, published books, census records, prison records, records from many other sources, and conducted personal interviews. We often found conflicting information, information that could not be confirmed, and old tombstones that were almost impossible to read. We used our best judgment to determine which information to use in bringing the stories together. For any inadvertent errors or omissions, we sincerely apologize.

Lawrence O. Greer
Benja Pittman Mize

Stories Beneath the Stones

Quiet. Peaceful.
I sit on a hill looking at the graves.
Did you die too young to fulfill your dreams?
Did you watch your children die despite your prayers?
Tell me your story. I will listen.

I will listen to your joys.
I will listen to your heartbreaks.
Tell me the stories beneath these stones.

Tell me your story. I will listen.
We will laugh together.
We will cry together.
Tell me your hopes, your dreams.
Tell me your stories. I will listen.
I will listen.

2017
Benja Pittman Mize

"Those who forget to cherish the memory of the dead
are not likely to be overly true in their affection
for the living."

ca. 1888
William Edmund "Ed" Foster
(Buried in Hillcrest Cemetery)

Acknowledgments

The authors are indebted to a great many people for invaluable help in bringing *Stories Beneath the Stones* into book form. It would have been virtually impossible to produce this book without the availability of material previously published by Van Zandt County Genealogical Society members. In addition to friends and family members who encouraged us to not give up, we want to thank the following for their special assistance:

Book Design:
Janis Dworkis for integrating these stories and pictures to help make it all come alive, and for her editorial contributions.

Research Material:
Sibyl Creasy for six volumes of *Early Van Zandt County Obituaries* and *Van Zandt County Civil War Veterans Books*,
Elvis Allen for *Commissioners Court Minutes, Volumes A, B, and C* and for *Building A County*,
Linda Mays for *Reconstruction in Van Zandt County*,
Betty Miller for her alphabetical listing of the Hillcrest Cemetery marked graves,
Cary Hilliard and Margaret Hoot for providing information on the Hilliard Family,
Kitty Wheeler for *Post Offices of Van Zandt County*.

Cemetery Photography:
Tom Tyler for special cemetery pictures,
Faith Caughron for excellent tombstone pictures and her dedication in researching the tombstone locations,
Dave Tunnel for comprehensive identification and photographs of all the tombstones in the Cemetery.

Family Photographs:
Dr. Billy Glenn Foster,
The Hilliard Family,
Diane Taylor Norrell.

Consultation:
Margaret Hoot for her editing of the final draft of the manuscript,
Mickie Greer for her proofreading of numerous drafts,
Vanessa Scott for her assistance with the African-American Section of the Cemetery,
Tom Tyler for his assistance with Find A Grave,
Sibyl Creasy for her assistance in drafting the manuscript,
Bert and Michele Fite, publishers of the "Grand Saline Sun."

Special Acknowledgment: Tommy Eubank, Brian Bass, and the staff at Eubank Funeral Home; Bryan Hilliard and the staff at Hilliard Funeral Home for providing access to their records

Contents

Foreword

I remember only one show-and-tell treasure from fourth grade.

A classmate brought in his family history, a bound volume in which the current family members provide their most recent information and the genealogy company fills in the rest all the way back to King John in 1215, along with a family crest that was probably more conjectural than authentic. It was something most of us had never seen before. But even as a 9-year-old, I sensed that it was impressive but not impactful. It was simply a bunch of names and dates with no meaning, no emotional connection to my classmate or his parents. It might as well have been random entries out of the phone book.

Had Lawrence O. Greer and Benja Pittman Mize gone only to that same depth in this book—merely indexing the names and dates of those buried in Hillcrest Cemetery—this book would have been a useful reference, but its impact would have stopped at the county line.

By going so much deeper, they have created a work much more meaningful and of a significantly broader appeal. In these compelling biographies, the authors have brought to life more than a thousand of their forebears and dearly departed friends.

Looking at the sources the authors consulted and receiving updates throughout the process, I can attest that countless hours have been spent adding layer upon layer of information and substance. The publication, this labor of love, reflects research in unexpected places and previously forgotten documents. Such underutilized sources such as funeral home records, occupation tax rolls, newspaper articles, and family interviews along with local and state archives combine to pay tribute to and revive the memories of those buried at Hillcrest Cemetery, including many dozens resting in unmarked graves. Many of the photographs and family stories collected here are being published for the very first time. You'll find that the joys and accomplishments, disasters and sorrows of these individuals have not been diminished by the passage of time. It is not only enjoyable but an honor getting to "know" these people, all of whose life stories deserve this retelling.

I hope this book gains a wide audience. Current and future citizens of Canton will benefit from absorbing an accurate and detailed history of how their town came to be. All who conduct research in local history can gain insight from the citations, methodology, and presentation to influence their own work. And all of us can relate to the stories told here of individuals, families, and a city, all shaped by a unique combination of tragedies and triumphs. This is a work not just for descendants or for residents, but for all of us.

May the legacy of *Stories Beneath the Stones* be the restored remembrance of the pioneers and neighbors of this community, a greater appreciation of those who have gone before us, and a better understanding of our own place in history.

"From one man he made all the nations, that they should inhabit the whole earth; and he marked out their appointed times in history and the boundaries of their lands." – Acts 17:26

Bob Brinkman
Texas Historical Commission
Austin, Texas
Summer, 2017

INTRODUCTION

Why would two aging genealogists from a small town in East Texas decide to write a biography of everyone buried in a city cemetery? All 1,263 of them? Why would we even start what would seem to be such an impossible project?

The truth is that all our many reasons can be summed up in one word: curiosity. Who were these people, these long-forgotten people who occupy the ground beneath the gravestones at Hillcrest Cemetery? Very simply, we wanted to know —and from the beginning, we believed their stories would be *worth* knowing. But there was no way we could have imagined the wonderful histories we would uncover, the courage and grit of these local pioneers, and the very many ways in which their stories would enrich our own.

Initially, we envisioned this book as a collection of brief narratives showing birth and death dates, marriage partners and parents' names. Like most researchers and writers, we intended to piggyback on the work of scholars who had already developed the style and outlay of material while publishing similar books. But we could not find books covering material we could use as an example.

After several attempts at various methods, we decided to create an alphabetical listing of the names. We started one name and one tombstone at a time. But if it sounds like the work would be plodding and boring, we assure you it never was. We began to uncover stories that had never been collected and written down. We felt as if we were on a treasure hunt with all its attendant excitement. As our work progressed, we realized we could construct rich biographical images from the past and offer an array of interesting local stories, stories that reflected not only the history of families in our area, but the history of Canton itself. Through this labyrinth of discovery, we had indeed found our treasure.

This is a unique group of people who lived very separate lives, but whose journeys all ended at rest in one little area of one little town. This collection of stories provides an amazing glimpse back into a 150-year period of time. Through these individual stories, the researchers—and now the readers—could glimpse a way of life that is now long gone. From those who entered Van Zandt County when it was nothing but wilderness, to slaves who lived to see emancipation and establish community, to the doctors and lawyers whose skills supported these pioneers, to the merchants who raised the town square, to the parents who buried child after child and somehow kept on going, to those buried under large monuments and those whose unmarked graves required hours of research to identify. Our lives are made larger by each of their stories, and it is our hope yours will be, too.

We know that one day, each of us will have passed on, and a time will come when no one remembers our name. That is the human condition. What an honor it was for us to have uncovered these stories, to help these individuals "live" again, to bring them back into the world by speaking their names and telling at least something of their life stories.

We tried our best to do them justice.

HILLCREST CEMETERY

History of Canton and Its Burial Ground

The earliest known settlers in the area that would become Canton, Texas were the Caddo Indians who had occupied the area for many generations before the white settlers arrived. Late in the eighteenth century disease and threats from other Indians forced the Caddos to leave the area. The Cherokee and associated tribes began to arrive during the early part of the 1800s when the Spanish were still in control of Mexico. Having been given certain squatters' rights to the land by the Spanish, the Cherokee eventually occupied a large portion of what would become the counties of Cherokee, Rusk, Smith, and Van Zandt. However, after Texas won its independence from Mexico, the new government refused to provide the Cherokee with permanent title to their lands, which created friction between the Cherokees and their neighbors, the white settlers. Eventually, their leader, Chief Bowl was killed; and the Cherokee were expelled from the area in 1839. In 1848, Van Zandt County was created by the Texas State Legislature from part of Henderson County and named for Republic of Texas leader Isaac Van Zandt. Jordan Saline was the first county seat. In 1850 Wood County was carved out of Van Zandt County; and the Texas State Legislature moved the Van Zandt county seat closer to the center of the county and named it Canton.

Few people lived in the area at that time, only about 500 to 600 in the whole county, having come from numerous locations for a variety of reasons. Those who came in during the 1850s more than likely had acquired a land grant. Later settlers came mostly to get away from wherever they had been living for one reason or another. Some individuals came who knew people already in the area, but mostly people immigrated to the area in groups. These early settlers were mostly from the South and brought with them their social and economic traditions of that region. The economy was largely subsistence farming until 1873 when the coming of the railroad opened the markets to other areas.

Hillcrest Cemetery is nearly as old as Canton itself. It is the town's first large burial ground and the oldest historic landmark in the city. No deed of record has ever been found, so the exact date the cemetery became active is not known. But we do know that the first people who died in Canton were not buried in the Cemetery. In 1851, a mother and child were buried in what would become a residential section of the city, although the exact location of these first graves has been lost to memory.

From the very beginning, anyone who died in the area could be buried there regardless of age, gender, race, ethnicity, religion, or economic status. However, for many years, the Cemetery was segregated by race, with African-Americans buried in the small northern section that was known historically as the Canton Colored Cemetery. It wasn't until 1888 that a physical boundary separated the two areas. That's when a barbed-wire fence was installed to delineate the boundaries of the entire Cemetery property and to establish a border between the white and "colored" burial areas.

The Cemetery was never platted into individual lots, and the early settlers of Canton and the surrounding area were allowed to select burial sites of their own choosing. Unfortunately, there is no record of the first person buried in the cemetery and it is impossible to precisely determine how many bodies lie in unmarked graves. In the early years, some of the settlers could not afford markers, and the passage of time has exacted a toll on many of the oldest markers and obscured the location of the earliest burials.

For eighty-five years, the burial ground was known as City Cemetery or Canton Cemetery. Then, in 1935, the Iris Garden Club, with Mae Stanford as president, held a contest to name the Cemetery and bring attention to the property. Mae Stanford herself submitted the winning name, and that same year an arch with the name Hillcrest Cemetery was placed over the main entrance. Eighty-two years later, that same arch still marks the Cemetery entrance.

Who's Buried Where?

Hillcrest Cemetery is composed of three sections: the original area for whites, the previously segregated African-American section, both of which are overseen by the City of Canton, and a private area known as the Hilliard Section. In 1916, Van Zandt County Commissioners transferred some land to the Hilliard Mercantile Company for use as a cemetery, and in 1925, the City of Canton transferred additional land to S. F. Hilliard, Sr., completing the Hilliard section as it is today. Within the confines of the cemetery are buried the farmers, merchants, businessmen, County Commissioners, County Judges, Sheriffs, Councilmen, State Representatives, U. S. Congressmen, attorneys, doctors, ministers, school teachers, and "just plain folks" who all together over many years formed a tightly knit extended community. Blacks, whites, slaves, slave owners, the strong, the weak, murderers, the murdered, paupers, and the wealthy are all buried in the Cemetery.

Hillcrest Cemetery is so deeply connected to the town of Canton that it could rightly be called its "Silent City of the Dead."

Canton citizens gathered together ca. 1900. Those buried in Hillcrest Cemetery include (l. to r.) back row: David Thompson "Tom" Riley, Morgan Gurley Sanders, Mattie "Fannie" Farmer, Albert Sidney "Mr. Sid" Nolen, Jessie Riley Nolen, Sidney James "Mr. Sid" McCauley, Mary Daisy Riley; middle row: Charles Thomas "Chuck" McCauley, Lucy Ethel Lively, Bird Riley, Minnie Maud Williams, Daisy Lucille Starnes, Spencer Starnes; front row: Charles Henry Grady Davis, Andrew Dean Mathis.

This gathering of Canton citizens ca 1890s includes three men now buried in Hillcrest Cemetery: David Love Riley, Jr. (back row) and Thomas Jones Foster Sr. and Thomas Jefferson "Captain" Towles (front row l. to r.)

Canton School Board early 1900s. Members now buried in Hillcrest Cemetery include (l. to r.): James Thomas "J.T." Todd, Jesse Taylor "J.T." Hodges, James Thomas "Tom" Beard, Jesse Smith, Claud L. "Judge" Stanford, George McIntosh Hilliard, Sr.

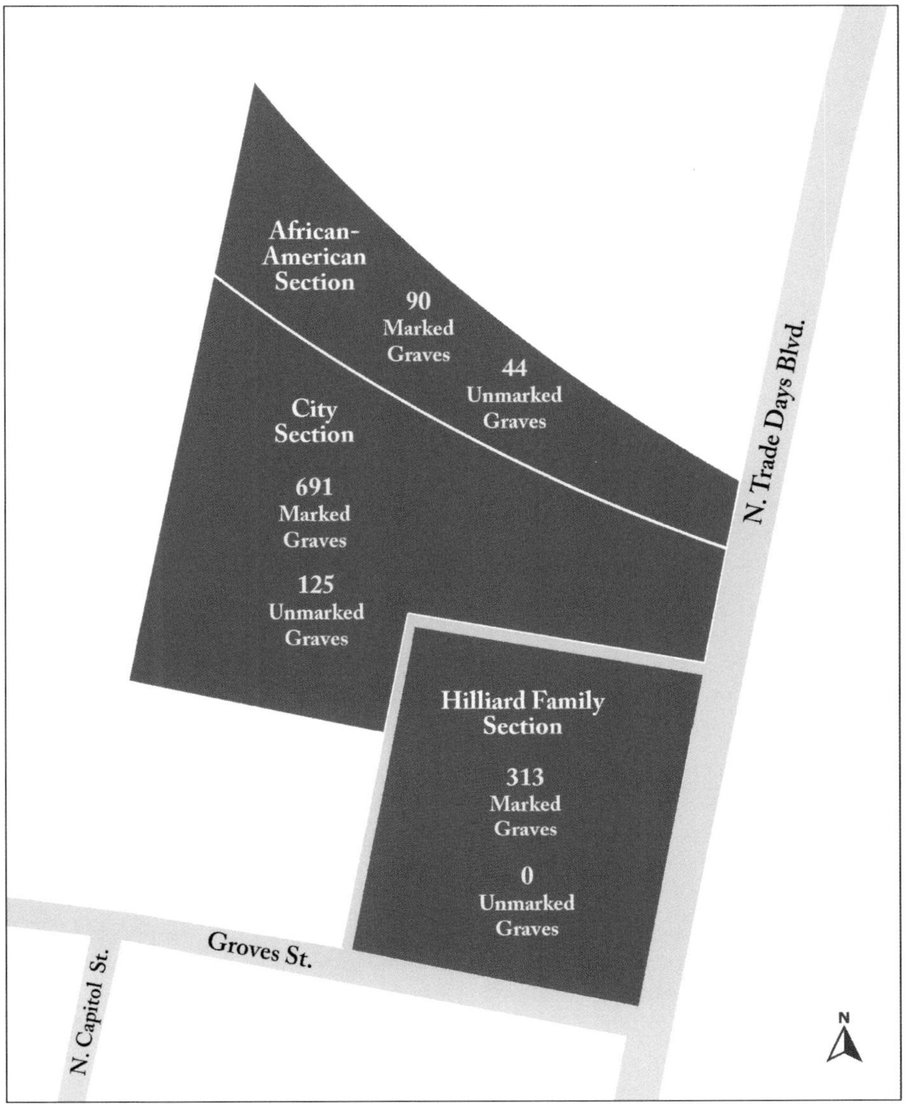

Hillcrest Cemetery
Canton, Texas
Schematic

The following pages contain lists of those buried in marked graves in each of the three sections of Hillcrest Cemetery. However, it's almost impossible to determine how many individuals are buried in unmarked graves. In the early years, some of the settlers could not afford markers of any kind. In addition, the passage of time has exacted a toll on many of the oldest markers and on the location of the earliest burials. But those buried in unmarked graves deserve to have their stories remembered as well as anyone else, and the authors have done their best to bring those stories to light in this book (***page 173***).

The authors have identified 1,263 burials in Hillcrest Cemetery. This includes 1,094 marked graves and 169 unmarked. The total includes 256 children of which 214 are marked and fifty-three are unmarked. The oldest marked grave is that of Matthew Wilhite, who died in 1858. The second oldest grave is that of Ann Calhoon in 1860. The authors found 134 African-Americans buried in the Cemetery, including fourteen who were born into slavery and lived through the Civil War to emancipation. Although some left the area after the War, several Freedmen stayed in the Canton area, setting down roots and purchasing land for themselves and extended family. Many of these families came together to create the Wynne Community.

Hillcrest Cemetery
Marked Graves in African-American Section

Aubrey, Jaceller "Jack"
Bell, William A.
Boles, Leroy
Bowles, Bessie Wynne
Bowles, John Wesley
Bowles, John Wesley
Bowles, Maggie
Bowles, Uyless
Bowman, Lela Francis
Brown, Ed
Castle, Sam
Cornelius, Owen C.
Cornelius, Tom G.
Davis, Sidney
Fitzgerald, Curtis Rudoph "Tinker"
Fitzgerald, Easter Mae
Fitzgerald, Eugene
Fitzgerald, Frank Lee
Fitzgerald, Infant
Fitzgerald, Jessie Henry
Fitzgerald, Perry
Fitzgerald, Walter Perry
Fitzgerald, Willie
Fitzgerald, Zeffie Telasca
Gray, Callie Mae
Gray, Dealy Burton "D.B."
Gray, John Wesley "Bud"
Greer, Anna Bell
Hardman, Fannie
Harris, Johnnie Ray
Howard, Lottie
Johnson, Elmer Lee "Soldier Boy"
Johnson, Hester
Johnson, Rachel
Johnson, Sandy
Jones, Charlie Lee
Mathes, Easter
Mathes, Thomas M.
Mathis, King William
Mathis, Linnie M.
Mathis, Naomi Ethelene
Matthews, Adam
Matthews, Sprig
McDaniel, Lovie
Mitchell, Kevon Lamont
Nelson, Baby Girl
Nelson, Bernice S.
Nelson, Virginia Lois
Pickens, Jarvis Eugene
Prestley, Rufus
Priesley, Infant
Priesley, J. S.
Read, Lennis H.
Rice, Maudella
Ross, L. V.
Sanders, Pauline B.
Scates, Jerry
Shamlin, Evelyn
Shamlin, Napoleon
Shamlin, Oscar, Sr.
Shamlin, Taylor
Shamlin, Willie Mae
Shannon, Buck
Shannon, Edmond Davis
Shannon, Lucy Ann
Shaw, Dave
Shaw, Donnel
Shaw, Douglas, Jr.
Shaw, Douglas, Sr.
Shaw, Lonnell
Shaw, Madelene "Mayde"
Smith, Annie
Smith, Berry
Smith, Henry Hawthorne
Smith, Lannie Bell
Smith, Mary
Smith, Walter
Taylor, Judy
Wells, Leta Belle
Williams, Louvennie "Vena"
Wilson, Emma Lou
Winn, Columbus
Wynne, Edmond Arnold
Wynne, Ella
Wynne, James Henry "Jim"
Wynne, Jesse Chapman "Bud"
Wynne, Jessie Captain
Wynne, Joseph E. "Uncle Bud"
Wynne, Martha
Wynne, Martha Louise

Hillcrest Cemetery
Marked Graves in Main City Section

Abbe, Margaret Caroline
Adams, Mollie B.
Albright, Alice
Albright, Dave Owens
Alexander, Matty W.
Allen, Anna Belle
Allen, Dewdrop
Allen, Hattie Belle
Allen, Henry D.
Allen, Nettie
Andrews, Bertha Josephine
Andrews, William Hatley
Arendall, Jesse H.
Bagby, Charlie
Bagby, Elizabeth Fountain
Bagby, Nannie Lou
Baker, Doris Maume
Baskin, Francis Amandaline Thomson
Baskin, William Leroy
Beard, George W.
Beard, Henry Britton
Beard, Jolly Truman
Beard, Sarah Ann
Blackwell, Henry Fisher, II
Blackwell, Henry Fisher, Jr.
Blackwell, Infant
Blackwell, Katie S.
Blackwell, Nancy Jane "Nannie"
Blount, Jessamine K.
Branson, Alice M.
Branson, Isadore A. "Dora"
Branson, James B.
Branson, Jimmy Wilson
Branson, (Carpenter) Mattie Lorene
Branson, Nettie Alice
Branson, Wesley B.
Brockeem, (Brackeen) M. J. M.
Brooks, Ambrose J.
Brooks, Infant
Brooks, Joe Ambrose
Brooks, Lucretia Martin "Cretia"
Brummett, Ida
Brummett, Samuel Rice
Bryant, Wesley Homer
Bunch, Verna Maxine
Burden, Cloyd
Burden, James Edward "Jim"
Burden, James Moore
Burden, Loyd
Burden, Myrtle
Burden, Nevada M. "Vada"
Burden, Nora Genettie
Burden, Viola Mae
Burge, Alex, Jr.

Burge, Alexander "Alex"
Burge, Howard
Burge, Josephine "Josie"
Burk, J. F.
Burk, M. E.
Burk, Willie
Burns, Alice C.
Burns, Missouri A.
Cain, David Lott
Calhoon, (Calhoun) Rachel Ann
Calhoun, Arthur
Calhoun, Baby Daughter
Calhoun, Mrs. Newtie
Canterbury, Clement Anna
Canterbury, John Franklin
Carroll, Ruth
Chaney, Annie Bell
Chaney, Annie Maude
Chaney, Benjamin Burgess
Chaney, Benjamin McClellan "Mack"
Chaney, Benjamin Oscar
Chaney, Gladys
Chaney, Lucy Phillip
Chaney, Ludy Pennington
Chaney, Margaret Ann
Chaney, Mary M. "Mollie"
Chaney, Robert Lee
Chaney, Thomas Washington
Chappell, Baby
Chappell, Hallie
Chappell, Jane
Chappell, Jeff David "J. D."
Chappell, Mastin
Chitty, Melvin Calvin
Chitty, Melvin, Jr.
Chitty, Owen Leonard
Chitty, (Hargrove) Viola "Ola"
Clancy, John E.
Clark, Artie May
Clark, Doc Franklin
Clark, Elizabeth Averilla
Clark, Fannie Aurellia
Clark, Francis May "Fannie"
Clark, Infant
Clark, Ophelia
Clark, Percy R.
Clark, Samuel Benjamin
Clark, Sarah Chapman
Clark, William Thomas "Tom"
Clifton, George Turner
Clifton, Kate Zora
Clifton, Mable
Coleman, Serena Rachel "Rena"
Coleman, William David
Cooper, Arthur
Cooper, Louis Henry "Ludie"
Couch, Clara Effie
Couch, Rube T.
Couch, Thomas W.
Couch, William Francis
Covert, May Virginia
Cox, Elizabeth Ann "Eliza"
Cox, George W.
Cox, Ida M.
Cox, Mattie E.
Cox, Ramon Loy
Cox, Richard
Cox, Richard E.
Cox, Unknown
Craft, Elizabeth E. "Bettie"
Craft, James A.
C.W.J.
Darden, Charlie
Davis, Alexander M.
Davis, Charles C. "Captain"
Davis, Charles Henry Grady
Davis, Jack
Davis, Little Sam
Davis, Nancy J.
Davis, Sarah Adelaide
Day, Darcy
Day, Felix
Day, Laddie Allen
Day, (Hutcherson) Martha Eula
Day, Sara Caroline
Dean, Melrose Chitty
Dodson, Ion
Dodson, James Frank
Dowdle, Eliza Jane
Downing, Charity Mira
Downing, Edith
Downing, Giles L.
Downing, Infant Daughter
Downing, Maggie
Downing, Nora Lee
Downing, Norah M.
Downing, Ollie
Downing, Thomas Jefferson "Tommy"
Dubose, Annie Lee
Dubose, Elmer Scott
Dubose, Fannie Beatrice
Dubose, Infant
Dubose, Mary Ann
Dubose, Milton Lee
Dunn, John D.
Dunn, Ola Hayes
Eads, William Alexander
Edwards, Cliddie "Clyde"
Engledow, Elvira Elizabeth
Evans, Jacob Alfred "Jake"
Everett, Elizabeth "Bettie"
Everett, George W.
Everett, Hugh Ellis
Everett, Lee Perry
Everett, Sidney Polk
Flatt, Annie Jewell
Flatt, James Arthur
Ford, B.
Ford, Blanche Mann
Ford, C.
Ford, Cora Bailey
Ford, Fredonia Catherine Hubbard
Ford, H.
Ford, Howell Elmore
Ford, J.
Ford, Jennie
Ford, M.
Ford, Robert Edward
Foster, Bessie
Foster, Eliza Willet "Willie"
Foster, Francis Ann
Foster, Infant
Foster, Infant
Foster, Marcus H.
Foster, Margaret Jane "Maggie"
Foster, Minnie Pulliam
Foster, Oscar Thompson
Foster, Thomas Jones, Jr.
Foster, Thomas Jones, Sr. "Judge"
Foster, William Edmund "Ed"
Fuller, Rev. James Marvin
Fuller, Janie Blackwell
Galloway, Francis Orman "Shorty"
Galloway, Francis Orman, Jr.
Galloway, Vernice Roberts
Gamel, Emily Christine
Gamel, John Cumby
Gamel, Johnny Lyman
Gamel, Melvin Lawrence
Gamel, Ora Frances
Gardenhire, Agnes Elizabeth
Gardenhire, Blanche Spinks
Gill, John T.
Gilmore, Bernard M.
Gilmore, Sarah Johanna
Gilmore, Wiley Coleman
Gordon, J. D.
Gossett, James P. "J. P."
Gossett, Sallie A.
Graham, Calvin B., Sr.
Griser, Blanche
Griser, Elizabeth M.
Griser, Eugenia Augusta May "Gussie"
Griser, Infant Daughter
Griser, Jesse Daryl
Griser, Jo Ann Williams
Griser, John Kasper
Griser, Kasper George
Groome, Ann Dora
Groome, Coot

Groome, John P.
Groome, Manerva E. "Nannie"
Groome, Sidney
Groome, Thomas
Groves, Carue
Groves, Georgia Davis
Groves, Harvey Addison
Groves, Joseph Alonzo "Joe"
Gullett, James Rufus Benjamin
Hale, James
Hale, Juliette Drinkwater "Julia"
Hale, Walter L.
Hale, Willis Jarrell
Hall, John H.
Hall, Julia Scott
Hall, Maggie Matilda
Hall, Nancy Julia
Hanes, Infant
Hardin, Billie Lyman
Harris, Victoria Jo Wright
Hartman, Mont M.
Hashert, Jerome
Hawkins, Coy
Hawkins, Joe Noel
Hawkins, Ruby R.
Haynes, Andrew Hunter
Haynes, Annie Lee
Haynes, Infant
Haynes, Isaac Edward
Henderson, Susan A.
Herston, Gladys Ona Seale
Highsmith, Brucie
Hilliard, Baby
Hilliard, Ella Thompson
Hilliard, George Mcintosh, Sr.
Hilliard, Ida Frances
Hilliard, Infant Son
Hocutt, John P.
Hodges, Guy
Hodges, Jesse Taylor "J. T."
Hodges, Nancy Ophelia "Nannie"
House, Timothy F.
Hulse, Mary Matilda
Hunt, Billy "Shine"
Hunt, Emogene "Jean"
Hunt, Garry W.
Hurst, Elizabeth P.
Hynes, Jane
Jaaland, Infant
Jackson, Johnie
Jackson, Thomas Eli "Tommie"
Jarvis, Armelia
Jarvis, Cora Allison
Jarvis, Josephine Amanda
Jarvis, Lewis Columbus
Jeter, Allen Yantis
Jeter, Dr. Joseph Joshua
Jeter, Mary Yantis
Johnson, Dr. William Goodman "W. G."
King, Charlie
King, Mary "Polly"
Knox, Anna Viola McClellen
Knox, Dora Effie
Knox, Flossie Vivian
Knox, Georgia Ann
Knox, Samuel Walter
Knox, Wallace Austin
Knox, Walter
Knox, William Montgomery
Lantrip, Delaine Franklin
Lantrip, Emma Etta
Lantrip, John Franklin "Frank"
Lapington, Manervia A.
Manning, Harvey
Manning, James Milo
Manning, John D. Keith
Manning, Martha
Marvin, Harold Wayne
Mathis, Hardy
Mathis, John Bennett "Johnie"
Matthews, Darling Freddie
Matthews,Georgia A.
Matthews, Dr. James L.
Matthews, Lilas Bruce
Maume, Mamie De Lois
McCarty, Benjamin F.
McCarty, Benna
McCarty, Dollie Bell
McCarty, E.
McCarty, Earl
McCarty, Elizabeth A. "Lizzie"
McCarty, Eva
McCarty, John Ross
McCarty, Johnnie
McCarty, Leonard E.
McCarty, Marion
McCarty, Martha Elizabeth
McCarty, Minnie Julia
McCarty, Nancy Averilla
McCarty, Pearley
McCarty, Riley
McCarty, Sarah Ellen
McCarty, Thompson
McCarty, W.
McCarty, William N.
McCarty, William Thompson
McCauley, Birdie Mae
McCauley, Charles Thomas "Chuck"
McCauley, Isaac
McCauley, Lucy Etheleen
McCauley, Lula Grace
McCauley, Richard C.
McCauley, W. E.
McClellen, Andrew Jackson "Jack"
McClellen, Edgar May "Edd"
McClellen, Elizabeth
McClellen, Frances Rachel "Fannie"
McClellen, Infant Daughter
McClellen, Robert, Jr.
McDavid, R. N. "Dick"
McKinnon, Lettie S.
McWilliams, Warren W. "Happy"
Medley, William P
Meredith, Katie P.
Meredith, Willis David
Mills, Cathern Ann
Mills, Cora Almeda
Mills, Edward Hughes
Mills, Homer
Mills, Infant Son
Mills, Infant Twin Daughters
Mills, James Harvey
Mills, Mary Missouri
Mills, Maudie M.
Mills, Robert Padian "Bobbie"
Mills, Roger Q.
Mills, William Samuel
Mitchell, Alice Victoria
Mitchell, Amy Eliza
Mitchell, Baby Girl
Mitchell, Mary M.
Mitchell, Willis Bunyan
Monroe, Jefferson Davis "Jeff"
Moore, Arlene F.
Moore, Bertha Ima
Moore, Dee Otis
Moore, Horace Erskin
Moore, James Elmer "Jimmie"
Moore, John Franklin "Johnny"
Moore, William C.
Morris, Alford Lee
Morris, Jettie Pearl
Morris, Mary Ola
Morris, Maston Alford "Buster"
Morris, Maston Luther
Morris, Myrtle Trava
Morrison, Elsie Josephine
Morrison, William Herbert
Morrissey, James Fair
Nash, Mirada Jane Tracy
Neely, Altha
Neely, Alvia Lee
Neely, Ivy Jane
Neely, James Abraham
Neely, Lela Roberta
Neely, Samuel Acie
Neely, William Carroll
Nolen, Mattie A.
Norman, America Emaline "Emma"
Norman, Jacob A. "Jake"

Nunnally, Sarah Tull
Overturf, Effa Ann
Overturf, Infant Daughter
Overturf, William Ira
Owens, David
Owens, Laura Virginia
Owens, Lucille
Owens, Mytra
Parker, M. J.
Paschall, Mary Mollie
Paschall, William James
Patrick, Annie
Patrick, Baby
Patterson, Elizabeth
Patterson, Francis "Frannie"
Patterson, James Duncan
Patterson, Lucretia
Patterson, Neill B.
Payne, Ruth
Payne, William Leroy
Peace, Clyde Augusta
Peace, Ettie L.
Peace, Everett
Peace, Fannie
Peace, Little Clyde
Penny, Infant (Twin)
Penny, Infant (Twin)
Penny, Josephine "Josie"
Perry, Bake
Perry, Sarah Jane
Petty, Nancy Alice
Petty, S. Jefferson "Jeff"
Petty, Sarah E.
Petty, Velma R.
Phillips, Alice "Allie"
Phillips, John Walter
Prier, Margaret
Prier, Mary A
Prier, William Cats
Pruiett, Myrtle Delilah
Pyron, Elizabeth Ann
Raglin, Baby
Ray, William J.
Redmon, Harold
Reese, Infant Son
Reese, Infant Son
Reese, Mary E
Reese, Walter
Reid, F. Z.
Reid, Luvena A.
Reid, Unknown
Rhodes, Agatha Mae
Richardson, Elisha Levi "Lit"
Richardson, Mary Elizabeth "Eliza"
Riley, Bird Richardson
Riley, Charles Pendleton "Charlie"
Riley, Claude Franklin
Riley, Corrie Richardson
Riley, David Love, Jr.
Riley, David Thompson "Tom"
Riley, Elizabeth
Riley, Infant Son
Riley, Jay Holt
Riley, Lina Hardy
Riley, Mamie Keys
Riley, Mary Daisy
Riley, Nancy Arrabella "Nannie"
Riley, Russell Steel
Roberts, Henry Oliver
Roberts, Mattie Jean "Jane"
Roberts, Sarah Elizabeth
Roberts, Theodore Earnest
Roberts, Thomas Ulysses
Robertson, Elsie Marie
Robertson, Irena
Robertson, John Porter
Robertson, Thomas E.
Rogers, J. E.
Rosinbaum, George Edward "Ed"
Ross, John William
Ross, Martha Onia
Rountree, Elizabeth Grace
Rusek, Madge Connie Lantrip
Russell, James L.
Russell, Jessie
Russell, Leila
Russell, Mary C.
Sambel, Walter William
Samples, Jesse F.
Samples, Jesse H.
Samples, Jettie
Samples, (Sherman) Nancy Jane
Sanders, Claud H.
Sanders, Cora Isabelle
Sanders, Henry
Sanders, James E.
Sanders, Jefferson H.
Sanders, Noma Louisa
Sanders, Sarah Jane
Sansom, George I.
Seale, Angus Truett
Seale, Clara Lavinia
Seale, Henry Jones
Seale, Susan Era
Sherman, Dada
Shettles, John E.
Shettles, Joseph S.
Shettles, Nancy E.
Shipp, Goldie Jewell
Shipp, Richard Dorman
Shivers, John William
Shivers, Mary Lou "Mickey"
Sides, Floy E.
Smith, Alonzo
Smith, Charles P., Jr.
Smith, Dr. Charles Pinkney "Dr. C.P."
Smith, Dorothy Tulula "Lula"
Smith, Dr. Edgar Eugene
Smith, Jesse
Smith, T. M.
Smithart, Jackson H.
Snodgrass, Infant
Snodgrass, Mary E.
Spears, A. Z.
Spears, Charlie L.
Spears, Effie Vesta
Spears, Johnnie A.
Spears, Laveta
Spears, Lucius Mack
Spears, Mary Elizabeth "Mollie"
Spears, Mary Jane
Spears, Mary Zulalee
Spears, Mollie Donnie
Spears, R. B.
Spears, Rufus B.
Spinks, Angus Thompson
Spinks, Elizabeth Z.
Spinks, Gladys Belle
Spinks, John S., Jr.
Spinks, John S., Sr. "Judge"
Spinks, Zollie T.
Springer, Infant Son
Springer, Owen
Staples, Isiah Rayshaun
Staton, Mary Josephine
Stephens, William H.
Strickland, Allen C.
Strickland, David Jackson "Jack"
Strickland, Infant Boy
Strickland, Margaret Ann "Tibbie"
Strickland, Mary A. "Polly"
Stuart, Lucinda C.
Sullivan, William Adolphus "Dot"
Sweatman, Dorothy Marie
Tawater, Helen Mae
Tawater, Noah Franklin "Frank"
Taylor, Little Nora
Taylor, Mitchell,
Taylor, Susan Y.
Teague, Hallie
Teague, Infant
Thames, Amos F.
Thompson, Albert
Thompson, Allen
Thompson, Anna Elizabeth
Thompson, Carlos
Thompson, Elvira
Thompson, Hattie
Thompson, James Carl "Dutch"
Thompson, James P. "Jim"
Thompson, James T.

Thompson, Jeptha Tolliver "Tull"
Thompson, Leah (Infant)
Thompson, Leah Elizabeth "Lizzie"
Thompson, Martha Isabella
Thompson, Molley
Thompson, Moses W.
Thompson, Nannie
Thompson, Obe D.
Thompson, Ora E.
Thompson, Ruby Irene
Thompson, Susan Rebecca
Thompson, William D. "Captain"
Thompson, Willie Fay
Thompson, Willis Milam
Thompson, Zorette
Tillery, N.S.
Tillison, William Preston
Todd, Barney
Todd, Emma Eugene "Toddy"
Todd, Harold Towles
Todd, Henry Grady "Buck"
Todd, James Kernon, Sr.
Todd, James Thomas "J.T."
Todd, Mae
Towles, Annie Alice
Towles, Howard Glenn
Towles, Infant Son
Towles, Johnnie
Towles, Minnie Merle
Towles, Nancy Ann "Nannie"
Towles, Thomas Bonner
Towles, Thomas Jefferson "Captain"
Travis, Eran A. "Eranaslee"
Tripp, James Alfred
Tripp, James T.
Tuggle, Lovie
Tull, Allie Estelle
Tull, Angeline
Tull, Baby
Tull, Bertie
Tull, Frendona Ruth "Dona"
Tull, George Washington, Sr. "G.W."
Tull, Mary Jane Cowen "Mollie"
Tull, Mary Martha Noble
Tull, Noble Napoleon "Polie"
Tull, Thomas G.
Tull, Walter H.
Tull, William Newton
Tumlinson, Horace K
Tumlinson, Louisa
Tunnell, Amphias Seaton "Amp"
Tunnell, May
Tunnell, Sarah "Sallie"
Tunnell, Wilson
Tunnell, Zorado Johnson
Tyler, Ula Lee
Tyler, W. J.
Tyson, John Henry
Utts, Albert J.
Utts, Allena May
Utts, Era Lucille
Utts, Jacob J. "Major"
Utts, Johnie Walter "Waltie"
Utts, Martha Elizabeth "Mattie"
Utts, Maudie D.
Valentine, Azilla House
Valentine, Carrie H.
Valentine, Clark
Valentine, Hardy W.
Valentine, James P.
Valentine, John Leslie, Jr.
Valentine, John Leslie, Sr.
Valentine, Wilma Annie Davis
Valentine, Zilla
Waldrip, Seabie
Walker, Clara Velma
Walker, E. A.
Walker, Francis Marion "Frank"
Walker, Peggy Ann
Walker, Roy Lee
Wallace, J. Frank
Wallace, Thomas W.
Walters, (Guess) Myrtle Mae
Walters, Thomas Jefferson
Ward, Henry Cozelle
Ward, Martha Arletha "Letha"
Ward, William Henry
Warren, Joseph W.
Warren, Josephine
Warren, Watson Norman
Weatherall, Charles L. "Charlie"
Weatherall, Martha Jane "Jennie"
White, Daniel Columbus "D.C."
White, Mary Elizabeth
White, William Franklin
Wilburn, Neppie A.
Wilburn, William Hardy "Bill"
Wilhite, John Harden
Wilhite, Louisa Anna
Wilhite, Matthew Herbert
Wilhite, Nancy Hanna
Wilhite, William Walter
Williams, Isaac Frank
Williams, James G. "Jim"
Williams, Laura
Williams, Merle
Williams, Millard
Williams, Minnie Maud
Williams, Minnie R.
Williams, Nora
Williams, R. Lee
Williams, Rebecca Christman
Williams, Richard "Dick"
Williams, Terah Pearl
Williams, William Oscar
Williams, Dr. William Oscar
Wilson, Eunice E.
Wilson, Vivian
Wood, J. White
Wood, Dr. W. P. "Billie"
Wyatt, Charles W. "Charley"
Yantis, Isabelle California "Belle"
Yantis, Robert Hobbs
Yantis, Thomas Rusk
Youngblood, James Marion
Youngblood, Mary Jane "Mollie"

Hillcrest Cemetery
Marked Graves in Hilliard Section

Allen, Lillian May "Lillie"
Ashworth, Charles W., Jr.
Ashworth, Jack Wesley
Ashworth, Katherine Lucille Kellam
Bailey, Millie Ann
Bandy, Bonnie Lue
Barber, Kathleen Stanford
Bateman, Cora Ann
Bateman, Dr. John Kearby
Bateman, John Willie
Bateman, Nelda Annette
Bateman, Norman Joel
Bateman, Norman Virgil
Beard, Cora Aletha
Beard, James Thomas "Tom"
Belcher, Ella Ruth
Blair, Eva Lee
Brewer, John Earl
Brewer, John Harold
Brewer, Lela Barnett
Campbell, Katie Geraldine "Gerry"
Campbell, Kenny Loyal
Campbell, William Loyal "Chili" "Judge"
Chaney, Charles Max
Chaney, James Clayton
Chaney, James Don
Chaney, Nora Mattie
Chaney, Ronald Lee "Red"
Chaney, Travis Aubrey "Jack"

Clower, Edith Mae
Clower, Walter Ashley
Corry, Frank Augustus
Cox, Altha Lee
Cox, Casey Lee
Cox, Helen Marie
Cox, Isaac Newton "Ike"
Cox, John Wesley
Cox, Lee
Cox, Marion Love
Cox, Millie
Cox, Silas Elam
Cozby, Jettie Sue
Cozby, Knox W.
Davidson, Leaston "Lete"
Davidson, Virginia M.
Davidson, Wiley A.
Dawson, Frank Albert
Dawson, Kathryn M.
Douthit, Calvin Riley
Douthit, Jewel Effiline
Douthit, Mary Elizabeth "Lessie"
Downing, Allen Riley
Downing, Nora Edna
Downing, Thomas Howard
Edwards, Eddie Ruth Terry
Farmer, Mattie "Fannie"
Farrell, Arthur Lee
Farrell, Connie Josephine Heard
Fitzgerald, Dorothy Mae
Fitzgerald, Harvey Joe
Fitzgerald, John Edward
Fitzgerald, Ronald Vernon "Ronnie"
Fizer, James L.
Fizer, Permelia Laura "Mattie"
Foster, Alfred "Alf"
Foster, Annie Velma
Foster, Corine Geddie "Dude"
Foster, Donald Geddie
Foster, Jeffie Lona
Foster, Marcus Columbus
Foster, Tate Ross
Gabbert, Luther Owen "Luke"
Gabbert, Wesson Bruner
Gentry, John William
Gentry, Mary Lou
Gore, George Washington "Wash"
Gray, Ben H.
Gray, Clemmie Lee
Green, Mattie Victoria
Greenway, Ellie Gladys
Greenway, William Bensen
Haynes, Allie
Haynes, William Francis "Bill"
Hays, Margie Mae
Heard, Eleazer Lee "E.A."
Heard, Susan Isabelle "Belle"
Heddins, Eva Jim Rascoe
Heddins, Lettrial
Helms, Effie Lee Oma Gore "Lela"
Hill, Gary Joel
Hill, Lurlyne Travis
Hill, Melvin Bernard
Hilliard, Cathaleen Green
Hilliard, Debbie Denice
Hilliard, Dr. Daniel Richardson
Hilliard, Dr. George Homer, Jr.
Hilliard, Dr. Horace Hampton
Hilliard, Faughlette Pickett
Hilliard, George Curtis
Hilliard, George Homer, Sr.
Hilliard, Gladys Eva
Hilliard, Ida Pina
Hilliard, Lois Marie
Hilliard, Mary Eleanor Bryan
Hilliard, Opal Malinda
Hilliard, Sally Lee
Hilliard, Samuel Foster, Jr. "Sam"
Hilliard, Samuel Foster, Sr. "Foster"
Hilliard, Seth Lee
Hilliard, Sonja Sue Caviness
Hilliard, William Foster "Butch"
Hurst, Joel Evans
Hutchinson, Frank G.
Hutchinson, Susan Elizabeth
Jensen, Gladys Agnes Rhodes
Jensen, Jens Peter
Jensen, Karen Kirstine
Jensen, Martin Peter
Jensen, Myrtle Marie
Johnston, Edith Mellisa
Johnston, Richard Marion
Jones, (Bass) Nora Hope
Jones, Bonteel
Kellam, Dr. Andrew Jackson "Jack"
Kellam, John Mayo
Kellam, Mary Duskie Hilliard
Kellam, William Christine
Knox, (Sumner) Bertha Orlene
Knox, Jesse Alton
Lambright, (Brown) Ida J.
Lambright, Gordon W.
Lewis, Frank McCoy
Lewis, Mary Elizabeth
Lively, Annie Julia Cannon
Lively, Anthony Gordon
Lively, Lucy Ethel
Lively, Robert Maclin
Loughmiller, Dwight Lyman
Loughmiller, George Jasper
Loughmiller, Mary Alice
Loughmiller, Max Edward
Loughmiller, Richard Leon
Loughmiller, Tommie West
Manasco, Lewis McKinzie
Manasco, Sam
Mann, Ben Hill
Mann, Eunice "Una Mae"
Mann, Paul Tillman
Massey, Annie Eleanor
Massey, Belle Nolen
Mathis, Alice Mae
Mathis, Andrew Dean
Mathis, Elizabeth "Bettie Belle"
Mathis, Hugh Nathan
Mathis, Roma Morris
Mathis, Sadie Elizabeth
McCauley, Florence Eva
McCauley, Sidney James "Mr. Sid"
McKenzie, Florence Elizabeth
McKenzie, Rena Sides
McMahon, Anna Beatrice Mayne
Milam, Martha Ann
Milam, Willis Andy
Mitchell, Berry Alvie
Mitchell, Nancy Elizabeth "Nannie"
Mitchell, Sarah Katherine
Mitchell, William B "Brian"
Nichols, Birdie Oleta Bartlett
Nichols, D. W.
Nichols, Daisy Louella
Nichols, Jeanie
Nichols, William Jesse "Willie"
Nolen, Albert Sidney "Mr. Sid"
Nolen, George Tate
Nolen, Jessie Riley
Nolen, Oscar Lee
Ogletree, Sylvia Shuttles
Parker, Eugene M.
Patrick, Mattie Alma
Patrick, Naomia Lucille
Patrick, Thomas Jefferson
Patrick, Virgil Avery
Paul, Emmett David
Paul, Eva Joe
Paul, James Winston
Paul, Mary Jane
Peace, Ada
Perry, Howard Carnelus
Phillips, Henry Lee
Phillips, Infant Son
Phillips, John Henry "Boose"
Phillips, Maudie Lee
Phillips, William Robert "Billy"
Pittman, John M.
Pittman, Sarah E.
Purkey, Lillie Belle
Rasco, Alton M. "Jack"
Rasco, Frank Monroe
Rasco, Mary Elizabeth "Lizzie"
Rasco, Minnie Bell
Rascoe, Jessie James "Jim" "Daddy Jim"
Rascoe, June Julia Oakley
Ratzlaff, Eva Jewell Green

Richards, Randall Elijah
Richards, Ruby Norene "Nonnie"
Richardson, Daniel D.
Richardson, Emily Belsora "Emma"
Riley, Lydia Colon
Riley, Mary Francis "Fannie"
Riley, William Edgar
Roberts, Cory Lee
Robinson, Minnie
Rodgers, Edna Mae
Rodgers, William Brown
Rosemand, Annie Lee
Ross, Clinton "Clint"
Ross, Lillian C.
Rushing, Grady Lee
Rushing, Ruby D.
Sanders, Florence W.
Sanders, Morgan Gurley
Sides, Billy Gene
Sides, Effie Letitia
Sides, Henry Monroe
Sides, James Love
Sides, John Emory
Sides, Katie
Sides, Lewis H. "Lude"
Sides, Lewis Lamar
Sides, Lila Belle
Sides, Lula L.
Sides, Minnie Lee
Sides, Stella M.
Sides, Walter Lee
Sides, William Roy
Simmons, Henry Scott
Simmons, Maude Green
Simmons, Williard G.
Simpson, Frances Merle
Simpson, Frank Foster
Simpson, Jessie Pinkney, Jr.
Simpson, Jessie Pinkney, Sr.
Slaughter, John W.
Slaughter, Manuel Owen "Jim"
Slaughter, Margaret Elizabeth Warren
Staley, Lottie Marie
Staley, Vergie Ina
Staley, Willie Raymond "Wid"
Stanberry, Clarence Teddy "Ted"
Stanberry, Lillie Mae
Stanford, Claud L, Sr. "Judge"
Stanford, Claud Leonidas, Jr. "C.L."
Stanford, Dealva K. "Dee"
Stanford, Georgia Hassell
Stanford, Roxie Mattie
Stanford, Dr. William Jonathan
Starnes, Cameron Spencer, Sr.
Starnes, Daisy Lucille
Starnes, Johnathan Ryan (Twin)
Starnes, Scott Harrison
Starnes, Weldon Bryan (Twin)
Starnes, Weldon F.
Steed, Florence
Steed, Walter Lee
Sumner (Cole) Alma Rivers
Sumner, Benjamin Franklin "Ben"
Sumner, Bonnie Lewis
Sumner, Estelle
Sumner, Homer L.
Sumner, Laymon Lewis
Sumner, Leonard Grady
Sumner, Mary Emma
Sumner, Mary Jeanette "Nettie"
Sumner, Oman
Sumner, Waymon Odell
Teel, Flora Pauline
Terry, Adde Mae
Terry, Eddie Obe
Travis, Allen T.
Travis, Lela Robison
Valdez, Olga Lydia
Venable, Sarah Allyne
Walker, Francis Jeanette "Nettie"
Walker, Frank Leslie
Walker, Mack Gibson
Walker, Scotty M.
Wann, Louis Homer
Wann, Ruby Rae Whitaker
Weatherall, Ernest Rushing
Weatherall, Thomas Dewey
Weatherall, Tula Ann
Weaver, Arthur Wilson
Weaver, Calvin Franklin
Weaver, Ethel Lee
Weldon, Joyce Juanita
Weldon, Nannie Eliza
Weldon, Wilson William
Whitaker, Earnest Glen
Whitaker, Rosa Pearl
White, Jessie G. Johnson
White, Junius Eugene "June"
Wilson, Drayton William
Wilson, Francis Henry "Frank"
Wilson, Gladys Ruth
Wilson, Mamie Wanda
Wilson, Mary Isabell
Wisdom, Gloria Ann
Wisenteiner, Betty Louise Nolen
Wisenteiner, Herman Francis
Woods, Martha Ann "Mattie"
Woods, Mittie Ann
Woods, William Forest
Woods, William Jasper

Hillcrest Cemetery
Unmarked Graves in African-American Section

Bell, Easter M.
Bell, Green
Bowles (Boles), Abe J.
Bowman, Charlie Percy
Brown, Nelce
Bunn, Alberta
Carr, Sallie
Cooper, Larry Ladell
Cooper, Lola
Fitzgerald, Albert
Fitzgerald, Cordy Mae
Fitzgerald, Earnest
Fitzgerald, Eddie Dean
Fitzgerald, Jessie "Red"
Fitzgerald, Lottie
Fitzgerald, Lum
Fitzgerald, May F.
Fitzgerald, Tiny
Fitzgerald, Victory
Floyd, De
Franklin, Irene
Gray, L. B.
Hambrick, Trim
Johnson, Pauline
Jones, Lucy
Ladd, Mrs. Lena
Ladd, (Lad) Robert
Lowry, Randal
Mathis, Tom, Jr.
McCoy, David Earl
McMillan, Dorothy
Morris, Baby Girl
Riggs, Mamie
Ross, Jim
Ross, Richard
Scates, Alford
Scates, Angelina
Scates, Henry
Scates, Minnie Bell
Scates, Willie Ruth
Smith, Paul L.
Wilson, J. D., Jr.
Winn, Emma
Wynne, Annie M.

Hillcrest Cemetery
Unmarked Graves in Main City Section

Alexander, Wiley Percy
Allen, A Little Boy
Ballard, Elizabeth
Ballard, John "Johnie"
Beasley, Payton
Bowers, George Henry
Bowers, Robie
Bowers, Sallie Lou
Brazelton, William L.
Brown, Ethel
Brown, R. L.
Brummett, Infant
Brunson, Bertha
Burns, John M.
Burrus, Carl Thomas, Jr.
Chaney, Sarah Elizabeth "Sacky"
Chaney, Zacharia Taylor " Zack"
Clark, Luther James
Compton, James M.
Compton, Josephus Gregory "Seath"
Compton, Mariah Alcey Austin "Lizzie"
Compton, Simpson P.
Cox, Baby
Cox, J. R.
Cullen, Elizabeth
Covert, Patricia
Darden, Charlie
Dearing, Carrie Frances
Dearing, Marvin L.
Dearing, William Conyer "Will"
Denton, Baby
Dubose, Glendora "Glenn"
Engledow, Elizabeth Exonia "Bettie"
Engledow, John Henry
Everett, A Little Child
Evine, Fannie
Ford, A Little Girl
Ford, Duck
Fuller, Edward C. "Uncle Ed "
Fulton, Mrs. Eugene
Goins, Allie Fay
Hashert, Mary, Elizabeth
Haynes Baby
Heard, Mary Matilda Ellen
Henderson, Mastin M.
Highsmith, Louis C.
Huggard, N.
Kellam, James Legitus
Kennedy, Infant
Keoun, J. B.
Kidd, John H.
Kitchens, Palestine "Grandma"
Knox, A Girl
Knox, Blanche
Knox, Jefferson Davis "Jeff"
Knox, Robert M. "Uncle Bob"
Knox, Robert Vasco
Koune, Johnie
Landrum, John W.
Lee, Kissiah Ann
Loughmiller, Reba Francine
Lummus, Eugene
Mansfield, Child
Mansfield, Elzy
Marshall, Georgia
Marshall, James Monroe
Maume, Alice R.
McClellen, Jimmie
McClellen, Sudie
McCord, Baby
McCoy, Earlie Omega
McCoy, Elbert Milton "E. M."
McDougal, Mrs. Walter
McGuire, Alexander H.
McKee, Infant
McKee, Maud
Meadows, Grandma
Melton, Mrs. John H.
Miller, Infant Daughter
Mullins, John Loftin "Uncle John"
Mullins, Mary Elizabeth
Nolen, Walter Andrew Webster
Peace, Baby
Peace, Baby
Pennington, Baby
Perry, Mrs. J. N.
Phelps, Charles
Phillips, Rosa
Phillips, Susan Darlene
Pompey, Martin
Red, Minnie L.
Reese, J. C.
Robertson, "Old Man"
Roe, Mrs. Harry
Rowland, Lanis Leslie
Russell, Ben F.
Russell, David
Russell, Phoeby
Stanford, Martha Jane
Starkey, Fannie
Stewart, Mrs.
Stoudenmire, Fannie K.
Strickland, Cynthia
Sudduth, Debbie Sophronia
Sumner, Monroe Lafayette "Fate"
Terry, Daughter
Thames, Mrs. T. T.
Thomas, Mr.
Thompson, Allen Fletcher
Thompson, Child
Thompson, Mollie
Tumlinson, Cora Merles
Valentine, James E.
Valentine, Murray Lockhart
Waldron, Elizabeth
Waldron, Mary Elizabeth "Bettie"
Walker, Hanna Cathern
Ward, James
Weatherall, Baby Boy
Womack, B. S.
Wortham, Elizabeth
Wortham, Infant
Wright, Jeff Davis
Yantis, Baby
Yantis, Ralph

The Authors Have Identified
1,094 in Marked Graves
169 in Unmarked Graves
1,263 Total
Buried in Hillcrest Cemetery

The Hillcrest Cemetery Restoration Project

Canton was an unincorporated town until 1919 with no ruling body to make decisions. Consequently, any and all improvements to the Cemetery required a volunteer effort. From the very beginning, the townspeople had difficulty adequately maintaining the Cemetery.

Eventually, the years of neglect took their toll and the Cemetery was in serious decline. Trees, shrubs, and vines grew up among the graves obscuring, and in some cases toppling, the grave markers. The aggressive Texas weather slowly destroyed some of the tombstones beyond recognition, particularly those made of softer materials. Inappropriate mowing and vandalism contributed to the steady deterioration and destruction. It finally became clear that without intervention, the elements would reclaim the Cemetery and permanently obscure the resting places and stories of these early settlers. They deserved better.

In 2012, City Councilman Ross Maris brought the situation to the attention of the City Manager, Mayor, and Council members. The City Council formed a twelve-member group called the Hillcrest Cemetery Restoration Committee, with the authors serving as historians on that committee. After some study, the city adopted and implemented a three-part plan to restore the Cemetery: a landscape and sculpture master plan to include tree removal / trimming as appropriate and proper mowing; the hiring of a professional cemetery restoration company to map the Cemetery, plot each marked grave, identify vacant spots, straighten and repair the damaged headstones, and mark with a metal cross any previously unmarked graves that could be found; and a volunteer effort to clean the headstones, removing the dirt and mold that had accumulated over the decades.

The project took more than three years to complete. On February 27, 2017, Preservation Texas honored the city of Canton by presenting the city with a Cemetery Preservation Award for its work on Hillcrest Cemetery. As the organization stated: "The oldest cemetery in Canton, Hillcrest Cemetery was threatened by neglect and vandalism until the Hillcrest Cemetery Restoration Committee formed and led city efforts to restore the cemetery."

Now, with a commitment to maintain the Cemetery and preserve its history, these early settlers and their descendants can rest peacefully, their resting places restored and their names and dates of birth and death legible once again.

But we know that's not all they were, these dedicated early settlers and others who formed the backbone of the Canton we know today—just their names and dates of birth and death. So the authors took the preservation effort one step further and brought their long-hidden history alive with *Stories Beneath the Stones.*

Hillcrest Cemetery

Located within the original 1850 town plat of Canton, this cemetery has served citizens of this area for well over a century. The oldest documented burial is that of Ann Calhoon (1807-1860). Among those buried here in marked and unmarked graves are Van Zandt County pioneers; veterans of the Civil War, World War I, and World War II; and business and community leaders. Serving as a reminder of Canton's pioneer heritage, the Hillcrest Cemetery is a reflection of the history of the town and its citizens. (1990)

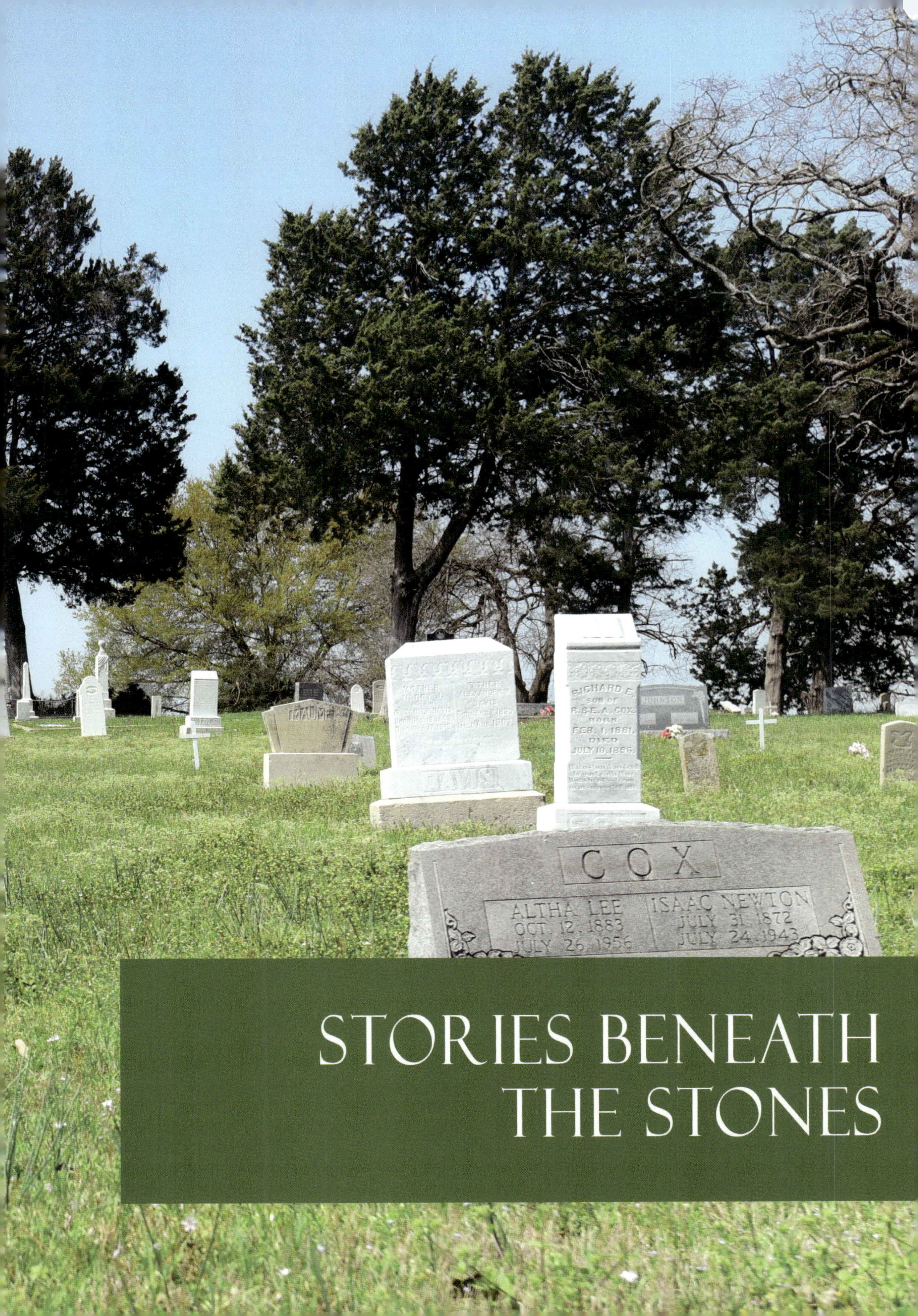

STORIES BENEATH THE STONES

A

ABBE, MARGARET CAROLINE

Born: July 18, 1850, Alabama. Died: July 6, 1892, Van Zandt County, Texas. Married: John C. Abbe, ca 1867, Caldwell Parish, Louisiana. Children: John L, William E., James L., Idonia, and Ella. Father: John Waldrip. Mother: Elizabeth J. Waldrip. Comments: Margaret Waldrip moved from Alabama to Louisiana and married John Abbe there about 1867. John was born in 1842 in Alabama and served with the 17th La. Regiment of the Confederate Army. John and Margaret were married after John's release from the Army and were in Van Zandt County before 1880. John was a farmer. He married Anna Barber after Margaret's death and lived in the Martins Mill, Texas area until his death in 1920. He is buried in the Holly Springs Cemetery in Van Zandt County. Sources: Tombstone; 1880 U. S. Census; *Canton Herald*, December 17, 1920; Find A Grave.

ADAMS, MOLLIE B.

Born: August 1, 1857. Died: June 6, 1884. Married: L. A. Adams. Father: Unknown. Mother: Unknown. Source: Tombstone.

ALBRIGHT, ALICE

Born: July 26, 1895. Died: October 12, 1977, Van Zandt County, Texas. Married: Dave Owens Albright. Father: Dr. Louis Edward Warrington. Mother: Ella Louise Hassell. Comments: Alice Albright lived in Canton and Wills Point for 25 years prior to her death. Sources: *Canton Herald*, October 20, 1977; Eubank Funeral Home records.

ALBRIGHT, DAVE OWENS

Born: October 12, 1893, Shelby County, Alabama. Died: December 2, 1974, Wood County, Texas. Cause of death: Heart failure. Married: Alice Warrington. Father: John Walter Albright. Mother: Martha Jane Weaver. Occupation: Farmer, cattleman. Comments: Dave Albright lived in Van Zandt County about twenty years prior to his death. Sources: *Canton Herald*, December 12, 1974; Eubank Funeral Home records.

ALEXANDER, MATTY W.

Born: August 15, 1867, Van Zandt County, Texas. Died: March 11, 1912, Van Zandt County, Texas. Father: Wiley P. Alexander. Mother: Lucinda Matilda Trammel. Comments: Matty Alexander died at the home of his sister and brother-in-law, Zula E. and R. L. Martin. His father is buried in an unmarked grave in Hillcrest. Source: *Grand Saline Sun*, March 14, 1912.

ALLEN, ANNA BELLE

Born: December 20, 1899. Died: April 16, 1912, Wood County, Texas. Father: B. F. Allen. Mother: Anna Lee Baskin. Comments: Anna Belle Allen's family lived in Wood County, Texas. Belle Massey, an aunt, lived in Canton, Texas. Two other Allen children are buried in Hillcrest Cemetery. Source: *Grand Saline Sun*, April 25, 1912.

ALLEN, DEWDROP

Born: September 29, 1890. Died: May 3, 1892. Father: B. F. Allen. Mother: Anna Lee Baskin. Source: Tombstone.

ALLEN, HATTIE BELLE

Born: September 11, 1888. Died: October 18, 1889, Wood County, Texas. Father: B. F. Allen. Mother: Anna Lee Baskin. Source: *Canton Telephone*, October 25, 1889.

ALLEN, HENRY D.

Born: November 14, 1861, Mississippi. Died: April 14, 1894, Van Zandt County, Texas. Cause of death: Gunshot wounds. Married: Josie Ella Compton, October 28, 1891. Father: Ezekael Nicholas Allen. Mother: Sara J. Blythe. Child: Winnie. Comments: Henry D. Allen was a resident of Canton, Texas for several years. He first was the manager of the Grange store. Later, he bought the business and continued in the family grocery business until the store burned in 1892. Henry then bought a livery business and was running it at the time of his death. He was a Mason and a member of the Knights and Ladies of Honor. The *Canton Telephone* reported his death as follows: "The killing of H. D. Allen last Saturday evening created quite an excitement in our town. Justice McClel-

The killing of **H. D. ALLEN** *last Saturday evening created quite an excitement in our town, as reported by the* Canton Telephone. *Justice McClellen rendered a verdict that he was accidently shot with a shotgun.*

The verdict was based upon the deceased's wife's testimony that the deceased was attempting to kill himself—and in a struggle to prevent it by his wife, the gun accidently discharged.

Charles W. Ashworth, Jr.

Jack Wesley Ashworth

Katherine Lucille Kellam Ashworth

len took testimony to ascertain how he was killed, and rendered a verdict that he was accidently shot with a shot gun. The verdict was based upon the evidence of deceased's wife's testimony, who stated that deceased was attempting to kill himself and a struggle to prevent it by his wife, the gun accidently discharged." Josie Allen married Nathaniel M. Crawford on November 1, 1898. He had a law practice in Grand Saline and later became County Attorney. Josie died in 1938 and is buried beside her second husband in Grand Saline. Her parents, S. P. and Mariah Austin Compton, are buried in unmarked graves in Hillcrest Cemetery. In 1935, the Canton Garden Club had a contest to rename the Canton Cemetery. Josie's daughter, Mae Crawford Stanford, submitted the name "Hillcrest Cemetery" and the judges selected her entry. The cemetery then became known as the "Hillcrest Cemetery." Sources: *Wills Point Chronicle*, April 14, 1894; *Canton Telephone*, April 20, 1894; Carol Baskin Tatum, Allen Family historian.

Allen, Lillian May "Lillie"

Born: January 9, 1867, Louisiana. Died: April 28, 1945, Van Zandt County, Texas. Married: (1) William Creed Morris. (2) W. M. Allen. Father: George Walker. Mother: Molly Key, Alabama. Comments: Lillie Allen was born near Mount Lebanon, Louisiana. She came to Texas in 1879, and the family located at Big Sandy. She came to Van Zandt County in 1923 after her husband's death. Two children had preceded her in death, leaving only a daughter, Mrs. Noah Frank Tawater, with whom she made her home until her death. Sources: Death Certificate; *Canton Herald*, May 3, 1945; Eubank Funeral Home records.

Allen, Nettie

Born: December 8, 1868. Died: October 14, 1892. Cause of death: Chronic myocastis. Married: Sim Allen, March 2, 1890. Father: James L. Matthews. Mother: Georgia A. Unknown. Comments: The *Canton Telephone* reported Nettie Allen's death as follows: "It becomes our sad and painful duty to chronicle the death of Mrs. Nettie Allen, which occurred at the residence of deceased's mother, Mrs. Georgia Matthews, this city, yesterday morning at 10 o'clock, after ten days of painful sickness with pneumonia. She had been a member of the Baptist church for several years. Just before she died she prayed 'Lord Jesus to receive her spirit,' repeating it several times. About thirty minutes before her spirit returned to God, she asked someone to sing a religious hymn." Sources: 1880 U. S. Census; *Canton Telephone*, October 14, 1892; Ancestry.com.

Andrews, Bertha Josephine

Born: January 17, 1878, Van Zandt County, Texas. Died: December 2, 1968, Dallas County, Texas. Cause of death: Heart disease. Married: Julius B. Andrews, April 21, 1898. Children: Joseph, William Hatley, Ruby, Julius Jr., Kathleen, and Maurine. Father: Jordon B. Hobbs. Mother: Paralee Walters. Comments: Julius Andrews was the son of Joseph William Andrews and Mrs. Susan Parker Simpson, widow of Freelin Simpson. Julius was buried in Holly Springs Cemetery, Van Zandt County, Texas. Bertha lived in Dallas for fifty years prior to her death. Sources: Death Certificate, Quana Barber's interview with Judy Andrews Bagby.

Andrews, William Hatley

Born: December 11, 1900. Died: January 7, 1902. Father: Julius B. Andrews. Mother: Bertha Josephine Hobbs. Source: *Free State Enterprise*, April 9, 1902.

Arendall, Jesse H.

Born: January 15, 1837, Franklin County, Georgia. Died: March 4, 1882, Van Zandt County, Texas. Married: Mary J. Galloway, April 25, 1859, Franklin County, Georgia. Father: John Arendall. Mother: Sarah (Sallie) Holbrook. Military: CSA, Ist Lt. 48th Ala. Inf. Co. E & G. Comments: Jesse Arrendall received his commission on April 12, 1862 from Governor Shorter of Alabama. Sources: *U. S. Civil War Soldiers 1861-1865*; Marriage Records, Franklin County, Georgia; Ancestry.com.

Ashworth, Charles W., Jr.

Born: October 1, 1907, Van Zandt County, Texas. Died: July 30, 1982, Dallas County, Texas. Married: Katherine Lucille Kellam. Children: Charles, Jack, and Mary Kathryn. Father: Charles Wesley Ashworth, Sr.. Mother: Amanda Mae Norman. Siblings: Joe Gee, W. W., Arlou, Mary Jo, Sue, Beola, Hazel, Alton, Guy, John Mac, and Jack. Occupation: Bookkeeper. Source: *Van Zandt News*, August 8, 1982.

Ashworth, Jack Wesley

Born: September 26, 1931, Van Zandt County, Texas. Died: June 12, 2012, Tarrant County, Texas. Never Married. Father: Charles W. Ashworth, Jr.. Mother: Katherine Lucille Kellam. Occupation: Cobol Software Developer, LTV, Texas Instruments. Military: U. S. Army. Comments: Jack Ashworth graduated from Dallas' Sunset High School and Texas Tech University, Lubbock, Texas. Source: Jane Hunter, Ashworth Family historian.

Ashworth, Katherine Lucille Kellam

Born: May 15, 1907, Van Zandt County, Texas. Died: August 10, 1998, Dallas County, Texas. Married: Charles W. Ashworth, Jr.. Children: Charles, Jack, and Mary Kathryn. Father: Dr. Andrew J. (Jack) Kellam. Mother: Duskie Hilliard. Comments: Katherine Ashworth was a Dallas resident for fifty-six years and had previously lived in Canton and San Antonio. She was a graduate of Canton High School and attended Texas Wesleyan University and North Texas State University. She was a national flower judge and taught school in Canton and San Antonio, Texas. Source: *Van Zandt News*, August 16, 1998.

Aubrey, Jaceller "Jack"

Born: April 14, 1925, Claiborne Parish, Louisiana. Died: July 23, 1989, Smith County, Texas. Father: Unknown Aubrey. Mother: Unknown. Occupation: Worked for CNO and BNO Railroad. Comments: Jack Aubrey was a member of the Ebenezer AME Church in Tyler. He had lived in Van Zandt County only four years. Source: *Van Zandt News*, July 30, 1989.

B

Bagby, Charlie

Born: August 13, 1872. Died: February 14, 1873. Father: Arthur P. Bagby. Mother: Elizabeth F. Turner. Source: Tombstone.

Bagby, Elizabeth Fountain

Born: May 15, 1832, Virginia. Died: February 5, 1873, Van Zandt County, Texas. Married: Arthur P. Bagby ca. 1850, Mississippi. Father: Unknown Turner. Mother: Unknown. Children: William Arthur, Alexander, Mary, Benjamin, Ada Cora, Thomas, Charlie, and Nannie Lou. Source: 1850, 1870 U. S. Census.

Bagby, Nannie Lou

Born: October 29, 1850. Died: August 4, 1869. Father: Arthur P. Bagby. Mother: Elizabeth F. Turner. Source: Tombstone.

Bailey, Millie Ann

Born: September 20, 1918, Dallas County, Texas. Died: January 7, 1920, Van Zandt County, Texas. Cause of death: Pneumonia. Father: C. C. Bailey, Dallas County, Texas. Mother: Emma Bell Williams, Dallas County, Texas. Source: Death Certificate.

Baker, Doris Nash Maume

Born: September 28, 1895, Blanco County, Texas. Died: February 25, 1937, Van Zandt County, Texas. Cause of death: Liver cancer. Married: J. Bonner Baker, July 7, 1920. Father: Edward W. Maume, Galveston County, Texas. Mother: Alice R. Nash, Iowa. Siblings: Mamie, Anna, and Ed. Occupation: Telephone operator. Comments: Doris Maume moved to Canton with her parents when she was 3 years old. From a young age she suffered from asthma. In 1920, just before Doris married Bonner Baker, she became a telephone operator. Back in those days, the telephone board was typically installed in the operator's home. The following is an item published in the *Canton Herald*: "Miss Doris Maume is now day operator at the local telephone board and is most pleasing and courteous in answering the multitudinous calls that pass and repass during the day." She had a major operation six weeks before her death at St. Paul Hospital in Dallas, Texas and returned after a month to stay with her sister, Mamie, at the Dixie Hotel in Canton. She soon died from liver cancer. Sources: Death Certificate; *Canton Herald*, June 18, 1920 and March 4, 1937.

Bandy, Bonnie Lue

Born: October 4, 1937. Died: April 5, 1972. Cause of death: Leukemia. Married: Raymond C. Bandy. Father: James Earl Brewer. Mother: Lela Burnett "Bonnie" Mack. Sources: Death Certificate, Find A Grave.

Barber, Kathleen Stanford

Born: July 5, 1925, Lamar County, Texas. Died: August 31, 2013, Van Zandt County, Texas. Married: (1) C. L. Stanford. (2) Brown Barber. Children: Ann and Elaine. Father: Lewis H. Jackson. Mother: Martha Jeffries. Comments: Kathleen Barber's mother died shortly after her birth, and she was reared by her maternal grandmother,

Renetta Jeffries. She attended high school in Cooper, Texas and college in Paris, Texas. After college, Kathleen worked for the Veteran's Administration in Dallas before moving to Van Zandt County, Texas. In Canton, she was active in the organization of the public library, a member of the DAR and Descendants of the Mayflower. She attended the First United Methodist Church and the Presbyterian Church. Source: Find A Grave.

BASKIN, FRANCES THOMSON
Born: April 1, 1816, Anderson District, South Carolina. Died: October 18, 1892, Van Zandt County, Texas. Married: William Leroy Baskin. Father: Matthew Thompson. Mother: Arabella Unknown. Occupation: Hotel owner. Comments: Frances Baskin joined the Old School Presbyterian Church at the age of 17 and attended until her death. The Baskin family owned the Phoenix Hotel in Canton, Texas. Source: *Canton Telephone*, October 21, 1892.

BASKIN, WILLIAM LEROY
Born: October 10, 1812, South Carolina. Died: December 25, 1883, Van Zandt County, Texas. Married: Frances Amandaline Thompson. Father: William Candor Baskin. Mother: Margaret Reid. Occupation: Hotel owner. Comments: William and Frances Baskin owned the Phoenix Hotel in Canton, Texas. Sources: 1880 U. S. Census, Ancestry.com, Find A Grave.

BATEMAN, CORA ANN
Born: January 19, 1873, Texas. Died: April 12, 1952, Cherokee County, Texas. Married: John Willie Bateman, February 27, 1887. Children: Charles, John, Nettie Ann, Hayden Tucker, Metta, Cora, and Lila Gertrude. Father: John Right Hobbs. Mother: Amanda Mayfield. Sources: *Canton Herald*, April 17, 1952; Bateman Family History.

BATEMAN, DR. JOHN KEARBY
Born: August 15, 1890, Van Zandt County, Texas. Died: September 28, 1954, Van Zandt County, Texas. Cause of death: Pancreatic cancer. Married: Nettie Lee Russell, June 20, 1916. Divorced. Father: John Willie Bateman. Mother: Cora Ann Hobbs. Occupation: Dentist. Comments: John Kirby Bateman's office was on the second floor of the First National Bank in Canton, Texas. He sold his practice to T. R. Keahey in February 1930 and opened an office in Tyler, Texas. Sources: Death Certificate; *Canton Herald*, February, 7, 1930 and September 30, 1954.

JOHN WILLIE BATEMAN *served as County Surveyor for twenty-eight years, qualifying him as the longest serving elected official in Van Zandt County history. He also served as a Constable for four years and Justice of the Peace for four years.*

BATEMAN, JOHN WILLIE
Born: July 23, 1865, Washington County, Alabama. Died: August 17, 1946, Van Zandt County, Texas. Married: Cora Ann Hobbs, February 27, 1887. Children: Charles, John, Nettie Ann, Hayden Tucker, Metta, Cora, and Lila Gertrude. Father: Charles I. Bateman. Mother: Elizabeth A. Cole. Occupation: Constable (four years), Justice Of The Peace (four years), surveyor (thirty-five years total—twenty-eight as County Surveyor), oil company employee. Comments: John Willie Bateman was a Van Zandt County resident for seventy-eight years. He came to Sabine County, Texas in a covered wagon pulled by a team of oxen. John Willie's father died in 1868 near the Texas-Louisiana border while en route to Texas. The family came to Van Zandt County that same year. His twenty-eight years as the County Surveyor qualifies as the longest serving elected official in Van Zandt County history. He also worked for the Pure Oil Company for seventeen years. He served the Baptist Church for most of his life and was a moderator of the Baptist Missionary Association for thirty-five years. Sources: *Canton Herald*, January 12, 1934, July 26, 1935, February 25, 1937, and August 22, 1946; information given to Quana Barber by family members.

BATEMAN, NELDA ANNETTE
Born: October 3, 1930, Van Zandt County, Texas. Died: October 24, 1997, Van Zandt County, Texas. Married: Norman Virgil Bateman, June 1, 1949. Children: Norman Joel, Paul, and Belinda Annett. Father: Henry Isham Brown. Mother: Mary Elizabeth Henson. Source: *Van Zandt News*, November 2, 1997.

BATEMAN, NORMAN JOEL
Born: January 8, 1952, Van Zandt County, Texas. Died: July 28, 1955, Van Zandt County, Texas. Cause of death: Electrocution. Father: Norman Virgil Bateman. Mother: Nelda Annette Brown. Comments: Norman Joel Bateman was the eldest child in the family. The family was living in the Mill Creek community near Canton. He was playing under the house and touched a propane pipe running to the cook stove. A hot electrical wire was touching the pipe, and he was electrocuted. The following was inscribed on

Norman Joel Bateman

Norman Virgil and Nelda Annette Bateman

James Thomas "Tom" Beard

Bessie Wynne Bowles

the tombstone: "Budded on earth to bloom in heaven." Sources: *Canton Herald*, August 4, 1955; Eubank Funeral Home records.

BATEMAN, NORMAN VIRGIL
Born: April 10, 1927, Van Zandt County, Texas. Died: April 30, 1987, Van Zandt County, Texas. Married: Nelda Annette Brown, June 1, 1949. Children: Norman Joel, Paul, and Belinda Annett. Father: Virgil Thomas Bateman. Mother: Ibera Johnson. Military: WWII, U. S. Navy. Occupation: Farmer. Source: *Van Zandt News*, May 3, 1987.

BEARD, CORA ALETHA
Born: October 26, 1879, Mississippi. Died: March 21, 1958, Dallas County, Texas. Cause of death: Heart disease. Married: James Thomas Beard, November 4, 1900. Father: W. W. Slaughter. Mother: Ellen Hawkins. Source: Death Certificate.

BEARD, GEORGE W.
Born: March 20, 1887. Died: October 8, 1896. Father: Henry Britton Beard. Mother: Sarah Ann Carlisle. Source: Tombstone.

BEARD, HENRY BRITTON
Born: July 9, 1850, Alabama. Died: February 7, 1897, Van Zandt County, Texas. Married: Sarah Ann (Babe) Carlisle, Bienville Parish, Louisiana, October 22, 1872. Children: George W., James Thomas, and Henry B. Father: James H. Beard, Cumberland County, North Carolina. Mother: Jane McDonald, Dallas County, Alabama. Occupation: Farmer. Sources: 1880 U. S. Census; *Van Zandt County History*; *Wills Point Chronicle*, February 11, 1897.

BEARD, JAMES THOMAS "TOM"
Born: November 4, 1873, Bienville Parish, Louisiana. Died: October 9, 1954, Van Zandt County, Texas. Married: Cora Slaughter, November 4, 1900. Father: Henry Britton Beard. Mother: Sarah Ann "Babe" Carlisle. Occupation: Drugstore owner, County Clerk. Comments: The Palace Drug Store was in business for forty years. Located on the south side of the square, it was a Canton landmark. Tom Beard purchased the drugstore in 1921. His brother, Sam H. Beard, became part owner of the business in 1949 and operated it until his death in 1962. Then the ownership of the building was transferred to Mrs. Sam Beard. In 1977, Glen McNeill, Jr. purchased the building from Mrs. Beard and moved the newspaper, the *Canton Herald*, into the building. Sources: Assumed Name Register; *Van Zandt County History*; *Canton Herald*, October 14, 1954 and March 17, 1977; Eubank Funeral Home records.

BEARD, JOLLY TRUMAN
Born: January 22, 1924. Died: February 2, 1927. Father: Hubert E. Beard. Mother: Elsie Groves. Sources: Tombstone, *Van Zandt County History*.

BEARD, SARAH ANN
Born: February 12, 1857, Louisiana. Died: November 14, 1928, Van Zandt County, Texas. Cause of death: Heart disease. Married: Henry Britton Beard, Bienville Parish, Louisiana, October 22, 1872. Children: George W., James Thomas, and Henry B. Father: Thomas Carlisle. Mother: Cynthia Pierce. Sources: Death Certificate, *Van Zandt County History*.

BELCHER, ELLA RUTH
Born: October 11, 1942. Died: December 27, 2015. Married: (1) Unknown May. (2) Porter L. Belcher, September 20, 1973. Children: Henry May, Karron and Jason Belcher. Father: John Henry Phillips. Mother: Maudie Lee Thompson. Occupation: Seamstress, City Cleaners, Mabank, Texas. Siblings: Henry Lee, Hobby, and Hubert. Sources: *Texas Marriage Collection, 1966-2002*; *The Monitor*, January 7, 2016.

Henry Fisher Blackwell II served as Deputy Sheriff and then Sheriff of Van Zandt County. During his tenure, a new modern jail facility was built in 1893. Blackwell began farming after his law enforcement days, but his interest in public affairs continued throughout his life. When he died in 1944, he was the oldest native resident of Canton. The house is now a Canton landmark and museum, and the oldest residence in the city.

Bell, William A.

Born: January 27, 1897. Died: August 25, 1927, Dallas County, Texas. Cause of death: Gunshot wounds, homicide. Single. Father: Bee Bell, Texas. Mother: Polly Williams, Texas. Comments: There are no details of the shooting. Source: Death Certificate.

Blackwell, Henry Fisher, II

Born: July 15, 1859, Van Zandt County, Texas. Died: June 20, 1944, Van Zandt County, Texas. Married: Nancy Jane "Nannie" Bartlett, December 16, 1885. Children: Katie S., Janie, Elsie Marie, Henry Fisher, Jr., R. E., R. L., Bonnie, and Rose. Father: Henry Fisher Blackwell, Sr., Virginia. Mother: Sarah Payne Engledow, Missouri. Occupation: Law enforcement. Comments: Henry Fisher Blackwell, II was one of seven children. His father, Henry F. Blackwell, Sr. was born in Virginia on December 21, 1826, was a soldier in the U. S. Mexican War, and went to California in the Gold Rush of 1849. He came back to Texas and married Sarah P. Engledow on September 22, 1852 in Nacogdoches. Sarah was born in Missouri in 1834, but moved to Nacogdoches with her parents at an early age and later married the senior Blackwell there. In 1852 the Blackwells moved to Canton, Texas. Henry Blackwell, Sr. opened one of the first business establishments on what was to become the courthouse square in Canton. Blackwell Sr. joined the Confederate Army and served as a 2nd Lt, TX 15th Cav. Co. I. On January 11, 1863 this unit surrendered at the defeat of Arkansas Post, Arkansas. Blackwell was a POW at Camp Chase, Ohio until he was released. He had started home to see his family when he became ill in Shelby County, Texas. He sent word for Sarah to come to see him. When she reached Shelby County on August 5, 1863, he had died and had been buried for about half an hour. Blackwell had been sick about seven days and was buried about eight miles southeast of Shelbyville. Sarah planned to move the body to Canton later, but never did. She died January 3, 1916 and is buried in the Pleasant Hill Cemetery, Polk County, Arkansas. Henry F. Blackwell II was born July 15, 1859 in Canton. As a boy, he kept books for his father's close friend, G. W. Tull, who was another of Canton's early merchants. At an early age, Henry became a Deputy Sheriff and served ten years in that capacity. He was elected Sheriff of Van Zandt County in 1886 and served four terms, which gave him a total of eighteen years in county law enforcement. A new modern jail facility was built in 1893 while he was Sheriff. Blackwell began farming after his law enforcement days, but his interest in public affairs continued throughout his life. When he died in 1944, he was the oldest native resident of Canton. After Henry and Nannie got married, the couple began building a house in Canton. They lived in the house until their deaths, and then it was passed down to their children. The house was continuously occupied by the immediate Blackwell family from 1887 -1975. On December 12, 1988, Rebel Blackwell, a son, presented the city of Canton with the deed to the Blackwell house and seven-and-a-half acres as a historical gift. The house is now a Canton landmark and museum. It is the oldest residence in the city. Sources: *Canton Herald*, Centennial Edition; *Canton Telephone*, June 24, 1887; *Wills Point Chronicle*, May 14, 1908; *Canton Herald*, June 10, 1937; undated articles from the *Canton Herald*; Joe Engledow, Blackwell Family historian; Sarah P. Blackwell's letter, August 1863; Eubank Funeral Home records.

BLACKWELL, HENRY FISHER, JR.
Born: July 5, 1888, Van Zandt County, Texas. Died: June 30, 1957, Dallas County, Texas. Married: Lillie Leona Youngblood, 1913. Children: Joyce Y. and Elsie Marie. Father: Henry Fisher Blackwell II. Mother: Nancy Jane "Nannie" Bartlett. Occupation: Wholesale gasoline and oil distributor. Sources: Marriage Announcement, 1913; *Canton Herald*, July 4, 1957 and March 6, 1975; Hilliard & Son Funeral Home records.

BLACKWELL, INFANT
Born: Unknown. Died: Unknown. Father: Henry F. Blackwell II. Mother: Nannie J. Bartlett. Source: Tombstone.

BLACKWELL, KATIE S.
Born: May 10, 1890. Died: August 29, 1891. Cause of death: Diphtheria. Father: Henry F. Blackwell II. Mother: Nannie J. Bartlett. Source: *Canton Telephone*, September 4, 1891.

BLACKWELL, NANCY JANE "NANNIE"
Born: April 11, 1861. Died: April 3, 1937. Married: Henry Fisher Blackwell II, December 16, 1885. Children: Katie S., Janie, Henry Fisher, Jr, R. E., R. L., Bonnie, and Rose. Father: Lucian L. Bartlett, Illinois. Mother: Martha J. Richardson, Alabama. Sources: *Canton Telephone*, July 24, 1891, Eubank Funeral Home records.

BLAIR, EVA LEE
Born: June 11, 1893. Died: November 7, 1918. Married: J. E. Blair. Father: James L. Fizer. Mother: Permelia Laura "Mattie" Miles. Comments: Eva Lee Blair's family had lived in the Canton area for eight years. Her father managed the Sanger Farm east of town. Source: *Canton Herald*, November 8, 1918.

BLOUNT, JESSAMINE K.
Born: February 2, 1883. Died: February 7, 1883. Father: Dr. J. P. Blount. Mother: J. Blount. Comments: Jessamine Blount's father practiced medicine in Canton for a number of years. He was also interested in politics and was a State Representative from Van Zandt County. His brothers-in-law were Jerome and Galatin Kearby, the most prominent attorneys in Van Zandt County in the 1880's. J. P. Blount moved to Denton about 1885 and practiced medicine there as well as owning a drugstore. He served as a school trustee and was the Chairman of the Executive Committee of the Democratic Party of Denton. Source: *Canton Telephone,* March 22, 1889.

BOLES, LEROY
Born: September 17, 1880, Texas. Died: November 17, 1957, Van Zandt County, Texas. Cause of death: Cancer. Father: Abe Boles. Mother: Rachel Johnson. Occupation: Texas & Pacific Railroad. Source: Death Certificate.

BOWLES, BESSIE WYNNE
(Photo page 25) Born: February 16, 1891. Died: February 3, 1981, Smith County, Texas. Married: (1) Jessie Captain Wynne, (2) John Wesley Bowles. Children: Karion, Vada, Opal L, Carrie, Elaine, Willie, James, George H., Elmer, and two unknown. Father: Jerry Mauldin, Williamson County, Texas. Mother: Lou Mauldin, Williamson County, Texas. Comments: Bessie Bowles was known locally as the Mother of the Wynne Community. She was active in the Methodist Church wherever she lived—Georgetown, Canton, San Antonio, Tyler, and Los Angeles, California. She received her fifty-year pin as a Stewardess at the Grant Memorial A. M. E. Church in Los Angeles. Source: *Canton Herald*, February 12, 1981.

BOWLES, JOHN WESLEY
Born: November 23, 1877, Texas. Died: August 2, 1955, Kaufman County, Texas. Cause of death: Heart disease. Married: (1) Maggie Payne, December 25, 1900. Divorced April 17, 1907. (2) Mrs. Bessie Mauldin Wynne, June. 8, 1935. Child: Salon. Father: Abe J. Bowles. Mother: Rachel Johnson. Occupation: Dixie Hotel employee in Canton. Comments: Wesley Bowles was a well-known person

in Canton. He worked at the Dixie Hotel doing a number of jobs, including being a waiter, for thirty-five years. Wesley was a member of the Wills Point Colored Masonic Lodge and of the Methodist Church. He was survived by his wife, the former Bessie Mauldin Wynne; one son, Salon Bowles; four stepsons, Willie D. Wynne, J. C. Wynne, George Wynne, and Elmer Wynne; five step-daughters, Vada, Elaine, Carrie, Opal, Karion, and Josie (foster daughter); and a brother, Roy. Sources: Death Certificate; *Van Zandt County Marriage Records 1909-1931*; *Canton Herald*, August 4, 1955; Eubank Funeral Home records.

Bowles, John Wesley

Born: May 29, 1927, Dallas County, Texas. Died: March 7, 1966, Dallas County, Texas. Cause of death: Gunshot wound. Father: Salon Bowles. Mother: Thelma Louise Punch. Military: WWII, Tec 5, 1692 Eng. COMBT Bn. Occupation: General contractor. Comments: John Wesley Bowles' death was ruled an accident. Source: Death Certificate.

Bowles, Maggie

Born: November 7, 1884, Henderson County, Texas. Died: June 4, 1934, Van Zandt County, Texas. Cause of death: Lung disease. Married: John Wesley Bowles, December 25, 1900. Divorced: April 17, 1907. Father: Cebe Payne. Mother: Fredonia Hubbard. Occupation: Cook at the Dixie Hotel, Canton, Texas. Comments: The *Canton Herald* reported Maggie Bowles' death as follows: "Maggie will be missed by the white people of Canton as well as among her own race. She has probably done more work for the white people than any other colored woman here. She has been working almost continuously for the past fifteen years at the Dixie Hotel and was considered one of the best cooks in town." Sources: Death Certificate; *Canton Herald*, June 8, 1934.

Bowles, Uyless

Born: April 26, 1887. Died: December 29, 1914. Father: Abe J. Bowles. Mother: Rachel Johnson. Source: Vanessa Scott, Wynne Community historian.

Bowman, Lela Francis

Born: May 10, 1918, Van Zandt County, Texas. Died: January 14, 2010, Van Zandt County, Texas. Married: Charlie P. Bowman, September 21, 1935. Children: Lacy, Kenneth, James, Sammie, Andrew, and Curtis. Father: Joe Bell. Mother: Easter McDaniel. Comments: The *Canton Herald* reported Lela Bowman's death as follows: "In 1944 Lela and her husband, Charlie P. Bowman, settled down in Chicago, Illinois. There she raised eight children and became a foster mother to several other children. In 1973 Lela moved to Dallas, Texas; and in 1974 to Canton to care for her brother, R. D. 'Buddy' Bell. While in Canton, she joined Evangelist Temple Church of God in Christ. She was the 'Mother' of the Church until her death." Sources: *Canton Herald*, January 24, 2010; Eubank Funeral Home records.

Branson, Alice M.

Born: November 23, 1890. Died: January 24, 1917. Married: Wesley B. Branson, December 24, 1912. Children: Donnie May and Nettie Alice. Father: Joseph Amplias Smith. Mother: Clara Smith. Siblings: Hope and Lottie. Comments: Alice Branson's sister, Hope, was the mother of Maurice Brown Eubank. Maurice's husband, Russell Eubank, owned Eubank Funeral Home in Canton, Texas for over fifty years. Sources: *Canton Herald*, February 2, 1917; *Van Zandt County Texas Biographies—Vol 2, 1848-1991.*

Branson, Isadore A. "Dora"

Born: March 30, 1856, Nacogdoches County, Texas. Died: October 10, 1936, Van Zandt County, Texas. Married: James B. Branson, June 20, 1874, Kaufman County, Texas. Children: William, Nettie Alice, Jim, Bertha, Hattie May (Hettie), Wesley B., Josephine "Josie," and Ida. Father: Oscar Bell, Alabama. Mother: Sara Jane Vaught, Texas. Siblings: John and Christopher. Comments: Dora Bell's father was a Confederate soldier. He died at Arkansas Post, Camp Hope, Arkansas on October 1, 1862 after his leg was amputated. Dora's ancestors, through the Vaught's and the Birdwell's, on her mother's side of the family, contributed much to the Republic of Texas and the early days of Texas statehood. Members of her family came into Texas as early as the 1830's and settled near Nacogdoches. John Birdwell, Dora's great grandfather, was one of the early settlers of Rusk County. Col. Allen Birdwell was elected to the Texas legislature in 1853, and again in 1863. His grandson, Dr. Alton William Birdwell, Dora's second cousin, was the first President of Stephen F. Austin College. Sources: *Van Zandt County Texas Biographies-Vol 2, 1848-1991*; *1890 In Van Zandt County*.

Branson, James B.

Born: December 25, 1844, Franklin County, Kentucky. (Tombstone birth date of 1840 is incorrect.) Died: May 13, 1933, Van Zandt County, Texas. Married: (1) Sarah Graves, January 26, 1868, Panola County, Texas. (2) Isadore A. (Dora) Bell, June 20, 1874, Kaufman County, Texas. Father: Charles Branson. Mother: Mary Slaughter. Military: CSA, Private, Regimental Drummer, 19th TX Inf., Walker's Texas Division. Siblings: Stephen and Ellen. Occupation: Farmer, general laborer. Comments: Records of The Episcopal Church of the Ascension, Frankfort, Kentucky lists James Branson's birthdate as December 25, 1844 and baptismal date as August 22, 1849. After his mother's death in 1858, he moved with his family to Panola County, Texas. During the Civil War, James served in the Trans-Mississippi Department primarily in Arkansas and Louisiana. In his Army career, he never rose above the rank of Private, but he lived to experience a full range

James B. Branson *was permanently transferred to the Regimental Band by order of Col. Waterhouse on January 1, 1864. His Division became known as Walker's Greyhounds because in a few months they did more marching than any other Division in the Confederate Army. James was known as the best drummer in the command. The drummers of the Civil War had the responsibility to establish order among units in the field. During battle, a drummer was always near a high ranking officer to hear the orders being given. Each order was represented by a specific series of drumbeats: meet here, attack now, or retreat, and all other commands of battlefield and camp. James was one of twenty-one soldiers from the 19th Infantry who were captured by the Union at Pleasant Hill. He was released in an exchange of prisoners a few days later. In 1915 he started receiving a Confederate pension of $25 per month.*

of Army life. He was detailed as a drummer boy in January and February of 1863 and was permanently transferred to the Regimental Band by order of Col. Richard Waterhouse on January 1, 1864. His Division became known as Walker's Greyhounds because in a few months they did more marching than any other Division in the Confederate Army. James apparently had a natural talent for playing "field" music. According to testimony in his pension records, James was known as the best drummer in the command. The drummers of the Civil War had an interesting, but too often overlooked, role in the Army. The drummers were not supposed to be fighters, but they did a very important job during battle. It was the drummers' responsibility to establish order among units in the field. During battle, a drummer was always near a high ranking officer so he could hear the orders being given. Each order was given a series of drumbeats to represent it. Both soldiers and drummers had to learn what each drum-roll meant: meet here, attack now, or retreat, and all other commands of battlefield and camp. The most feared drum call was the "long roll" which was a signal to attack. In between sounding calls, the drummer worked as a stretcher bearer or walked around the battlefield looking for the wounded. The 19th Texas Infantry participated in several engagements, the most notable being the battles of Milliken's Bend, Mansfield, and Pleasant Hill. Milliken's Bend is notable in that it was the first important engagement of the Union Army's new regiments comprised entirely of men of "African Descent" and the percentages of casualties of both Union and Confederates were one of the highest during the Civil War. The Battles of Mansfield (April 8, 1864) and Pleasant Hill (April 9, 1864) were known as the Battles that saved Texas from Union invasion. James was one of twenty-one soldiers from the 19th Infantry who were captured by the Union at Pleasant Hill. He was released in an exchange of prisoners a few days later. After the War, James moved back to Panola County, Texas and later moved to Kaufman County where he married Dora. She was the daughter of Oscar Bell, a Confederate soldier, who died in Arkansas in 1862 and Sara Jane Vought. James and Dora moved to Van Zandt County before 1880 and first settled in the Jackson community before moving to the Starr/Wentworth community. They had eight children, six who lived to adulthood. In addition, they helped rear Dora's brothers, the Bell boys. James farmed and worked for others most of his adult life. In 1915 he started receiving a Confederate pension of $25 per month. The highlight of his life had been leading his regiment into battle beating on his drum. Source: *Van Zandt County Texas Biographies, 1848-1991, Fold 3 Confederate Records.*

Branson, Jimmy Wilson

Born: October 2, 1933, Van Zandt County, Texas. Died: January 26, 1997, Van Zandt County, Texas. Married: (1) Unknown. (2) Mrs. Mattie Lou Asberry Weehunt. Father:

Wesley B. Branson. Mother: Mattie Lorene Berry. Military: U. S. Navy, Korea. Siblings: Gloria Ann and one half-sister, Donnie May. Sources: *Van Zandt County Texas Biographies-Vol 2, 1848-1991*; *Canton Herald*, April 6, 2008.

BRANSON, (CARPENTER) MATTIE LORENE
(Photo page 34) Born: July 2, 1906, Lampasas County, Texas. Died: May 13, 1984, Van Zandt County, Texas. Married: (1) Wesley B. Branson, October 13, 1930. Children: Jimmy Wilson and Gloria Ann. (2) Robert Henry Carpenter. Father: William Wilson Berry. Mother: Sara Francis Seay. Siblings: Ellen, Elgin, Mary Corine, Bill, Margie, and Francis. Occupation: Restaurant cook. Comments: Mattie Lorene Carpenter chose to be buried next to Wesley Branson, her first husband. Sources: *Van Zandt County Texas Biographies-Vol 2, 1848-1991*; *Van Zandt News*, May 21, 1984.

AMBROSE J. BROOKS *taught school for a number of years before serving as Van Zandt County District Clerk from 1908 to 1912. He was a member of the Board of Deacons of the Canton Baptist Church, a member of the W.O.W., and a Royal Arch Mason. He was Vice President of the First National Bank of Canton and President of the Canton Lumber Company. In addition, he was in the real estate and abstract business. At his death in 1920, his funeral was the largest ever witnessed in Canton.*

BRANSON, NETTIE ALICE
Born: November 18, 1915. Died: April 9, 1916. Father: Wesley B. Branson. Mother: Alice Smith. Source: Tombstone.

BRANSON, WESLEY B.
Born: November 12, 1883, Van Zandt County, Texas. Died: February 3, 1951, Van Zandt County, Texas. Cause of death: Appendicitis. Married: (1) Alice M. Smith, December 24, 1912. Children: Donnie May and Nettie Alice. (2) Mattie Lorene Berry, October 13, 1930. Children: Jimmy and Gloria Ann. Father: James B. Branson. Mother: Isadore (Dora) Bell. Siblings: William, Jim, Nettie Alice, Josie, Hattie May, Bertha, and Ida Rebecca. Occupation: Farmer. Source: *Van Zandt County Texas Biographies-Vol 1, 1848-1991.*

BREWER, JOHN EARL
Born: January 16, 1897, Van Zandt County, Texas. Died: August 16, 1966, Van Zandt County, Texas. Cause of death: Heart disease. Married: (1) Lela Barnett "Bonnie" Mack, Hunt County, Texas. Children: John Harold, William George, Lee Gee, G. W., and Bonny Lue. (2) Ovilla Beaver. Father: George W. Brewer. Mother: Pearl Katherine "Kate" Armstrong. Sources: Ancestry.com, Find A Grave.

BREWER, JOHN HAROLD
Born: August 28, 1920, Van Zandt County, Texas. Died: May 29, 1944, North Africa. Cause of death: Killed in action. Single. Father: John Earl Brewer, Van Zandt County, Texas. Mother: Lela Barnett Mack, Hunt County, Texas. Siblings: William George, Lee Gee, G. W., and Bonny Lue. Military: WWII, Pvt. 6 Armor, 1st Arm. Div. Comments: John Brewer was killed in action in North Africa in 1944. The body was re-buried in Hillcrest Cemetery in 1948. Source: Death certificate.

BREWER, LELA BARNETT
Born: August 8, 1900, Hunt County, Texas. Died: October 9, 1953, Cherokee County, Texas. Cause of death: Intestinal obstruction. Married: John Earl Brewer. Children: John Harold, William George, Lee Gee, G. W., and Bonny Lue. Father: W. A. Mack, Georgia. Mother: Minnie Lee Brown, Georgia. Sources: Death Certificate, Eubank Funeral Home records, Find A Grave.

BROCKEEM (BRACKEEN) M.J.M.
Comments: The grave has a broken marker with no information other than the name. Source: Tombstone.

BROOKS, AMBROSE J.
Born: 1882, Wood County, Texas. Died: March 2, 1920. Cause of death: Pneumonia. Married: Lucretia Martin, September 15, 1907. Children: Joe A. and Margaret. Father: J. S. Brooks. Mother: Unknown. Comments: Ambrose Brooks moved to Canton as a young adult and died at the age of 38 years. He taught school for a number of

years and was then elected District Clerk. Ambrose was a member of the Board of Deacons of the Canton Baptist Church, a member of the W. O. W., and a Royal Arch Mason. He was Vice President of the First National Bank of Canton, and President of the Canton Lumber Company. In addition, he was in the real estate and abstract business. He served as Van Zandt County District Clerk from 1908-1912. The obituary stated that the funeral was the largest ever witnessed in Canton. Sources: 1920 U. S. Census; *Grand Saline Sun*, March 25, 1920; *Canton Herald*, March 26, 1920.

BROOKS, INFANT
No dates.

BROOKS, JOE AMBROSE
Born: May 17, 1915. Died: April 25, 1986. Father: Ambrose J. Brooks. Mother: Lucretia Martin. Source: Death Certificate of Lucretia Brooks.

BROOKS, LUCRETIA MARTIN "CRETIA"
Born: September 9, 1885, Van Zandt County, Texas. Died: February 26, 1972, Dickens County, Texas. Cause of death: Heart disease. Married: Ambrose J. Brooks, September 15, 1907. Children: Joe A. and Margaret. Father: J. W. Martin. Mother: Margaret Burns. Occupation: School teacher. Source: Death Certificate.

BROWN, ED
Born: January 18, 1920. Died: August 6, 2005. Father: Nelce Brown. Mother: Mary Marietta Stephens. Military: WWII, US Army. Sources: U. S. Social Security Applications and Claims Index, U. S. Veterans Gravesites Index.

BRUMMETT, IDA TAYLOR
Born: 1870. Died: 1913. Married: (1) James P. Thompson, July 15, 1886. Children: James Earl and Elijah Tull. (2) Robert E. Taylor, 1894. Children: Jewel and Ellen. (3) Samuel Rice Brummett, April 9, 1899. Father: John William Phillips. Mother: Edna Hunt. Source: Kitty Wheeler, Chaney Family historian.

BRUMMETT, SAMUEL RICE
Born: 1862, Wood County, Texas. Died: 1907, Van Zandt County, Texas. Married: (1) Mary J. Stroud, 1885. Children: James, Julius, Cora, Ora, and Virgie. (2) Ida Taylor, April 9, 1899. Father: Samuel Jackson Brummett. Mother: Martha Jane Moore. Sources: *Van Zandt County Marriage Book 1848-1908*, Ancestry.com.

BRYANT, WESLEY HOMER
Born: October 7, 1872, Crawford County, Georgia. Died: May 11, 1937, Van Zandt County, Texas. Cause of death: Heart disease. Never married. Father: William Henry Bryant. Mother: Francis Clementine Gordon. Occupation: Painter. Comments: Wesley Homer Bryant came with his family from Crawford County, Georgia and settled in Smith County, Texas in 1873. He lived in various places before he arrived in Canton. He had seven brothers and sisters. Source: Death Certificate.

BUNCH, VERNA MAXINE
Born: August 28, 1930, Van Zandt County, Texas. Died: August 16, 1933, Van Zandt County, Texas. Cause of death: Whooping cough. Father: J. A. Bunch. Mother: Bertha Philips. Source: Death Certificate.

BURDEN, CLOYD
Born: January 14, 1934. Died: January 14, 1934. Father: James Moore Burden. Mother: Vernice Reeves. Source: Death Certificate.

BURDEN, JAMES EDWARD "JIM"
Born: March 13, 1871, Alabama. Died: August 22, 1944, Van Zandt County, Texas. Married: Nevada Moore, De-

Samuel Rice Brummett and Ida Taylor Brummett

cember 4, 1895. Children: Viola Mae and James Moore. Father: William Harrison Burden, Alabama. Mother: Mary Jean English, Alabama. Source: Eubank Funeral Home records.

BURDEN, JAMES MOORE
Born: January 29, 1908, Van Zandt County, Texas. Died: June 22, 1934, Van Zandt County, Texas. Cause of death: Pneumonia. Married: Vernice Irene Reeves, March 23, 1930. Father: James Edward Burden. Mother: Nevada "Vada" Moore. Occupation: Farming. Comments: James Moore Burden died at the age of 26 and was survived by his wife. Twins, Cloyd and Loyd, died in January 1934. Vernice later married Raymond Scott. Sources: Death Certificate; *Canton Herald*, January 26, 1934.

BURDEN, LOYD
Born: January 14, 1934. Died: January 14, 1934. Father: James Moore Burden. Mother: Vernice Reeves. Source: Death Certificate.

BURDEN, MYRTLE
Born: 1902. Died: 1904. Father: James E. Burden. Mother: Vada Moore. Comments: Myrtle Burden's father moved to Horatio, Arkansas. He was expecting his family to follow him there when she died. Source: *Wills Point Chronicle*, January 7, 1904.

BURDEN, NEVADA M. "VADA"
Born: February 10, 1876, Texas. Died: November 30, 1958, Van Zandt County, Texas. Cause of Death: Pneumonia. Married: James Edward Burden, December 4, 1895. Children: Viola Mae and James Moore. Father: James Elbert Moore. Mother: Josephine Jane Faulk. Siblings: Elizabeth, Ubie, Fenton, Corbin, and Carbon. Source: Death Certificate.

BURDEN, NORA GENETTIE
Born: May 25, 1894. Died: April 23, 1895. Father: William Harrison Burden. Mother: Mary Jane English. Source: Tombstone.

BURDEN, VIOLA MAE
Born: June 23, 1900 Van Zandt County, Texas. Died: August 15, 1940, Victoria County, Texas. Cause of death: Automobile accident. Never married. Father: James Edward Burden. Mother: Nevada M. Moore. Occupation: Nurse. Comments: Viola Mae Burden had moved from Van Zandt County to Victoria and was a practicing nurse. She was killed in an automobile accident on State Highway 87 near Victoria. Source: Death Certificate.

BURGE, ALEX, JR.
Born: January 30, 1880. Died: November 4, 1892. Father: Alexander Burge. Mother: Josephine "Josie" Smith. Source: *Canton Telephone*, November 18, 1892.

DAVID LOTT CAIN *was a young man of unusual ability as a minister and possessed the many traits of character so necessary in one of his high calling. He was well known in the county and his high Christian character, upright life, and genial disposition won for him the highest respect from all—saint and sinner alike. He was in his second year as pastor in charge of the Canton circuit composed of Canton, Edgewood and Morris Chapel, and he was bending every effort to advance the Master's cause in that field.*
—Wills Point Chronicle

BURGE, ALEXANDER "ALEX"
Born: August 10, 1848, Indiana. Died: July 2, 1892, Van Zandt County, Texas. Married: Josephine "Josie" Smith, April 4, 1876. Father: Hamilton Burge. Mother: Sarah A. Walters (Waters). Occupation: Attorney. Source: *Canton Telephone*, August 5, 1892.

BURGE, HOWARD
Born: May 15, 1889, Van Zandt County, Texas. Died: January 28, 1909, Dallas County, Texas. Father: Alex Burge. Mother: Josephine Smith. Comments: Howard Burge had been reared in Canton but moved to Beaumont where he lived for four years. He was living in Dallas when he died. Sources: *Wills Point Chronicle*, February 4, 1909; *Grand Saline Sun*, February 4, 1909.

BURGE, JOSEPHINE "JOSIE"
Born: July 2, 1856, Baltimore County, Maryland. Died: May 26, 1930, Harris County, Texas. Cause of death:

Nephritis. Married: Alexander Burge, April 4, 1876. Father: J. F. Smith. Mother: Unknown. Source: Death Certificate.

Burk, J.F.
Born: October 6, 1856. Died: October 1, 1878. Married: M. E. Koonse, September 12, 1877. Father: Unknown Burk. Mother: Unknown. Comments: J. F. Burk died less than a year after his marriage. Source: Tombstone.

Burk, M.E.
Born: February 23, 1858. Died: January 23, 1881. Married: J. F. Burk. Father: Unknown. Mother: Unknown. Comments: M. E. Burk died three years after her husband's death. Source: Tombstone.

Burk, Willie
Born: July 22, 1878. Died: September 12, 1878. Father: J. F. Burk. Mother: M. E. Koonse. Source: Tombstone.

Burns, Alice C.
Born: December 17, 1874. Died: February 24, 1899. Married: J. F. Burns. Father: Unknown. Mother: Unknown. Source: Tombstone.

Burns, Missouri A.
Born: September 9, 1857. Died: February 5, 1895. Father: Unknown. Mother: Unknown. Married: H. B. Burns, March 22, 1888. Sources: Tombstone; *Van Zandt County Marriage Book, 1848-1908*.

C

Cain, David Lott
Born: November 4, 1869, Mississippi. Died: July 10, 1903, Van Zandt County, Texas. Cause of Death: Flux. Married: Fannie M. Fowler, November 9, 1897, Van Zandt County, Texas. Children: Marvin Wesley and Mary Bell. Father: Leonard Cain, South Carolina. Mother: Louisa G. Cain, Alabama. Occupation: Methodist minister. Comments: The *Wills Point Chronicle* reported the death of D. L Cain as follows: "Rev. D. L. Cain, Canton, died on July 10 of flux, aged 33. Mention was made last week of the serious illness of Rev. D. L. Cain of Canton. He lingered till Friday morning when death relieved him of his suffering and his spirit winged its way to God. Bro. Cain was a young man of unusual ability as a minister and possessed the many traits of character so necessary in one of his high calling. He was well known in the county and his high Christian character, upright life, and genial disposition won for him the highest respect from all—saint and sinner alike. He was in his second year as pastor in charge of the Canton circuit composed of Canton, Edgewood and Morris Chapel, and he was bending every effort to advance the Master's cause in that field. The remains were necessarily interred Friday afternoon, but services were not held till Saturday morning that many people who desired to attend from a distance might reach there. The impressive service was conducted by Presiding Elder J. T. Smith, with short talks from Revs. Kidd, Methvin and Turrentine. A wife and two children, mother, sisters and other relatives are left in sadness by his death. A brother, Rev. L. W. Cain, Kossuth Miss., arrived before his death." David moved from Mississippi to Texas and was admitted on trial to the Texas Methodist Conference in 1893. He ministered in various places in East Texas prior to accepting his position with the Canton Circuit. When he died, he had been married almost six years to Fannie Fowler. Her father was Rev. Littleton Fowler, a prominent and respected minister in Texas. Fannie never remarried. She died in 1942 in New Hanover County, North Carolina and was buried in Forest Park Cemetery, Harris County, Texas. Sources: Death Certificate of Regina Fowler Cain; *Wills Point Chronicle*, July 16, 1903; Ancestry.com.

Calhoon, (Calhoun) Rachel Ann
Born: March 12, 1807, North Carolina. Died: August 24, 1860, Van Zandt County, Texas. Married: Elizy A. Calhoun. Father: Unknown Harper. Mother: Unknown. Comments: Ann Calhoon's (Calhoun) grave is the second oldest marked grave in the Hillcrest Cemetery. In 1860 her husband was a wagon maker in the Canton, Texas area. In 1870 he was living with the family of Robert P. Parker in Van Zandt County. Source: Tombstone; 1860, 1870 U. S. Census.

Calhoun, Arthur
Born: 1886. Died: 1904. Cause of death: Unknown. Father: Unknown Calhoun. Mother: Mrs. Newtie Calhoun Comments: The *Wills Point Chronicle* reported Arthur Calhoun's death as follows: "Arthur Calhoun, aged 19 years, and a nephew of Rev. J. Calhoun of this city, was found dead in a bed at the house of Walter Clark at Mt. Sylvan, this county, this morning. Arthur had been in bad health for some time, but heart failure is assigned as the immediate cause of his sudden demise. Deceased has lived with Rev. J. C. Calhoun in this city for several years and had been at the home of Walter Clark, to whom he is related, for a few weeks. His father lives at Spring Hill, Upshur County. The remains will be expressed to Canton, where interment will be beside his mother." Arthur's uncle, John Caldwell Calhoun, was a Methodist minister at Canton and elsewhere in Van Zandt County. He died in 1935 and is buried in the Starrville Cemetery in Smith County, Texas. Sources: Tombstone; *Wills Point Chronicle*, December 15, 1904.

Ruth Carroll

Mattie Lorene (Carpenter) Branson

Katie Geraldine "Gerry" Campbell

Chili Campbell *was a lifelong resident of Canton. He served 19 years as a City Judge and 18 years as Justice of the Peace Precinct 2. In addition, he was past President of the Canton Lions Club and The Kiwanis Club, served on the East Texas Council of Governments, Canton Fire Department, and the Canton City Council.*

Calhoun, Baby Daughter
Born: unknown. Died: 1889. Father: unknown Calhoun. Mother: Newtie Calhoun. Source: Tombstone.

Calhoun, Newtie
Born: 1860. Died: 1889. Married: Unknown Calhoun. Father: Unknown. Mother: Unknown. Comments: The *Wills Point Chronicle* reported Mrs. Newtie Calhoun's death as follows: "Mrs. Calhoun, wife of Prof. Calhoun, of Canton died Monday and was buried Tuesday. She had been sick a long time. She leaves a husband and three children, one infant, to mourn her loss. Professor Calhoun has been at Canton a few months. He is the brother to Rev. J. C. Calhoun, the pastor of the Methodist church at that place." (Canton) Source: *Wills Point Chronicle*, August 22, 1889.

Campbell, Katie Geraldine "Gerry"
Born: September 9, 1927, Van Zandt County, Texas. Died: May 8, 2007, Smith County, Texas. Married: William Loyal Campbell, December 29, 1945. Children: Jed and Kenny. Father: Walter A. Clower. Mother: Edith Morris. Occupation: Bank officer for Athens Federal Savings and Loan. Source: *Van Zandt News*, May 13, 2007.

Campbell, Kenny Loyal
Born: August 24, 1948, Texas. Died: June 29, 1954, Van Zandt County, Texas. Father: William Loyal Campbell. Mother: Katie Geraldine Clower. Comments: Kenny Campbell's father was a long-time Justice of the Peace in Van Zandt County, Texas. Source: Eubank Funeral Home records.

Campbell, William Loyal "Chili" "Judge"
Born: September 8, 1924, Van Zandt County, Texas. Died: July 15, 2006, Van Zandt County, Texas. Married: Katie Geraldine Clower, December 29, 1945. Children: Jed and Kenny. Father: Alfred Campbell. Mother: Grace Jeanette Emerson. Occupation: City Judge, Justice of the Peace Precinct 2. Comments: Chili Campbell was a lifelong resident of Canton. He served nineteen years as a City Judge and eighteen years as Justice of the Peace Precinct 2. In addition, he was past President of the Canton Lions Club and The Kiwanis Club, served on the East Texas Council of Governments, Canton Fire Department, and the Canton City Council. He was a member of the Canton Church of Christ at Big Rock for over fifty years. Source: *Van Zandt News,* July 23, 2006.

Canterbury, Clement Anna
Born: April 20, 1884, McLennan County, Texas. Died: November 1, 1953, Van Zandt County, Texas. Married: John Franklin Canterbury, December 23, 1903. Father: George Rayford. Mother: Julia Turner. Sources: *Canton*

Herald, November 5, 1953; Eubank Funeral Home records.

CANTERBURY, JOHN FRANKLIN
Born: May 29, 1880, Red River County, Texas. Died: January 23, 1964, Van Zandt County, Texas. Cause of death: Heart disease. Married: (1) Clement Anna Rayford, December 23, 1903. (2) Lou Canterbury. Father: John Canterbury. Mother: Mary Jane Berry. Occupation: Certified Public Accountant. Comments: John F. Canterbury was head of the Accounting Department of the Whitney Dam Project. Sources: Death Certificate; *Canton Herald*, January 30, 1964; Eubank Funeral Home records.

CARROLL, RUTH
Born: May 8, 1902, Van Zandt County, Texas. Died: May 12, 1998, Henderson County, Texas. Married: (1) Owen Springer, June 12, 1932. Children: One child died in infancy. (2) Odes Boyd Carroll, August 31, 1957. Father: Thomas Rusk Yantis. Mother: Belle Coy Riley. Occupation: Dean of Women at Mary Hardin Baylor, Belton, Bell County, Texas. Siblings: David, Mary, Albert, Robert Hobbs, Ralph, and Baby. Other siblings died young. Comments: Ruth Carroll lived most of her life in Van Zandt County. Her parents were pioneer settlers and prominent citizens of the county. Her first husband was a popular Canton druggist. Ruth retired as Dean of Women at Mary Hardin Baylor College in Belton, Texas in 1972. She is buried next to her first husband. Her second husband died in 1972 and is not buried in Hillcrest Cemetery. Sources: *Van Zandt News*, May 17, 1998; Tom McKinnon, Yantis Family historian

CASTLE, SAM
Born: December 25, 1894, Angelina County, Texas. Died: October 31, 1963, Dallas County, Texas. Cause of death: Heart disease. Married: Louise Bell, August 8, 1924. Father: Babe Castle. Mother: Francis Black. Occupation: Café owner. Military: WWI, Pvt. U. S. Army. Sources: Death Certificate; *Van Zandt County Marriage Records, 1909-1931.*

CHANEY, ANNIE BELL
Born: 1896. Died: February 13, 1910. (Tombstone date is incorrect.) Cause of death: Burns. Father: Benjamin McClellan "Mack" Chaney. Mother: Lucy Steed Phillips. Siblings: Kitty A., William Gordon, Odis Maude, Ollie Lee, Nora Lee, Homer Henry, and Mary Etta. Comments: After her parents' deaths, Annie Chaney and her younger siblings lived with their sister, Nora Lee and her husband, Les Lapington, in the Highland community of Van Zandt County, Texas. Annie and her sister, Mary, were in the house alone, and Annie was cleaning the lamps and filling them with oil. She spilled some kerosene on her dress. When she went to the fireplace mantle to get a needle to repair her dress, her clothes ignited and she burned to death. Sources: Tombstone; *Grand Saline Sun*, February 17, 1910; Kitty Wheeler, Chaney Family historian.

Benjamin Oscar Chaney and Annie Maude Chaney

CHANEY, ANNIE MAUDE
Born: January 21, 1879, Tennessee. Died: January 31, 1941, Van Zandt County, Texas. Cause of death: Fall. Married: Benjamin Oscar Chaney, May 6, 1900. Father: J. W. Webb, Tennessee. Mother: Unknown. Children: Elmer Benjamin, Velma Lee, Alva, Jesse Raymond, Annie Lillie, Willie Jo, and Charity Elizabeth. Comments: Annie Maude Chaney was at home in the Central Community of Van Zandt County when she fell. Her head injury caused her death. Sources: Death Certificate; *Canton Herald*, February 6, 1941. Find A Grave.

CHANEY, BENJAMIN BURGESS
Born: November 19, 1810, Tennessee. Died: July 9, 1878, Van Zandt County, Texas. Married: (1) Mary Melissa McClellan, November 20, 1833, St. Clair County, Alabama. Children: William J., Thomas W., James Marion, Evaline, and Zacharia Taylor "Jack." (2) Margaret G. McClellan, 1852, St. Clair County, Alabama. Children: Margaret, Benjamin "Mack," and Lucinda. Occupation: Farmer. Comments: Benjamin Chaney was the patriarch of the

Chaney family who came to Van Zandt County with the McClellan's in the 1870's. Ben married two daughters of Thomas McClellan. His first wife died in 1851. He married her sister in 1852. Source: *Van Zandt County Texas Biographies-Vol II, 1848-1991.*

CHANEY, BENJAMIN MCCLELLAN "MACK"
Born: August 1859. Died: 1903. Cause of death: Consumption (Tuberculosis). Married: (I) Louisa "Eliza" Ballard, October 4, 1878, Van Zandt County, Texas. (2) N. Ludy Pennington, September 29, 1883, Van Zandt County, Texas. (3) Mrs. Lucy A. Steed Phillips, November 15, 1893, Van Zandt County, Texas. Father: Benjamin Burgess Chaney. Mother: Margaret G. McClellan. Siblings: William J., Thomas W., and Zacharia. Sources: *Van Zandt County Marriage Records, 1848-1908;* Kitty Wheeler, Chaney Family historian.

CHANEY, BENJAMIN OSCAR
(Photo page 35) Born: November 7, 1874. Died: November 17, 1957. Cause of death: Stomach cancer. Married: Annie Maude Webb, May 6, 1900. Father: Thomas Washington Chaney. Mother: Mary M. McClellan. Children: Lessie Mae, Elmer Benjamin, Velma Lee, Alva Berlin, Jessie Raymond, and William Ovalie. Sources: Death Certificate, Kitty Wheeler, Chaney Family historian.

CHANEY, CHARLES MAX
Born: September 21, 1948, Van Zandt County, Texas. Died: June 14, 2004, Van Zandt County, Texas. Never married. Father: James Clayton Chaney. Mother: Nora Mattie Windham. Source: Eubank Funeral Home records.

CHANEY, GLADYS
Born: February 9, 1905. Died: October 23, 1905. Father: William Ovalie Chaney. Mother: Bertie Hartman. Sources: Tombstone; *Van Zandt County Marriage Records 1848-1905;* Kitty Wheeler, Chaney Family historian.

CHANEY, JAMES CLAYTON
Born: September 26, 1915. Died: May 16, 1988. Married: Nora Mattie Windham, September 11, 1937. Children: James Don, Charles Max, Ronald Lee, Winell, and Bobbie Fern. Father: Charlie Pinkney Chaney. Mother: Carrie Lenora Staley. Occupation: Heavy equipment operator, Baptist minister. Sources: 1920 U. S. Census; U. S. Social Security Index; *Van Zandt News*, May 22, 1988.

CHANEY, JAMES DON
Born: July 10, 1941. Died: February 17, 1956. Cause of death: Automobile accident. Father: James Clayton Chaney. Mother: Nora Mattie Windham. Siblings: Charles Max, Ronald Lee, Winell, and Bobbie Fern. Comments: Two Canton High School students were killed, and three injured in a head-on collision at the intersection of Hwy 64 and Hwy 17. Neither James Don Chaney (age 14) nor Sidney Elgine Pool (age 21) survived the accident. The accident occurred in front of the Chaney home. Donald Pool and Ronnie Don Cox were injured in the accident. Mrs. Ruby Faye Stewart, 48, of Lubbock was the driver of the 1953 Buick involved in the collision. Sources: *Canton Herald*, February 23, 1956, Hilliard Funeral Home records.

CHANEY, LUCY PHILLIP
Born: 1872, Alabama. Died: 1906, Van Zandt County, Texas. Married: Benjamin McClellen "Mack" Chaney, November 15, 1893. Father: John William Phillip. Mother: Edna Hunt. Children: Annie, Homer, and Mary Etta. Source: Kitty Wheeler, Chaney Family historian.

CHANEY, LUDY PENNINGTON
Born: 1868. Died: March 1892. Married: Benjamin "Mack" Chaney, September 29, 1883. Father: Unknown Pennington. Mother: Unknown. Source: Tombstone.

CHANEY, MARGARET ANN
Born: August 14, 1881, Jasper County, Missouri. Died: April 7, 1957, Dallas County, Texas. Cause of death: Myocardial failure. Married: Robert Lee Chaney, August 7, 1899, Van Zandt County, Texas. Children: Thomas Monroe, Adie, Clyde, Claude, Warren, Farris, Herron, Houston, Ethel, Randa Mae, and Octavia. Father: Francis M. "Fred" Hinkle. Mother: Sara Ann Foster. Sources: *Canton Herald*, April 11, 1957; Eubank Funeral Home records; Find A Grave.

CHANEY, MARY M. "MOLLIE"
Born: 1845, Talladega County, Alabama. Died: October 14, 1924, Van Zandt County, Texas. Married: Thomas Washington Chaney, February 8, 1867. Children: Amanda Adella, James C, Robert Lee, Alice, Benjamin Oscar, and William O. Father: Robert McClellan. Mother: Elizabeth Knox. Comments: Mary McClellan came to Van Zandt County, Texas in the 1870's with her family and her husband's family, the Chaneys. They were neighbors in Alabama. Mary's husband was a Confederate veteran. She received a pension for his service. Sources: *Civil War Records of Van Zandt County;* Kitty Wheeler, Chaney Family historian.

CHANEY, NORA MATTIE
Born: June 21, 1920. Died: January 13, 2006. Married: James Clayton Chaney, September 11, 1937. Children: James Don, Charles Max, Ronald Lee, Winell, Bobbie Fern. Father: Will Windham. Mother: Purity Smith. Sources: *Van Zandt News*, January 22, 2006; Hilliard Funeral Home records.

CHANEY, ROBERT LEE
Born: November 19, 1870, Talladega County, Alabama. Died: October 17, 1944, Jim Wells County, Texas. Cause

Thomas Washington Chaney *Mary M. "Mollie" Chaney*

Margaret Ann Chaney and Robert Lee Chaney

of death: Heart disease. Married: Margret Ann Hinkle, August 7, 1899. Children: Ethel, Thomas Monroe, Claude, Clyde, Warren, Farris, Herron, Houston, Randa Mae, and Octavia. Father: Thomas W. Chaney. Mother: Mary M. McClellen. Sources: Death Certificate; 1910 U. S. Census; *Canton Herald*, October 19, 1944.

CHANEY, RONALD LEE "RED"
Born: September 26, 1952. Died: October 18, 2016. Never married. Father: James Clayton Chaney. Mother: Nora Mattie Windom. Siblings: James Don, Charles Max, Bobbie Fern, and Winell. Source: Hilliard Funeral Home records.

CHANEY, THOMAS WASHINGTON
Born: October 23, 1837, Talladega County, Alabama. Died: March 10, 1903, Van Zandt County, Texas. Cause of death: Black Jaundice. Married: Mary M. "Mollie" McClellan, February 8, 1867. Father: Benjamin Burgess Chaney. Mother: Melissa McClellan. Occupation: Farmer. Military: CSA, Co. A. 8th Mississippi. Cavalry. Comments: The Chaney's and McClellan's were friends, neighbors, and relatives in Talladega County, Alabama. Thomas Chaney's wife was his first cousin. She was the daughter of Robert McClellan, Melissa's brother. The McClellan and Chaney families came to Texas together sometime after 1870 and settled in Van Zandt County. Source: Kitty Wheeler, Chaney Family historian.

CHANEY, TRAVIS AUBREY "JACK"
Born: February 6, 1910. Died: October 10, 1976. Single. Father: Vernon Lee Chaney. Mother: Maude Wolf. Source: Death Certificate.

CHAPPELL, BABY
Born: Unknown. Died: 1896. Father: Unknown Chappell. Mother: Unknown. Comments: The baby is buried next to Jane Chappell. Source: Broken Tombstone.

CHAPPELL, HALLIE
Born: September 11, 1900. Died: October 2, 1900. Father: A. B. Chappell. Mother: Unknown. Sources: Tombstone; *Free State Enterprise*, October 4, 1900.

CHAPPELL, JANE
Born: July 13, 1823, Clark County, Mississippi. Died: August 3, 1912, Van Zandt County, Texas. Cause of death: Dropsy. Married: Mastin Chappell, January 19, 1854. Father: Unknown Williams. Mother: Unknown. Children: Albert, Davis, Columbus, and Mary (two infant deaths). Comments: Jane Chappell died at the home of her son, Columbus. She came to Van Zandt County in 1852 with her father's family. Source: *Wills Point Chronicle*, August 12, 1912.

CHAPPELL, JEFF DAVID "J.D."
Born: February 16, 1857, Texas. Died: March 5, 1908, Van Zandt County, Texas. Single. Father: Mastin Chappell, Mississippi. Mother: Jane Chappell, Mississippi. Occupation: Farmer. Sources: 1880 U. S. Census; *Wills Point Chronicle*, August 8, 1912.

CHAPPELL, MASTIN
Born: February 28, 1830, Mississippi. Died: March 28, 1873, Van Zandt County, Texas. Married: Jane Williams, January 19, 1854. Military: CSA, 11 TX Inf. Co.1. Comments: Mastin Chappell was born in Mississippi but was in Van Zandt County by 1854. He received a Texas Land Patent on July 28, 1871 for his Civil War service which granted him 160 acres in Van Zandt County. Sources: Texas General Land Office; *Wills Point Chronicle*, August 8, 1912.

CHITTY, MELVIN CALVIN
Born: August 19, 1901, Van Zandt County, Texas. Died: March 4, 1951, Van Zandt County, Texas. Cause of death: Drowning. Married: Viola Wilburn. Children: Larry Joe, Wilburn, Owen Leonard, Shirley Ann, Jessie Mae,

John E. Clancey *was a practicing attorney but was also involved in the affairs of the county. He served on numerous committees working to benefit the city and county—schools, land, and the Courthouse building, among others. He was appointed Postmaster of Canton on January 4, 1864. John's wife, Frances, was one of the first Canton residents to open a boarding house. In 1858 she bought lots on the northwest side of the courthouse square, where she later built the Clancey Hotel.*

Melrose, and Melvin Jr. Father: George Price Chitty. Mother: India Rosella Thurman. Occupation: Farmer. Comments: Melvin Chitty drowned in the Mathis Lake which was located about one mile from Canton on the Old Kaufman Hwy on the A. D. Mathis farm. He had gone out to check on some tomato hot beds. When he didn't return, searchers found his body in the lake. It was ruled an accidental drowning. Sources: Death Certificate; *Canton Herald*, March 8, 1951; Hilliard and Sons Funeral Home records.

Chitty, Melvin, Jr.

Born: June 6, 1951. Died: June 6, 1951. Father: Melvin C. Chitty. Mother: Viola Wilburn. Source: Hilliard and Sons Funeral records.

Chitty, Owen Leonard

Born: March 15, 1932, Van Zandt County, Texas. Died: August 10, 1965, Dallas County, Texas. Married: Olene Inice Unknown. Father: Melvin C. Chitty. Mother: Viola Wilburn. Occupation: Cook. Sources: Death Certificate; *Canton Herald*, August 12, 1965.

Chitty, (Hargrove) Viola "Ola"

Born: April 26, 1907, Van Zandt County, Texas. Died: May 24, 1978, Harris County, Texas. Buried under "Chitty" next to her first husband. Cause of death: Pneumonia. Married: (1) Melvin Calvin Chitty. Children: Larry Joe, Wilburn, Owen Leonard, Shirley, Jessie Mae, Melrose, and Melvin, Jr. (2) Sterling Hargrove. Father: William H. Wilburn. Mother: Neppie A. Burns. Occupation: Seamstress. Comments: Viola Wilburn was born in the Old Bethel Community of Van Zandt County. Her husband was a farmer who died from an accidental drowning in 1951 near Canton. She later married a Hargrove who preceded her in death. She lived in Canton for 38 years prior to moving to Houston where she died. Sources: Death Certificate; *Canton Herald*, June 1, 1978.

Clancey, John E.

Born: ca 1811, New York, New York. Died: November 30, 1871, Van Zandt County, Texas. Married: Frances F. Unknown, Alabama. Occupation: Attorney. Comments: John E. Clancey moved his family to Van Zandt County in 1854 from Spring Fields, Limestone County, Texas. On February 24, 1859, he received a Nacogdoches 3rd Class Land Grant of 319 acres of land in Henderson and Van Zandt Counties (Patent #1044). He was a practicing attorney but was also involved in the affairs of the county. He served on various committees including schools, land, repairing of the courthouse and others which benefited the county and Canton. He was appointed Postmaster of Canton on January 4, 1864 and served until October 15, 1864. John's wife, Frances, is known to have been one of the first Canton residents to open a boarding house (Clancey Hotel). In 1858, she bought lots in Canton on the northwest side of the courthouse square and later built the hotel. The building was of pole construction with the walls and floors of several rooms covered with rough lumber while the kitchen and dining rooms had dirt floors. After her husband's death in 1871, Frances continued to run the boarding house serving local residents. She later married J. T. Davis, January 20, 1876; and in 1880, she sold her holdings in Canton and moved to Grand Saline, Texas. She opened a restaurant alongside the railroad tracks. Frances operated the restaurant in Grand Saline until she was an elderly woman. Sources: 1860, 1870 U. S. Census; Texas General Land Office; *History of Van Zandt County by W. S. Mills*; *Van Zandt County Court Minutes, Volumes A & B.*

Clark, Artie May

Born: July 22, 1913. Died: July 22, 1913. Father: Samuel Benjamin Clark. Mother. Sarah O. Clark. Source: Tombstone.

Elizabeth Averilla Clark

Owen C. Cornelius

Percy R. Clark *was one of Canton's earliest newspaper editors / publishers. He worked at several papers during his career, including managing the Canton weekly, the* Free State Enterprise. *He left the newspaper in 1901 to become Deputy City Marshall of Grand Saline, Texas.*

Clark, Doc Franklin

Born: February 25, 1853, Alabama. Died: December 17, 1923, Dallas County, Texas. Married: Fannie Aurelia McCurley, March 12, 1876. Children: Percy R., Mattie, and Loy. Father: William Clark. Mother: Rebecca Dulaney. Occupation: Drugstore owner, stockholder in Texas State Bank, Canton, Texas; part owner Canton Telephone Exchange. Comments: Doc Franklin Clark came from Alabama in the early 1870's. The *Wills Point Chronicle* reported his death as follows: "The deceased died at a sanitarium in Dallas Monday. He was for years a prominent citizen and druggist at Canton, associated with his brother Tom Clark, who died a few years ago at Canton. D. F. Clark was engaged in the drug business in Dallas at the time of his death. He leaves a son and daughter." Sources: *Wills Point Chronicle*, December 10, 1923; Ancestry.com.

Clark, Elizabeth Averilla

Born: September 29, 1861. Died: September 19, 1896. Married: Nathan S. Clark. Father: William Thompson McCarty. Mother: Nancy Zilpha Averilla Barton. Siblings: James Madison and William Jr. Source: Find A Grave.

Clark, Fannie Aurellia

Born: April 11, 1857, Alabama. Died: March 17, 1920, Tarrant County, Texas. Cause of death: Hit by a train. Married: Doc Franklin Clark, March 12, 1876. Father: U.S. McCurley. Mother: Jinnie Moore. Comments: *The Ft. Worth Star-Telegram* on March 25, 1920 reported Fannie Clarks death as follows: "The body of Mrs. Fannie Clark, 70, of 1522 East Murphy Street, was found on the I.&G.N. railroad tracks near the Cobb brick factory, at 7 o'clock Wednesday morning by Charles Webner, telegraph operator, who was going to work. The body was badly mutilated. It is supposed that the I.&G.N, ran over her about 6:30 o'clock. Mrs. Clark had left home at 4 o'clock Wednesday morning clad in her night clothes and a dressing gown. The family had been hunting her for several hours. Her body was shipped back to Canton for burial." Sources: T*exas Deaths, 1890-1976*; *Ft. Worth Star Telegram*, March 25, 1920; Ancestry.com.

Clark, Francis May "Fannie"

Born: August 27, 1868, Smith County, Texas. Died: July 21, 1896, Van Zandt County, Texas. Married: Samuel Benjamin Clark, December 25, 1884. Father: William Thompson McCarty. Mother: Nancy Averilla Barton. Source: Ancestry.com.

Clark, Infant

Born: December 28, 1914. Died: December 28, 1914. Father: Samuel Benjamin Clark. Mother: Sarah O. Clark. Source: Tombstone.

Clark, Ophelia

Born: 1875. Died: January 1915. Married: Samuel Benjamin Clark, April 13, 1898. Father; James Chesley Couch Mother: Paralee Johnson. Siblings: William F., James Henry, Victor, and Mattie Jane. Source: Find A Grave.

Clark, Percy R.
Born: December 31, 1876. Died: October 30, 1915. Cause of death: Tuberculosis. Single. Father: Doc Franklin Clark. Mother: Fannie A. McCurley. Occupation: Newspaper editor and publisher. Comments: In 1898 Percy Clark began working for Morgan G. Sanders who published a weekly newspaper, in Canton, Texas. When Sanders left to become Assistant Journal Clerk for the Texas State Senate, he turned the newspaper over to Clark to manage. Clark left the newspaper in August, 1901 to become Deputy City Marshall of Grand Saline, Texas. Clark had always been a newspaper man by trade. He worked at various newspapers during his lifetime. In August of 1913, while suffering from tuberculous, he sold his paper in Sinton, Texas. He relocated to Denver, Colorado for health reasons. He died in his father's house in Canton in October of 1915 when he was 39. Sources: *Wills Point Chronicle*, August 14, 1913 and November 4, 1915; *Canton Herald*, November 5, 1915.

Clark, Samuel Benjamin
Born: May 12, 1866, Van Zandt County, Texas. Died: July 13, 1942, Van Zandt County, Texas. Cause of death: Heart disease. Married: (1) Francis May "Fannie" McCarty, December 25, 1884. (2) Ophelia Couch, April 13, 1898. Father: Samuel Rosamond Clark, Alabama. Mother: Sarah Chapman Martin, Alabama. Occupation: Farmer. Sources: Death Certificate; *Canton Herald*, July 23, 1942.

Clark, Sarah Chapman
Born: February 5, 1838, Alabama. Died: April 11, 1879, Van Zandt County, Texas. Married: Samuel Rosamond Clark, February 12, 1856, Alabama. Children: Martha Ann, Samuel, Henry, and Waltie. Father: Elijah Martin. Mother: Catherine Greer. Comments: Sarah Clark and her family moved from Alabama to Freestone County, Texas. Her father received a Texas Land Grant near Martin's Mill in Van Zandt County. Samuel and Sarah had six children before she died in 1879. Samuel went to Ada, Oklahoma Territory with his son Henry. Samuel died January 11, 1911 and is buried in the Rosedale Cemetery, Ada, Oklahoma. Sources: *Van Zandt County History Book, Volume I*; Find A Grave.

Clark, William Thomas "Tom"
Born: March 12, 1838, Calhoun County, Alabama. Died: April 13, 1915, Van Zandt County, Texas. Single. Father: William Clark. Mother: Rebecca Dulaney. Occupation: Druggist. Military: CSA, 4th Alabama Battalion, which later became a regiment. Comments: Tom Clark came to Van Zandt County in 1866 and moved to Canton in 1875. In 1881 he and his brother, Doc Franklin, opened a drugstore. They became prominent businessmen, owning a drugstore, a telephone exchange; and they chartered the Texas State Bank of Canton in 1909. Source: *Van Zandt County History Book, Volume I.*

Frank Augustus Corry *was a resident of Canton most of his life. He and his wife opened the first mobile-home sales business in the city.*

Clifton, George Turner
Born: January 20, 1866, Hopkins County, Texas. Died: July 21, 1938, Kaufman County, Texas. Cause of death: Paralysis. Married: Kate Z. McCoy. Father: James Clifton, Tennessee. Mother: Liza Hudson, Hopkins County, Texas. Occupation: Farmer. Source: Death Certificate.

Clifton, Kate Zora
Born: January 14, 1867, Hopkins County, Texas. Died: December 23, 1945, Stephens County, Texas. Cause of death: Stomach cancer. Married: George Turner Clifton. Father: Oliver Cromwell McCoy. Mother: Martha Gaddis. Sources: Death Certificate; *Canton Herald*, January 3, 1946.

Clifton, Mable
Born: June 2, 1904, Grant County, Arkansas. Died: November 11, 1920, Van Zandt County, Texas. Cause of death: Malaria. Single. Father: F. H. Clifton. Mother: Marian A. Vaughn. Source: Death Certificate.

Clower, Edith Mae
Born: September 10, 1910, Van Zandt County, Texas. Died: June 29, 1954, Van Zandt County, Texas. Cause of death: Automobile accident. Married: Walter Ashley Clower. Child: Katie Geraldine. Father: H. L. Morris. Mother: Hesta Pearl Stroud. Sources: Death Certificate, Hilliard Funeral Home Records.

Clower, Walter Ashley
Born: July 4, 1907. Died: January 19, 1976. Cause of death: Meningitis. Married: (1) Edith May Morris. Child: Katie Geraldine. (2) Verba Clower. Father: John Clower. Mother: Ina Smith. Occupation: Butane Salesman. Source: Death Certificate.

Coleman, Serena Rachel "Rena"
Born: January 7, 1853, Texas. Died: July 14, 1904, Van Zandt County, Texas. Married: William D. Coleman, July 29, 1873. Father: James Terrell Copeland. Mother: Elizabeth "Eliza" Austin. Sources: *Wills Point Chronicle*, August 18, 1904; Ancestry.com.

Coleman, William David
Born: May 28, 1853, Alabama. Died: April 19, 1928, Dallas County, Texas. Cause of death: Influenza. Married: (1) Serena Rachel Copeland, July 29, 1873, Smith County, Texas. (2) Sara Ann Copeland. Father: John G. Coleman Mother: Isabella L. Nolen. Occupation: Farmer. Sources: Death Certificate, Ancestry.com.

Cooper, Arthur
Born: August 20, 1877, St. Tammany Parish, Louisiana. Died: August 10, 1953, Van Zandt County, Texas. Cause of death: Heart attack. Married: Louis "Ludie" Traxler, September 22, 1898. Children: S. F., K. F., and Mrs. L. C. Turner. Father: Emile Cooper, Virginia. Mother: Victoria Stringer, Van Zandt County, Texas. Source: Eubank Funeral Home records.

Cooper, Louis Henry "Ludie"
Born: August 19, 1878, Hinds County , Mississippi. Died: February 12, 1959, Van Zandt County, Texas. Married: Arthur Cooper, September 22, 1898. Children: S. F., K. F., and Mrs. L. C. Turner. Father: Henry Traxler, North Carolina. Mother: Caladonia Unknown, Mississippi. Sources: Death Certificate, 1880 U. S. Census, Eubank Funeral Home records.

Cornelius, Owen C.
(Photo page 39) Born: January 2, 1896, Van Zandt County, Texas. Died: November 1, 1971, Dallas County, Texas. Cause of death: Heart disease. Married: Willie May Green, March 21, 1923. Father: Henry Cornelius. Mother: Lou Bradley. Occupation: Farmer, janitor. Military: WWI, TX PFC, Co. A. 507 Ser. Bn., 5 Serv. Co. 20 Engrs. Source: Death Certificate.

Cornelius, Tom G.
Born: February 27, 1892. Died: October 12, 1932. Cause of death: Heart disease. Married: Roxie Preisley, July 6, 1920. Father: Henry Cornelius. Mother: Lou (Lue) Bradley. Occupation: Farmer. Military: WWI, Pvt., TX 20 Engrs. USMC. Sources: Death Certificate, Marriage License, Texas Death Index, WWI Draft Card.

Clara Effie Couch and William Francis Couch

Clara Effie Byrd *graduated from East Texas Normal College in Commerce, Texas. She then taught school for several years and worked in a dry goods store before marrying* **William Francis Couch,** *who owned a livery stable. In 1914, Couch opened the first Ford dealership in Canton. During the early years, when he sold a car, he had to teach each buyer how to drive.*

Corry, Frank Augustus
Born: July 21, 1933. Died: February 21, 2017. Married: Norma Jean Terry. Children: Frank Jr., Diane, Donna, and Brenda. Father: Clifton White Corry, Sr. Mother: Thelma Lometa Swepston. Siblings: Cliff Jr., Florence, Mary, and Martha. Occupation: Businessman. Comments: Frank Corry had been a resident of Canton most of his life. He and his wife opened the first mobile home sales business in Canton. Source: Hilliard Funeral Home records.

Marion Love Cox *taught school in Van Zandt County for a short time before attending Kentucky School of Medicine and graduating in 1894. In 1905, he and his wife Millie Youngblood moved to Canton where he practiced medicine for twenty-six years and was recognized as one of the leading physicians in all of East Texas. Dr. Cox was also very active in the business and civic affairs of Van Zandt County serving as President of the First National Bank, Canton Lumber Company, and the Van Zandt County Medical Society. He was a charter member of the East Texas Chamber of Commerce and served on its Board of Directors.*

Couch, Clara Effie
(Photo page 41) Born: August 28, 1888, Van Zandt County, Texas. Died: March 4, 1968, Van Zandt County, Texas. Married: William Francis Couch, August 16, 1914. Children: Lorene (stepdaughter), Naoma, Etta Ruth, and Willie Byrd. Father: William B. Byrd. Mother: Mary Elizabeth Livesey. Comments: Effie Couch graduated from East Texas Normal College in Commerce, Texas. In 1908 she taught school in Clarendon, Texas; and in 1912, she taught school at Cobb Switch, near Wills Point. Effie also worked in Wills Point at Rose Dry Goods before marrying William Couch in 1914, and at Riley Richardson Dry Goods in Canton. Sources: Shirley Estes Poulan, Couch Family historian, Eubank Funeral Home records.

Couch, Rube T.
Born: April 4, 1894, Cherokee County, Texas. Died: November 19, 1970, Van Zandt County, Texas. Father: James Chesley Couch. Mother: Paralee Johnson. Comments: Rube Couch often lived with family members William, Effie, and Eva Couch. Eva was married to Henry Jones, one of the largest syrup producers in East Texas. Sources: Eubank Funeral Home records, Shirley Estes Poulan, Family historian.

Couch, Thomas W.
Born: January 27, 1870. Died: February 25, 1907. Cause of death: Pneumonia. Married: May Virginia Mills, February 25, 1900. Father: Henry Andrew Couch. Mother: Ida Holder. Sources: Tombstone, Find A Grave.

Couch, William Francis
(Photo page 41) Born: November 15, 1878, Cherokee County, Texas. Died: June 7, 1952, Van Zandt County, Texas. Cause of death: Stroke. Married: (1) Tabitha Francis Tomlin. Child: Lorene. (2) Clara Effie Byrd, August 16, 1914. Children: Naoma, Etta Ruth, and Willie Byrd. Father: James Chesley Couch, Cherokee County, Texas. Mother: Paralee Johnson, Cherokee County, Texas. Siblings: Ophelia, James Henry, Victor, and Mattie Jane. Comments: William Couch owned a livery stable in Canton from 1900-1914. He owned the first Ford dealership in Canton, 1914-1925. During the early years, when William sold a car, he had to teach each buyer how to drive. From 1925-1935, he was a cotton buyer for the government at Wills Point, grading and selling the cotton. In his later years, he milked cows and sold their milk to a local dairy. Sources: Death Certificate; Eubank Funeral Home Records; Shirley Estes Poulan, Family historian.

Covert, May Virginia
Born: March 25, 1880, Texas. Died: June 4, 1960, Bexar County, Texas. Cause of death: Heart disease. Married: (1) Thomas W. Couch, February 25, 1900. (2) Frederick W. Covert, July 2, 1911. Children: Mary Ruth, Frederick B., Howell Mills, and James Grady. Father: James Harvey Mills, Tuscaloosa County, Alabama. Mother: Mary Missouri Samuel, Alabama. Sources: Death Certificate; *Canton Herald*, June 9, 1960; Dr. Billy Glenn Foster, Foster Family historian; Find A Grave.

Cox, Altha Lee
Born: October 12, 1883, Robertson County, Texas. Died:

July 26, 1956, Van Zandt County, Texas. Married: Isaac Newton Cox, 1908. Father: Willie Jordon Moore. Mother: Sallie Gipson. Comments: Altha Cox's husband and five of her children preceded her in death. She had two surviving daughters. Sources: Canton Herald, August 2, 1956; Eubank Funeral Home records.

Cox, Casey Lee

Born: October 15, 1949. Died: January 6, 1998, Smith County, Texas. Married: Beverly Newman. Children: Christi, and stepsons Jason Warren, Jamie Warren, and Joshua Warren. Father: Lee Cox. Mother: Helen Marie Duncan. Occupation: Texas Power and Light. Military: Texas National Guard. Source: *Van Zandt News*, January 11, 1998.

Cox, Elizabeth Ann "Eliza"

Born: September 14, 1838, Martin County, Indiana. Died: April 6, 1910, Van Zandt County, Texas. Married: Richard Cox, Sr., December 6, 1860. Children: George W., John Wesley, Mary J., Margaret J., Isaac Newton, James T. , Grace P., and Richard E.. Father: Thomas Mitchell. Mother: Mary Wagaman. Siblings: George A., David, Dr. John Charles, and James Joseph. Comments: Richard and Elizabeth Cox moved from Illinois to Indiana in 1875 and to Van Zandt County in 1879. Sources: *Grand Saline Sun*, April 14, 1910; Find A Grave.

Cox, George W.

Born: October 3, 1862. Died: January 2, 1932, Van Zandt County, Texas. Married: Mattie E. Wolfe, February 7, 1910. Father: Richard Cox, Sr. Mother: Elizabeth Ann Mitchell. Siblings: John Wesley, Isaac Newton, and Richard E. Occupation: Farmer. Sources: Death Certificate, Find A Grave.

Cox, Helen Marie

Born: March 10, 1927, Navarro County, Texas. Died: August 4, 1993, Van Zandt County, Texas. Married: Lee Cox, October 11, 1946. Father: W. D. Duncan. Mother: Georgia Collier. Occupation: Nurse's aide. Source: *Canton Herald*, August 9, 1993.

Cox, Ida M.

Born: January 20, 1872, Van Zandt County, Texas. Died: December 26, 1944, Van Zandt County, Texas. Cause of death: Nephritis. Married: John Wesley Cox, January 22, 1891. Children: Henry Grady, and Adis Blanche. Father: Blake Perry, Alabama. Mother: Sarah J. McClellan, Alabama. Siblings: Howard O., Dora Effie, and Anna Blanche. Sources: Death Certificate, Hilliard Funeral Home records.

Cox, Isaac Newton "Ike"

Born: July 31, 1872, Martin County, Indiana. Died: July 24, 1943, Van Zandt County, Texas. Married: Altha Lee Moore. Father: Richard Cox, Indiana. Mother: Elizabeth Ann Mitchell, Indiana. Comments: Ike Cox came to Van Zandt County with his parents at the age of 3. He lived in the Willow Springs Community and had been a member of the Baptist Church for over forty years. Sources: *Canton Herald*, July 29, 1943; Eubank Funeral Home records.

Cox, John Wesley

Born: September 15, 1864, Martin County, Indiana. Died: April 4, 1946, Van Zandt County, Texas. Married: Ida M. Perry, January 22, 1891. Children: Henry Grady and Adis Blanche. Father: Richard Cox, Indiana. Mother: Elizabeth Ann Mitchell, Indiana. Occupation: Farmer. Sources: *Canton Herald,* April 11, 1946; Hilliard Funeral Home records.

Cox, Lee

Born: April 30, 1915, Van Zandt County, Texas. Died: September 29, 1958, Dallas County, Texas. Married: Helen Marie Duncan, October 11, 1946. Father: Dr. Marion Love Cox. Mother: Mollie Hassell Youngblood. Occupation: Farmer. Military: WW II. Sources: Death Certificate, Hilliard Funeral Home records.

Cox, Marion Love

Born: February 22, 1870, Van Zandt County, Texas. Died: October 29, 1931, Van Zandt County, Texas. Cause of death: Apoplexy (Stroke). Married: Millie Hassell Youngblood, August 12, 1894. Children: Dr. Kelley, Lila, Ben, and Lee. Father: Tillman Lindsey Cox, Alabama. Mother: Nancy A. Riley, Talladega County, Alabama. Siblings: Matilda, Louisa Susan, Kate, Silas Elam, and Ben. Occupation: Physician. Comments: M. L. Cox was born at Martins Mill on the 192-acre family farm. The land was a Texas Land Grant his father had received on August 11, 1858. He grew up working on this farm with his family. Marion graduated from the Alamo Institute at Ben Wheeler, one of the top schools in Van Zandt County at the time. He taught school for a short time, then he went to Lewisville, Kentucky to attend the Kentucky School of Medicine. He graduated in 1894. After his graduation in August, he married Millie Youngblood, the daughter of Mr. and Mrs. E. H. Youngblood of Ben Wheeler, Texas. He then began his medical practice. In 1905, Marion moved to Canton and purchased the practice of Dr. T. P. Davis. He was a practicing physician in Canton for twenty-six years and was ranked as one of the leading physicians of Van Zandt County and all of East Texas. He was also very active in business and civic affairs of Van Zandt County. In 1905, Harry Houston, a relative of Sam Houston, helped form the First National Bank, the first bank organized in Canton, Texas. Cox assumed control of this bank from Houston in 1907 and served as its President until his death. He was also involved in the real estate business with A. J. Brooks; and together, during World War I, they helped organize the Canton Lumber Company. Cox served as its president until he died. He was a charter member of the East Texas Chamber of Commerce and served on their Board of Directors. He also served as President of the Van Zandt County Medical Society, a Shriner in the Masons, and as a delegate to the State and National Democratic Conventions. Sources: Death Certificate; Texas General Land Office; *The Southland Vol XII*; 1880, 1920, 1930 U. S. Census; *Canton Herald,* October 30, 1931 and November 6, 1931.

COX, MATTIE E.
Born: August 12, 1881, Lee County, Mississippi. Died: December 21, 1932, Van Zandt County, Texas. Cause of death: Heart disease. Married: George Washington Cox, February 7, 1910. Father: Joe Wolfe, Georgia. Mother: Mary Jennings, Alabama. Source: Death Certificate.

Leaston "Lete" Davidson

LEASTON "LETE" DAVIDSON *joined the Confederate Army when the Civil War began, along with his father and two brothers. When the war ended, he came home to farm, later building a cotton gin and running a general mercantile store. At age 50, Davidson became a lawyer and served two terms as County Judge.*

COX, MILLIE
Born: October 12, 1874, Van Zandt County, Texas. Died: December 7, 1956, Cherokee County, Texas. Married: Dr. Marion Love Cox, August 12, 1894. Children: Dr. Kelly, Ben, Lee, and Lila. Father: Elidge H. Youngblood, Texas. Mother: Millie H. Chandler. Sources: *Canton Herald,* December 13, 1956; Hilliard & Sons Funeral Home records.

COX, RAMON LOY
Born: August 18, 1906. Died: September 18, 1906. Father: John Thomas Cox. Mother: Mrs. R. E. Reynolds. Sources: Tombstone, *Van Zandt County Marriage Records* 1848-1909.

COX, RICHARD
Born: May 10, 1842, Indiana. Died: January 6, 1907, Van Zandt County Texas. Married: Elizabeth Ann Mitchell, December 6, 1860. Children: George Washington, John Wesley, Mary J., Margaret J., Isaac N., John Thomas, Richard E., and Gracie. Father: Isaac Cox. Mother: Mary Williams. Military: Union-Co. H 67th Indiana Regiment. Comments: Richard Cox's family moved to Sumner County, Illinois by 1875. By 1879, the family was living in Van Zandt County. Source: Ancestry.com.

COX, RICHARD E.
Born: February 1, 1881. Died: July 10, 1896. Father: Richard S. Cox. Mother: Elizabeth Ann Mitchell. Siblings: George W., John Wesley, and Isaac Newton. Source: Tombstone.

COX, SILAS ELAM
Born: July 4, 1882, Van Zandt County, Texas. Died: February 15, 1942, Van Zandt County, Texas. Married: Sybil Verner, 1933. Father: Tillman Lindsey Cox. Mother: Nancy A. Riley. Occupation: Businessman, Postmaster. Comments: Elam Cox was born near Martins Mill. He was the son of early pioneers of Van Zandt County, Texas. He graduated from Martins Mill High School and then went to Dallas to pharmacy school. He graduated with a Pharmacy Degree in 1910. He returned to Martins Mill and established a drug business there. His first building was destroyed by a tornado in 1911. He moved to Canton, Texas in 1920, and worked with his brother, Dr. M. L. Cox at the First National Bank. He was President of the bank for a number of years. Elam spent one year in Washington D.C as Secretary to Congressman Morgan G. Sanders. In 1935, he was appointed Postmaster of the Canton Post Office and served about a year. Except for the time in school in Dallas, Texas and the time he spent in Washington, D. C., he lived in Van Zandt County all of his life. Sources: *Canton Herald*, February 19, 1942; Hilliard Funeral Home records.

Cox, Unknown
Comments: There is no first name or date on the tombstone. Source: Tombstone.

Cozby, Jettie Sue
Born: July 24, 1882, Washington County, Texas. Died: January 17, 1977, Van Zandt County, Texas. Married: Knox W. Cozby. Father: Andrew Monroe Jackson. Mother: Anna M. Jackson. Source: Eubank Funeral Home Records.

Cozby, Knox W.
Born: August 30, 1868. Died: April 17, 1929. Married: Jettie Sue Jackson. Father: John Cozby, Alabama. Mother: Elizabeth Smelley. Source: Eubank Funeral Home records.

Craft, Elizabeth E. "Bettie"
Born: September 15, 1832, Tennessee. Died: November 29, 1890. Married: James A. Craft. Children: Thomas Marvin, George R., Henry Jefferson, and Mary Bell. Father: Unknown Miller. Mother: Unknown. Comments: The Craft family was living in Kaufman County, Texas by 1860. They moved to Van Zandt County in the 1880's.. Sources: *Canton Telephone*, December 5, 1890; Find A Grave.

Craft, James A.
Born: January 9, 1812, Tennessee. Died: July 26, 1894, Van Zandt County, Texas. Married: Elizabeth "Bettie" E. Miller. Children: Thomas, M., George R., Edward, William A., Henry J., Bettie, and Mary. Occupation: Farmer. Comments: James and Bettie Craft moved to Kaufman County in 1860. They moved to Van Zandt County in the 1880's. After Bettie's death, James moved into the home of Henry Jefferson Craft (his son). They lived on a farm near Ben Wheeler, Texas. Henry was elected Van Zandt County Tax Assessor, District Clerk, County Clerk and Tax Assessor. Sources: 1860, 1870, 1880 U.S. Census, *History of Van Zandt County by W. S. Mills*, *Wills Point Chronicle*, August 2, 1894

C., W. J.
Born: Unknown. Died: Unknown. Father: Unknown. Mother: Unknown. Comments: W. J. C.'s grave only has a footstone with initials.

D

Darden, Charlie
Born: November 12, 1871. Died: May 17, 1892. Cause of death: Heart congestion. Father: Unknown Darden. Mother: Unknown. Comments: *The Canton Telephone*, May 20, 1892 reported Charlie Darden's death as follows: "Died: Tuesday evening at 1 o'clock of congestion. He had come to town with some pork to sell Monday Morning, and soon after making the sale, he was found by J. R. Kennedy in an unconscious state at an old house unoccupied, having spasms. His remains were interred in the Canton cemetery Wednesday at noon." There was no other information about this individual. Source: *Canton Telephone*, May 20, 1892.

Davidson, Leaston "Lete"
Born: January 1, 1847, Gadsden County, Florida. Died: January 25, 1924, Dallas County, Texas. Cause of death: Accident. Married: (1) Mary Anna "Annie" Germany, July 6, 1868. (2) Virginia Mae "Jennie" Germany, March 26, 1877. Children: John Wesley, Ada Virginia, and Wiley A. Father: John Wesley Davidson, Georgia. Mother: Emaline Spence, Georgia. Occupation: Farmer, cotton gin owner, merchant, lawyer, County Judge. Military: CSA, Private Co. D. 13th Texas Infantry. Comments: The Davidson family left Florida in 1853 and came to Texas. Leaston's father was a farmer; and his grandfather, William, was a carpenter. When the Civil War began, Leaston, along with his father and two brothers, joined the Confederate Army. After the end of the War, Leaston came home and farmed with his father. In 1868, he married Annie, the daughter of J. W. Germany. Annie died in 1872, and Leaston married her sister, Virginia, in 1877. He and his brother, James, built a cotton gin in the Davidson community and also ran a general mercantile store. When he was 50 years old, he became a lawyer and established his practice in Canton. He served two terms as County Judge (1917-1920), a position his son, John Wesley Davidson, held from 1901-1905. After his term as Judge, he moved to Dallas and opened a feed store with his grandson, W. H. Cole. On their way home from work, while riding in a hack, they were hit by an automobile; and Leaston died as a result. Sources: Death Certificate; *Grand Saline Sun*, February 7, 1924; Ancestry.com.

Davidson, Virginia M.
Born: September 24, 1845, Mississippi. Died: December 4, 1917. Married: Leaston Davidson, March 26, 1877. Children: John Wesley, Ada Virginia, and Wiley A. Father: John W. Germany. Mother: Elizabeth Jane Morris. Sources: *Canton Herald*, December 7, 1917; Ancestry.com.

Davidson, Wiley A.
Born: December 4, 1877, Texas. Died: July 30, 1920, Potter County, Texas. Cause of death: Pneumonia. Married: Emily Minnaugh, December 28, 1904. Father: Leaston Davidson, Florida. Mother: Virginia M. Germany, Mississippi. Occupation: Attorney at Law. Comments: Wiley Davidson's mother was the daughter of J. W. Ger-

The tombstone of Martha Eula Day reads: "Eula, Wife of Felix Day."

In February 1906, the widow **MARTHA EULA DAY** *married her second husband W.D. Hutcherson, a barber and Justice of the Peace. As reported in the* Grand Saline Sun, *her daughter said the couple "got along reasonably well except at times when Mr. Hutcherson had spells, caused principally by drink and various drugs." After three years, Eula decided she could no longer tolerate the marriage and told Mr. Hutcherson she was leaving. He begged her to give him one more chance. He then, in the presence of her daughter and "with his arm around his wife's neck, fired two very rapid shots and she fell in the hall. The third shot was at his own head, and he fell backwards upon the floor, dead." The murder was described as one of the saddest affairs in the history of Canton.*

many, an early pioneer of Van Zandt County. His uncle, Eugene Germany, was one of the more prominent oil men in Texas. Sources: Death Certificate; *Wills Point Chronicle*, August 5, 1920; *Grand Saline Sun*, August 5, 1920.

DAVIS, ALEXANDER M.
Born: August 8, 1835, Tennessee. Died: August, 1907, Van Zandt County, Texas. Married: (1) E. C. Jones, December 20, 1877. (2) Mrs. Nancy J. Price Bunch, December 16, 1879. Father: Unknown Davis. Mother: Unknown. Occupation: Farming. Sources: 1880 U. S. Census, Marriage Records of Van Zandt County 1848-1909.

DAVIS, CHARLES C. "CAPTAIN"
Born: December 6, 1837, Tennessee. Died: July 7, 1900, Van Zandt County, Texas. Cause of death: Stroke and paralysis. Married: Sarah Adelaide Varnell. Children: Thomas Porter and Sam. Father: Unknown Davis. Mother: Unknown. Occupation: W. & A Railroad Conductor. Comments: Charles Davis was born in Tennessee and moved to Georgia as a small boy. In 1893, he moved from Georgia to Florida. Charles was a conductor on the Western & Atlantic Railroad where he obtained the name "Captain." In 1896, he moved to Wichita County, Texas; and in 1899 he moved to Canton to live with his son, Dr. T. P. Davis. Thomas Porter was a prominent doctor in Van Zandt County for 25 years. In 1905, he moved to Kaufman County, Texas leaving three children and his parents buried in the Canton Cemetery. Sources: *Free State Enterprise*, July 12, 1900; *Willis Point Chronicle*, July 12, 1900; *Marriage Records of Van Zandt County, 1848-1909*; Ancestry.com.

DAVIS, CHARLES HENRY GRADY
Born: October 14, 1886, Van Zandt County, Texas. Died: October 27, 1890, Van Zandt County, Texas. Father: Dr. Thomas Porter "T. P." Davis. Mother: Julia Rusk Kellam. Sources: *Canton Telephone,* October 24, 1890 and November 7, 1890.

DAVIS, JACK
Born: April 17, 1900. Died: January 1, 1902. Father: Dr. Thomas Porter "T.P" Davis. Mother: Julia Rusk Kellam. Source: *Free State Enterprise*, January 2, 1902.

DAVIS, LITTLE SAM
Born: November 18, 1888. Died: October 16, 1889. Father: Dr. Thomas Porter "T. P." Davis. Mother: Julia Rusk Kellam. Source: *Canton Telephone,* October 18, 1889.

DAVIS, NANCY J.
Born: December 18, 1843, Claiborne Parish, Louisiana. Died: December 17, 1912, Van Zandt County, Texas. Married: (1) William Bunch. November 21, 1866. Children: Claborn, Margaret E., Josiah Frazier, and Archibald Henry. (2) Alexander M. Davis, December 16, 1879. Father: Josiah W. Price. Mother: Mary Ann Wilbanks. Sources: *Marriage Records of Van Zandt County, 1848-1908*; Ancestry.com.

Davis, Sarah Adelaide
Born: July 9, 1838. Died: January 19, 1902. Married: Charles C. Davis. Children: Thomas Porter and Sam. Father: Unknown Varnell. Mother: Unknown. Source: *Free State Enterprise*, January 23, 1902.

Davis, Sidney
Born: May 11, 1901, Louisiana. Died: June 5, 1962, Texas. Cause of death: Heart disease. Married: Floyd Davis. Father: Scott Johnson. Mother: Lisa Williams. Source: Death Certificate.

Dawson, Frank Albert
Born: April 14, 1892, Van Zandt County, Texas. Died: March 28, 1941, Van Zandt County, Texas. Cause of death: Farming accident. Married: Kathryn M. Smith, November 19, 1919. Father: Frank Alexander Dawson, Mississippi. Mother: Ella Barnett, Rusk County, Texas. Military: WWI, US Army 36 Division. Occupation: Farmer. Comments: Frank Dawson was a well-known farmer in the Dawson community which was named after his father. On the day of his death, Frank's hired hand stuck a tractor in the wet ground, and Frank was assisting him in getting the tractor unstuck. Frank was attempting to drive the tractor out and gave it too much gas. The tractor reared and fell over crushing him to death. Sources: Death Certificate; *Canton Herald*, April 3, 1941.

Dawson, Kathryn M.
Born: 1897. Died: June 1, 1984. Married: Frank Albert Dawson, November 19, 1919. Father: Dr. C. P. Smith. Mother: Lula D. Peel. Source: *Van Zandt News*, June 3, 1984.

Day, Darcy
Born: February 5, 1889. Died: November 6, 1894. Father: Felix Day. Mother: Eula Spears. Source: *Wills Point Chronicle*, November 7, 1894.

Day, Felix
Born: May 30, 1853. Died: January 23, 1900, Van Zandt County, Texas. Cause of Death: Pneumonia. Married: (1) Sarah Caroline Sumner, February 10, 1876. (2) Eula Spears, March 12, 1885. Children: Darcy and George Thomas. Occupation: Tonsorial Artist (Barber). Comments: Felix Day owned a barber shop on the courthouse square throughout his adult life. His first wife, Caroline Sumner, was the daughter of Monroe "Fate" Sumner, a pioneer Van Zandt County settler and county official. His second wife, Eula, after his death, married W. D. Hutcherson, February 1, 1906. Hutcherson murdered Eula, August 23, 1909. She is buried next to Felix under the Day name. Sources: *Marriage Records of Van Zandt County, 1848-1908*; *Free State Enterprise*, January 25, 1900.

Day, Laddie Allen
Born: 1952. Died: April 16, 1955. Father: Luther V. Day. Mother: Helen Day. Source: Eubank Funeral Home records.

Day (Hutcherson), Martha Eula
Born: March 18, 1868. Died: August 23, 1909, Van Zandt County, Texas. Cause of death: Homicide. Married: (1) Felix Day, March 12, 1885. Children: Darcy and George Thomas. (2) W. D. Hutcherson, February 1, 1906. Father: Lucius Mack "L. M." Spears. Mother: Mary Jane Barnes. Occupation: Owner of the Day Hotel, Canton, Texas. Comments: Eula Day's first husband was Felix Day, a Canton barber. He died from pneumonia. Later, Eula married her second husband, W. D. Hutcherson, in 1906; and he killed her in 1909. Information taken from the *Grand Saline Sun* is as follows: "The killing of Eula: One of the saddest affairs in the history of Canton took place at the Day Hotel last night about 9:30. W. D. Hutcherson, barber and Justice of the Peace, Precinct No. 1, took a revolver and shot his wife through the head and in an instant placed the same deadly weapon to his own mouth and shot, tearing a great hole through his own head. Mrs. Ed Haynes was with her mother when this terrible tragedy occurred, and before the court this morning, stated that they got along reasonably well except at times when Mr. Hutcherson had spells caused principally by drink and various drugs. The immediate trouble came when Mrs. Hutcherson said she could stand him no longer, and was going to leave him. They, with Mrs. Haynes, sat together in front of the hotel and talked of the separation, and after a time Mrs. Haynes with her mother started to Mrs. Haynes home. Mr. Hutcherson followed them to the corner of the garden about 30 yards from yard gate, begging her to return and give him one more chance. They all turned back to the hotel, Hutcherson with his arm about his wife's neck. They stepped upon the gallery and Mrs. Haynes had entered the screen door to the hall when Hutcherson pushed the door closed and placed his back against the door. Mrs. Hutcherson asked Mrs. Haynes to phone Mr. Kellis, deputy sheriff, to come to their assistance. Hutcherson said 'Yes, phone for him,' but Mrs. Haynes shoved on the door getting her mother by the arm and about half way through the door, Hutcherson with his arm around his wife's neck fired two very rapid shots and she fell in the hall. The third shot was at his own head and he fell backwards upon the floor, dead. They will be buried here this afternoon." Source: *Grand Saline Sun*, August 26, 1909.

Day, Sara Caroline
Born: June 12, 1860. Died: Before 1885. Married: Felix Day, February 1, 1876. Father: Monroe L. Sumner. Mother: Martha Jane Burns. Comments: Sara Day's father was an early settler and county official in Van Zandt County. Her husband, Felix Day, was a barber in Canton, Texas. After her death, Felix married Eula Spears, March 12, 1885. He died January 23, 1900 and is buried beside her

in Hillcrest Cemetery. Sources: 1870 U. S. Census, Ancestry.com.

DEAN, MELROSE CHITTY

Born: January 16, 1927, Van Zandt County, Texas. Died: September 8, 1972, Dallas County, Texas. Cause of death: Gunshot wounds. Married: Unknown Dean. Father: Melvin Chitty. Mother: Ola Wilburn. Siblings: Larry Joe, Wilburn, Owen Leonard, Shirley Ann, Jessie, and Melvin, Jr. Occupation: Office work, Security Tool Products Co. Dallas, Texas. Sources: Death Certificate; *Canton Herald*, September 14, 1972.

DODSON, ION

Born: February 25, 1901, Collin County, Texas. Died: April 27, 1971, Dallas County, Texas. Married: James Frank Dodson, October 1, 1921. Child: Lilla Belle. Father: William Chambers. Mother: Martha Andrews. Occupation: School teacher. Sources: *Canton Herald*, April 29, 1971; Eubank Funeral Home records.

DODSON, JAMES FRANK

Born: April 7, 1892, Van Zandt County, Texas. Died: October 22, 1952, Lynn County, Texas. Cause of death: Heart attack. Married: Ion Chambers, October 1, 1921. Child: Lilla Belle. Father: John Henry Dodson. Mother: Nancy Eliza Brasher. Military: WWI, U. S. Army, Pvt. Medical unit. Occupation: School Teacher, County Treasurer (1929-1930), Deputy Sheriff, Assistant County Auditor, rural mail carrier. Comments: Frank Dodson had a number of jobs during his lifetime. One job that he held was Deputy Sheriff. Ethel Burnett became the first woman Sheriff of Van Zandt, County when her husband died. On April 30, 1934, she appointed Frank as her Deputy. Frank was visiting a cousin in Tahoka, Texas when he had a heart attack and died. Sources: *Canton Herald*, October, 1952; Army Discharge; Deputation (Deputy Sheriff) Records Van Zandt County; Eubank Funeral Home records.

DOUTHIT, CALVIN RILEY

Born: March 15, 1876, Van Zandt County, Texas. Died: June 8, 1946, Van Zandt County, Texas. Father: George Washington Douthit. Mother: Mary Elizabeth Josephine Burke. Occupation: Farmer. Comments: Calvin Douthit came from a family of eleven children. The Douthits were some of the earliest pioneers of Texas. Calvin's father was born in Palestine, Texas on September 11, 1851. Calvin's paternal grandfather and grandmother, James and Mary Daniel Douthit, migrated from Illinois and settled in Anderson County before 1836. James enlisted in the Texas Army and served under General Sam Houston during the Texas Revolution. He fought in several battles, including the decisive Battle of San Jacinto. For his service during the Texas Revolution, James was awarded a league and a labor of land (4,405 acres) in 1845 in what would become Van Zandt County. James Douthit never settled on this land. He died in 1851 and is buried in Anderson, County. The land was divided among James' heirs, and George Washington received a 1,100 acre share adjacent to Canton, Texas. George Washington and Mary Douthit farmed and reared their eleven children on this property. Calvin never married. He lived with his sisters, Jewell and Lessie, and farmed part of the Douthit land. According to family stories, Lessie never married, and Jewell's marriage lasted only about a month due to conflicts within the family. These stories also note that at times—to get away from his sisters' nagging—Calvin would move into the storm cellar and live there. At his death, the *Canton Herald* expressed this about Calvin: "He was of unusual character, one who expressed very little interest in public affairs, even his trips to town being rare and could always be counted a specific reason or personal business. Certainly he was not selfish but was a genuine neighbor, honest friendly and kind to his fellow man. He worked hard and many have enjoyed the fruits of the labor of Calvin Douthit,

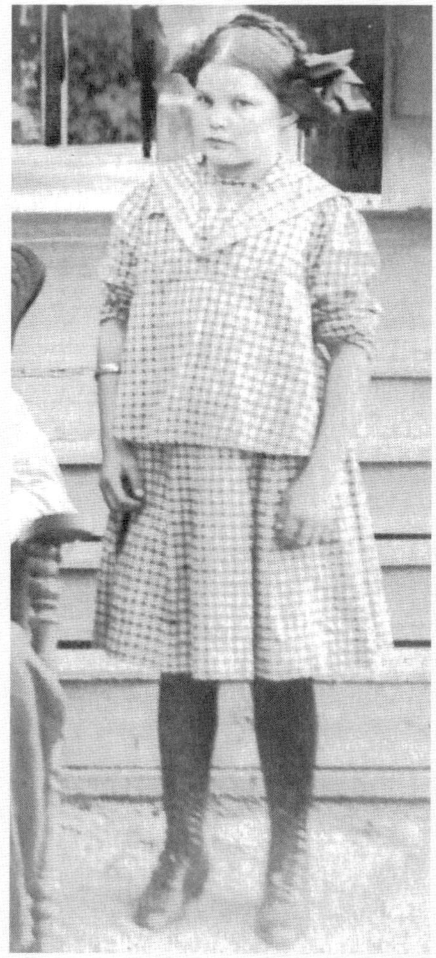

Mary Elizabeth "Lessie" Douthit

who was never known to intrude on the personal of others but his life was an expression of a strong belief which he practiced, 'Just tending to his own business' for which he merits commendation in sacred memory." Source: Texas General Land Office; Van Zandt County Biographies, Vol. I; *Canton Herald*, June 1946; Hilliard Funeral Home records; interviews with Douthit family members.

Douthit, Jewell Effiline

Born: November 20, 1890, Van Zandt County, Texas. Died: October 27, 1970, Van Zandt County, Texas. Cause of death: Heart disease. Married: J. E. Covert, April 17, 1916. Divorce: October 24, 1916. Father: George Washington Douthit. Mother: Mary Elizabeth Josephine Burke. Occupation: Farmer. Comments: Jewell Douthit's ancestors were some of the earliest pioneers in Texas. She lived most of her life with her brother, Calvin, and sister, Lessie, farming family land. After her marriage, she and J. E. only lived together for about a month. Douthit family stories relate that Covert left Jewell because Calvin and Lessie were creating problems for him and pressuring Jewell to leave him. Covert later became a Constable in Van Zandt County. In December of 1921, he along with Sheriff Orsborn, and Constable Clay Hollifield, raided a still on W. R. Stringer's farm near Ben Wheeler. In that conflict, one of the bootleggers shot Covert in the shoulder, and he bled to death before help could arrive. Family stories indicate that Jewell was very despondent at the death of her former husband, because apparently, she never recovered from his leaving her five years earlier. Sources: Death Certificate; Divorce Records of Van Zandt County; *Canton Herald*, December 30, 1921; Interviews with Douthit family members.

Douthit, Mary Elizabeth "Lessie"

Born: May 30, 1900, Van Zandt County, Texas. Died: January, 1989, Van Zandt County, Texas. Father: George Washington Douthit. Mother: Mary Elizabeth Josephine Burke. Comments: Lessie Douthit never married. She spent most of her life farming family land with her brother, Calvin, and sister, Jewell. She was a member of the Ladies Auxiliary of Veterans of WWI, Chapter 2496. Source: *Van Zandt News*, January 22, 1989.

Dowdle, Eliza Jane

Born: March 14, 1844, Mississippi. Died: February 29, 1916, Van Zandt County, Texas. Married: Robert Padian Dowdle. Children: Delila Elizabeth, James Dudley, Etta, Eliza Willet, Delila Willet, and Robert Padian. Father: George Washington Tyler. Mother: Delila Melvina Bennett. Comments: Eliza Jane Tyler's mother died when Eliza was at the age of 17. Her father was fighting in the Civil War at the time which left her responsible for her seven siblings. The training she received looking after a family during those trying times gave her the experience to overcome many frontier hardships. During the early part of the War, she married while her husband was on furlough. They

Eliza Jane Dowdle

had six children; all lived to be adults except one. Robert died in 1873 leaving Eliza alone again with her children. She and her family came to Van Zandt County about 1887 and settled in the Walton community where they stayed about four years. She then moved to Canton and ran the Wortham Hotel on the square. After four years, she gave up the hotel and lived with her married children until her death. Sources: *Van Zandt County History Book, Vol. I*; *Canton Herald*, March 17, 1916; Dr. Billy Glenn Foster, Dowdle Family historian.

Downing, Allen Riley

Born: January 7, 1885, Van Zandt County, Texas. Died: May 8, 1953, Dallas County, Texas. Cause of death: Kidney disease. Never married. Father: Giles L. Downing, Alabama. Mother: Mary C. Riley, Alabama. Occupation: Produce market employee. Comments: Allen Downing spent the majority of his life farming near Canton, Texas. He moved to Dallas in 1942 and worked in the produce business. Sources: Death Certificate; *Canton Herald*, May 14, 1953; Hilliard Funeral Home Records.

Downing, Charity Mira

Born: October 11, 1814, Georgia. Died: January 19, 1893, Van Zandt County, Texas. Married: Thomas Jefferson "T. J." Downing Sr., November 18, 1832, Alabama. Father: Cornelius Autry. Mother: Nancy Eaves. Comments: Charity Downing became the matriarch of the Downing family after her husband's death in 1859 at the age of 44. The Downings apparently were large-scale farmers—maybe even plantation owners. In 1860, Charity was living in Calhoun County, Alabama as a widow with five children and nine slaves. Sometime shortly after the end of the Civil War, they migrated to Van Zandt County, Texas. Sources: 1850, 1860, 1870, 1880 U. S. Census; *1860 Slave Schedules, Calhoun County, Georgia*; *Van Zandt County Texas Marriage Records, 1848-1909*; Ancestry.com.

DOWNING, EDITH
Born: July 4, 1882. Died: July 4, 1882. Father: Thomas J. Downing. Mother Sarah E. Smith. Source: Tombstone.

DOWNING, GILES L.
Born: September 28, 1854, Calhoun County, Alabama. Died: November 13, 1895, Van Zandt County, Texas. Married: Mary C. Riley, November 18, 1874. Father: Thomas Jefferson Downing, Sr., Tennessee. Mother: Charity M. Autry, Georgia. Occupation: Farming. Sources: 1860 U. S. Census; *Marriage Records of Van Zandt County, 1848-1909.*

DOWNING, INFANT DAUGHTER
Born: August 9, 1883, Van Zandt County, Texas. Died: August 9, 1883, Van Zandt County, Texas. Father: Thomas Jefferson Downing. Mother: Sarah E. Smith. Source: Tombstone.

DOWNING, MAGGIE
Born: February 1, 1891. Died: October 21, 1894. Father: Thomas Jefferson Downing. Mother: Sarah E. Smith. Source: Tombstone.

DOWNING, NORA EDNA
Born: April 8, 1889. Died: December 30, 1974, Tarrant County, Texas. Cause of death: Kidney disease. Married: Thomas Howard Downing, December 28, 1909. Father: Bob Robertson. Mother: Cansady Sumner. Source: Death Certificate.

DOWNING, NORA LEE
Born: 1868. Died: February 22, 1870. Father: Unknown Downing. Mother: Unknown. Source: Tombstone.

DOWNING, NORAH M.
Born: May 31, 1880. Died: June 2, 1881. Father: Thomas Jefferson Downing. Mother: Sarah E. Smith. Source: Tombstone.

DOWNING, OLLIE
Born: January 4, 1878. Died: August 16, 1891. Not married. Father: Thomas Jefferson Downing. Mother: Sarah E. Smith. Source: Tombstone.

DOWNING, THOMAS HOWARD
Born: September 16, 1880, Van Zandt County, Texas. Died: March 5, 1959, Van Zandt County, Texas. Cause of death: Heart disease. Married: Nora Roberson, December 28, 1909. Father: Giles L. Downing. Mother: Mary C. Riley. Occupation: Railroad worker. Source: Death Certificate.

DOWNING, THOMAS JEFFERSON, "TOMMIE"
Born: October 29, 1859, Calhoun County, Alabama. Died: November 17, 1894, Van Zandt County, Texas. Married: Sarah Elizabeth "Sallie" Smith, December 26, 1876, Van Zandt County, Texas. Children: Nora Lee, Ollie, Norah M., Edith, Infant Daughter, Bee, Tee, and Maggie. Father: Elijah Berryman Downing. Mother: Sarah Ann King. Occupation: Farmer. Comments: Sarah Elizabeth married J. W. Barrier on April 18, 1895 in Van Zandt County five months after Tommy Downing's death. Sources: 1860, 1870, 1880 U. S. Census; Ancestry.com.

DUBOSE, ANNIE LEE
Born: April 19, 1910. Died: November 1, 1912. Father: Milton Lee Dubose. Mother: Mary Ann Quinn. Sources: Tombstone; *Grand Saline Sun*, November 7, 1912.

DUBOSE, ELMER SCOTT
Born: January 6, 1912. Died: February 27, 1912. Father: Milton Lee Dubose. Mother: Mary Ann Quinn. Source: Tombstone.

DUBOSE, FANNIE BEATRICE
Born: June 23, 1913. Died: March 10, 1915. Father: Milton Lee Dubose. Mother: Mary Ann Quinn. Source: Tombstone.

DUBOSE, INFANT
Born: April 28, 1909. Died: April 28, 1909. Father: Milton Lee Dubose. Mother: Mary Ann Quinn. Source: Tombstone.

DUBOSE, MARY ANN
Born: October 4, 1886, Tarrant County, Texas. Died: December 16, 1945, Dallas County, Texas. Married: Milton Lee Dubose. Children: Infant, Annie Lee, Elmer Scott, Fannie Beatrice, Milton Lee, Jr., and Edgar Thomas. Father: Steven F. Quinn. Mother: Sara Francis Walton. Source: Eubank Funeral Home records.

DUBOSE, MILTON LEE
Born: February 14, 1877, Alabama. Died: December 16, 1945, Van Zandt County, Texas. Cause of death: Heart disease. Married: Mary Ann Quinn. Children: Infant, Annie Lee, Elmer Scott, Fannie Beatrice, Milton Lee Jr., and Edgar Thomas. Father: Middleton Dubose, Alabama. Moth-

er: Sally Jordon, Alabama. Occupation: Farmer. Sources: Death Certificate; *Canton Herald*, January 3, 1946.

DUNN, JOHN D.
Born: June 26, 1881, Morgan County, Alabama. Died: September 12, 1951, Van Zandt County, Texas. Cause of death: Stroke. Married: Ola Hays Thompson, 1930. Children: David, John, Anna Lee, and Lillie. Father: James K. Polk Dunn, Alabama. Mother: Julia Wiley Homes, Alabama. Sources: Death Certificate; 1900 U. S. Census; *Canton Herald*, September 1951; Eubank Funeral Home records; Ancestry.com.

DUNN, OLA HAYES
Born: April 21, 1907, Tennessee. Died: July 7, 1991, Smith County, Texas. Married: John D. Dunn, 1930. Children: David, John, Anna Lee, and Lillie. Father: Unknown Thompson. Mother: Unknown. Occupation: School teacher. Comments: Ola Dunn lived in Canton most of her life. Her husband died in 1951. Source: *Van Zandt News*, July 14, 1991.

JACOB "JAKE" ALFRED EVANS *had been sitting in his house talking to family during a storm, when he walked out on the porch to look at the clouds. A bolt of lightening struck a stove flue, ripping it from the house, and followed some tin guttering down the roof of the main building and to the roof of the porch. The lightening passed through Evans, tearing his garments to shreds and killing him.*

E

EADS, WILLIAM ALEXANDER
Born: April 9, 1839, Arkansas. Died: November 28, 1892, Van Zandt County, Texas. Cause of death: Asthma. Married: (1) Mary Ann R. Murphy, Claiborne Parish, Louisiana, November 24, 1859. Children: James Thomas, Mary S., Samuel B., John Ben, George C., and Luther. (2) Martha Ann Davis Garrison, Van Zandt County, Texas, April 5, 1888. Father: Matthias Eads. Mother: Nancy Ann Griffith. Military: CSA, 4th SGT, 24 Reg. Co. B. Ark. Infantry. Sources: *Van Zandt County Confederate Pension Records*; *Canton Telephone*, December 2, 1892; Ancestry.com.

EDWARDS, CLIDDIE "CLYDE"
Born: June 27, 1904. Died: August 22, 1904. Father: John Robert Edwards. Mother: Ann Thomas Byrant. Comments: Clyde Edwards' family moved from Mississippi to Collin County, Texas. In 1902, They bought 125-acre farm in the Highland Community of Van Zandt County where they farmed. John and Ann Edwards had nine children. Clyde was the only one who died as an infant, and the only one of the family buried in the Hillcrest Cemetery. Ann died November 15, 1924; and John died April 17, 1945. Sources: *Wills Point Chronicle*, September 1, 1904; Edwards Family History.

EDWARDS, EDDIE RUTH TERRY
Born: February 1, 1935, Van Zandt County, Texas. Died: May 5, 1979, Smith County, Texas. Cause of death: Epilepsy. Married: Sam Edwards. Divorced. Father: Eddie Obe Terry. Mother: Adde Mae Craft. Siblings: Norma Jean, Ina Mae, Hazel, Bill, and Robert. Sources: Death Certificate; *Canton Herald*, May 18, 1879.

ENGLEDOW, ELVIRA ELIZABETH
Born: February 28, 1812, Warren County, Tennessee. Died: June 1, 1896, Van Zandt County, Texas. Cause of death: Injuries sustained in a fall. Married: Creed S. Engledow, ca 1833. Father: Henry Randolph. Mother: Sarah Nancy Pogue. Children: Creed Jr., Sarah, and John Henry. Comments: There are several Engledow family members buried in Hillcrest Cemetery in unmarked graves. Sources: *Wills Point Chronicle*, June 9, 1896; Ancestry.com.

EVANS, JACOB ALFRED "JAKE"
Born: April 30, 1870, Louisiana. Died: July 23, 1898, Van Zandt County, Texas. Cause of death: Struck by lightning. Married: Arrena "Rena" Samples, October 17, 1894, Van Zandt County, Texas. Father: Henry Adams Evans. Mother: Lavinia Elizabeth Threeton. Comments: The *Wills Point Chronicle* reported Jacob Evans' death as follows: "On last Saturday night, about 8:30 o'clock, during

Ronald Vernon "Ronnie" Fitzgerald *was a printer by trade. He worked for the* Rains County Leader *and the* Kaufman Herald *before joining* The Dallas Morning News *in 1966. He retired from the* Morning News *after thirty years as a linotype operator and assistant foreman of the composing department.*

an electrical and rain storm, Jake E. Evans was killed by lightning at his residence in South Canton. He had been sitting in the house talking to his family and walked out on the porch to look at the clouds, when a bolt came, which struck a stove flue, completely tearing it from the house. Apparently the bolt that struck the flue followed some tin guttering down the roof of the main building to the roof of the gallery porch, passing through it with the result above stated. Every garment he had on was completely torn to shreds." Sources: *Van Zandt County Marriage Records, 1848-1909*; *Wills Point Chronicle*, July 28, 1898; Ancestry.com.

Everett, Elizabeth "Bettie"

Born: January 27, 1850. Died: January 5, 1909, Van Zandt County, Texas. Married: George W. Everett, 1871. Father: William Gillispie. Mother; Sarah Gillispie. Comments: Bettie Everett's husband was traveling in Oklahoma when she was taken very ill on a Sunday. She died on Tuesday of the same week. He did not attend the funeral. Bettie was the only sister of J. H. Gillispie, who was living in the Oakland Community at the time of her death. She was survived by her husband, three daughters, and a son, A. W. Everett. Sources: 1870 U. S. Census; *Grand Saline Sun*, January 7, 1909; *Wills Point Chronicle*, January 14, 1909.

Everett, George W.

Born: January 27, 1850. Died: February 2, 1911. Married: Elizabeth "Bettie" Gillispie, 1871. Father: James S. Everett. Mother: Isabella Stamps. Sources: 1900 U. S. Census, Ancestry.com.

Everett, Hugh Ellis

Born: ca 1873. Died: August 25, 1899, Van Zandt County, Texas. Married: Gracie Milstead, July 17, 1896. Father: George W. Everett. Mother: Elizabeth "Bettie" Gillispie. Occupation: Clerk for W. P. Robinson and Company, Grand Saline, Texas. Comments: Hugh Everett was in the process of building a new residence in Grand Saline, Texas when he died. He was only 26 years old. Source: *Free State Enterprise*, August 31, 1899.

Everett, Lee Perry

Born: January 16, 1878. Died: March 9, 1881. Father: George W. Everett. Mother: Elizabeth "Bettie" Gillispie. Source: Tombstone.

Everett, Sidney Polk

Born: ca 1880. Died: December 9, 1893. Father: George W. Everett. Mother: Elizabeth "Bettie" Gillispie. Source: Tombstone.

F

Farmer, Mattie "Fannie"

Born: January 7, 1878, Van Zandt County, Texas. Died: October 14, 1944, Dallas County, Texas. Cause of death: Heart disease. Married: J. A. Farmer. Child: Mildred. Father: J. Tull Thompson. Mother: Martha Blare (Blair). Occupation: School teacher. Comments: The following information was found in an insert in the Hilliard Funeral Home Records file, "Mrs. Mattie Farmer, born January 7, 1878 in Canton, daughter of Mr. & Mrs. Tull Thompson, one of the oldest families of this county. Married to J. A. Farmer thirty-six years ago. To this union one child, Mildred Farmer, was born. Both husband and daughter preceded Mrs. Farmer in death twenty-six years ago in Fargo, Oklahoma. At the loss of her family, she returned to Canton and Wills Point where she made her home until ten months ago when she went to Dallas in order to be under the care of a nurse. Mrs. Farmer taught school in the Wallace community seventeen years before failing health necessitated her giving up this profession which she sincerely loved and enjoyed. During the present World Conflict (WWII), she eagerly scanned the daily papers in search of

Walter Perry Fitzgerald — Zeffie Telasca Fitzgerald

news from 'her boys' on the front—men, whom she taught as beginners only a few years ago." Sources: Death Certificate; Hilliard Funeral Home Records, Insert in file, author unknown.

Farrell, Arthur Lee

Born: May 15, 1889, Kaufman County, Texas. Died: June 9, 1948, Tarrant County, Texas. Married: Connie Josephine Heard, May 15, 1917. Father: James C. Farrell. Mother: Sarah Elizabeth Farrell. Comments: Note: There is a duplicate headstone for Arthur Lee Farrell in the Wetumka Cemetery, Hughes County, Oklahoma. The Hillcrest tombstone might be a memorial stone. Source: 1920 Census; Martha Heard, Heard Family historian.

Farrell, Connie Josephine Heard

Born: November 20, 1897, Van Zandt County, Texas. Died: August 13, 1941, Van Zandt County, Texas. Cause of death: Cancer. Married: Arthur Lee Farrell, May 15, 1917. Father: Eleazer. A. Heard, Van Zandt County, Texas. Mother: Bell Hobbs, Van Zandt County, Texas. Sources: Death Certificate; Martha Heard, Heard Family historian.

Fitzgerald, Curtis Rudolph "Tinker"

Born: April 14, 1939. Died: November 20, 2006. Father: Perry Fitzgerald. Mother: Zeffie Telasca Smith. Military: PFC, U. S. Army. Comments: Curtis Fitzgerald lived in the Wynne Community in Van Zandt County. He attended the Wynne School and later the Cartwright School in Wills Point, Texas. Sources: 1940 U. S. Census, Find A Grave.

Mattie "Fannie" Farmer — *Curtis Rudolph Fitzgerald "Tinker"*

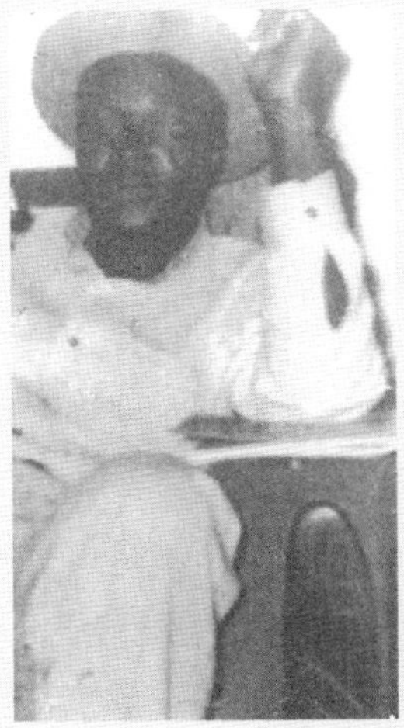

Perry Fitzgerald — *Jessie Henry Fitzgerald*

Fitzgerald, Dorothy Mae

Born: April 18, 1911, Kansas. Died: January 17, 1996, Kansas. Married: John Edward Fitzgerald. Father: Charles Mohr. Mother: Addie Eddy Mohr. Occupation: Bookkeeper. Comments: Dorothy Fitzgerald lived in Dayton, Oregon and Lafayette, Kansas. Source: *Van Zandt News*, January 21, 1996.

Fitzgerald, Easter Mae

Born: March 12, 1918, Van Zandt County, Texas. Died: February 23, 2007, Smith County, Texas. Married: Willie Fitzgerald, April 19, 1933. Children: Eugene, Herman, Dorothy, Shirley Ann, Susie Ann, Patricia, and Peggy. Father: Nelce Brown. Mother: Marietta Stevens. Sources: *Van Zandt News*, January 21, 1996; Hilliard Funeral Home records.

James L Fizer *managed the farms of Sanger Brothers, a pioneer wholesale dry-goods and retail company started in McKinney, Texas in 1857. Fizer began managing their largest farm in 1903, about two miles east of Canton. In addition to farm crops, the place was stocked with hogs, sheep, goats, Jersey cattle, and a large stable of brood mares. He was trained in the most modern methods of scientific farming and stock raising, and developed this farm into one of the most successful in Van Zandt County. Fizer managed the farm for seventeen years before his untimely death due to an accidental gunshot.*

Fitzgerald, Eugene
Born: July 9, 1934. Died: November 11, 2008. Father: Willie Fitzgerald. Mother: Easter Mae Brown. Source: 1940 U. S. Census.

Fitzgerald, Frank Lee
Born: March 12, 1935, Van Zandt County, Texas. Died: September 22, 1987, Dallas County, Texas. Married: Martha Ann Scates. Father: Willie Fitzgerald. Mother: Easter Mae Brown. Occupation: Chef, Margo's Cafeteria, Dallas, Texas. Sources: *Van Zandt News*, October 4, 1987; Vanessa Fitzgerald Scott, Wynne Community historian.

Fitzgerald, Harvey Joe
Born: July 19, 1937, Dallas County, Texas. Died: September 6, 1990, Dallas County, Texas. Father: John Edward Fitzgerald. Mother: Dorothy May Mohr. Occupation: Electronics technician, television consultant. Source: *Van Zandt News*, September 16, 1990.

Fitzgerald, Infant
Born: August 10, 1941. Died: August 10, 1941. Cause of death: Stillborn. Father: Perry Fitzgerald. Mother: Telasca Smith. Source: Death Certificate.

Fitzgerald, Jessie Henry
(Photo page 53) Born: October 26, 1937. Died: August 18, 2004. Single. Father: Perry Fitzgerald. Mother: Telasco Smith. Occupation: Eagle Drug Store employee, Canton, Texas. Military: U. S. Army, Private. Source: Vanessa Scott, Wynne Community historian.

Fitzgerald, John Edward
Born: September 29, 1891, Grayson County, Texas. Died: October 30, 1965, Van Zandt County, Texas. Cause of death: Heart disease. Married: Dorothy May Mohr. Father: A. T. Fitzgerald. Mother: Emma E. Grafton. Occupation: Printer, tax consultant, owner of Dallas Suburban Publications, Baptist minister. Sources: Death Certificate; *Canton Herald*, November 4, 1965.

Fitzgerald, Perry
(Photo page 53) Born: December 24, 1897, Van Zandt County, Texas. (Tombstone year of birth 1896 is incorrect.) Died: April 24, 1961, Van Zandt County, Texas. Cause of death: Heart disease. Married: Zeffie Telasca Smith, December 30, 1930. Father: Jerry Fitzgerald. Mother: Lena Ladd. Military: WWI, Pvt. Co. D. 412 Labor Bn. QMC. Sources: Death Certificate, Eubank Funeral Home records.

Fitzgerald, Ronald Vernon "Ronnie"
Born: July 21, 1934, Dallas County, Texas. Died: November 23, 1997, Dallas County, Texas. Father: John Edward Fitzgerald. Mother: Dorothy May Mohr. Occupation: Newspaper printer. Comments: Ronald Fitzgerald was born in Dallas. He later moved to Canton, Texas where he graduated from high school in 1951. He was a printer. Ronald worked for the *Rains County Leader* and the *Kaufman Herald* before joining *The Dallas Morning News* in 1966. He retired after thirty years as a linotype operator and assistant foreman of the composing department. Source: *The Dallas Morning News*, November 26, 1997.

Fitzgerald, Walter Perry
(Photo page 53) Born: January 18, 1934. Died: June 23, 1994. Married: Claudia Shaw. Father: Perry Fitzgerald. Mother: Zeffie Telasca Smith. Occupation: Maintenance work. Source: *Canton Herald*, June 1994.

Fitzgerald, Willie
Born: July 29, 1910, Kaufman County, Texas. Died: February 14, 2007, Van Zandt County, Texas. Married: Eas-

ter May Brown, April 19, 1933. Children: Francis, Carter May, Eddie Dean, Frank, Eugene, Herman, Dorothy Jean, Shirley Ann, Murry, Susie Ann, Patricia Ann, and Peggie Jean. Father: Herman Fitzgerald. Mother: Leonora Shamlin. Occupation: Car dealer employee. Comments: Willie Fitzgerald worked for Canton Motors for forty years. Sources: *Tyler Morning Telegraph*, February 16, 2007; Eubank Funeral Home records.

Fitzgerald, Zeffie Telasca

(Photo page 53) Born: March 15, 1905, Van Zandt County, Texas. Died: April 14, 1978, Van Zandt County, Texas. Married: Perry Fitzgerald, December 30, 1930. Children: Louise, Lena, Walter P., Jesse F, and Rudolph. Father: Walter Smith. Mother: Lannie Bell Wynne. Siblings: Henry Hawthorn, Leta Bell, Maudella, and Ethelene. Sources: Eubank Funeral Home records; Find A Grave.

Fizer, James L.

Born: December 12, 1864, St. Clair County, Missouri. Died: November, 1925, Van Zandt County, Texas. Cause of death: Accidental death, gunshot. Married: Permelia Laura "Mattie" Miles. Children: Lena May, Ollie, and Thomas Preston. Father: John B. Fizer. Mother: Unknown. Occupation: Sanger Brothers' farm manager. Comments: James Fizer was born in Missouri and came to Texas at an early age. He had been in the employ of Sanger Brothers, Dallas, Texas since about 1900 as Manager of their farms. He worked in Collin and Hunt Counties prior to coming to Canton about 1903. Sanger Brothers was a pioneer wholesale dry-goods and retail company which started in McKinney, Texas in 1857. The Company opened a store in Bryan, Texas which was the first to carry the Sanger Brothers name. The Company entered the farming business largely out of necessity. By 1872, they had opened a store in Dallas, Texas and had expanded their wholesale operation by selling to retail establishments in East Texas. G. W. Tull was one of the early merchants in Canton, Texas; and Sanger Brothers became his largest suppliers of goods. In the middle 1890's, a major nationwide recession occurred, and merchants of Van Zandt County were affected. Several declared bankruptcy. G. W. Tull was on the verge of bankruptcy, and in order to stay in business, he worked an arrangement with Sanger Brothers to transfer farm land to them in order to pay his debt in full. Their largest farm was about two miles east of Canton on what is now Hwy. 64 and now includes a roadside park. This is the farm that J. L. Fizer came to manage in 1903. He was trained in the most modern methods of scientific farming and stock raising, and this particular farm was one of the most successful in Van Zandt County. The Sangers owned almost a thousand acres of farm land in Van Zandt County. The farm improvements included a large house for the manager, substantial outbuildings, and excellent roads around the property. In addition to farm crops, the place was stocked

Eliza Willet "Willie" Foster

with hogs, sheep, goats, Jersey cattle, and a large stable of brood mares. The farm provided work for a large number of workers. Fizer managed the farm for seventeen years and became an honored member of the Canton community before his tragic death. His death was caused by an accidental gun-shot wound which occurred a few hundred yards from his house. The *Canton Herald* describes Fizer's death as follows: "He had been hunting and was returning home. As no one was with him at the time, and the wound was inflicted on the left side of his face, severing his tongue, those who visited the scene of the tragedy arrived at the conclusion that the deceased had rested the double barrel shot gun against the wire fence, then making his way through the wire strands, caught his clothing on the barbs and fell, the gun also falling and being discharged with the above mentioned result. This theory was substantiated by signs and gestures of the mortally wounded man, who was speechless, but conscious and anxious to describe the horrible accident." James died on his way to the hospital. Sources: *Wills Point Chronicle*, April 20, 1911; *Canton Herald*, November, 1925.

FIZER, PERMELIA LAURA "MATTIE"
Born: September 17, 1882, Mississippi. Died: February 20, 1960, Bee County, Texas. Cause of death: Heart disease. Married: James L. Fizer, November 18, 1896, Hunt County, Texas. Children: Lena May, Ollie, and Thomas Preston. Father: John Thomas Miles. Mother: Permelia M. "Pollie" Parish. Sources: Death Certificate, Eubank Funeral Home records, Ancestry.com.

FLATT, ANNIE JEWELL
Born: February 13, 1889. Died: October 13, 1986. Married: James Arthur Flatt, October 12, 1919. Father: Ben F. Clark. Mother: R. A. Geddie. Children: Orville, Willis Earl, and Emma Jean. Source: Tombstone.

FLATT, JAMES ARTHUR
Born: September 15, 1895. Died: July 13, 1944, Dallas County, Texas. Married: Annie Jewell Clark, October 12, 1919. Children: Orville, Willis Earl, and Emma Jean. Father: George W. Flatt. Mother: Annie Eliza Barnett. Military: WWI, U. S. Army. Sources: *Canton Herald*, July 20, 1944; Eubank Funeral Home records.

FORD, BLANCHE MANN
Born: December 2, 1876, Texas. Died: March 2, 1943, Van Zandt County, Texas. Married: Robert Edward Ford, February 2, 1902. Child: Arlene. Father: Rufus Brooks Mann, North Carolina. Mother: Mary Eudora Fanning, Indiana. Sources: Eubank Funeral Home records, Ancestry.com.

FORD, CORA BAILEY
Born: March 20, 1874, Texas. Died: November 18, 1893, Van Zandt County, Texas. Married: Robert Ford, December 16, 1891. Father: William Henry Bailey. Mother: Amanda Sexton. Source: Ancestry.com.

FORD, FREDONIA CATHERINE HUBBARD
Born: March 23, 1838, Tennessee. Died: June 5, 1921, Van Zandt County, Texas. Married: Howell E. Ford, October 26, 1854. Children: Sallie, Robert E., Margaret E., Fredonia, and Duck. Father: James B. Hubbard. Mother: Sarah Ann Taggert. Comments: Fredonia Hubbard came to Texas with her family in 1849 at the age of 11. She married H. E. Ford. In their 33 years of marriage, eight children were born, five dying in infancy. The following is an article she published in *The Canton Telephone* in March, 1888 after her husband's death: "Having lost my husband and having no one with experience to carry on the business, I offer for sale, in the Town of Canton, a—mill and cotton gin, a 20 horse-power engine-all in good working order; also a 4-acre lot of land, known as the Howell Ford lot. I need money to settle the debt of the said Howell Ford. For prices and terms apply to me at my residence 3 miles West of Canton on Prairieville road." Sources: Death Certificate; *Canton Telephone*, March 9, 1888; *Canton Herald*, June 10, 1921.

Marcus Columbus Foster and Jeffie Lona Foster with children Bessie, Frances Merle, and Mary Mildred

Jeffie Lona Foster and Marcus Columbus Foster

FORD, B.
FORD, C.
FORD, H.
FORD, J.
FORD, M.
These five are children of Fredonia and Howell E. Ford who died as infants. They have only footstones with no dates.

Ford, Howell Elmore
Born: December 2, 1826, Alabama. Died: November 20, 1887, Van Zandt County, Texas. Married: Fredonia C. Hubbard, October 27, 1854. Children: Sallie, Robert, Margaret E., Fredonia, and Duck. Occupation: Farmer, mill, cotton gin owner. Military: CSA, Sgt., 15 TX Cav. Co. I. Sources: *Wills Point Chronicle*, November 24, 1887; Ancestry.com.

Ford, Jennie
Born: August 14, 1854. Died: October 22, 1902. Married: Thomas D. Ford. Sources: 1880 U. S. Census, Tombstone.

Ford, Robert Edward
Born: August 13, 1870, Van Zandt County, Texas. Died: February 24, 1948, Dallas County, Texas. Married: (1) Cora Bailey, December 16, 1891. (2) Blanche Mann, February 1902. Father: Howell Elmore Ford. Mother: Fredonia Hubbard. Sources: Texas Death Index; *Canton Herald*, February 26 and March 4, 1948.

Foster, Alfred "Alf"
Born: March 12, 1914, Van Zandt County, Texas. Died: November 23, 1991, Smith County, Texas. Married: Corine Geddie, June 20, 1936. Children: Don and Jerry. Father: Tate Ross Foster. Mother: Annie Velma Bolin. Comments: Alf Foster was born in Canton and lived there all of his life. He was involved in preserving local history and was a Charter Member of the Van Zandt County Historical Commission, a member of the Van Zandt County Genealogical Society, and Friends of the Library. He was also a deacon at the First Baptist Church in Canton for forty-three years. Source: *Van Zandt News*, December 1, 1991.

Foster, Annie Velma
Born: September 21, 1892, Louisiana. Died: March 5, 1986, Van Zandt County, Texas. Husband: Tate Ross Foster. Children: Alf, Jack, Thomas, Billy, and Agnew. Father: Jay Bolin, Alabama. Mother: Fannie G. Bolin, Louisiana. Occupation: Dairy farmer. Sources: 1910, 1920, 1930 U. S. Census; *Van Zandt News*, March 27, 1986.

Foster, Bessie
Born: August 7, 1895. Died: April 16, 1907. Father: Marcus C. Foster. Mother: Jeffie Lona Thompson. Sources: Tombstone; *Wills Point Chronicle*, May 23, 1907.

Foster, Corine Geddie "Dude"
Born: October 26, 1912, Van Zandt County, Texas. Died: June 25, 1996, Van Zandt County, Texas. Married: Alfred "Alf" G. Foster, June 20, 1936. Children: Don and Jerry. Father: Arthur Daniel Geddie. Mother: Beulah B. Oliver. Siblings: Mable Ellen and Emily Mae. Sources: 1920, 1930, U. S. Census; Social Security Death Index, 1936-2007; *Van Zandt News*, June 30, 1996.

Tate Ross Foster and Annie Velma Foster

Thomas Jones Foster, Jr. and Eliza Foster
with children from his first marriage to Maggie Jane Walker

Foster, Donald Geddie
Born: February 14, 1941, Kaufman County, Texas. Died: February 21, 2004, Dallas County, Texas. Married: Ruth Ann Platter. Child: Donna. Father: Alfred "Alf" Foster. Mother: Corine "Dude" Geddie. Comments: Donald Foster's family were pioneer settlers of Canton and Van Zandt County, Texas. He had lived in Canton for years. He was a long-time member of the First Baptist Church of Canton and a member of the Lions Club. He was "Lion Of The Year" in 2003. Source: *Tyler Courier Times Telegraph,* February 22, 2004; Ancestry.com.

Foster, Eliza Willet "Willie"
(Photos pages 55, 57) Born: January 4, 1869, Mississippi. Died: March 2, 1958, Van Zandt County, Texas. Married: Thomas Jones Foster, Jr., November, 1893. Children: Julia Francis, William Jennings Bryan, Thomas Porter, Janie Herma, William Dudley, and Robert Padian. Father: Robert P. Dowdle, Mississippi. Mother: Eliza Jane Tyler, Mississippi. Source: Hilliard Funeral Home records.

Foster, Francis Ann
Born: August 12, 1842. Died: September 6, 1925. Married: Thomas Jones Foster, Sr., December 20, 1860. Children: Mary Ellen, Thomas Jones Jr., William Edmund, John Calvin, Marcus Columbus, Jerome Kearby, Marshall Alexander, Robert Lee, Jesse Miller, Grover Blunt, and Tate Ross. Father: John Thomas Tate. Mother: Nancy Reed Taylor. Source: Dr. Billy Glenn Foster, Foster Family historian.

Foster, Infant
Born: March 8, 1888. Died: March 8, 1888. Father: Thomas Jones Foster, Jr. Mother: Margaret Jane "Maggie" Walker. Source: Tombstone.

Foster, Infant
Born: November 30, 1894. Died: November 30, 1894. Father: William Edmund Foster. Mother: Minnie Pulliam. Source: Tombstone.

Foster, Jeffie Lona
(Photo page 56) Born: March 21, 1873, Van Zandt County, Texas. Died: March 21, 1947, Van Zandt County, Texas. Married: Marcus Columbus Foster, November 13, 1890. Children: Oscar Thompson, Francis Merle, Bessie, Marcus Homer, Mary Mildred, Jessie Lona, and Marcus Glen. Father; Jeptha Tolliver "Tull" Thompson. Mother: Isabella Martha Blair. Comments: In January 1921, Jeffie Foster purchased the Dixie Hotel in Canton from Mamie Maume and managed it for a short time. She later sold it back to Miss Maume. Source: Dr. Billy Glenn Foster, Foster Family historian.

Foster, Marcus Columbus
(Photo page 56) Born: January 15, 1869, Van Zandt County, Texas. Died: May 12, 1946, Van Zandt County, Texas. Married: Jeffie Lona Thompson, November 13, 1890. Children: Oscar Thompson, Francis Merle, Bessie, Marcus Homer, Mary Mildred, Jessie Lona, and Marcus Glen. Father: Thomas Jones Foster. Mother: Francis Ann Tate. Occupation: Farmer, merchant, mail carrier. Comments: Marcus Foster joined the Postal Service in 1911 and retired in 1934 after twenty-three years of service. He was the first postal service employee in Van Zandt County to retire with a pension of $1,100 per year. Sources: *Canton Herald*, May 16, 1946; Dr. Billy Glenn Foster, Foster Family historian.

Foster, Marcus H.
Born: June 1, 1898. Died: August 30, 1900. Father: Marcus C. Foster. Mother: Jeffie L. Thompson. Source: Tombstone.

Foster, Margaret Jane "Maggie"
Born: February 4, 1869. Died: September 25, 1892. Married: Thomas Jones Foster, Jr. Children: Unnamed child, Mary Ines, and Margaret Lorine. Father: Frank M. Walker. Mother: Hannah Cathern Martin Walker. Sibling: Georgia Ann Walker. Source: Dr. Billy Glenn Foster, Foster Family historian.

Foster, Minnie Pulliam
Born: September 25, 1858, Mississippi. Died: May 3, 1936, Harris County, Texas. Cause of death: Stroke. Married: William Edmund Foster. Father: John Pulliam, Mississippi. Mother: Betty Stell. Source: Death Certificate.

Foster, Oscar Thompson
Born: February 6, 1892. Died: August 10, 1892. Father: Marcus C. Foster. Mother: Jeffie L. Thompson. Source: Tombstone.

Foster, Tate Ross
(Photo page 57) Born: March 10, 1886. Died: December 26, 1919. Married: Annie Velma Bolin, March 22, 1911. Children: Alf, Jack, Thomas, Billy, and Agnew. Father: Thomas Jones Foster, Sr. Mother: Francis Ann Tate. Source: Dr. Billy Glenn Foster, Foster Family historian.

Foster, Thomas Jones, Jr.
(Photo page 57) Born: June 30, 1863. Died: February 21, 1905. Cause of death: Pneumonia. Married: (1) Maggie Jane Walker. (2) Eliza Willet "Willie" Dowdle. Children: Unnamed infant, Mary Inez, Margaret Lorine, Julia Francis, William Jennings, Thomas Porter, Janie Hanna, William Dudley, and Robert Padian. Father: Thomas Jones Foster, Sr. Mother: Francis Anne Tate. Occupation: School teacher, store clerk, worker in Clark Brothers Saloon, saloon owner, farmer. Sources: *Wills Point Chronicle*, February 23, 1905; Dr. Billy Glenn Foster, Foster Family historian.

Foster, Thomas Jones, Sr. "Judge"
Born: June 15, 1826, Wilkes County, North Carolina. Died: August 6, 1906, Van Zandt County, Texas. Married: Francis Ann Tate, December 20, 1860. Children: Mary Ellen, Thomas Jones, Jr., William Edmund, John Calvin, Marcus Columbus, Jerome Kearby, Marshall Alexander, Robert Lee, Jesse Miller, Grover Blunt, and Tate Ross. Father: Ambrose Foster. Mother: Mary Ellen Miller. Occupation: Deputy Sheriff, Wilkes County, North Carolina, six years; school teacher, farmer, Probate Judge (County Judge), County Clerk, and County Commissioner. Military: CSA, Captain 11Th Tex. Inf. Co. I. Thomas Foster was a First Lt. serving under Captain Thomas B. Smith, who prior to the War, had been a school teacher in Van Zandt County, Texas. When Captain Smith became ill with pneumonia and died at Princeton, Arkansas on May 9, 1864, Thomas was promoted to the rank of Captain of the company. Comments: A death notice in the *Wills Point Chronicle* stated: "Few men ever resided in the county who were better known or more universally liked than this good man and his death removes from the ac-

Francis Ann Foster and baby William Edmund "Ed"

Minnie Pulliam Foster and William Edmund Foster

Minnie Pulliam Foster

William Edmund "Ed" Foster

Foster on the porch of The Canton Telephone, *a forerunner of the* Canton Herald, *still published today.*

William Edmund "Ed" Foster

Having always been interested in writing, William Edmund "Ed" Foster purchased The Canton Telephone *after his high-school graduation in 1884 and became known as "the boy editor." He worked as editor and publisher of the paper for about ten years before selling it to a relative. He then decided to become a minister and enrolled in the Baptist Theological Seminary. He preached at several churches across the state and served as the Secretary of the State Sunday School Board of the Southern Baptist Convention.*

Thomas Jones "Judge" Foster, Sr.

Thomas Jones "Judge" Foster, Sr. and Francis Ann Foster

tivities of life one of the oldest citizens of the county and one who has been a useful, upright citizen, identified at all times with the best interests of the county." Judge Foster came to Van Zandt County in 1857 and settled in the Big Rock area. After teaching for two years, he returned to North Carolina in January of 1859 only to return to Van Zandt County in May of the same year. A large part of his family from North Carolina followed in the winter of 1859. Thomas married his former student, Francis Ann Tate, in 1860. On February 8, 1862, he joined the Confederate Army as a Sergeant and was a Captain by the end of the War. In 1866, he was elected Probate Judge (County Judge) but was removed by the Reconstruction government a few months later. In order to hold office or vote, citizens were required to take an oath known as "An Ironclad Oath," which stated you had never fought against the Union. This eliminated thousands of ex-Confederates from the political process. In 1878, he was elected County Clerk and served six years. In 1888, he was appointed to fulfill a vacated post as County Commissioner. In the mid 1880's, he was a dealer in fine wines, brandies, liquors, tobaccos, cigars, etc., on the Canton Square. He also owned over 500 acres of land adjacent to Canton on which he farmed and raised cattle. He was a lifetime Mason. Judge T. J. Foster and his wife, Francis Tate, had 12 children, all boys except one daughter who died at the age of 12. Sources: *Southland Magazine*; *Wills Point Chronicle*, August 9, 1906; Dr. Billy Glenn Foster, Foster Family historian.

FOSTER, WILLIAM EDMUND "ED"

(Photo page 59) Born: September 20, 1865, Van Zandt County, Texas. Died: February 10, 1956, Harris County, Texas. Cause of death: Heart disease. Married: Minnie Pulliam. Father: Thomas Jones Foster, Sr., North Carolina. Mother: Francis Ann Tate, Tennessee. Occupation: Newspaper owner/publisher, minister. Comments: Edmund Foster obtained his education at the local schools and graduated near the top of his class. He was interested in writing. After his high school graduation in 1884, he purchased a local newspaper, *The Canton Telephone*. He was known as the "boy editor." When people review those early day newspapers now, it is simply amazing how well he wrote at such an early age. These early newspapers, although slanted toward which political party the editor belonged to, has preserved more local history than any other source available today. Edmund met Minnie Pulliam, while she was visiting others at the C. A. Wortham hotel, which was next door to the newspaper office. She was seven years older than Edmund, but this didn't deter him from marrying her. They had one child who died at birth. He was editor and publisher of the newspaper for about ten years before selling to a relative. The paper was a forerunner of the *Canton Herald* which is still published today. Ed became dissatisfied with the newspaper business and moved to Louisville, Kentucky to prepare himself for the ministry. He enrolled in the Baptist Theological Seminary. After receiving his training, he held pastorates in Kentucky, came back to Texas as Secretary of the State Sunday School Board of the Southern Baptist Convention, then preached at several churches across the state. They moved to Harris County and lived there until his death. His wife, Minnie, died in 1936. Sources: Death Certificate; *The Texan*, March 30, 1883; Dr. Billy Glenn Foster, Foster Family historian.

Fuller, Rev. James Marvin
Born: June 27, 1886, Van Zandt County, Texas. Died: March 23, 1939, Smith County, Texas. Married: (1) Janie Blackwell. Children: Lola Mae and Mrs. Edwin Chambers. (2) Henrietta Unknown. Father: Benjamin Franklin "Frank" Fuller. Mother: Margret Elizabeth Short. Occupation: Methodist minister. Comments: Marvin Fuller attended Van Zandt County schools. He then became a minister for more than 25 years. He started his ministry at the Methodist Church in Canton and preached at numerous places in Texas. He was pastor of the Methodist Church at Bullard, Texas when he died. He first wife was from a prominent pioneer Canton family. Sources: *Canton Herald*, March 30, 1939; Ancestry.com.

Fuller, Janie Blackwell
Born: September 29, 1886, Van Zandt County, Texas. Died: July 17, 1938, Collin County, Texas. Cause of death: Heart disease. Married: James Marvin Fuller. Children: Lola Mae and Mrs. Edwin Chambers. Father: Henry Fisher Blackwell, Jr. Mother: Nannie Jane Bartlett. Comments: Janie Blackwell came from pioneer Canton settlers. Her grandfather was Henry Fisher Blackwell, Sr., one of the first merchants in Canton; and her father was a former Van Zandt County Sheriff. Her father built the Blackwell house in June and July of 1887; and in 2016, it remains the oldest surviving house in Canton, Texas. Source: Death Certificate.

G

Gabbert, Luther Owen "Luke"
Born: December 5, 1910, Oklahoma. Died: February 13, 1965, Dallas County, Texas. Cause of death: Emphysema. Married: Geraldine Eaten, December 24, 1943. Father: Erastus Malone Gabbert. Mother: Myra Eva Williams. Occupation: Baker, County Treasurer. Comments: Luke Gabbert had lived in Van Zandt County for twenty-nine years, twenty-three of them as County Treasurer. He was the longest-serving County Treasurer in Van Zandt County history. Sources: Death Certificate; *Canton Herald*, February 18, 1965.

Gabbert, Wesson Bruner
Born: August 22, 1893, Calhoun County, Mississippi. Died: January 6, 1961, Caddo Parish, Louisiana. Married: Bessie Lee Cooksey. Father: Erastus Malone Gabbert. Mother: Myra Eva Williams. Occupation: Bookkeeper. Military: WWI, Okla. Wagoner, Sup. Co. 358 Inf. Sources: *Canton Herald*, January 12, 1961; Hilliard and Sons Funeral Home records.

Galloway, Francis Orman "Shorty"
Born: September 28, 1919, Thomas County, Kansas. Died; July 7, 2009, Dallas County, Texas. Children: Debbie and Frank. Married: Vernice Faye Roberts. Father: Martin LoAllen Galloway. Mother: Mary Angeline Fuller. Military: WWII, PFC U. S. Army, Purple Heart. Sources: *Van Zandt News*, July 19, 2009; Eubank Funeral Home records.

Galloway, Francis Orman, Jr.
(Photo page 62) Born: January 12, 1947, Kansas. Died: May 22, 1987, San Diego County, California. Married: Deanna Marie Bennett, January 21, 1980. Father: Francis Orman Galloway, Sr. Mother: Vernice Faye Roberts. Military: ROTC, University of Texas, U.S. Army. Comments: Francis Galloway, Jr. was born in Kansas, but soon moved to Dallas, Texas with his family. He graduated from Bryan Adams High School in 1965 and the University of Texas in 1970. He participated in ROTC at the University of Texas and graduated with a B. S. Degree. He served in the U. S. Army. Sources: Nevada Marriage Index 1956-2005, Ancestry.com.

Galloway, Vernice Roberts
Born: March 31, 1927, Van Zandt County, Texas. Died: October 18, 2008, Dallas County, Texas. Married: Francis Orman "Shorty" Galloway. Children: Debbie and Frank. Father: Thomas V. Roberts. Mother: Mattie Jane Couch. Occupation: Veterans of Foreign Wars, forty years. Sources: *Van Zandt News*, October 26, 2008; Eubank Funeral Home Records.

Luther Owen "Luke" Gabbert *was the longest-serving County Treasurer in Van Zandt County history, having held the post for twenty-three years. He is buried with his brother, Wesson.*

Francis Orman Galloway, Jr.

George Washington "Wash" Gore and Effie Lee "Lela" Gore Helms

Gamel, Emily Christine
Born: June 17, 1922, Van Zandt County, Texas. Died: March 13, 1979, Bosque County, Texas. Cause of death: Gunshot wound. Married: Melvin Lawrence Gamel, 1941. Children: J. L., Thomas R., Charletta, and Stephen. Father: John Lyman Hardin. Mother: Vinnie Ware. Sources: 1930 U. S. Census, Death Certificate, Birth Certificate.

Gamel, John Cumby
Born: March 3, 1880, Webster Parish, Louisiana. Died: January 31, 1971, Gregg County, Texas. Cause of death: Heart disease. Married: Ora Francis Pettit. Children: Norman J., W. A., Pearl, Ruth, Isabell, Minnie, and Mrs. Maxie Nugent. Father: Zack Gamel. Mother: Emily Baird. Occupation: Farmer, U. S. Department of Agriculture. Sources: Death Certificate; *Canton Herald*, February 4, 1971.

Gamel, Johnny Lyman
Born: June 2, 1942, San Diego County, California. Died: June 20, 2009, Tarrant County, Texas. Married (1): Marretta I. Compton. Divorced. (2) Sandra C. Unknown. Divorced. (3) Betty J. Unknown. Divorced. Father: Melvin Lawrence Gamel. Mother: Emily Christine Hardin. Military: Vietnam, U. S. Navy. Sources: Texas Marriage Collection, Texas Divorce Index, Hilliard Funeral Home records, Ancestry.com.

Gamel, Melvin Lawrence
Born: April 19, 1916, Haskell County, Texas. Died: December 24, 1954, Dallas County, Texas. Married: Emily Christine Hardin, 1941. Children: J. L., Thomas R., Charletta, and Stephen. Father: John Cumby Gamel. Mother: Ora Francis Pettit. Military: WWII, Chief Bosn USN. Sources: *Dallas Morning News*, December 29, 1954; Eubank Funeral Home records.

Gamel, Ora Frances
Born: April 17, 1888, Georgia. Died: June 17, 1964, Gregg County, Texas. Married: John Cumby Gamel. Children: Norman J., W. A., Pearl, Isabell, Ruth. Father: William P. Pettit. Mother: Mary G. Boseman. Sources: *Canton Herald*, June 25, 1964; Eubank Funeral Home records.

Gardenhire, Agnes Elizabeth
Born: March 29, 1916, Rockwall County, Texas. Died: June 27, 1953, Dallas County, Texas. Cause of death: Breast cancer. Married: Unknown. Divorced. Father: George H. Gardenhire. Mother: Blanche Spinks. Occupation: School teacher. Source: Death Certificate.

Gardenhire, Blanche Spinks
Born: January 15, 1889, Van Zandt County, Texas. Died: April 14, 1953, Rockwall County, Texas. Cause of death: Automobile accident. Married: George H. Gardenhire. Father: John S. Spinks, Mississippi. Mother: Zollie Thompson, Texas. Occupation: Cleaning plant worker. Comments: Blanche Gardenhire's father was the longest serving County Judge in Van Zandt County history. Source: Death Certificate.

Gentry, John William
Born: October 10, 1867, Alabama. Died: December 6, 1931, Van Zandt County, Texas. Cause of death: Kidney disease. Married: (1) Laura Ann Goode, January 3, 1895. Child: Vevie. (2) Sudie "Susie" Rusk, December 23, 1909. Children: Lila Maurine, Willie Ilene, Faye Exre, Mary Lou, and J. W., Jr. Father: Daniel Harrison (Buck) Gen-

try, Alabama. Mother: Mary E. Mitchell. Occupation: Deputy Sheriff, Sheriff, mercantile store owner, farmer. Comments: The Gentry family plot has footstones but the headstones are missing. John Gentry lost his bid for a third term as sheriff in 1910. He ran again for sheriff at various times but was never re-elected. He later served as City Marshal of Grand Saline with his last term ending May 2, 1916. Later he became associated with A. M. Herrin in the mercantile business in the Hayden Community and farmed until his death in 1931. One of his first appointments as Sheriff was John Rusk Kellis as a deputy. He later became a very well-known sheriff of Van Zandt County. John Gentry's first wife was the daughter of Dr. C. A. Goode of the Owlet Green community. She died in childbirth with Vevie. Vevie was reared by John's sister, Lou Gentry Bryant. John's second wife was the daughter of Cicero Rusk, the former Sheriff whom he had served as a deputy. Sudie survived John by 40 years, dying in 1971 in Irving, Texas. Sources: Death Certificate; 1880 U.S. Census; *Desperate Characters of Van Zandt County*; *Canton Herald*, December 12, 1931; Ancestry.com; Find A Grave.

GENTRY, MARY LOU
Born: 1916. Died: March 1919. Cause of death: Pneumonia. Father: John W. Gentry. Mother: Sudie Rusk. Comments: Mary Lou Gentry is buried in the Gentry Family plot. There are footstones but no headstones. Source: *Canton Herald*, March 7, 1919.

GILL, JOHN T.
Born: December 19, 1847, Alabama. Died: September 29, 1887, Van Zandt County, Texas. Married: Missouri Blackwell, November 30, 1871. Child: William V. Father: William Karr Gill. Mother: Arena Staggs. Occupation: Farmer, Deputy Sheriff, Deputy U. S. Marshall. Military: CSA Private 9th Georgia Infantry. Comments: John Gill was in Van Zandt County by June of 1873 when he was appointed Deputy Sheriff under Sheriff Parker He was a farmer; but at least for a time, he served as a Deputy U. S. Marshall. Family stories report that Gill suffered an injury while in the War and never fully recovered, and this contributed to his early death. His wife, Missouri, was part of the Blackwell's, a pioneer Van Zandt County family. Less than a year after John Gills death, Missouri married B. F. Eleazer in Van Zandt County. Sources: 1880 U. S. Census; *Civil War Veterans of Van Zandt County*; *Van Zandt County Court Minutes, Volumes A&B, 1848-1871*; *Texan Telephone*, January 6, 1887; *Canton Telephone*, September 9, 1887; Ancestry.com.

GILMORE, BERNARD M.
Born: March 9, 1882, Texas. Died: January 20, 1902, Van Zandt County, Texas. Cause of death: Playground accident. Father: Wiley C. Gilmore, Butts County, Georgia. Mother: Sarah J. Monroe. Occupation: School teacher. Comments: Bernard Gilmore was playing baseball with his students at Silver Lake Community School. He was hit in his diaphragm with a ball. His diaphragm ruptured which led to his death. Sources: 1900 U. S. Census; *Wills Point Chronicle*, January 23, 1902.

GILMORE, SARAH JOHANNA
Born: September 9, 1843. Died: May 6, 1898. Married: Wiley C. Gilmore, February 17, 1867. Children: George E., Clarence E., and Raymond M. (Plus two deceased children). Father: James J. Monroe. Mother: Blanche Narcissa Kelley. Source: *Van Zandt County Texas Biographies.*

GILMORE, WILEY COLEMAN
Born: February 14, 1839, Butts County, Georgia. Died: January 25, 1923, Van Zandt County, Texas. Married: Sarah Johanna Monroe, February 17, 1867, Newton County, Mississippi. Children: George E., Clarence E., and Raymond M. (Plus two deceased children). Father: Humphrey James Wiley Gilmore. Mother: Sarah R. Colemen. Occupation: Farmer, Constable of Precinct 1, Van Zandt County, Texas. Military: CSA, Company I 45th Georgia Infantry (Surrendered at Appomattox Courthouse with Robert E. Lee's Army). Comments: Wiley C. Gilmore and his wife moved to Van Zandt County from Mississippi in 1872 and settled near Canton. They remained for fifty-three years, forty-three on the same place. He was highly respected, but even respected people could have family squabbles. Here is one example as reported by the Texas Telephone "A difficulty between Messrs. W. C. Gilmore and R. M. Knox has not terminated as serious, as first suspected. The combat took place in the woods near town; in the meantime, Mr. Gilmore received a painful gash from the blade of an axe, also a painful wound on the hand from the blade of a knife. The wounded man is not considered to be in a dangerous condition. Mr. Knox is at home. They are brothers-in-law, and it is said that the fight is the result of an old feud." Sources: 1880 U. S. Census; *Texas Telephone*, June 1888; *Canton Herald*, January 26 and February 2, 1923.

GORDON, J.D.
Born: August 23, 1845. Died: March 15, 1908. Father: Unknown Gordon. Mother: Unknown. Comments: The *Grand Saline Sun* related J. D. Gordon's death as follows: "J. D. Gordon, a rather peculiar character, died at the John Bass home one mile east of town Sunday. Mr. Gordon, as far as could be found out had no relatives in Texas. He held papers for large tracts of land in Texas and is supposed to be worth several thousand dollars. He has been making his home with Mr. Bass at intervals for several years, but Bass says it was next to impossible to get any information regarding relatives or business." Source: *Grand Saline Sun*, February 19, 1908.

GORE, GEORGE WASHINGTON "WASH"
Born: January 19, 1892, Alabama. Died: October 1, 1967,

Van Zandt County, Texas. Cause of death: Heart disease. Married: (1) Maggie Inez Frye, 1912, Kaufman County, Texas. Divorced. (2) Effie Lee Oma "Lela" Stanbery Helms, 1933. Children: Irene, T. J., Dorothy, Fay, and Glenna Mae. Father: James Pinkney Gore. Mother: Lou Cindy Hopkins. Occupation: Farmer. Comments: George Washington Gore was born in Alabama and came to Texas about 1901. He spent most of his life in Kaufman and Van Zandt Counties, Texas. After Wash's death in 1967, Effie married Alvin Helms who died 1977. Effie died December 29, 1998 at the age of 100 years. Sources: Death Certificate; 1920 U. S. Census; *Canton Herald*, October 5, 1967; Ancestry.com; Find A Grave.

GOSSETT, JAMES P. "J.P."

Born: September 11, 1834, Union County, South Carolina. Died: October 2, 1897, Van Zandt County, Texas. Married: (1) Sallie A. Manuel, July 26, 1857. Children: Mrs. W. J. Greer, Mrs. F. B. Mason, Mrs. Erwin, M. H., T. J., and Floyd, Alton. (2) Mrs. M. A. Arnold, May 17, 1893. Military: CSA, 17th Texas Cavalry. Father: Unknown Gossett. Mother: Unknown. Occupation: Van Zandt County Treasurer. Comments: James P. Gossett moved from Union County, South Carolina to Cherokee County, Texas when he was a young boy. He eventually moved to Van Zandt County; and in 1892, he was elected County Treasurer on the Democratic ticket. James was nominated again in 1894; but was defeated by the Populist candidate. He ran again for County Treasurer in 1896, was elected, and served until his death in 1897. He had always been interested in singing. In 1869, while living at Goshen, Texas, he, along with his brother-in-law, Frank Manuel, formed the Central Texas Musical Convention and adopted the Sacred Harp as its textbook. This convention lasted for many years promoting Sacred Harp singing. Source: *Wills Point Chronicle*, October 7, 1897.

GOSSETT, SALLIE A.

Born: February 26, 1840. Died: January 14, 1892. Married: James P. Gossett, July 26, 1857. Children: Mrs. W. J. Greer, Mrs. F. B. Mason, Mrs. Erwin, M. H., T. J., Floyd, and Alton. Father: Unknown Manual. Mother: Unknown. Source: *Canton Telephone*, January 16, 1892.

GRAHAM, CALVIN B., SR.

Born: June 3, 1821, Warren County, Tennessee. Died: December 1, 1864, Kaufman County, Texas. Cause of death: Killed in an ambush. Married: Nancy Bailes, ca 1850, Tennessee. Father: Samuel Graham, North Carolina Mother: Nancy (unknown). Military: CSA, Van Zandt County Enrolling Officer. Comments: Calvin Graham came to Van Zandt County from Tennessee about 1854. He first was a Deputy Sheriff and then was elected Sheriff, August 4, 1856; reelected August 2, 1858. He served until August 6, 1860. Calvin was Sheriff during the building of the Van Zandt County courthouse in 1857. In the 1860 census, he was listed as a merchant. He was appointed Postmaster of Canton, August 21, 1860. At the beginning of the Civil War, he was selected as the Confederate Enrolling Officer of Van Zandt County. His title was "Captain," and it was his duty to enforce the Confederate Conscription Laws. Starting in 1862, every able-bodied man between the ages of 18 and 35 was subject to serve 3 years in the Confederate Army. In 1864, the age requirement changed to people 18 to 45 being subject to active service. One of the duties of the enrolling officer was to hunt down draft dodgers and deserters. *The Galveston Weekly News* reported the following article: "From the *Kaufman Enquirer*: We regret to learn that on last Thursday night, Capt. Graham, enrolling officer of Van Zandt County, while searching with a small company of men in Kaufman County for a squad of deserters, was ambushed and shot." He died from his wounds, and the deserters were never captured. Calvin Jr., the youngest of C. B. Graham's children, was born November 1, 1864, a month before his father died. He grew to manhood in Van Zandt County and was elected sheriff in 1896 which made them the first father and son to serve as Van Zandt County Sheriff. Sources: 1860 U. S. Census; *Van Zandt County Court Minutes, Volumes A&B*; *Desperate Characters of Van Zandt County; Early Murders & Bizarre Deaths in Kaufman County, 1860-1930*; *Galveston Weekly News*, December 14, 1864; Ancestry.com.

GRAY, BEN H.

Born: February 21, 1888, Van Zandt County, Texas. Died: November 15, 1950, San Francisco, California. Married: Clemmie Lee Heard, December 1, 1912. Child: Benja. Father: John W. Gray. Mother: Adeline Burns. Occupation: School teacher, government auditor (fourteen years in California). Comments: Ben Gray moved to California sometime after his wife's death and was living there until his death. Source: *Canton Herald*, November 16, 1950.

GRAY, CALLIE MAE

Born: April 13, 1917, Texas. Died: May 4, 1967, Dallas County, Texas. Cause of death: Cancer. Married: D. B. Gray. Father: Charlie Morris. Mother: Mamie Riggs. Occupation: Domestic, private home. Source: Death Certificate.

GRAY, CLEMMIE LEE

Born: July 28, 1892, Van Zandt County, Texas. Died: August 20, 1938, Dallas County, Texas. Cause of death: Cancer. Married: Ben H. Gray, December 1, 1912. Father: Eleazer A. Heard. Mother: Susan Isabella Hobbs. Source: Death Certificate.

GRAY, DEALY BURTON "D.B."

Born: November 17, 1902, Texas. Died: June 29, 1979, Van Zandt County, Texas. Married: Callie Mae Morris. Father: John Wesley "Bud" Gray. Mother: Hester John-

Calvin B. Graham, Sr. *served as Sheriff of Van Zandt County for four years, during the building of the County Courthouse. In 1860, he was appointed Postmaster of Canton. When the Civil War began, he was selected as the Confederate Enrolling Officer of Van Zandt County, charged with enforcing the Confederate Conscription Laws and hunting down draft dodgers and deserters. In 1864, he was ambused and killed by a squad of deserters.*

Mattie Victoria Green

son. Occupation: Shoe-shine stand in Jiggs Reynolds Barber Shop, Canton, Texas. Comments: D. B. Gray's job at his shoe-shine stand brought him in contact with many people. He did many favors for people of all walks of life and was universally known and liked throughout Van Zandt County. Source: Eubank Funeral Home records.

Gray, John Wesley "Bud"

Born: March 12, 1871, Texas. Died: May 2, 1963, Van Zandt County, Texas. Cause of death: Pneumonia. Married: Hester Johnson. Father: Elbert Gray. Mother: Unknown. Occupation: Carpenter. Comments: Bud Gray was the father of D. B. Gray who ran a shoe-shine stand and was very well known in Canton. Another son, Elbert Gray, was awarded the Carnegie Hero Medal for saving a small boy from a well in 1912. He is the only recipient of this Medal in Van Zandt County, Texas. Minnie Watts, a daughter, owned a café in Wills Point, Texas. Source: Death Certificate.

Green, Mattie Victoria

Born: August 3, 1892, Smith County, Texas. Died: December 31, 1985, Smith County, Texas. Married: John Wesley Green. Children: W. T., Cathaleen, and Eva Jewell. Father: J. W. Terrell. Mother: Ellen Malvinenie Wilson. Sources: Death Certificate of Ellen Wilson Terrell; 1910 U. S. Census; *Canton Herald*, January 9, 1986.

Greenway, Ellie Gladys

Born: July 17, 1914, Van Zandt County, Texas. Died: July 1, 2002, Van Zandt County, Texas. Married: William Bensen Greenway, September 11, 1937. Father: John Franklin Staley. Mother: Florence Lelia Bailey. Comments: The Staley's were early settlers in the Starr- Wentworth community of Van Zandt County. Ellie Greenway was reared in that community and was a lifelong resident of Van Zandt County. Sources: 1940 U. S. Census; *Canton Herald*, July 2002; Ancestry.com.

Greenway, William Bensen

Born: November 21, 1916, Fisher County, Texas. Died: October 22, 1991, Van Zandt County, Texas. Married: Ellie Gladys Staley, September 11, 1937. Father: Mitchel L. Greenway, Sr. Mother: Ollie May Salling. Source: Ancestry.com.

Greer, Anna Bell

Born: August 15, 1902, Van Zandt County, Texas. Died: January 5, 1977, Kaufman County, Texas. Cause of death: Leukemia. Married: Unknown Greer. Father: Ed Fitzgerald. Mother: Fannie Toles. Source: Death Certificate; *Canton Herald*, January 12, 1977.

Griser, Blanche

Born: 1891, Van Zandt County, Texas. Died: 1907, Van Zandt County, Texas. Cause of death: Meningitis. Father: Kasper George Griser. Mother: Eugenia Augusta

John P. Groome *graduated with honors from the Kentucky Military Institute in Frankfort, Kentucky and was granted a law license in Mississippi. When he arrived in Canton without money or acquaintances, he was allowed to practice law in the southwest corner of the Van Zandt County Courthouse. As payment for his rent on that space, he agreed to serve as County Attorney, earning a percentage of the fines and forfeitures he collected for the County.*

"Gussie" May Mullins. Sources: Tombstone; 1900 U. S. Census; *Wills Point Chronicle*, December 12, 1907; Ancestry.com.

Griser, Elizabeth M.
Born: September 17, 1887, Van Zandt County, Texas. Died: January 13, 1979, Van Zandt County, Texas. Married: John Kasper Griser. Children: Delles, Darryl, W. E., Howard, Lyndon, Rosalyn, and Lila Faye. Father: Martin Anderson. Mother: Adaline Blaylock. Source: Eubank Funeral Home records.

Griser, Eugenia Augusta May "Gussie"
Born: March, 1856, Alabama. Died: December 31, 1927, Van Zandt County, Texas. Married: Kasper George Griser, December 2, 1883, Kaufman County, Texas. Children: Mrs. Andrew Haynes, Mrs. Jessie Wallace, and Kasper. Father: John Loftin Mullins. Mother: Mary Ann Elizabeth "Mollie" Perdue. Source: Ancestry.com.

Griser, Infant Daughter
Born: October 3, 1946. Died: October 4, 1946. Father: Bill Griser. Mother: Clorene Griser. Source: Tombstone.

Griser, Jesse Daryl
Born: October 8, 1924. Died: September 16, 1990. Married: Jo Ann Williams. Children: Hugh, David, Daryla, Debbie, Diane, Donna. Father: John Kasper Griser. Mother: Elizabeth "Bettie" Anderson. Military: WWII, S/Sgt. US Army. Source: Ancestry.com.

Griser, Jo Ann Williams
Born: May 25, 1928, Dallas County, Texas. Died: July 2, 2010, Dallas County, Texas. Married: Jesse Daryl Griser. Children: Hugh, David, Daryla, Debbie, Diane, and Donna. Father: Hugh B. Williams. Mother: Maud S. Varley. Source: Eubank Funeral Home records.

Griser, John Kasper
Born: March 3, 1889. Died: October 31, 1984. Married: Elizabeth Anderson, November 7, 1909. Father: Kasper George Griser. Mother: Gussie May Mullins. Source: Ancestry.com.

Griser, Kasper George
Born: October 1, 1856, Wuizburg, Bavaria, Germany. Died: March 19, 1934, Taylor County, Texas. Cause of death: Cancer. Married: Gussie May Mullins, December 2, 1883, Kaufman County, Texas. Father: Kasper George Griser. Mother: Barbara Margaretha Kleinschroth. Occupation: Café owner. Comments: Kasper Griser was living at the home of his daughter, Mrs. Leroy Payne, Abilene, Texas, when he died. His remains were brought home for burial. Sources: Canton Herald, March 24, 1934; Ancestry.com.

Groome, Ann Dora
Born: November 27, 1858, Upshur County, Texas. Died: August 19, 1947, Van Zandt County, Texas. Married: (1) John P. Groome, May 1, 1880. Children: Hallie, Coot, Thomas, and Sidney (All died before 1892). (2) William W. Graham, May 25, 1896. Father: Robert W. Nolen. Mother: Sarah Darden. Source: Ancestry.com.

Groome, Coot
Born: 1885. Died: 1890. Father: John P. Groome. Mother: Ann Dora Nolen. Sources: Canton Telephone, October 17, 1890; Ancestry.com.

Groome, John P.
Born: September 7, 1852, Louisiana. Died: January 16, 1892, Wood County, Texas. Cause of death: Pneumonia. Married: (1) Manerva E. "Nannie" Blackwell, November 15, 1874. Children: One child died as an infant. (2) Ann Dora Nolen, May 1, 1880. Children: Hallie, Coot, Thomas, and Sidney. (All died before 1892.) Father: J. R. Groome.

Mother: Susan M. Groome. Occupation: Attorney, County Attorney. Comments: John P. Groome was born in Louisiana, but grew up in Hazelburst, Mississippi. He graduated with honors from the Kentucky Military Institute, Frankfort, Kentucky. He was granted a law license in Mississippi, but left in 1874 and arrived in Van Zandt County without money or acquaintances. In March of 1875, he was allowed to occupy the southwest corner of the Van Zandt County Courthouse to practice law. In exchange for free rent, he was to serve as the County Attorney. He held this position for a number of years. This was beneficial for John and the county. The county had no money to pay an attorney, and he needed an office. The only income he received was a percentage of the fines and forfeitures which were collected for the county, and he received free rent. Sources: *Canton Telephone*, February 6, 1892; *Van Zandt County Court Minutes, Volume C, 1872-1881.*

Groome, Manerva E. "Nannie"

Born: August 13, 1853. Died: October 3, 1875. Married: John P. Groome, November 15, 1874. Father: Henry Fisher Blackwell, Sr. Mother: Sarah Payne Engledow. Sources: Tombstone, *Van Zandt County Marriage Records 1848-1909*, Ancestry.com.

Groome, Sidney

Born: 1890. Died: 1890. Father: John P. Groome. Mother: Ann Dora Nolen. Sources: *Canton Telephone*, October 17, 1890 and February 6, 1892; Ancestry.com

Groome, Thomas

Born: 1891. Died: 1891. Father: John P. Groome. Mother: Ann Dora Nolen. Sources: *Canton Telephone*, February 6, 1892; Ancestry.com.

Groves, Carue

Born: Unknown. Died: August 1899, Van Zandt County, Texas. Father: Joe Groves. Mother: Georgia D. Goodwin. Comments: The *Free State Enterprise* reported Carue Groves' death as follows: "Carue, son of Mr. and Mrs. Joe Groves living two and a half miles south of town died Monday evening." Source: *Free State Enterprise*, August 24, 1899.

Groves, Georgia Davis

Born: September 2, 1861. Died: May 26, 1929. Cause of death: Heart disease. Married: Joseph Alonzo "Joe" Groves, March 26, 1882. Father: George Washington Goodwin. Mother: Mary Dennis. Sources: Death Certificate; *The History of Van Zandt County, Texas.*

Groves, Harvey Addison

Born: July 6, 1888, Van Zandt County, Texas. Died: June 26, 1963, Stephens County, Texas. Cause of death: Cancer. Married: Alice Sims. Father: Joseph Alonzo Groves. Mother: Georgia Davis Goodwin. Occupation: Farmer. Sources: Death Certificate; *The History of Van Zandt County, Texas.*

Groves, Joseph Alonzo "Joe"

Born: February 27, 1857, Mississippi. Died: April 14, 1932, Van Zandt County, Texas. Cause of death: Kidney disease. Married: Georgia Davis Goodwin. Father: Harvey F. Groves, Virginia. Mother: Mary Ward, Mississippi. Occupation: Farmer. Sources: Death Certificate; *The History of Van Zandt County, Texas.*

Gullett, James Rufus Benjamin

Born: May 8, 1862, Louisiana. Died: May 1, 1907, Van Zandt County, Texas. Cause of death: Struck by a train. Married: (1) Nellie E. Evans. Children: Katie Mae, Bessie Louise, Hallie Lucile, and Vergie Marie. (2) Ada Maude Evans Beck. Children: William Thomas, Frank Edwin, and Walter Vernon. Father: Rufus Young Gullett, Georgia. Mother: Paulina McLean, North Carolina. Occupation: Cotton gin repairer. Comments: Ben Gullett was married twice—first to Nellie E. Evans, and second to her younger sister, Ada Maud Evans Beck. Ben's death was reported by the *Wills Point Chronicle* as follows; "Ben Gullett of Canton at Grand Saline last Wednesday night: Mr. Gullett was a gin repairer by trade and was doing work there. It is reported that he had attended a show given there that night and when returning to his boarding house was struck by a train. He leaves a wife and four sweet little girls to mourn his death. He leaves his family in good shape as his life was insured for $2,000 and he had a good home in Canton." Sources: 1870 U. S. Census; *Wills Point Chronicle*, May 9, 1907; Ancestry.com, Find A Grave.

H

Hale, James

Born: February 8, 1883. Died: January 6, 1884. Father: W. J. Hale. Mother: Juliette D. Monroe. Source: Tombstone.

Hale, Juliette Drinkwater "Julia"

Born: January 6, 1848, Newton County, Mississippi. Died: July 9, 1929, Van Zandt County, Texas. Married: Willis Jarrell Hale, February 27, 1870, Newton County, Mississippi. Children: Edna, Walter L., Metza Don, and Carl. Father: James Joseph Monroe. Mother: Blanche Narcissa Kelly. Comments: Julie Hale's father served as a Circuit Clerk of Newton County, Mississippi soon after the county was formed in 1836. He was a prominent lawyer of Decatur, Mississippi and served as a State Senator, 1854-56. He died in 1867. Sources: *Van Zandt County Texas Biographies 1848-1991*, Ancestry.com.

HALE, WALTER L.

Born: May, 1873, Texas. Died: April, 1922, Pulaski County, Arkansas. Married: May Hale, December 23, 1897. Father: Willis Jarrell Hale. Mother: Julia D. Monroe. Occupation: Newspaper publisher, realtor. Military: Spanish-American War 1898, Co A, 6 Massachusetts Infantry. Comments: Walter Hale was in the newspaper business at Grand Saline, Texas prior to moving to Little Rock, Arkansas about 1902. He became a realtor there. His brother, Metsa D. Hale, was a teacher in Van Zandt County. Sources: *Canton Herald*, April 7, 1922; Ancestry.com.

HALE, WILLIS JARRELL

Born: August 25, 1844, Monroe County, Georgia. Died: May 9, 1910, Van Zandt County, Texas. Married: Juliette Drinkwater Monroe, February 27, 1870, Newton County, Mississippi. Children: Edna, Walter L., Metsa Don, and Carl. Father: James Hale, North Carolina. Mother: Ann McCarty. Military: CSA, 24 MS Cav. Co. E. Occupation: Farmer, syrup maker. Comments: Van Zandt County, in its early days, was widely known for its production of ribbon cane syrup; and almost all farmers raised a patch of ribbon cane for their own use. But of all the farmers to grow ribbon cane and manufacture syrup, none garnered as much publicity for the large production and quality of syrup than the pioneer grower, W. J. Hale and later his successor, Henry D. Jones. The Hale family came to Texas in 1871 and moved to Van Zandt County in 1874. In 1884, Willis started farming and growing ribbon cane on what became known as the "Hale Farm" 2-1/2 miles east of Canton. He developed the land so that he could irrigate the cane by the flood method by using the water coming from a large spring on the property, and frequently made 600 gallons of syrup to the acre. He developed a reputation for a superior quality of syrup which made Van Zandt County known as the best syrup producers all over Texas as well as nationally. He produced the "Hale Farm Syrup" for 23 years. His last year of production was 1906, and he sold the farm due to ill health to Henry D. Jones. Mr. Jones kept producing syrup until 1962—making a total of 75 years of syrup production. Sources: *The Southland*; *Wills Point Chronicle*, May 12, 1910; Van Zandt County's Most Famous Syrup Makers, W. J. Hale and Henry Jones, by Lawrence Greer and Paulette Reid Boswell, *Our Heritage*, August 2001.

HALL, JOHN H.

Born: April 8, 1834, Alabama. Died: February 22, 1904, Van Zandt County, Texas. Married: Julia Scott. Children: Maggie and Nancy Julia. Father: Andrew J. Hall. Mother: Mary Hall. Military: CSA, Pvt. 23 MS Inf. Co I, F, S. Sources: 1850, 1880 U. S. Census; *Civil War Veterans in Van Zandt County, Texas.*

HALL, JULIA SCOTT

Born: October 30, 1851. Died: January 24, 1897. Married: John H. Hall. Children: Maggie and Nancy Julia. Father: Unknown Scott. Mother: Unknown. Source: Tombstone.

HALL, MAGGIE MATILDA

Born: December 18, 1889. Died: September 21, 1895. Father: John H. Hall. Mother: Julia Scott. Source: Tombstone.

HALL, NANCY JULIA

Born: December 19, 1896. Died: January 8, 1897. Father: John H. Hall. Mother: Julia Scott. Source: Tombstone.

HANES, INFANT

Born: unknown. Died: June, 1892. Father: J. B. Hanes. Mother: M. A. Matthews. Comments: *The Canton Telephone* reported the death of infant Hanes as follows. "A little infant of Mr. J. B. Hanes and wife of Lawndale died on Thursday of last week and its remains were brought to Canton for interment." The infant's mother was the daughter of James L. and Georgia Matthews. The Matthews were early settlers in Canton. James was the pastor of the First Baptist Church of Canton for about ten years until 1882. Note: Lawndale was a boomtown that sprang up in 1886 along the Van Zandt and Kaufman County border. The town dissolved in the early 1890's. Source: *Canton Telephone*, June 24, 1892.

HARDIN, BILLIE LYMAN

Born: September 11, 1933, Van Zandt County, Texas. Died: February 15, 1982. Cause of death: CEV. Father: Lyman Escue Hardin, Comanche County, Texas. Mother: Vinnie Orlene Peavy, Alabama. Occupation: Farmer. Source: Birth Certificate.

HARDMAN, FANNIE

Born: 1878, Louisiana. Died: 1952. Father: Tower Hardman, California. Mother: Lottie Hardman, California. Siblings: Dorset and Ella. Occupation: Cook. Sources: 1880, 1940 U. S. Census.

HARRIS, JOHNNIE RAY

Born: January 13, 1954, Harris County, Texas. Died: May 11, 2016, Van Zandt County, Texas. Married: Peggy Jean Fitzgerald. Children: Chris McCleveland, Johnny Ray Jr., Frank, Joshua, and Latisha. Father: John Neal Harris. Mother: Sarah Lee Flemons. Siblings: Herman, Kelvin, Willie, O'Neal, Wanda Faye, and Patrina. Military: US

Lettrial Heddins and his wife, Eva Jim Rascoe Heddins.

Army, Paratrooper, 82nd Airborne. Source: Eubank Funeral Home records.

HARRIS, VICTORIA JO WRIGHT

Born: September 22, 1977, Dallas County, Texas. Died: January 31, 2003, Sacramento County, California. Cause of death: Homicide. Married: Johnny Ray Harris, May 25, 1998. Father: Tom Wright. Mother: Vickie J. Wright. Comments: Vickie Jo Harris was murdered in Sacramento, California. Details are not known. Source: Hilliard Funeral Home records.

HARTMAN, MONT M.

Born: March 5, 1876, Tennessee. Died: August 25, 1968, Smith County, Texas. Cause of death: Chronic Brain Disorder. Single. Father: William M. Hartman. Mother: Hester Hazelwood. Occupation: Farmer. Sources: Death Certificate; *Canton Herald*, August 29, 1968; Eubank Funeral Home records.

HASHERT, JEROME

Born: September 16, 1873. Died: August 22, 1885. Father: William H. Hashert, Georgia. Mother: Unknown. Siblings: John W. and George H. Comments: *The Canton Telephone* reports Jerome Hashert's death as follow: "About one minute before his death, he and his father were sitting on the Piazza, during the time, a cow, which had been breaking in the field, came walking up the lane and he asked his father if he had not better go and drive her back. His father's reply was yes. The little fellow started and had gone about 30 yards from the house, where he fell dead in the road. The physician pronounced the case sunstroke, which a great many people are of the opinion that it was a heart disease. It was a terrible blow to his father and two little motherless brothers." Sources: 1880 U.S. Census; *Canton Telephone*, August 29, 1885.

HAWKINS, COY

Born: 1928. Died: 1928. Father: Joe Noel Hawkins. Mother: Ruby Ross. Source: Tombstone.

HAWKINS, JOE NOEL

Born: August 7, 1890, Dallas County, Texas. Died: September 14, 1975, Smith County, Texas. Cause of death: Heart attack. Married: Ruby Ross, October 28, 1921, Van Zandt County, Texas. Father: Dudley S. Hawkins. Mother: Millie Larahe. Occupation: Auto Mechanic. Sources: Death Certificate; *Marriage Records Van Zandt County 1909-1931*.

HAWKINS, RUBY R.

Born: October 28, 1899, Grant County, Arkansas. Died: March 12, 1985, Van Zandt County, Texas. Married: Joe Noel Hawkins, October 28, 1921. Father: John Ross. Mother: Onia Lites Ross. Siblings: Bert, Tony Ross, Amy, Myrtle, and Mary Lou. Sources: Onia Ross' Death Certificate; *Canton Herald*, March 14, 1985; Ancestry.com.

HAYNES, ALLIE

Born: February 5, 1905, Pontotoc County, Oklahoma. Died: April 25, 1999, Williamson County, Texas. Married: William Francis Haynes, August 5, 1925. Child: Earnest Lee. Father: Earnest Felgar Bellamy. Mother: Maggie Leota Buck. Occupation: Seamstress. Comments: Allie Haynes lived most of her life in Canton, Texas. She moved to Georgetown, Texas in 1996 and lived there until she died. Source: *Van Zandt News*, May 2, 1999.

Effie Lee "Lela" Helms

Haynes, Andrew Hunter

Born: February 7, 1877, Van Zandt County, Texas. Died: September 12, 1956, Van Zandt County, Texas. Cause of death: Heart attack. Married: Annie Lee Griser, October 13, 1907. Children: Vivian Juanita and James Leon. Father: William L. "Judge" Haynes. Mother: Parthenia "Fannie" Flowers. Comments: Andrew Haynes' father was in Van Zandt County by the mid 1870's. He was elected as the County Commissioner of Precinct 3 in 1876 and served in that position until 1884. He was elected County Judge and served one term 1906-1907. Sources: Death Certificate, Eubank Funeral Home records.

Haynes, Annie Lee

Born: July 17, 1886, Van Zandt County, Texas. Died: October 6, 1935, Kaufman County, Texas. Cause of death: Struck by automobile. Children: Vivian Juanita and James Leon. Married: Andrew Hunter Haynes, October 13, 1907. Father: Kasper George Griser. Mother: Gussie Mullins. Comments: Annie Lee Haynes was struck by an automobile on October 5, 1935 while in Canton, Texas. She suffered a concussion and a mangled left arm and leg. She was taken to a hospital in Terrell, Texas and died as a result of her injuries. Source: Death Certificate.

Haynes, Infant

Born: 1911. Died: 1911. Father: Andrew Hunter Haynes. Mother: Annie Lee Griser. Source: Tombstone.

Haynes, Isaac Edward

Born: August 26, 1881, Van Zandt County, Texas. Died: October 2, 1961, Van Zandt County, Texas. Cause of death: Burns. Married: Zeffie Day, March 8, 1903. Divorced: March 27, 1916. Remarried: February 3, 1918. Father: William L. "Judge" Haynes. Mother: Parthenia "Fannie" Flowers. Comments: Isaac Haynes was burned to death. It is assumed that his clothes caught on fire from a heater. Isaac's father was in Van Zandt County by the mid 1870's. He was elected County Commissioner of Precinct 3 and served from 1876 through 1884. He was also elected County Judge and served one term 1906-07. He also operated a drugstore in Wills Point, Texas, as W. L. Haynes and Son. Sources: Death Certificate; *Canton Herald*, October 5, 1961; Eubank Funeral Home records.

Haynes, William Francis "Bill"

Born: August 8, 1889, Van Zandt County, Texas. Died: June 25, 1943, Pontotoc County, Oklahoma. Married: (1) Lyda Haynes, 1918. Filed for divorce November 24, 1920. Child: Billy. (2) Allie Bellamy, August 5, 1925. Child: Earnest Lee. Father: William L. "Judge" Haynes. Mother: Parthenia "Fannie" Flowers. Siblings: Andrew and Isaac Edward. Military: WWI, WWII, Chief, U. S. Navy, (served thirty-four years). Comments: William F. Haynes joined the U. S. Navy as a young man and served during WWI. He married Lyda in 1918 in California, and they divorced in 1920. He went into the Reserves, married Allie Bellamy in 1925, and moved back to Van Zandt County, Texas. He was called to active duty at the beginning of WWII and reported to Corpus Christi, Texas for a few months. Then he transferred to Grand Prairie, Texas where he became ill. He was transferred to the Base Hospital in Ada, Oklahoma for treatment and died there. Sources: Tombstone; *Canton Herald*, June, 1943.

Hays, Margie Mae

Born: January 18, 1883, Van Zandt County, Texas. Died: September 4, 1941, Rusk County, Texas. Cause of death: Cancer. Married: James S. Hays, Mississippi. Father: J. R. Travis, Mississippi. Mother: Nan Williams, Canton, Texas. Sources: Death Certificate, 1920 U.S. Census.

Heard, Eleazer Lee "E.A."

Born: December 15, 1866, Van Zandt County, Texas. Died: August 26, 1946, Van Zandt County, Texas. Married: Susan Isabelle "Belle" Hobbs, January 31, 1889. Children: Jordan Ansel, Clemmie Lee, Sarah Maude, Connie Josephine, Howard Burnell, and Laurice B. Father: Ansel Cunningham Heard, Georgia. Mother: Cordelia Rains, Texas. Occupation: Banker, cotton gin owner. Comments: E. A. Heard owned a cotton gin for fifty-six years. His first gin was located in the Mt. Pisgah community where he first established his family home. He later bought and operated a gin at Canton until he sold it to the East Texas Oil Company. After selling the business, he continued his employment with East Texas Oil Company as business manager. He helped to organize the Texas State Bank in Canton in 1909 and was serving as President when the institution was consolidated with the First National Bank. He was named to the Board of Directors and later served as Vice President of the First National Bank, and then

President before retiring. Sources: *Canton Herald*, August 29, 1946; Eubank Funeral Home records; Martha Heard, Heard Family historian.

HEARD, SUSAN ISABELLE "BELLE"
Born: July 25, 1873, Van Zandt County, Texas. Died: May 28, 1958, Van Zandt County, Texas. Married: Eleazer Lee "E.A." Heard, January 31, 1889. Children: Jordan Ansel, Clemmie Lee, Sarah Maude, Connie Josephine, Howard Burnell, Irma, and Laurice B. Father: Jordan William Hobbs. Mother: Susan Josephine Cook. Sources: Eubank Funeral Home records; Martha Heard, Heard Family historian.

HEDDINS, EVA JIM RASCOE
(Photo page 69) Born: October 23, 1906, Van Zandt County, Texas. Died: February 2, 1991, Smith County, Texas. Cause of death: Heart disease. Married: Lettrial Heddins, August 18, 1942, Sherman County, Kansas. Father: Jessie James Rascoe. Mother: June Julia Oakley. Occupation: School teacher, retail clerk, personal companion. Source: *Van Zandt News*, February 10, 1991.

HEDDINS, LETTRIAL
(Photo page 69) Born: August 30, 1906, Van Zandt County, Texas. Died: February 4, 1995, Kaufman County, Texas. Cause of death: Heart failure. Married: Eva Jim Rascoe, August 18, 1942. Father: Thomas L. Heddins. Mother: Emma K. Herron. Occupation: Clerk, Van Zandt County Tax Office. Military: WWII U. S. Army Air Corp. Sources: *Van Zandt News*, February 12, 1995; R. J. Heddins, Heddins Family historian.

HELMS, EFFIE LEE OMA GORE "LELA"
(Photos pages 62, 70) Born: January 25, 1898. Died: December 29, 1998. Married: (1) Judson James Helms, May 24, 1914. (2) George Washington Gore, 1933. (3) George "Alvin" Helms, May 9, 1970. Father: Van Buren Stanbery. Mother: Mary Emeline Mandy Aliminta Bond Stanbery. Comments: Lela Helms was the eighth child of seventeen children. She married three times, the first and third husbands were brothers. Lela outlived all three husbands and lived to be 100 years old. She is buried beside her second husband, George Washington Gore. Sources: R. J. Heddins, Helms Family historian; Find A Grave.

HENDERSON, SUSAN A.
Born: ca 1844. Died: March 1, 1876. Married: Mastin Henderson. Father: unknown Thompson. Mother: unknown. Comments: Susan A. Henderson was the third wife of Mastin Henderson. She married him after his divorce from his second wife, Betsy Blair Scates, in January 1861. Mastin had moved into Van Zandt County in the 1850's and was a Canton businessman. He served as County Judge of Van Zandt County from August 1860 until July of 1862. Mastin was elected County Treasurer in 1875 and served until 1876. He died in 1881; and it is believed that he is buried beside Susan in an unmarked grave in the Hillcrest Cemetery. Source: Ancestry.com.

HERSTON, GLADYS ONA SEALE
Born: April 8, 1907, Van Zandt County, Texas. Died: June 18, 1964, Van Zandt County, Texas. Cause of death: Colon cancer. Married: W. E. Herston. Children: Louise and Betty. Father: Henry Seale. Mother: Era Milam. Siblings: Marvin, Angus, and Avis. Sources: *Canton Herald*, June 5, 1964; Eubank Funeral Home records.

HIGHSMITH, BRUCIE
Born: September 12, 1882. Died: January 29, 1890. Father: Louis C. Highsmith. Mother: Cyntha P. Highsmith. Source: Tombstone.

Cathaleen Ellen Hilliard

Dr. Daniel Richardson Hilliard and Sally Lee Hilliard

Debbie Denice Hilliard

Faughlette Pickett Hilliard

Historical Marker
Hilliards of Canton

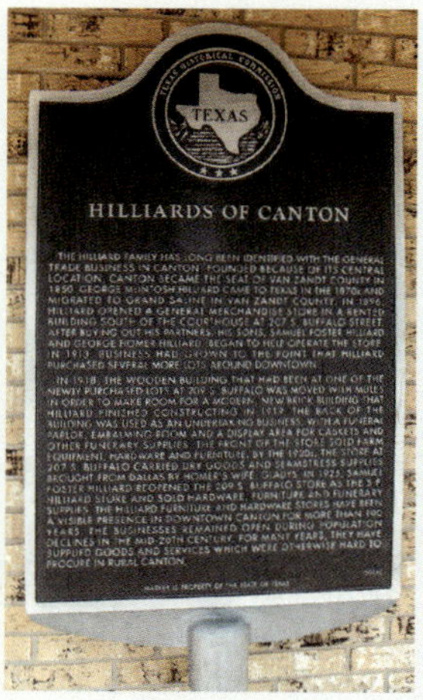

The Van Zandt County Historical Commission dedicated a Historical Marker in honor of the Hilliard Family of Canton in June, 2017. Located in front of the Hilliard furniture store on Buffalo Street in downtown Canton—now owned and operated by Mary Lynn Hilliard Baugh and Jimmy Baugh—the Marker reads as follows:

The Hilliard Family has long been identified with the general trade business in Canton. Founded because of its central location, Canton became the seat of Van Zandt County in 1850. George McIntosh Hilliard came to Texas in the 1870s and migrated to Grand Saline in Van Zandt County. In 1896, Hilliard opened a general merchandise store in a rented building south of the courthouse at 207 S. Buffalo Street. After buying out his partners, his sons, Samuel Foster Hilliard and George Homer Hilliard, began to help operate the store. In 1913, business had grown to the point that Hilliard purchased several more lots around downtown.

In 1918, the wooden building that had been at one of the newly purchased lots at 209 S. Buffalo was moved with mules in order to make room for a modern, new brick building that Hilliard finished constructing in 1919. The back of the building was used as an undertaking business, with a funeral parlor, embalming room and a display area for caskets and other funerary supplies. The front of the store sold farm equipment, hardware and furniture. By the 1920s, the store at 207 S. Buffalo carried dry goods and seamstress supplies brought from Dallas by Homer's wife, Gladys. In 1925, Samuel Foster Hilliard reopened the 209 S. Buffalo store as the S.F. Hilliard store and sold hardware, furniture and funerary supplies. The Hilliard Furniture and Hardware Stores have been a visible presence in downtown Canton for more than 100 years. The businesses remained open during population declines in the mid-20th Century. For many years, they have supplied goods and services which were otherwise hard to procure in rural Canton.

Hill, Gary Joel
Born: December 22, 1944, Cherokee County, Texas. Died: March 23, 2017, Harris County, Texas. Married: Pamela Weigel. Father: Melvin Bernard Hill. Mother: Lurlyne Travis. Child: Joel. In addition to Joel, he helped support and considered Darren Johnson, Matt Germany, and Paul Germany his sons. Occupation: Attorney. Source: Eubank Funeral Home records.

Hill, Lurlyne Travis

Born: October 25, 1912. Died: December 7, 1999. Married: Melvin Bernard Hill, December 24, 1938. Child: Gary Joel. Father: Allen Travis. Mother: Lela Robison. Siblings: Angus, J. R., and Ruth. Occupation: Home Economics teacher. Comments: Lurlyne Hill taught school at Whitewright, Iowa Park, Canton, and Spring Hill for a total of almost fifty years. She retired from Spring Hill Independent School District in Gregg County, Texas after teaching there for thirty-two years. Source: *Van Zandt News*, December 12, 1999.

Hill, Melvin Bernard

Born: March 5, 1911. Died: March 22, 1947. Cause of death: Stomach cancer. Married: Lurlyne Travis, December 24, 1938. Child: Gary Joel. Father: William C. Hill. Mother: Cora Payne. Siblings: Mrs. George Outlaw, Mrs. R. L. Willis, Mrs. E. L. Foster, Mrs. R. L. Sims, and Mrs. W. E. Anthony. Occupation: Vocational Agriculture teacher, Assistant County Agent, and County Agent. Comments: Melvin Bernard Hill was a graduate of Texas A&M College. He was a Vocational Agriculture teacher in Canton, Assistant County Agent for Van Zandt County, and County Agent for Nacogdoches and Smith Counties, Texas. Sources: Death Certificate; *The Dallas Morning News*, March, 24, 1947; Eubank Funeral Home records.

Hilliard, Baby

Born: March 19, 1903. Died: March 19, 1903. Father: George M. Hilliard, Sr. Mother: Ella Thompson. Source: Margaret Scott Hoot, Hilliard Family historian.

Hilliard, Cathaleen Green

(Photo page 71) Born: March 17, 1916, Smith County, Texas. Died: April 1, 2008, Van Zandt County, Texas. Married: (1) E. B. Honea, November 12, 1940. (2) George Curtis Hilliard, August 7, 1948. Children: Susan, Mary Lynn, and Michael Lee. Father: John Wesley Green. Mother: Mattie Victoria Terrell. Occupation: Owner of Hilliard's Furniture & Appliance, Canton, Texas. Sources: *Marriage Records Van Zandt County, 1932-1950*; *Van Zandt News*, April 6, 2008; Hilliard Funeral Home records.

Hilliard, Dr. Daniel Richardson

(Photo page 71) Born: January 31, 1933, Van Zandt County, Texas. Died: February 7, 2011, Van Zandt County, Texas. Married: (1) Sally Dawson. Children: Dennis Conrad and Jeffery Allen. (2) Ester Thompson Weaver. Father: George Homer Hilliard, Sr. Mother: Gladys Richardson. Occupation: Physician. Comments: Dan Hilliard graduated from Canton High School in 1950, Texas A&M University in 1953, and Baylor Medical School in 1957. He interned at Hermann Hospital in Houston. Dan established a medical practice with his brother, Dr. George Homer Hilliard, Jr., in 1958 at Canton, Texas. In 1973, he began a solo practice which lasted until his retirement. He practiced medicine for more than forty-eight years and delivered over 1,000 babies. In addition, he served as Chief of Staff, Cosby Germany Hospital, Grand Saline, Texas; served on the local school board as President; and on the Board of Directors of the First National Bank of Canton. Sources: Hilliard Funeral Home Records; *Canton Herald*, February 10, 2011.

Hilliard, Debbie Denice

(Photo page 71) Born: May 16, 1957, Taylor County, Texas. Died: May 7, 2014, Denton County, Texas. Married: (1) Rocky F. Timmons, October 5, 1973. (2) Howard E. Darby, September 20, 1984. (3) Michael Lee Hilliard, June 7, 1989. Children: Eric Michael, Lauren Michelle, and Ellen Nicole. Father: Henry "Sonnie" Woerner, Jr. Mother: Connie B. Luckett. Sibling: Vick-

Ella Thompson Hilliard

George Curtis Hilliard

Ida Frances Hilliard

Dr. George Homer Hilliard, Jr.

George Homer Hilliard Sr. and Gladys Eva Hilliard

Dr. Horace Hampton Hilliard

Ida Pina Hillard

Mary Eleanor Hillard

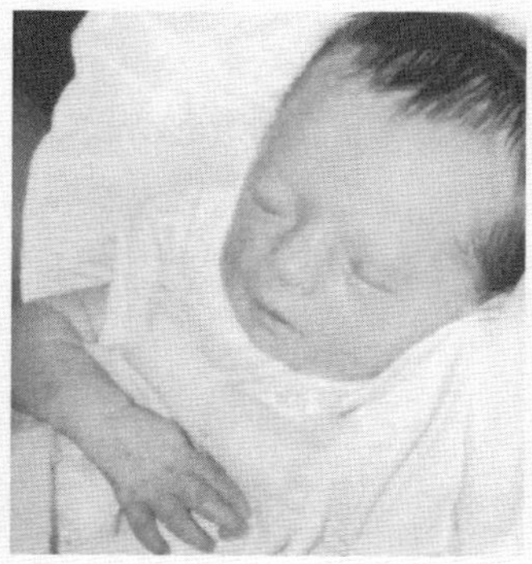

Seth Lee Hilliard

William Foster "Butch" Hilliard and Sonja Sue Hilliard

ie. Sources: Birth Certificate; *Van Zandt News*, May, 2014; State of Texas Marriage and Divorce records.

HILLIARD, ELLA THOMPSON

(Photo page 73) Born: August 6, 1875, Van Zandt County, Texas. Died: November 6, 1939, Dallas County, Texas. Married: George McIntosh Hilliard, Sr., April 6, 1902 (his fourth wife). Father: J. Tolliver "Tull" Thompson. Mother: Martha Blair. Source: Hilliard Funeral Home records.

HILLIARD, FAUGHLETTE PICKETT

(Photo page 71) Born: May 18, 1924. Died: April 29, 2013. Married: (1) Dr. George Homer Hilliard, Jr. Children: Cary, Andrea, and George Homer III. (2) Les Durzo. (3) Ned Jackson. Father: Dr. Walter Faugh Pickett. Mother: Thelma Lea Adams. Occupation: LVN; owner of Canton Health Food Store. Comments: Faughlette Hilliard assisted her husband in his medical practice. She also was the owner of the Canton Health Food Store. Faughlette was named "Van Zandt County Woman of the Year" in 2000. Sources: *Van Zandt News*, May 5, 2013; Cary Hilliard, Hilliard Family historian.

HILLIARD, GEORGE CURTIS

(Photo page 73) Born: August 21, 1913. Died: February 2, 1999. Married: (1) Connie Ruth Mills. Children: Joanna and James Curtis. (2) Mrs. Cathaleen E. Green Honea, August 7, 1948. Children: Susan, Mary Lynn, and Michael Lee. Father: Samuel Foster Hilliard. Mother: Mary Eleanor Bryan. Occupation: Merchant. Comments: Curtis Hilliard was the owner of Hilliard Furniture and Appliance in Canton, and licensed funeral director, mortician and embalmer for sixty-five years for Hilliard's and Son Funeral Home. He raised cattle and was on the Board of Directors of the First National Bank of Canton. He also served thirty-five years on the Canton Fire Department and was a member the Canton City Council. Curtis was named "Man of The Year" for the City of Canton in 1985. Sources: *Marriage Records Van Zandt County, 1932-1950*; *Van Zandt News*, February 7, 1999.

HILLIARD, DR. GEORGE HOMER, JR.

Born: March 9, 1921, Van Zandt County, Texas. Died: November 17, 1973, Smith County, Texas. Cause of death: Respiratory arrest. Married: (1) Faughlette Pickett. Children: Cary, Andrea, and George Homer III. (2) Lois Marie Bowers. Father: George Homer Hilliard, Sr. Mother: Gladys Eva Richardson. Occupation: Physican. Military: WWII Ensign U. S. Navy Doctor. Comments: George Homer Hilliard received his Bachelor of Science degree from Baylor University in 1942. After World War II, George received his medical degree from Baylor and started his medical practice with Dr. Baker in Wills Point, Texas. He moved his practice to Canton in 1947. His office was above the Eagle Drug Store. In 1956, he built his own office and clinic. In addition to being a doctor, George had a farm and cattle business with his father. He also served on the local school board for thirteen years. Sources: Death Certificate; Cary Hilliard, Hilliard Family historian.

George McIntosh Hilliard, Sr. & George McIntosh Hilliard, Jr.

George McIntosh Hilliard, Sr.

Hilliard, George Homer, Sr.

Born: February 12, 1894. Died: August 22, 1959. Married: Gladys Eva Richardson, July 9, 1916. Children: Emma Lou, George Homer, Jr. Marjory, and Daniel. Father: George McIntosh Hilliard, Sr. Mother: Ida Pina White. Military: WWI. Occupation: Mercantile business, rancher. Comments: George Homer Hilliard's mother died at his birth. He was reared into his teens by his maternal grandparents. He owned a mercantile business in Canton most of his adult life. He was Mayor of Canton for three terms. In his later years, Gladys managed the mercantile store in Canton while George operated his cattle business. Sources: Hilliard Funeral Home Records; Margaret Scott Hoot, Hilliard Family historian.

Hilliard, George McIntosh, Sr.

Born: September 21, 1856, Hilliard's Crossroads, Alabama. Died: November 23, 1931, Van Zandt County, Texas. Cause of death: Chronic nephritis, diabetes. Married: (1) Ira Bellamy, 1878; died 1879 in childbirth. Child: Ira Bellamy. (2) Ida Pina White, August 27, 1884. Children: Mary Duskie, Samuel Foster, Horace H., and George Homer. (Ida died in childbirth with Homer). (3) Era Lee Whaley, November 9, 1895, divorced, October 27, 1896. (4) Ella Thompson Hilliard, April 6, 1902. Children: Baby Hilliard (died 1903) and George McIntosh, Jr. Father: George Washington Hilliard, Georgia. Mother: Melvina LaDuske Parramore, Georgia. Occupation: Merchant. Comments: George M. Hilliard became an orphan at an early age and lived with his uncle until he was 16 or 17 years old. In 1877, he left Georgia for Texas and settled in the Providence community of Van Zandt County. George was a farmer while living in the Providence community. He moved to Canton about 1891 and went into the saloon business. In 1896, he opened a mercantile store in partnership with Sid and Chuck McCauley at 207 S. Buffalo Street in Canton. About a year later, he bought the McCauley Brothers' share of the business. George brought his sons into the business; and in 1908, the name was changed to Hilliard Mercantile. Eventually the business included hardware, furniture and a funeral home. The business prospered, and the Hilliards became one of the more prominent and involved families in Van Zandt County. The family business continues to operate today and is the oldest continually operated business in Van Zandt County. Sources: Death Certificate; *Canton Herald*, December 4, 1931; Cary Hilliard, Hilliard Family historian.

Hilliard, Gladys Eva

Born: July 24, 1896. Died: March 20, 1984. Married: George Homer Hilliard, Sr., July 9, 1916. Children: Emma Lou, George Homer, Jr. Marjory, and Daniel. Father: Daniel D. Richardson. Mother: Emily Belsora Rose. Occupation: Assisted her husband in running a general mercantile business in Canton, Texas. Source: *Southland 1903; Van Zandt News*, April 1, 1984.

Hilliard, Dr. Horace Hampton

Born: March 12, 1890, Van Zandt County, Texas. Died: October 14, 1940, Van Zandt County, Texas. Cause of death: Heart attack. Married: Metta Delila Bateman, October 6, 1926. Child: Joe Bob. Father: George McIntosh Hilliard, Sr. Mother: Ida Pina White. Occupation:

Physician. Military: WWI, Medical Corp Captain. Comments: Dr. Horace Hilliard was born in the Providence community and came with his family to Canton when he was about 1 year old. He attended the Canton Schools before graduating from Denton Normal. He returned to Van Zandt County and taught school before attending Baylor Medical College where he graduated in 1917. He volunteered for the Medical Corps and served as a Captain during World War I. Upon his discharge on October 21, 1919, he returned to Canton and began his private medical practice. He developed a very large and successful medical practice in Van Zandt County and served his community as President of the local school board. He and his wife had one child, Joe Bob Hilliard, who also became a doctor. On October 14, 1940, Dr. Hilliard made a night call to a patient and was last seen alive at 4 a.m. He was found dead in his car parked beside the side of the road about 3 miles from Canton. Sources: *Canton Herald,* October 17, 1940; Hilliard Funeral Home records.

HILLIARD, IDA FRANCES

(Photo page 73) Born: February 20, 1912. Died: September 13, 1977. Never Married. Father: Samuel Foster Hilliard, Sr. Mother: Mary Eleanor Bryan. Occupation: School teacher. Comments: Ida Frances Hilliard was partially deaf from birth and spoke in the monotone common to the deaf. She was a graduate of East Texas State Teachers College and received her Master's Degree from North Texas State University. She taught in the Canton Independent School District for almost forty-five years. Students said that they doubted she was deaf because she always knew what they whispered behind her back. Sources: *Canton Herald*, September 22, 1977; Margaret Scott Hoot, Hilliard Family historian.

HILLIARD, IDA PINA

(Photo page 74) Born: February 11, 1867. Died: September 9, 1894. Cause of death: Childbirth. Married: George McIntosh Hilliard, Sr., August 27, 1884. Children: Duskie, Foster, Horace, and Homer. Father: William Franklin White. Mother: Mary E. Guy. Comments: Ida Pina Hilliard died in childbirth on delivery of George Homer Hilliard, Sr. Source: Margaret Scott Hoot, Hilliard Family historian.

HILLIARD, INFANT SON

Born: 1916. Died: 1916. Father: Samuel Foster Hilliard, Sr. Mother: Mary Eleanor Bryan. Source: Tombstone.

HILLIARD, LOIS MARIE

Born: November 27, 1925, Hunt County, Texas. Died: June 2, 1972, Van Zandt County, Texas. Married: George Homer Hilliard, Jr. Father: Ishmal E. Bowers. Mother: Gracie Stephens. Occupation: Clinic Nursing. Source: Death Certificate.

HILLIARD, MARY ELEANOR BRYAN

(Photo page 74) Born: June 19, 1883, Cass County, Texas. Died: February 12, 1941, Dallas County, Texas. Married: Samuel Foster Hilliard. Children: Curtis, Samuel, Jr., Bryan, Ida Frances, and Andrea Laurie (one died in infancy). Father: Harvey Curtis Bryan, Cass County, Texas. Mother: Verona Frances "Dona" Hardy. Occupation: Teacher, assisted her husband in his business in Canton. Comments: Mary Hilliard lived in Canton thirty-five years. Sources: Death Certificate; *Canton Herald*, February 20, 1941; Hilliard Funeral Home records.

HILLIARD, OPAL MALINDA

Born; December 4, 1914, Erath County, Texas. Died: January 7, 1988, Smith County, Texas. Married: Samuel Fos-

Samuel Foster "Foster" Hilliard, Sr.

Samuel Foster "Sam" Hilliard, Jr. and Opal Malinda Hilliard

ter Hilliard, Jr., December 12, 1935. Children: William F. "Butch" and Charles. Father: William Jesse Nichols. Mother: Daisy Louella Kelly. Source: *Van Zandt News*, January 10, 1988.

Hilliard, Sally Lee

(Photo page 71) Born: November 11, 1933. Died: August 7, 1998. Married: Dr. Dan Hilliard. Children: Dennis Conrad and Jeffrey Allen. Father: Blanks Jefferson "Doc" Dawson. Mother: Lottie Bell Pittmon. Siblings: Perry Max, Harold, Ben, Ronald, Charles, Jerry, and Allen. Occupation: Office Manager Hilliard Clinic. Comments: Sally Hilliard graduated from Canton High School Class of 1951 and married Dan Hilliard, Class of 1950. Dan became a doctor and established the Hilliard Clinic in Canton. Sally was his office manager. Dan married Esther Thompson Weaver after Sally's death. Sources: *Canton Herald*, August, 1998; Find A Grave.

Hilliard, Samuel Foster, Jr. "Sam"

Born: December 12, 1915. Died: September 20, 1993. Married: Opal Malinda Nichols, December 12, 1936. Children: William Foster (Butch) and Charles Kelley. Father: Samuel Foster Hilliard, Sr. Mother: Mary Eleanor Bryan. Occupation: Owner Hilliard Hardware Store, Canton, Texas. Military: WWII. Comments: Sam Hilliard was a graduate of Canton High School and attended Draughon Business College. He was employed by the U. S. Department of Agriculture, Farm Administration until 1942 as Chief Clerk and Auditor for nineteen northeast Texas counties. He was owner of Hilliard Hardware until 1981 when he sold the business to his son, Butch. He was Mayor of Canton from 1959 to 1965, City Councilman from 1972 to 1976, and Van Zandt County Judge from 1981 to 1986. He was a Volunteer Fire Department member and had served as a Director of The First State Bank of Ben Wheeler. Source: *Van Zandt News*, September 26, 1993.

Hilliard, Samuel Foster, Sr. "Foster"

Born: April 17, 1886, Van Zandt County, Texas. Died: September 2, 1965, Smith County, Texas. Cause of death: Heart failure. Married: Mary Eleanor Bryan, April 21, 1911. Father: George M. Hilliard. Mother: Ida P. White. Occupation: Mercantile store owner. Comments: Foster Hilliard became a partner with his father in Hilliard Mercantile Store on the Canton Square in 1907. He remained in that business until 1947. Sources: Death Certificate; *Canton Herald*, September 9. 1965.

Hilliard, Seth Lee

(Photo page 74) Born: May 6, 1999. Died: May 13, 1999. Father: Jeff Hilliard. Mother: Beth Hall. Source: Van Zandt News, May 16, 1999.

Jesse Taylor "J.T." Hodges

Billy "Shine" Hunt

Hilliard, Sonja Sue Caviness

(Photo page 74) Born: October 24, 1942, Dallas County, Texas. Died: December 14, 2003, Van Zandt County, Texas. Married: William Foster "Butch" Hilliard. Children: Amy and Bill. Father: Clifford Caviness. Mother: Laura May Smith. Occupation: Teacher, Canton Elementary School. Source: Hilliard Funeral Home records.

Hilliard, William Foster "Butch"

(Photo page 74) Born: May 12, 1940. Died: December, 2014. Married: Sonja Sue Caviness. Children: Amy and Bill. Father: Samuel Foster Hilliard, Jr. Mother: Opal Malinda Nichols. Sibling: Charles Kelly. Occupation: Hilliard Hardware Store owner. Comments: Butch Hilliard was the Mayor of Canton for four years, City Council Member, and served on the Canton ISD School Board for twenty-two years. Source: *Van Zandt News*, December 28, 2014.

Hocutt, John P.

Born: January 17, 1860, Alabama. Died: July 6, 1892, Van Zandt County, Texas. Single. Father: Festus J. Hocutt, Alabama. Mother: Sarah Jane Clements, Alabama. Source: Ancestry.com.

Hodges, Guy

Born: 1882. Died: September 1895. Father: J. T. Hodges. Mother: Nancy Ophelia Wood. Source: *Wills Point Chronicle*, September 19, 1895.

Hodges, Jesse Taylor "J.T."

Born: October 1, 1854, Smith County, Texas. Died: January 21, 1943, Van Zandt County, Texas. Married: Nancy "Nannie" Ophelia Wood, February 6, 1878. Child: Guy. Father: Jessie Henderson Hodges, Tennessee. Mother: Lucinda Jane Ballew, Tennessee. Occupation: Pharmacist, drugstore owner. Comments: J. T. Hodges came to Canton in 1890. In 1892, G. W. Tull, a local merchant, built the first brick building on the west side of the Canton,

Dr. Joseph Joshua Jeter *Mary Yantis Jeter*

Texas square. J. T. Hodges, built the second building next to Tull and opened a drugstore at that location. Today the building is still standing with J. T. Hodges' name on the façade. His is the only name of those early merchants that is still there. He was an active pharmacist until 1942. Sources: Death Certificate, *Canton Herald*, January 28, 1943; Eubank Funeral Home records; Ancestry.com.

HODGES, NANCY OPHELIA "NANNIE"

Born: May 5, 1859, Smith County, Texas. Died: January 6, 1947, Van Zandt County, Texas. Married: J. Taylor Hodges, February 6, 1878. Child: Guy. Father: William Wood. Mother: Rhoda C. Gates. Sources: *Canton Herald*, June 5, 1947; Hilliard Funeral Home Records; Ancestry.com.

HOUSE, TIMOTHY F.

Born: April 17, 1894. Died: December 9, 1897. Father: T. F. House. Mother: J. F. House. Source: Tombstone

HOWARD, LOTTIE

Born: 1875. Died: 1932. Married: William Howard. Father: unknown. Mother: unknown. Source: 1930 U. S. Census.

HULSE, MARY MATILDA

Born: July 13, 1859. Died: October 13, 1888. Married: F. G. Hulse, February 15, 1887. Father: James L. Riley. Mother: Sarah Hobbs. Siblings: John and Rose. Comments: The *Canton Telephone* reported her death as follows: "It was on Saturday noon that the sad message was heralded from place to place of the lamentable death of Mrs. Mary Hulse—a Christian, kind and true lady. She had been in a low state of health for several months, but her death was unexpected at the time. She seemed to be apparently as well as she had been up to a few moments before her death as she had been for several months. After it was discovered that the monster death had seized her, she expired before the family circle could get to her bedside. Her remains were interred in the Canton cemetery Sunday evening at 2:30; Rev. Mr. McConnell, a Baptist minister of Wills Point, conducting the burial ceremonies. The Telephone extends condolence to the bereaved ones." Source: *Canton Telephone*, October 19, 1888.

HUNT, BILLY "SHINE"

(photo page 77) Born: October 26, 1928, Terrell, Kaufman County, Texas. Died: March 29, 1996, Dallas County, Texas. Married: Emogene Morris. Children: Billy G., Janette, Mary Jean, and Tommy. Father: Archie Albert Hunt. Mother: Willie Mae Cook. Occupation: Carpenter. Sources: *Van Zandt News*, April 7, 1996; Find A Grave.

HUNT, EMOGENE "JEAN"

Born: December 23, 1928. Died: March 8, 2016. Married: Billy Hunt. Children: Billy G., Janette, Mary Jean, and Tommy. Father: Mastin Luther Morris. Mother: Mary Ola Bussey. Comments: Emogene Hunt grew up in the Starr/Wentworth communities of Van Zandt County. She moved to Dallas in the 1940's after her marriage. She lived there for most of her life. Source: Eubank Funeral Home records.

HUNT, GARRY W.

Born: October 9, 1958, Dallas County, Texas. Died: July 14, 1989, Smith County, Texas. Father: Tony Dewitt Hunt. Mother: Evelyn Virginia Black. Source: *Van Zandt News*, July 23, 1989.

HURST, ELIZABETH P.

Born: 1804, Georgia. Died: February 8, 1882, Van Zandt County, Texas. Married: Samuel Hurst, February 17, 1824, Wilks County, Georgia. Father: Unknown Leverette. Mother: unknown. Comments: Elizabeth Hurst had at least seven children before she left Georgia as a widow. By 1880, she was in Van Zandt County living with her son, Joel E Hurst. She was 74 years old. Sources: 1880 U. S. Census, Tombstone, Ancestry.com, Find A Grave.

HURST, JOEL EVANS

Born: May 16, 1835, Georgia. Died: October 24, 1903, Van Zandt County, Texas. Married: Louisa Owen Phelps. Father: Samuel Hurst. Mother: Elizabeth P. Leverett. Occupation: Farmer. Military: CSA, Pvt. 30th Regiment, Georgia Infantry. Comments: Tombstone is in pieces and difficult to read. It was erected by H. E. and M. E. Rogers. Sources: 1880 U. S. Census, Tombstone, Ancestry.com.

HUTCHINSON, FRANK G.

Born: February 20, 1858, Choctaw County, Alabama. Died: January 12, 1920, Van Zandt County, Texas. Cause of death: Tuberculosis. Married: Susan Elizabeth Gibson. Father: Dr. Augustus "Alex" Henderson Hutchinson, Virginia. Mother: Martha Ann Sabina Bloomfield. Occupation: Farmer. Sources: Death Certificate, Ancestry.com.

Hutchinson, Susan Elizabeth
Born: October 28, 1857, Giles County, Tennessee. Died: June 30, 1942, Dallas County, Texas. Married: Frank G. Hutchinson, ca 1882. Father: Joseph Perry Gibson, Tennessee. Mother: Nancy Catherine Morrow, Tennessee. Sources: Death Certificate, Ancestry.com.

Hynes, Jane
Born: Unknown. Died: November 2, 1882. Married: E. Hynes. Father: Unknown. Mother: Unknown. Source: Tombstone.

J

Jaaland, Infant
Born: September 15, 1892. Died: September 18, 1892. Father: O. M. Jaaland. Mother: R. A. Jaaland. Source: Tombstone.

Jackson, Johnie
Born: March 24, 1900, Texas. Died: June 1, 1943, Bell County, Texas. Cause of death: Heart disease. Married: Thomas E. Jackson, 1918. Father: William Robert Haley. Mother: Elizabeth Zenobia Morgan. Sources: Death Certificate, Ancestry.com.

Jackson, Thomas Eli "Tommie"
Born: March 22, 1895, Coryell County, Texas. Died: May 16, 1943, Dallas County, Texas. Married: Johnnie E. Haley, 1918. Father: James William Jackson. Mother: Mary Alsie "Polly" Griffin. Sources: Eubank Funeral Home records, Ancestry.com.

Jarvis, Armelia
Born: July 31, 1882. Died: September 16, 1883. Father: R. R. Jarvis. Mother: Josephine A. Hamilton. Source: Tombstone.

Jarvis, Cora Allison
Born: January 10, 1890, Tarrant County, Texas. Died: May 23, 1971, Blanco County, Texas. Cause of death: Pulmonary edema. Married: Lewis C. Jarvis. Children: Ben E, Billie, and Mozelle. Father: Unknown Allison. Mother: Willie E. Allison. Source: Death Certificate.

Jarvis, Josephine Amanda
Born: October 11, 1859, Smith County, Texas. Died: March 11, 1897, Van Zandt County, Texas. Married: Robert Reeves Jarvis. Children: Loy, Lula, Leslie William., and Armelia. Father: Robert William Hamilton. Mother: Rosabella Flynn. Sources: *Wills Point Chronicle*, March 18, 1897; Ancestry.com.

Jarvis, Lewis Columbus
Born: December 16, 1883, North Carolina. Died: February 28, 1955, Van Zandt County, Texas. Married: Cora Holt Allison. Father: Warren Jarvis. Mother: Elizabeth Ketner. Source: Eubank Funeral Home records.

Jensen, Gladys Agnes Rhodes
Born: February 1, 1908. Died: November 24, 1968. Married: Martin Peter Jensen. Father: Leo Nicholas Rhodes Mother: Louise Marie Roddy. Source: Ancestry.com.

Jensen, Jens Peter
Born: September 7, 1887, Denmark. Died: December 29, 1966, Smith County, Texas. Cause of death: Heart disease. Married: Karen Kirstine Hansen, January 11, 1908, Cook County, Illinois. Children: Myrtle, Eleanor, Elaine,

Sandy Johnson *was born into slavery in 1855 in Alabama. After the Civil War, he settled in Van Zandt County in the area that became known as the Wynne Community. He lived until the age of 92, successfully farming 150 acres just north of Canton. Although he and his wife Rachel had no children of their own, they were among the largest financial contributors to the schools of the Canton area and also supported local churches.*

and Clarence. Father: Mat Jensen, Denmark. Mother: Unknown. Occupation: Road contractor. Sources: Death Certificate; *The Dallas Morning News*, January 3, 1967.

JENSEN, KAREN KIRSTINE
Born: February 8, 1889, Denmark. Died: January 10, 1962, Van Zandt County, Texas. Cause of death: Heart disease. Married: Jens Peter Jenson, January 11, 1908, Cook County, Illinois. Children: Clarence, Myrtle, Elaine, and Eleanor. Father: Unknown Hansen. Mother: Unknown. Sources: Death Certificate; *Canton Herald*, January 18, 1962.

JENSEN, MARTIN PETER
Born: August 16, 1908, Cook County, Illinois. Died: January 23, 1948, Calcasieo Parish, Louisiana. Married: Gladys Agnes Rhodes. Father: Jens Peter Jensen, Denmark. Mother: Karen Kristine Hansen, Denmark. Occupation: Contractor. Source: Hilliard Funeral Home records.

JENSEN, MYRTLE MARIE
Born: November 15, 1910, Cook County, Illinois. Died: September 24, 1997, Rockwall County, Texas. Father: Jens P. Jensen. Mother: Karen K. Hansen. Source: U. S. Social Security Applications and Claims Index.

JETER, ALLEN YANTIS
Born: March 30, 1923, Van Zandt County, Texas. Died: November 12, 1929, Taylor County, Texas. Cause of death: Intestinal obstruction. Father: Dr. Joseph J. Jeter. Mother: Mary Yantis. Comments: Allen Jeter's father delivered him. Sources: Death Certificate, Tombstone, Find A Grave.

JETER, DR. JOSEPH JOSHUA
(Photo page 78) Born: March 6, 1875, Van Zandt County, Texas. Died: January 16, 1948, Smith County, Texas. Cause of death: Stomach cancer. Married: (1) Eva Mae High, September 4, 1898; Divorced: Filed July 14, 1907. Child: Buck. (2) Mary Yantis, September 21, 1916. Children: Joy Belle, Mary Jo, George T., Ella Ruth, Jerry, and Allen. (3) Ida LaDora Cruse. Father: Allen William Jeter, Mississippi. Mother: Susan Seale, Mississippi. Occupation: Physician. Sources: Death Certificate; *Canton Herald*, January 22, 1948.

JETER, MARY YANTIS
(Photo page 78) Born: December 29, 1892, Van Zandt County, Texas. Died: October 2, 1932, Van Zandt County, Texas. Cause of death: Pancreatic cancer. Married: Dr. Joseph Joshua Jeter, September 21, 1916. Children: Joy Belle, Mary Jo, George T., Ella Ruth, Jerry, and Allen. Father: Judge Thomas Rusk Yantis. Mother: California Belle Riley, Van Zandt County, Texas. Siblings: Ruth, Robert, Albert, and D. L. Sources: Death Certificate; *Canton Herald*, October 7, 1932; Find A Grave.

JOHNSON, ELMER LEE "SOLDIER BOY"
Born: May 31, 1929, Rusk County, Texas. Died: January 25, 1993, Dallas County, Texas. Married: Joan E. Pickens. Father: Frank Clay Johnson. Mother: Mandy Johnson. Occupation: Construction, Dallas Power & Light Company. Source: *Van Zandt News*, January 31, 1993.

JOHNSON, HESTER
Born: March 12, 1888, Van Zandt County, Texas. Died: July 21, 1944, Van Zandt County, Texas. Cause of death: Cerebral hemorrhage. Married: (1) John Wesley "Bud" Gray. (2) Will Johnson, May 17, 1913; Filed for divorce, January 4, 1916. Children: Minnie, Elbert, D. B., and three others. Father: John Whitaker. Mother: Sarah Scates. Comments: One of Hester Johnson's children, D. B. Gray, worked at Jiggs Reynolds Barbershop in Canton for several years and was a well-known Canton resident. Another son, Elbert, was awarded the Carnegie Hero Medal in 1913 for saving a boy from a well in 1912. He is

DR. WILLIAM GOODMAN "W.G." JOHNSON, *reared on a farm in Smith County, Texas, graduated from Vanderbilt Medical College in Nashville, Tennessee in 1882 at age 22. Two years later he moved to Canton with his wife and child and opened his medical practice in the Meredith Building on the Canton Square. He practiced medicine in Canton for ten years, also serving as Secretary of the Van Zandt County Medical Society and as Medical Examiner of Masonic Lodge 141. He died at age 34.*

the only person who has received this medal in Van Zandt County. Minnie Watts, a daughter, owned a café in Wills Point, Texas. Source: Death Certificate.

JOHNSON, RACHEL

Born: 1865. Died: 1953. Married: Sandy Johnson. Father: Unknown. Mother: Unknown. Source: Tombstone.

JOHNSON, SANDY

Born: 1855, Alabama (slave). Died: December 14, 1947, Van Zandt County, Texas. Cause of death: Heart disease. Married: (1) Annie Dorough, December 24, 1884. (2) Rachel Johnson. Father: Unknown. Mother: Unknown. Occupation: Farmer. Comments: After the Civil War, Sandy Johnson settled in Van Zandt County in what later became the Wynne Community. He lived his life farming 150 acres of land near Canton. The *Canton Herald* reported Sandy Johnson's 86th birthday as follows: "Sandy Johnson, who is one of Canton's most highly respected Negroes was in town Monday relating that he observed his 86th birthday on Friday, Aug. 30. Sandy stated that he was born a slave in Alabama, but has been in Canton more than fifty years. He owns a 150-acre farm north of town which he has quite successfully operated for many years. Sandy and his wife have never had any children but are among the largest contributors to the schools and churches for the up building of their race in this vicinity. He is very appreciative of his white friends and a number of them remembered him kindly on his birthday." Sources: Death Certificate; *Canton Herald*, September 5, 1940.

JOHNSON, DR. WILLIAM GOODMAN "W.G."

Born: November 28, 1859, Ashley County, Arkansas. Died: October 31, 1893, Van Zandt County, Texas. Married: Zorado E. Wallace, November 5, 1882. Father: S. E. D. Johnson, South Carolina. Mother: M. E. Johnson, South Carolina. Occupation: Physician. Comments: The following information was extracted from a biographical sketch printed in the *Canton Telephone*. William Goodman Johnson, the fourth son of S. E. D. and M. E. Johnson, was born in Ashley County, Arkansas November 28, 1859. William Johnson's mother and father were born in South Carolina, came to Arkansas in 1854, remaining there until 1862, when they moved to Smith County, Texas. Johnson was reared on a farm in Smith County, receiving a common school education. At the age of sixteen he moved with his parents to Ellis County, Texas and again helped his father on the farm while attending the county schools. At the age of 19 he began teaching penmanship in the local schools and reading medicine alternately for two years. Johnson then attended the Vanderbilt Medical College at Nashville, Tennessee, graduating February 27, 1882. In March 1883 he returned to Ellis County, and began the practice of medicine at Ennis. On November 5, 1882, he married, Zorado E. Wallace, a daughter of Jesse W. and Elizabeth Hubbard Wallace, of Wills Point, Van Zandt County. They had one child, Minnie. In April, they moved to Canton to establish a medical practice in the Meredith Building on the Canton Square. In the ten years that he practiced medicine in Canton, Johnson became fully engaged in the activities of the town. He lived in a two story house on West Main Street, became Secretary of the Van Zandt County Medical Society, Medical Examiner of Masonic Lodge 141, and a Member of the Knights and Ladies of Honor. Johnson became a doctor at the age of 23 and died at the age of 34. His widow, Zorado, became the third wife of A. S. Tunnell in 1901. Sources: 1800 U. S. Census; *Texas Telephone,* February 14, 1885; *Canton Telephone*, August 14, 1891, November 3, 17, and 24, 1893.

Dr. Andrew Jackson "Jack" Kellam and his wife Mary Duskie Hilliard Kellam

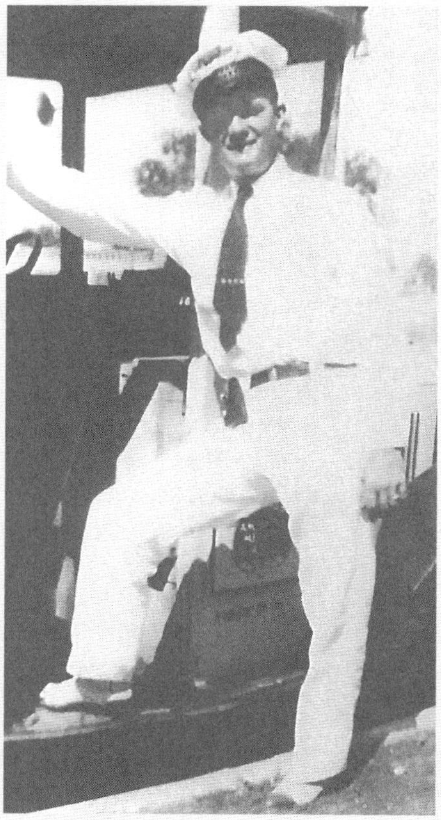

John Mayo Kellam, Sr.

JOHNSTON, EDITH MELLISA
Born: April 6, 1866, Georgia. Died: July 8, 1943, Gregg County, Texas. Married: Richard Marion Johnston, 1887. Children: Fred, Jessie V, Alonzo M., Paul R., Hugh L., Carl, Ruby, and Clayton C. Father: James Petit. Mother: Cynthia Clayton. Sources: 1940 U. S. Census, Find A Grave.

JOHNSTON, RICHARD MARION
Born: January 27, 1861, Madison County, Arkansas. Died: September 8, 1942, Van Zandt County, Texas. Cause of death: Cancer. Married: Edith Mellisa Petit, 1887. Children: Fred, Jessie G., Alonzo M., Paul R., Hugh L., Carl, Ruby, and Clayton C. Father: Dennis Johnson, Madison County, Arkansas. Mother: Patsy Jane Frazier, McDonald County, Missouri. Occupation: Farmer. Sources: Death Certificate, Eubank Funeral Home records.

JONES, BONTEEL
Born: July 15, 1921, Henderson County, Texas. Died: September 13, 1985, Dallas County, Texas. Married: Nora "Jo" Hope Frailey. Children: Kenneth and Casey. Father: Eugene Jones. Mother: Myrtle Jones. Occupation: Truck driver, service station owner. Military: WWII U. S. Air Force. Comments: Bonteel Jones owned Jones Allied Service Station in Canton. He also served as Canton's Chief of Police for four years. Source: *Canton Herald*, September 19, 1985.

JONES, CHARLIE LEE
Born: April 2, 1898, Bibb County, Georgia. Died: August 25, 1969, Van Zandt County, Texas. Cause of death: Cancer. Married: Adelaide Jones. Father: John Henry Jones. Mother: Lena Jones. Occupation: Auto agency employee. Military: WWI, Texas PFC. Co. D. 24 Infantry. Sources: Death Certificate, 1910 U. S. Census, Eubank Funeral Home records, Find A Grave.

JONES (BASS), NORA HOPE
Born: April 13, 1924, Illinois. Died: February 28, 2007, Dallas County, Texas. Married: (1) Bonteel Jones. Children: Kenneth and Casey. (2) Denver Bass. Father: James Lyman Frailey. Mother: Lola Madge unknown. Occupation: Owner of Jo's Beauty Shop, Canton and Edgewood, Texas. Comment: She is buried next to her first husband Bonteel Jones. Source: *Van Zandt News*, March 11, 2007.

K

KELLAM, DR. ANDREW JACKSON "JACK"
(Photo page 81) Born: April 17, 1880, Van Zandt County, Texas. Died: October 23, 1945, Van Zandt County, Texas. Cause of death: Heart attack. Married: Mary Duskie Hilliard, May 6, 1906. Children: John Mayo and Katherine Lucille. Father: John Mosby Kellam, Arkansas. Mother: Cynthia Polk Wise, Arkansas. Occupation: Medical doctor. Comments: Jack Kellam and his twin brother, Jim R. Kellam, were born April 17, 1880, in the Colfax community. Jack's father died when he was quite young, and his mother struggled to raise five boys alone. Jack finished high school in Grand Saline and then worked for the T.B. Meeks and J. C. Mason Companies in Grand Saline. He married Duskie Hilliard from Canton in 1906, and later decided to become a doctor. Jack entered Baylor Medical College in 1909 graduated in May of 1913. In August, he bought the medical practice of Dr. C. P. Smith and established an office on the second floor of the Nolen Bros. drugstore on the Canton Square. Jack developed a successful medical practice which lasted for over thirty years, starting in the horse and buggy days, and lasting into the modern era. In addition to his successful medical practice, Jack developed a reputation for being somewhat of a rounder. He apparently liked to drink; and when he was drunk, he liked to fight. These altercations sometimes led

to serious consequences. The following is a story reported in the *Canton Herald* in September 1919 about one such altercation that could have cost Jack his life. "The timely interference of Sheriff Joe Carpenter probably prevented a tragedy Saturday night in Canton. In a personal difficulty between Dr. A. J. Kellam and Levi Teel, in the Palace Drug Store, the latter drew a gun and had it not been for the presence of Mr. Carpenter, Bruce Marshall and others, there doubtless would have been a shooting. The men had previously been in one or more settos, it being alleged that Dr. Kellam started the fight by striking Teel from behind. Anyhow a fight ensued and the physician got the worst end of it. Teel is said to have gone to his room and secured a gun and after he had returned to the store the quarrel was renewed and the gun came into play. After a struggle the gun was gotten possession of by someone assisting the sheriff in putting a stop to the trouble. Dr. Kellam was taken home and the difficulty ended with the men each paying fines for fighting and making friends." Note: On April 30, 1938, this writer (Lawrence Greer) was delivered by Dr. A. J. Kellam in a farm house about four miles east from Canton on what is now Hwy. 1255. Sources: *Wills Point Chronicle* May 29, July 10, and August 14, 1913; *Canton Herald*, September 5, 1919 and November 1, 1945; *The Dallas Morning News*, October 24, 1945; Hilliard and Son Funeral Home.

Kellam, John Mayo, Sr.

Born: December 23, 1913, Van Zandt County, Texas. Died: August 8, 1977, Dallas County, Texas. Married: William Christine Bailey. Children: John Mayo, Jack William, and Ann. Father: Andrew Jackson Kellam. Mother: Mary Duskie Hilliard. Occupation: Cates Pharmacy, Desoto, Texas. Sources: *The Dallas Morning News*, August 10, 1977; *Canton Herald*, August 11, 1977.

Kellam, Mary Duskie Hilliard

(photo page 81) Born: July 7, 1885, Smith County, Texas. Died: June 9, 1960, Dallas County, Texas. Married: Dr. Andrew Jackson Kellam, May 6, 1906. Children: John Mayo and Katherine Lucille. Father: George M. Hilliard. Mother: Ida P. White. Source: Hilliard Funeral Home records.

Kellam, William Christine

Born: November 20, 1916, Van Zandt County, Texas. Died: February 19, 2004, Tarrant County, Texas. Married: John M. Kellam, Sr. Children: John Mayo, Jack William, and Ann. Father: William J. Bailey. Mother: Elnora Annice Daugherty. Source: Hilliard Funeral Home records.

King, Charlie

Born: 1858, Alabama. Died: Unknown (tombstone is in pieces, and death date is unreadable). Father: Unknown. Mother Unknown. Comments: The 1870 Census shows

Wallace Austin Knox

Lucy Ethel Lively

that Charlie King was 10 years old, born in Alabama and living in Milam County, Texas. He was living in the household of Susan King with no father listed. The 1880 census shows that he was 21 years old, a laborer living in the household of Jane Chappell. He may be connected to Isaac King, Mary Childress King, and Sarah Ann King who married E. B. Downing. All three are buried in Hillcrest Cemetery. Charlie King is buried between T. J. and Giles L. Downing. Source: 1870, 1880 U. S. Census.

King, Mary "Polly"

Born: May 8, 1804, South Carolina. Died: April 14, 1887, Van Zandt County, Texas. Married: Isaac King. Children: Jessie, Elizabeth, Francis, and Sarah. Father: Unknown Childress. Mother: Unknown. Comments: Mary Childress was born in South Carolina, but the family had moved to Alabama before 1828. She married Isaac King in Alabama. Isaac's place of death is unknown. Mary was living in Van Zandt County in 1870 with her daughter, Sarah, and son-in-law, Elija Downing. Sources: 1870, 1880 U. S. Census; Ancestry.com.

Knox, Anna Viola McClellen

Born: May 16, 1879. Died: January 23, 1916. Married: Hugh Alden Knox III, October 7, 1906. Children: Lois Inez and Deward. Father: Robert McClellen, Alabama. Mother: Frances Bowden "Fannie" McClellen, Alabama. Siblings: Mary Alabama, T. Oscar, Edgar May, Saphronia Adelin, Florence, and Ollie. Sources: Death Certificate, Ancestry.com.

Knox (Sumner), Bertha Orene

Born: January 24, 1895, Van Zandt County, Texas. Died: March 26, 1930, Van Zandt County, Texas. Buried under the name "Sumner." Cause of death: Pulmonary tuberculosis. Married: Perry C. Knox, December 23, 1925. Father: Benjamin Franklin Sumner. Mother: Julie Baker, Rockwall County, Texas. Sources: *Canton Herald*, April 4, 1930, Ancestry.com.

KNOX, DORA EFFIE
Born: December 5, 1876. Died: June 11, 1947. Cause of death: Heart failure. Married: Samuel Walter Knox, January 23, 1898. Children: Flossie Vivian, Perry, Marvin Lee, Jessie, Buster Brown, Wallace A., and Ray. Father: Bake Perry, Alabama. Mother: Sara Jane McClellan. Sources: Death Certificate, Eubank Funeral Home Records, Find A Grave.

KNOX, FLOSSIE VIVIAN
Born: August 12, 1898, Van Zandt County, Texas. Died: July 18, 1984, Smith County, Texas. Father: Samuel Walker Knox. Mother: Dora Effie Perry. Siblings: Perry, Marvin Lee, Jessie Lee, Buster Brown, Wallace Austin, and Ray. Source: *Van Zandt News*, July 29, 1984.

KNOX, GEORGIA ANN
Born: January 20, 1867, Henderson County, Texas. Died: January 1, 1908, Van Zandt County, Texas. Married: Hugh Alden Knox, Sr., May 23, 1895. Child: Charlie M. Father: Francis Marion Walker. Mother: Hanna Cathern Martin. Comments: Georgia Ann Knox's husband was the son of Hugh Alden Knox II and Bethany Lambert. He was born in Talladega County, Alabama and moved to Van Zandt County, Texas. After Georgia died in 1908, Hugh married Mary Inez Foster and had several other children. He died in Harris County, Texas April 8, 1946 and is buried in the Rest Haven Cemetery in Houston. Source: Ancestry.com.

KNOX, JESSE ALTON
Born: June 5, 1906, Van Zandt County, Texas. Died: February 11, 1946, Live Oak County, Texas. Cause of death: Automobile accident. Married: Willie Jo Chaney, September 1, 1933. Father: Samuel W. Knox. Mother: Dora Effie Perry. Comments: Jesse Knox was living in Sinton, Texas when he had an automobile accident and died from his injuries. His companion, Clarence Tawater, was injured; but after receiving medical aid, he was released from the hospital. Sources: *Canton Herald*, February 14, 1946; Find A Grave.

KNOX, SAMUEL WALTER
Born: February 14, 1868, Alabama. Died: January 20, 1942, Van Zandt County, Texas. Cause of death: Heart attack. Married: Dora Effie Perry, January 23, 1898. Children: Flossie Vivian, Perry, Marvin Lee, Buster Brown, Jessie Alton, Ray, and Wallace A. Father: Hugh Alden Knox, South Carolina. Mother: Bethany Lambert, Georgia.Occupation: Farmer. Sources: *Canton Herald*, January 22, 1942, Ancestry.com.

KNOX, WALLACE AUSTIN
(Photo page 83) Born: November 28, 1913, Van Zandt County, Texas. Died: June 23, 1994, Van Zandt County, Texas. Father: Samuel Walter Knox. Mother: Dora Effie Perry. Siblings: Flossie, Perry, Marvin Lee, Buster Brown, Jessie Alton, and Ray. Military: WWII, CPL U. S. Army. Source: *Canton Herald*, June 25, 1994.

KNOX, WALTER
Comments: No dates given. Walter Knox's name is inscribed on the same tombstone as Annie and Ed McClellan. Source: Tombstone.

KNOX, WILLIAM MONTGOMERY
Born: February 5, 1831, Talladega County, Alabama. Died: September 27, 1905, Van Zandt County, Texas. Married: (1) Frances McClellan, February 3, 1853, Alabama. Children: Robert and Edd. (2) Nancy McClellan, 1868, Alabama. Children: John W., Linnie Lee, and Edith May. Father: William Knox. Mother: Martha Knox. Occupation: Farmer, carpenter, boarding house proprietor. Comments: William Montgomery Knox came to Van Zandt County between 1870 and 1873 and settled in the Snider Springs area. He later moved to Canton and lived there for twenty years before he moved to Grand Saline. Sources: *Wills Point Chronicle*, October 5, 1905; Ancestry.com.

L

LAMBRIGHT, GORDON W.
Born: September 15, 1883, Texas. Died: May 22, 1931, Tarrant County, Texas. Cause of death: Pneumonia. Married: Ida J. McCarty, September 14, 1902. Father: Benjamin Davis "Dee" Lambright, Arkansas. Mother: Laura Jane Barnet, Texas. Occupation: Machinist. Sources: Death Certificate, Ancestry.com.

LAMBRIGHT, (BROWN) IDA J.
Born: January 14, 1883, Van Zandt, County, Texas. Died: 1938. Married: (1) Gordon W. Lambright, September 14, 1902. (2) Unknown Brown. Father: Benjamin F. McCarty. Mother: Martha E. Plumlee. Comments: Ida Lambright is buried beside her first husband with a double marker. Sources: Van Zandt County, *Texas Biographies, 1848-1991 Vol. 2*; Ancestry.com.

LANTRIP, DELAINE FRANKLIN
Born: September 29, 1922, Mississippi. Died: April 24, 1929, Van Zandt County, Texas. Cause of death: Drowning. Father: John Franklin Lantrip. Mother: Emma E. Ivey. Comments: Delaine Lantrip was a first grader at Wentworth School when he met his untimely death. Normally he would have walked home after school with his sister, but this day he went home alone. Torrential rains had caused raging water in Mustang Branch. When Delaine reached the normal crossing place, the crossing

log was under water. He went up the creek to a ford and walked off into the water which was about ten feet deep. His older sister had gone home by a longer route, and the children's father had started after both of them. He did not arrive as soon as school was out, and they had already left for home. When Delaine was missed, a search party was formed. The boy's hat and coat were the first traces found, and later his body was found lodged among tree roots. Source: *Grand Saline Sun*, May 2, 1929.

Lantrip, Emma Etta
Born: March 12, 1884, Mississippi. Died: June 8, 1961, Dallas County, Texas. Cause of death: Heart disease. Married: John Franklin Lantrip, January 30, 1903. Children: Clinton Elvis, Mary Fannie, Madge, Norma Jewel, Ethelene, and Delaine Franklin. Father: Eli Ivey. Mother: Mary Sherman. Source: Death Certificate.

Robert Maclin Lively *was admitted to the Texas bar in 1876 at age 22. He established his law practice in Wills Point and then moved to Canton. He continued his private practice throughout the years but also served his community as Van Zandt County Attorney, County Judge, and Representative in the United States Sixty-First Congress.*

Lantrip, John Franklin "Frank"
Born: April 24, 1884, Mississippi. Died: November 12, 1936, Van Zandt County, Texas. Cause of death: Brain tumor. Married: Emma Ivey. Children: Clinton Elvis, Mary Fannie, Madge, Norma Jewel, Ethelene, and Delaine Franklin. Father: Lawrence Van Vuron "Lat" Lantrip. Mother: Fannie Brasher. Occupation: Farmer. Comments: Frank Lantrip came to Van Zandt County in 1922, first settling in the Wallace Community. During the last twenty years of his life, he rented a farm from Mrs. M. L. Cox in the Wentworth Community. Frank suffered from a brain tumor for more than a year. He went to Dallas, Texas for an operation but it was not successful. Source: Death Certificate; *Canton Herald*, November 19, 1936; James Erwin and Ivolue Lantrip, Lantrip Family historian.

Lapington, Manervia A.
Born: February 28, 1857, Alabama. Died: May 22, 1915, Van Zandt County, Texas. Cause of death: Surgery complications. Married: (1) Unknown Batts. (2) H. P. Lapington. Father: William F. Greenhaw. Mother: Emily S. Horton. Comments: Manervia Lapington had surgery to remove a tumor. She went into shock after the surgery and died as a result. Source: *Canton Herald*, May 27, 1915.

Lewis, Frank McCoy
Born: September 11, 1889, Navarro County, Texas. Died: August 24, 1973, Dallas County, Texas. Cause of death: Lung disease. Married: (1) Bessie Lou Mauldin. (2) Mary Elizabeth Jones. Father: John F. Lewis. Mother: Martha Youngblood. Occupation: Automobile mechanic. Military: WWI. Sources: Death Certificate, Ancestry.com.

Lewis, Mary Elizabeth
Born: December 7, 1910. Died: February 11, 1988 (date incorrect on tombstone). Married: Frank McCoy Lewis. Father: Charles C. Jones. Mother: Sallie J. Jones. Sources: Van Zandt News, February 21, 1988; Ancestry.com.

Lively, Annie Julia Cannon
Born: July 24, 1864, Montgomery County, Alabama. Died: November 19, 1934, Dallas County, Texas. Cause of death: Cancer. Married: Robert Maclin Lively, November 24, 1878. Children: Anthony Gordon, James Cannon, Lucy Ethel, and Estelle Elizabeth. Father: James A. Cannon, Alabama. Mother: Francis E. Smith, Texas. Source: Death Certificate.

Lively, Anthony Gordon
Born: September 22, 1879, Van Zandt County, Texas. Died: July 22, 1932, Dallas County, Texas, Cause of death:

James Milo Manning *was a Whig and a friend of Henry Clay—U.S. Representative, U.S. Senator, and Secretary of State under President John Quincy Adams. Manning moved to Van Zandt County in 1858, and settled just a few miles from Canton. He was opposed to the Ordinance of Secession, joining the Union Reconstruction efforts with two of his sons after the Civil War. He was elected to the Texas House of Representatives, serving under Governor Edmund Davis in 1869. Manning, his wife, and their children played an integral role in the development of Canton and Van Zandt County.*

Cancer. Never Married. Father: Robert M. Lively. Mother: Julia Cannon. Occupation: Newspaper printer and editor. Comments: Gordon Lively learned the printing trade in Canton. He was an associate with Morgan G. Sanders (future Congressman) in the *Free State Enterprise*, a weekly newspaper. Gordon spent about ten years as editor of the *Lufkin Daily News*. He also was an editor for many years on the *Wills Point Chronicle* and the *Canton Herald*. His father was a prominent lawyer, County Judge, and U. S. Congressman. Sources: Death Certificate; Canton Herald, July 20, 1932.

Lively, Lucy Ethel

(Photo page 83) Born: October, 1883. Died: January 15, 1968. Father: Robert Maclin Lively. Mother: Annie Julia Cannon. Siblings: Anthony Gordon, Ethel, James Cannon, and Estelle Elizabeth. Sources: 1900 U. S. Census; A. G. Lively's (brother) obituary in *The Dallas Morning News*, July 25, 1932; Ancestry.com.

Lively, Robert Maclin

(Photo page 85) Born: January 6, 1854, Washington County, Arkansas. Died: January 13, 1929, Van Zandt County, Texas (middle name on tombstone incorrect). Married: Annie Julia Cannon, November 24, 1878. Children: Anthony Gordon, Ethel, James Cannon, and Estelle. Father: Rev. Louis P. Lively. Mother: Amanda Lively. Occupation: Lawyer, County Prosecuting Attorney, County Judge, U. S. Congressman. Comments: Robert Lively's family moved to Texas in 1864, and they settled in Kaufman County. He attended the schools in East Texas and chose the practice of law as his profession. In 1875 he studied law under George D. Marion and Z. T. Adams in Kaufman and was admitted to the bar in 1876. In 1877 he moved to Wills Point and established his law practice. He later moved his practice to Canton. He was elected Van Zandt County Attorney in 1880 and served one term. He then returned to his law practice. In 1910 he was appointed County Judge to fill an unexpired term due to Judge John Spinks' death. In 1910 he won a special election as a Democrat to United States Sixty-first Congress due to the resignation of James Gordon Russell. Robert served from July 23, 1910, to March 3, 1911; but he did not run for reelection. He served one additional term 1915-16, as County Judge before returning to private practice. Source: The Handbook of Texas Online, Southland, 1903; *Wills Point Chronicle*, March 10, 1910.

Loughmiller, Dwight Lyman

Born: April 30, 1903, Van Zandt County, Texas. Died: April 23, 1924, Van Zandt County, Texas. Cause of death: Pneumonia. Single. Father: George Jasper Loughmiller. Mother: Tommy West Richards Dawson. Occupation: College Student. Comments: Dwight Loughmiller graduated from Canton High School in 1922 and was a student at Denton Normal in Denton, Texas. He became ill and returned home to Canton. About three weeks later, he developed pneumonia which led to his death. Sources: *Wills Point Chronicle*, March 6, 1924; *Canton Herald*, March 7, 1924.

Loughmiller, George Jasper
Born: December 18, 1860, McMinn County, Tennessee. Died: May 16, 1940, Van Zandt County, Texas. Married: (1) Julia Eudora Richards, 1891, Van Zandt County, Texas. Children: Aubrey Ophir "A.O." and Bertha Parilee. (2) Tommie West Richards Dawson. July 1, 1902. Children: Dwight Lyman, George Campbell., Mary Ellen, Max Edward, Wiley Wilton, and Richard Leon. Father: George Washington Loughmiller, Tennessee. Mother: Nancy A. Hester. Occupation: Farmer, grist mill owner. Comments: George Loughmiller's second wife was his first wife's half-sister. She was formerly married to Donald (David) D. Dawson and had three children, Athol, Leonard, and Margaret Eudora. George's family came to Texas about 1872 and settled in Cherokee County. Later his family moved to Van Zandt County and farmed in the Wallace community. In 1920, they moved to Canton, built a home on Buffalo Street, and lived there until George's death. Source: *The History of Van Zandt County, Texas*; Eubank Funeral Home records; Ancestry.com.

Loughmiller, Mary Alice
Born: December 31, 1932, Limestone County, Texas. Died: March 2, 2006, Texas. Married: Richard Leon Loughmiller. Children: Joe, Mark, Ann, Mary Kay, and Brett Shelton. Father: Homer Storey, Hopkins County, Texas. Mother: Mary E. Bryant, Callahan County, Texas. Occupation: Smith County Clerk's office. Sources: Birth Certificate; *Van Zandt News*, March 12, 2006.

Loughmiller, Max Edward
Born: May 5, 1911, Van Zandt County, Texas. Died: April 1, 1951, Smith County, Texas (incorrect date of death on tombstone). Cause of death: Automobile accident. Married: Eleanor Loughmiller. Father: George Jasper Loughmiller, McMinn County, Tennessee. Mother: Tommy West Richards Dawson. Occupation: Cotton Belt Railroad clerk, Tyler, Texas. Comments: Max Loughmiller lost control of his car and hit a bridge on the Tyler-Kilgore highway. Sources: Death Certificate, 1940 U. S. Census, Eubank Funeral Home records.

Loughmiller, Richard Leon
Born: August 19, 1919, Texas. Died: April 2, 1976, Smith County, Texas. Cause of death: Heart attack. Married: Mary Alice Storey. Father: George Jasper Loughmiller. Mother: Tommie West Richards Dawson. Occupation: Insurance salesman. Military: WWII, U. S. Navy. Source: Death Certificate.

Loughmiller, Tommie West
Born: April 3, 1879, Van Zandt County, Texas. Died: March 11, 1962, Smith County, Texas. Cause of death: Kidney disease. Married: (1) Donald (David) D. Dawson. Children: Athol, Leonard, Margaret, and Eudora. (2) George J. Loughmiller, 1902. Children: Dwight, George Campbell, Mary Ellen, Max Edward, Wiley Wilton, and Richard Leon. Father: Thomas West Richards. Mother: Margret Paralee Hubbard. Sources: Death Certificate; *The History of Van Zandt County, Texas.*

M

Manasco, Lewis McKinzie
Born: November 27, 1900, Johnson County, Texas. Died: February 19, 1973, Smith County, Texas. Cause of death: Cancer. Divorced. Father: Samuel Houston Manasco. Mother: Mary M. Carroll. Siblings: William Asbery, Terry A., Rosa M., Nancy Jane, Sam, Alma, and John. Occupation: Farming. Sources: Death Certificate; *Canton Herald*, February 11, 1965.

Manasco, Sam
Born: October 5, 1905, Johnson County, Texas. Died: February 4, 1965, Van Zandt County, Texas. Cause of death: Cardiac arrest. Married: Unknown. Father: Sam Houston Manasco. Mother: Mary M. Carroll. Occupation: Farming. Comments: Sam Manasco died in his home and was found by a neighbor. Military: WWII, PVT. Co. M. 358 INF. Sources: Death Certificate; *Canton Herald*, February 11, 1965.

Mann, Ben Hill
Born: August 3, 1882, Texas. Died: November 7, 1951, Dallas County, Texas. Cause of death: Cancer. Single. Father: Asberry Tillman Mann, Georgia. Mother: Saba Augusta Tennison. Occupation: Insurance salesman. Sources: Death Certificate, Eubank Funeral Home records, Ancestry.com.

Mann, Eunice "Una Mae"
Born: October 16, 1893, Van Zandt County, Texas. Died: July 26, 1952, Van Zandt County, Texas. Married: Paul Tillman Mann, September 29, 1912. Children: Irby L., Infant son Mann, H. C., John Paul, and Herbert Gerald. Father: John Simpson McLemore. Mother: Milbrey Harrington McDougal. Occupation: Van Zandt County Tax Assessor/Collector. Sources: T*he Dallas Morning News*, July 30, 1952; Hilliard Funeral Home Records; Ancestry.com.

Mann, Paul Tillman
Born: January 8, 1894, Grayson County, Texas. Died: June 29, 1948, Van Zandt County, Texas. Married: Eunice "Una May" McLemore, September 29, 1912. Father: Asberry Tillman Mann, Georgia. Mother: Saba Augusta

Tennison, Georgia. Occupation: Farmer, Van Zandt Tax Assessor Collector. Siblings: Ben Hill, Laura F., Lexie Lee, and Hyma C. Comments: Paul Mann moved with his family to Van Zandt County in 1898, settled, and farmed in the Mt. Pisgah community. He was elected Van Zandt County Tax Assessor/Collector in 1946. He died during his term, and his wife succeeded him. Sources: *Canton Herald*, June 29, 1948; Hilliard Funeral Home records; Find A Grave.

MANNING, HARVEY

Born: August 30, 1883. Died: July 25, 1884. Father: Henry Clay Manning. Mother: Mary Mellissa Keith. Comments: Henry Manning was in business with his brother, Wentworth, in Canton. After his two children's death (according to family legends), his wife was so overcome by grief that she spent most of the day crying in the cemetery. Because of Mellissa's anguish, Henry sold his business interest in Canton, bought 1,200 acres of land near Wills Point, and lived there until his death in 1912. Source: *Some History of Van Zandt County.*

MANNING, JAMES MILO

(Photo page 86) Born: December 2, 1805, Pennsylvania. Died: March 20, 1874, Van Zandt County, Texas. Cause of death: Dropsy. Married: Martha Harvey, January 28, 1828. Children: Harriet Guilliford, Delila, Nancy, Henry, Abigail, John Oliver, Wentworth, Thomas Dudley, Winfield Scott, and Margaret Ann "Tibbie." Father: Elisha Manning. Mother: Lucy Ingersoll. Occupation: Farmer, Cooper (barrel maker). Note: Milo Manning's granddaughter, Dr. Mary Evelyn Blagg Huey, was named the first woman President of Texas Women's University, Denton, Texas on August 19, 1976. Comments: Milo Manning came from patriotic ancestors. His grandfather, William Manning, fought at the Battle of Bunker Hill and spent the winter of 1777-78 at Valley Forge with George Washington. Milo's father served in the War of 1812. Milo was born in Pennsylvania near the border of New York. He moved to Ohio, then to Pendleton County, Kentucky where he was a Whig and a friend of Henry Clay. Milo moved his family to Texas in 1857 and settled in Red River County. In 1858, he and his family came to Van Zandt County and settled about three miles from Canton. Milo had deep seated patriotic feelings toward the United States and never changed his view. He was opposed to the Ordinance of Secession and remained a Republican throughout his life. During the Civil War, one son, Henry Clay, refused to join the Confederate Army. Instead he joined a Rangers Company to fight Indians on the frontier. Another son, John Oliver, joined the Confederate Army. At the Battle of Murfreesboro, he was placed on the Confederate Roll of Honor, which was similar to the Union's Medal of Honor. John was killed in action a few weeks later. After the Civil War, Milo and his sons, Henry and Wentworth, joined the Union's Reconstruction efforts. Henry was appointed Sheriff of Van Zandt County. Wentworth became a Captain in the State Militia. Milo was elected to the Texas House of Representatives; and as a radical Republican, he served under the first term of Governor Edmund Davis in 1869. After the Reconstruction Period, Henry and Wentworth joined the business community of Canton, but remained Republicans all of their lives. Wentworth wrote *Some History of Van Zandt County* in 1919, the first book covering the county's history. Milo and Martha had eleven children, and the Manning's were an integral part of the development of Canton and Van Zandt County. Their daughter, Margaret, married Gideon Strickland whose father was the first permanent settler along the Saline Creek. Another daughter, Delilah, married James D. Wright, who was the first District Clerk of Van Zandt County and the first doctor to settle and practice in Canton. Source: *Van Zandt County Texas Histories and Biographies 1848-1991, Vol. II.*

THOMAS M. MATHES *was born into slavery in Virginia in 1819. His owner moved with his family and slaves to the Cream Level community of Van Zandt County in 1858 and to Canton in 1861. After gaining his freedom at the end of the Civil War, Mathes and his wife,* **EASTER MATHES,** *moved to an area just north of Canton where he purchased and successfully farmed 275 acres, and they raised their nine children.*

MANNING, JOHN D. KEITH
Born: September, 1876. Died: September, 1876. Father: Henry Clay Manning. Mother: Mary Mellissa Keith. Source: Tombstone.

MANNING, MARTHA
Born: March 20, 1811. Died: March 16, 1882. Married: James Milo Manning, January 28, 1828, Pendelton County, Kentucky. Children: Harriet Gulliford, Delila, Nancy, Henry, Abigail, John Oliver, Wentworth, Thomas Dudley, Winfield Scott, and Margaret Ann "Tibbie." Father: Gresham Harvey. Mother: Unknown. Source: *Van Zandt County Texas Histories and Biographies 1848-1891, Vol. II.*

MARVIN, HAROLD WAYNE
Born: June 16, 1950. Died: June 17, 1950. Father: Billy Jack Marvin. Mother: Jo Marie McCord. Sources: Tombstone; *Marriage Records, Van Zandt County 1932-1950.*

MASSEY, ANNIE ELENOR
Born: October 13, 1883, Texas. Died: April 17, 1974, Van Zandt County, Texas. Cause of death: CVA. Single. Father: F. W. Massey. Mother: Arabella Elizabeth "Annie Bell" Baskin. Source: Death Certificate.

MASSEY, BELLE NOLEN
Born: August 2, 1848, Chickasaw County, Mississippi (incorrect date of birth on tombstone). Died: October 25, 1918 Van Zandt County, Texas. Cause of death: Apoplexy. Married: (1) Albert A. Nolen, February 5, 1869. Children: Oscar Lee, Albert Sidney, and George Tate. (2) F. W. Massey, February 19, 1880. Child: Annie Eleanor. Father: William Leroy Baskin. Mother: Frances Amandaline Keys Thompson. Comments: After her husband's death, Belle Nolen came to Van Zandt County in 1879. Her sons, George Tate and Albert Sydney, owned Nolen Brothers Drug Store; and they were among Canton's best known and most popular citizens. Sources: *Canton Herald*, November 1, 1918; Ancestry.com.

MATHES, EASTER
Born: 1844 Georgia (a slave). Died: August 20, 1899, Van Zandt County, Texas. Married: Thomas M. Mathes. Children: Matthew, Ann, John, Adam, Robert, Sprig, Siss, and Lark. Father; Unknown. Mother: Unknown. Source: 1870 U. S. Census.

MATHES, THOMAS M.
Born: 1819, Virginia (a slave). Died: March 24, 1915, Van Zandt County, Texas. Married: Easter Unknown. Children: Matthew, Ann, John, Adam, Spring Robert, Siss, and Lark. Father: Unknown. Mother: Unknown. Comments: Tom Mathes has an interesting background. He was a slave for forty-six years. His obituary indicates that he was born in Rome, Georgia; but the 1870 U. S. Census reflects that he was born in Virginia. Tom came to Texas with his master, Sherard Mathis, before the Civil War and settled in Anderson County. It is here that Sherard married Louisa Posey Woodall. The family, along with their slaves, moved to the Cream Level community of Van Zandt County in 1858 and to Canton in the early part of 1861. Slave schedules show that Tom was valued by his owner at $1,800 with his sisters valued somewhat less. On October 31, 1861, Tom's owner, at age 35, joined the Confederate Army as a bugler and was assigned to Co. E, 6th Texas Cavalry. He died from the effects of typhoid fever just after the noted Battle of Corinth in Mississippi in 1862. Sometime after the close of the Civil War and freedom, Tom moved his family just north of Canton. They settled in what later became the Wynne community where Tom purchased a 275-acre farm. He, along with Edmond Wynne and other freedmen, developed a self-sufficient Black community that is still in existence today. *Wills Point Chronicle* reported his death as follows: "'Uncle Tom" remained at Canton and reared a family of well-to-do children, including seven boys and two girls, and it is a matter of common knowledge that not one of them have ever been connected with anything of a questionable character and at no time have they ever had any dealing with the courts. His conduct was exemplary and his word was his bond, and he so lived that he had an abiding friend in the white folks from the least little tot to the old, gray haired and feeble." Sources: 1870 U. S. Census; Confederate Army Records; *Wills Point Chronicle,* March 5, 1908 and April 1, 1915.

Andrew Dean Mathis *Naomi Ethelene Mathis*

MATHIS, ALICE MAE
Born: October 24, 1889. Died: August 5, 1985. Married: Roma M. Mathis, 1912. Father: Aaron Perry McDaniel. Mother: Miranda Mae Dawson. Sources: Eubank Funeral Home records, Ancestry.com.

Mamie DeLois Maume and Canton's Dixie Hotel just after its construction in 1915. Maume owned and operated the hotel for almost forty years. Known for its famous guests, cooks, and excellent food, the hotel was closed the night Maume died and the building torn down soon after.

MATHIS, ANDREW DEAN
(Photo page 89) Born: August 6, 1889. Died: August 11, 1953. Married: Sadie Elizabeth French, 1908. Child: Hugh. Father: Johnie B. Mathis. Mother: Elizabeth "Bettie Belle" Nolan. Occupation: Grocery store and meat market owner. Comments: Dean Mathis was in business in Canton for over fifty years. Sources: *Canton Herald*, August 20, 1953; Eubank Funeral Home records.

MATHIS, ELIZABETH "BETTIE BELLE"
Born: September 17, 1863, Upshur County, Texas. Died: January 10, 1941, Van Zandt County, Texas. Married: Johnie B. Mathis, March 25, 1883. Children: Andrew Dean, Roma Morris, and Hardy. Father: Robert Wilson "Whit" Nolan. Mother: Sarah Catherine Darden. Sources: Death Certificate, Ancestry.com.

MATHIS, HARDY
Born: 1886. Died: 1897. Father: Johnie B. Mathis. Mother: Elizabeth "Bettie Belle" Nolan. Source: Ancestry.com.

MATHIS, HUGH NATHAN
Born: February 1, 1909. Died: October 21, 1976, Van Zandt County, Texas. Father: Andrew Dean Mathis. Mother: Sadie E. French. Occupation: Grocery store owner. Sources: Death Certificate; *Canton Herald*, October 28, 1976.

MATHIS, JOHN BENNETT "JOHNIE"
Born: April 27, 1860. Died: January 27, 1890. Married: Elizabeth "Bettie Belle" Nolan, March 25, 1883. Children: Andrew Dean, Roma Morris, and Hardy. Father: Sharard Mathis. Mother: Louisa Posey Woodall. Comments: The *Canton Telephone* reported the death of Johnie Mathis as follows: "After three months of very excruciating pain and suffering, Johnie Mathis died Monday morning. He leaves a wife and three small children, a mother and sister, relatives and friends to mourn his death. He was buried by the Knights and Ladies of Honor of which society he was a member, and carrying a policy of $1,000 for the benefit of his wife and children. All that was mortal of J. B. Mathis was deposited in the Canton cemetery Tuesday morning at 11 O'clock. J. W. Staton assisted in the funeral services." Sources: *The Canton Telephone*, January 31, 1890; *Van Zandt County Texas Histories Texas and Biographies 1848-1991*.

MATHIS, KING WILLIAM
Born: August 15, 1876. Died: November 11, 1951. Married: Linnie M. Smith, March 27, 1904. Father: Thomas M. Mathes. Mother: Easter Thompson. Occupation: Farmer. Sources: Death Certificate; 1880, 1910, 1940 U. S. Census.

MATHIS, LINNIE M.
Born: January 15, 1881, Fulton County, Georgia. Died: June 5, 1962, Potter County, Texas. Married: King W. Mathis, March 27, 1904. Father: Berry Smith. Mother: Unknown. Source: Death Certificate.

MATHIS, NAOMI ETHELENE
(Photo page 89) Born: July 3, 1907, Texas. Died: June 4, 1980, Van Zandt County, Texas. Cause of death: Heart disease. Married: (1) Isaac Bowman, October 14, 1931. Children: Henry Paul. (2) Joe E. Mathis, September 24, 1944. Father: Walter Smith. Mother: Lannie Belle Wynne. Sources: Death Certificate; *Van Zandt County Marriage Records, 1909-1931, 1932-1950.*

Mathis, Roma Morris
Born: December 28, 1883, Van Zandt County, Texas. Died: December 19, 1949, Dallas County, Texas. Married: Alice Mae McDaniel. Father: John Bennett Mathis. Mother: Elizabeth "Bettie Bell" Nolan. Occupation: Meat Market Owner, Van Zandt County Tax Collector. Comments: Roma Mathis opened one of the first meat markets in Canton, Texas and was well known during his lifetime. He served as Tax Collector from 1931 to 1934. Sources: *Van Zandt County Texas Biographies 1848-1991*, Eubank Funeral Home records, Ancestry.com.

Mathis, Sadie Elizabeth
Born: September 24, 1889. Died: December 19, 1973. Cause of death: Stroke. Married: Dean Mathis, 1908. Father: George N. French. Child: Hugh. Mother: Mollie Craft. Occupation: Assisted her husband in their grocery store which was open for 50 years. Comments: Sadie Mathis had resided at 603 Athens Street in Canton for sixty-two years. Sources: Death Certificate, *Canton Herald*, December 27, 1973.

Matthews, Adam
Born: July 1862. Died: April 1872. Father: T. M. Matthews (Mathes). Mother: E. Matthews (Mathes). Comments: There is some confusion about Adam Matthew's parents. It is believed that Adam's parents were Thomas M. and Easter Thompson Mathes whose graves are nearby. Source: Tombstone.

Matthews, Darling Freddie
Born: 1876. Died: June 4, 1878. Father: James L. Matthews. Mother: Georgia A. Matthews. Source: Tombstone.

Matthews, Georgia A.
Born: May 19, 1844, Georgia. Died: May 9, 1913, Kaufman County, Texas. Cause of death: Heart disease. Married: Dr. James L. Matthews, November 2, 1860. Children: Amanda, Virginia, Bettie, Ann Nettie, Charles, Jessie, John, and Lilis Bruce. Comments: Georgia A. Matthews was born in Georgia, but later moved to Mississippi. They moved to Texas in 1869 and to Canton in 1874. Georgia's husband, a Baptist minister, organized the Providence Baptist Church in 1873. He was called as pastor of the Canton First Baptist Church in 1874, and he served in that position until 1882. He was also pastor of the Wills Point Baptist Church. He died in December of 1883. Georgia joined the Baptist Church at Canton soon after moving there. She was the mother of eight children. At her death, Georgia had thirteen living grandchildren. Several of their mothers had died, and she helped to rear them. She was helping her son-in-law, Dr. I. E. Russell, at Petrolia, Clay County, care for his children when she was stricken with dropsy of the heart. She was brought to her daughter, Mrs. J. B. Hanes, in Kaufman where she lived several months before she died. Rev. Tom Post, an old-time minister in Van Zandt County, conducted the funeral. Source: *Wills Point Chronicle*, May 15, 1913.

Matthews, Dr. James L.
Born: July 7, 1831, Georgia. Died: December 7, 1883, Van Zandt County, Texas. Married: Georgia A. Matthews, December 2, 1860. Children: Amanda, Virginia, Bettie, Ann Nettie, Charles, Jessie, John, and Lilis Bruce. Military: CSA, Sergeant 8th Regt., Miss. Inf. Occupation: Minister. Comments: Dr. James L. Matthews and his family moved to Texas in 1869. As a minister, he organized the Providence Baptist Church in Van Zandt County in 1873 and then moved to Canton. He was pastor of the First Baptist Church there until 1882. He was also pastor of the Wills Point Baptist Church. He died in 1883. Georgia lived for another 30 years and died in Kaufman County at the home of their daughter, Mrs. J. B. Haynes. Sources: 1880 U. S. Census, *Ministers of Van Zandt County.*

Matthews, Lilas Bruce
Born: Unknown. Died: February 15, 1887. Cause of death: Pneumonia. Father: Dr. James L. Matthews. Mother: Georgia A. Unknown. Sources: Tombstone; *Canton Telephone,* February 18, 1887.

Matthews, Nettie Allen
Note: See Allen, Nettie

Matthews, Sprig
Born: 1875. Died: November 8, 1897. Father: T. M. Matthews (Mathes). Mother: E. Matthews (Mathes). Comment: There is some confusion about Sprig Matthews' parents. They were Tom Mathes and Easter Mathes, not Matthews. Source: Tombstone.

Maume, Mamie De Lois
Born: November 13, 1891, Blanco County, Texas. Died: May 5, 1954, Van Zandt County, Texas. Cause of death: Cancer. Never Married. Father: Edward Walston Maume, Adams County, Mississippi. Mother: Alice R. Nash, Missouri. Occupation: Owner and operator of the Dixie Hotel, Canton, Texas. Comments: The Dixie Hotel was a landmark in Canton for almost forty years. It was built in 1915 by John R. Kellis, Sheriff of Van Zandt County, and Dr. M. L. Cox, an enterprising young doctor. The hotel was located across from the courthouse and named after the Dixie Highway (now Highway 64) which ran in front of it. Mamie Maume, who had been a telephone operator for the local exchange, took over the hotel operations in 1916. She owned and ran the hotel, except for a short time, until her death. The hotel was known for its famous guests, its cooks and excellent food. These cooks, Maggie Bowles, Aarona Maxie, and Nannie Hambrick

Charles Thomas "Chuck" McCauley *Sidney James "Mr. Sid" McCauley*

The McCauley Brothers were two of Canton's earliest and most successful merchants.

are mentioned since they were equally responsible for the hotel's excellent reputation. Mamie was known for her kindness and charitable attributes. She never married. The hotel was closed the night she died, and the building torn down by relatives. Sources: *Canton Herald*, May 13, 1954 and Centennial Edition; Eubank Funeral Home records.

McCarty, Benjamin F.
Born: January 15, 1847, Rusk County, Texas. Died: September 3, 1926, Van Zandt County, Texas. Married: Martha E. Plumlee, January 31, 1867. Children: Robert Thompson, Elizabeth A., James Monroe, William N., Mary Isbell, Edward, Frank M, Jess B., Andrew Jackson, Ida I., Pearly, Benjamin H., and Leona Ona. Father: William Thompson McCarty. Mother: Nancy Averilla Barton. Military: CSA, Co. A. Slayback's Missouri Cavalry Comments: Benjamin McCarty moved with his family to Van Zandt County in 1869. He received a Nacogdoches Preemption Land Grant of 160 acres in Van Zandt County, August 12, 1870. He was a farmer and lived in Van Zandt County for over fifty-six years. Source: Texas General Land Office; *Wills Point Chronicle*, March 20, 1926; Ancestry.com.

McCarty, Benna
Born: November 28, 1888. Died: August 19, 1892. Father: Benjamin F. McCarty. Mother: Martha E. Plumlee. Source: Barbara Corbin, McCarty Family historian.

McCarty, Dollie Belle
Born: June 15, 1871. Died: February 8, 1899. Cause of death: Pneumonia. Married: William Thompson McCarty, July 30, 1883. Father: Unknown Petitt. Mother: Unknown. Sources: *Free State Enterprise*, February 16, 1899; Ancestry.com.

McCarty, E.
Born: June 2, 1855. Died: Unknown. Father: Unknown. Source: Tombstone.

McCarty, Earl
Born: February 1, 1877. Died: July 9, 1877. Father: James F. McCarty. Mother: Fredonia N. Riley. Source: Tombstone.

McCarty, Elizabeth A. "Lizzie"
Born: October 27, 1869, Texas. Died: October 20, 1873, Van Zandt County, Texas. Father: Benjamin Franklin McCarty. Mother: Martha Elizabeth Plumlee. Source: Find A Grave.

McCarty, Eva
Born: September 8, 1905. Died: June 30, 1907. Father: Edward McCarty. Mother: Debbie Stanford. Source: Barbara Corbin, McCarty Family historian.

McCarty, John Ross
Born: August 8, 1889. Died: July 21, 1890. Father: James Matthew McCarty. Mother: M. A. Clark. Source: Tombstone.

McCarty, Johnnie
Born: September 12, 1896. Died: February 2, 1900. Father: Robert T. McCarty. Mother: Saphronia Williams. Source: Tombstone.

McCarty, Leonard E.
Born: October 28, 1903. Died: February 4, 1905. Father: Edward McCarty. Mother: Debbie Stanford. Source: Barbara Corbin, McCarty Family historian.

McCarty, Marion
Born: April 3, 1911. Died: Unknown. Father: Dr. James F. McCarty. Mother: Iola McCarty. Source: Ancestry.com.

McCarty, Martha Elizabeth
Born: August 25, 1847, Scott County, Missouri. Died: April 22, 1918, Van Zandt County, Texas. Married: Benjamin F. McCarty, January 31, 1867. Father: Robert M. Plumlee, Clay County, Tennessee. Mother: Anna E. Bell, Tennessee. Sources: Death Certificate; *Canton Herald*, April 29, 1918; Ancestry.com.

McCarty, Minnie Julia
Born: June 24, 1892. Died: March 20, 1912. Cause of death: Meningitis. Father: W. Thompson McCarty. Mother: Dollie Bell Petitt. Comments: Minnie McCarty

was born and reared at Center near Grand Saline, Texas. At her father's death in 1907, she and her younger sister moved to Dallas to make their home with another sister, Mrs. Jeff Smith. After an illness of about six weeks, Minnie died. Source: Tombstone; *Wills Point Chronicle*, March 28, 1912.

McCarty, Nancy Averilla

Born: August 17, 1830, Pickens County, South Carolina. Died: July 31, 1884, Van Zandt County, Texas. Married: William Thomson McCarty, October 28, 1845. Children: Zilpha Ann, Thomas Jefferson, Samuel Houston, Robert, Elizabeth Averilla, Ava, Thompson, and Fannie Mae. Father: Benjamin Franklin Barton. Mother: Zilpha Baker. Sources: Ancestry.com, Find A Grave.

McCarty, Pearley

Born: October 1, 1886. Died: November 19, 1890. Father: Benjamin F. McCarty. Mother: Martha Elizabeth Plumlee. Source: Ancestry.com.

McCarty, Riley

Born: August 16, 1880. Died: October 4, 1881. Father: James F. McCarty. Mother: Fredonia N. Riley. Source: Tombstone.

McCarty, Sarah Ellen

Born: January 22, 1849. Died: November 4, 1874. Married: Dr. James Franklin McCarty, September 28, 1873 Father: James Douthitt. Mother: Mary Douthitt. Source: 1850, 1870 U. S Census; *Marriage Records Van Zandt County, Texas 1848-1909*; Ancestry.com.

McCarty, Thompson

Born: November 15, 1862. Died: March 1, 1907. Married: (1) Dollie Bell Petitt, July 30, 1883. (2) Mrs. Ella Nora Tull Roberts, November 23, 1899. Father: William Thompson McCarty. Mother: Nancy Averilla Barton. Source: Ancestry.com.

McCarty, W.

Born: Unknown. Died: Unknown. Father: Unknown. Mother: Unknown. Comments: This tombstone has been damaged. No other information available.

McCarty, William N.

Born: January 7, 1874. Died: December 24, 1904. Cause of death: Pneumonia. Never married. Father: Benjamin F. McCarty. Mother: Martha E. Plumlee. Occupation: School teacher. Comments: William McCarty's death was reported in the Wills Point Chronicle as follows: "Prof. W.N. McCarty died at the home of Bob Martin in the Willow Springs community last Saturday of pneumonia. His remains were interred at Canton the day following with Masonic honors, the Edgewood and Canton lodges conducting same. Prof. McCarty was teaching the Willow Springs School at the time of his death. He was sick only a short time, being attacked at first with a severe cold which developed rapidly into a very malignant type of pneumonia. He was a son of B. F. McCarty, near Myrtle Springs and was one of the rising young teachers of the county." Source: *Wills Point Chronicle*, December 29, 1904.

McCarty, William Thompson

Born: October 10, 1821, Jefferson County, Alabama. Died: January 13, 1882, Van Zandt County, Texas. Married: Nancy Averilla Barton, October 28, 1845. Children: Zilpha Ann, Thomas Jefferson, Samuel Houston, Robert, Elizabeth Averilla, Ava, Thompson, and Francis Mae. Father: William McCarty. Mother: Jane "Mary" Anderson Brown. Siblings: Elizabeth Ann, James, Nancy E., Benjamin F., and Early. Occupation: Farmer. Comments: William Thompson McCarty came to Texas in 1841 and settled in Rusk County. He received two land grants: one from the Republic of Texas and one from the State of Texas. He came to Van Zandt County in the 1860s and lived there for the remainder of his life. Thompson in a will dated November 26, 1881 bequeathed all of his estate to his wife. His estate included a 320-acre farm near Canton. Sources: Will of Thompson McCarty dated November 26, 1881; *Van Zandt County Texas Biographies, 1848-1991*; Family Tree Maker; Ancestry.com.

McCauley, Birdie Mae

Born: March 30, 1881, Van Zandt County, Texas. Died: October 29, 1900, Van Zandt County, Texas. Married: Charles Thomas McCauley, January 28, 1900. Child: Mary Lou. Father: Daniel D. Thames, Mississippi. Mother: Mary L. "Mollie" Miller. Comments: Birdie Mae Thames only lived nine months after her marriage. Birdie's father owned a general merchandise store in Canton for over 20 years. His business failed in the Depression of 1897, and he lost it. After the Canton business failure, her father moved to Grand Saline and owned another business for eight more years. Chuck McCauley married two more times before his death in 1964. He had been a successful businessman in Canton for many years. Source: *Wills Point Chronicle*, November 1, 1900.

McCauley, Charles Thomas "Chuck"

Born: April 28, 1873, Van Zandt County, Texas. Died: May 28, 1964, Van Zandt County, Texas. Married: (1) Birdie Mae Thames, January 28, 1900. Child: Mary Lou. (2) Stella Longmire, June 21, 1903. Children: Charles Richard, and Lucy Etheleen. (3) Lula Grace Youngblood Moore. Father: Richard Charles McCauley, Georgia. Mother: Anna Elizabeth Alexander. Occupation: Café owner, partner and owner of McCauley Brothers Dry Goods and Groceries. Comments: Chuck McCauley and his brother, Sidney, worked close together for most of their lives. About 1896, they both worked with the Hilliards when they were establishing their various busi-

WARREN W. "HAPPY" McWILLIAMS *(above and in the dark shirt in his barber shop) earned his nickname due to his cheerful disposition and genial hospitality—right up until he was shot and killed at age 30 by former Deputy Sheriff R.E. Parker in a Canton restaurant. Although the reason for the shooting was never publicly discussed, rumors indicated McWilliams might have been paying too much attention to Parker's wife. Five separate trials over a period of years resulted in verdicts of "guilty," hung juries, and eventually "not guilty." Five trials and one defendant might be a record still in Van Zandt County.*

nesses on the Canton square. The McCauley Brothers owned and operated a café for a short time before they bought a mercantile store on the northwest corner of the town square. The McCauley's also owned and operated the local telephone exchange in Canton for a time. The mercantile store operated as "McCauley Brothers" and carried dry goods, groceries, hardware, farm implements, furniture and funeral supplies. It supported Chuck and Sid's families for a lot of years. Chuck eventually sold his portion of the store to Sid and finished his career working at Liberty Hardware and later Eubank Hardware Store. The McCauley's were in business for 47 years. Sid operated the business until November of 1945 when he retired and leased the building to Garth and Jake Slaughter who opened a Whites Auto store. Sources: *Van Zandt County Texas Biographies, 1848-1991, Volume II*; *Canton Herald*, November 28, 1945; Eubank Funeral Home records.

McCAULEY, FLORENCE EVA

Born: October 14, 1894, Van Zandt County, Texas. Died: August 29, 1980, Smith County, Texas. Married: Sidney James McCauley, October 27, 1912. Children: Florence Elizabeth, Dr. Lloyd Cecil, Dorothy Sidney, and Rose Mary. Father: William Erb Prather. Comments: Florence McCauley was born in the Garden Valley Community. Before she married, she was a telephone operator working for her father, William Prather. He owned the local telephone exchange. This is how she met Sid McCauley. He was partners with his brother, Chuck McCauley, in the Canton Telephone Exchange. Sid was filling in as an operator and just happened to talk to Florence. This conversation led to more communication and eventually to their marriage. Florence worked with her husband, Sid, in the general merchandise store for over forty years. Sources: *Canton Herald*, September 4, 1980; *Van Zandt County Texas Biographies Vol. II, 1848-1991.*

McCAULEY, ISAAC

Born: February 14, 1875. Died: September 30, 1880. Father: Richard C. McCauley. Mother: Anna Elizabeth Alexander. Source: Tombstone.

McCAULEY, LUCY ETHELEEN

Born: February 6, 1905. Died: October 3, 1906. Father: Charles T. McCauley. Mother: Stella Longmire. Source: Tombstone.

McCAULEY, LULA GRACE

Born: November 18, 1889, Van Zandt County, Texas. Died: September 29, 1975, Kaufman County, Texas. Married: Charles T. "Chuck" McCauley. Father: Basil B. Youngblood. Mother: Josephine Cantrell. Source: Eubank Funeral Home records.

McCAULEY, RICHARD C.

Born: 1848, Alabama. Died: October 3, 1881, Van Zandt County, Texas. Married: Anna Elizabeth "Babe" Alexander, May 30, 1872. Children: Charles Thomas (Chuck), Isaac, W. E., and Sidney James. Father: Unknown McCauley. Mother: Unknown. Comments: Richard McCauley has two young children (Isaac, W. E.) buried in the family plot in the Hillcrest Cemetery. Richard died at the age of 33. He never got to see the successful business operations of his sons, Sid and Chuck. Richard's wife married J. Tull. Thompson, January 13, 1884, and he helped rear her children. Sources: *Van Zandt County Texas Biographies, 1848-1891;* Ancestry.com.

McCauley, Sidney James "Mr. Sid"

(Photo page 92) Born: October 18, 1880, Van Zandt County, Texas. Died: October 28, 1965, Van Zandt County, Texas. Married: Florence Eva Prater, October 27, 1912. Children: Loyd Cecil, Florence Elizabeth, Dorothy Sidney, and Rose Mary. Father: Richard C. McCauley. Mother: Anna Elizabeth Alexander. Siblings: Charles Thomas (Chuck), Isaac, and W. E. Comments: Sid McCauley was born near Saline Creek between Canton and Colfax in 1880. In 1881 Richard McCauley, Sid and Chuck's father, died, and their mother moved the family to Canton. She married the widower Tull Thompson in 1883. The McCauley brothers, Chuck and Sid, were in business together for most of their career. About 1896, when Chuck was 23 and Sid was 18, they started to work for the Hilliard's in their startup mercantile business. They shortly left the Hilliards' employment. They owned and operated a café for a while. They next bought a general merchandise store on the northwest side of the Canton square. It is possible that they bought the merchandise of Chuck's father-in-law, D. D. Thames', failed business which was in the same location. The mercantile store, operating as "McCauley Brothers," carried almost everything including caskets. The popular store operated for forty-seven years. Chuck sold his part in the store to Sid and worked at Liberty Hardware and then Eubank Hardware until he retired. Sid ran the business until November of 1945 when he retired and leased the building to Garth and Jake Slaughter, who opened a White's Auto Store. Sources: *Van Zandt County Texas Histories and Biographies 1848-1991 Vol. II*; *Canton Herald*, November 4, 1965.

McCauley, W.E.

Born: October 25, 1877. Died: December 25, 1877. Father: Richard C. McCauley. Mother: Anna Elizabeth Alexander. Source: Tombstone.

McClellen, Andrew Jackson "Jack"

Born: February 2, 1828, Alabama. Died: July 15, 1903, Van Zandt County, Texas. Married: Mrs. Ellen Adams Nolan, January 11, 1891. Child: Minnie Lee. Father: Thomas McClellen. Mother: Mary Townsend. Occupation: Farmer and mercantile business. Comments: Andrew Jackson McClellen was a pioneer citizen of Van Zandt County. He was 62 years old when he married. Andrew had one surviving child, Minnie Lee McClellen. Minnie married Henry Sides and died in 1972. Sources: *The Canton Telephone*, March 25, 1887; *Wills Point Chronicle*, July 16, 1903; Ancestry.com.

McClellen, Edgar May "Edd"

Born: March 30, 1877, Texas. Died: March 23, 1937, Henderson County, Texas. Cause of death: Heart disease. Single. Father: Robert McClellen. Mother: Frances Rachel Bowden. Occupation: Farmer. Siblings: Mary Alabama, T. Oscar, Annie V., Saphronia Adeline, Florence W., and Ollie. Sources: Death Certificate, Find A Grave.

McClellen, Elizabeth

Born: January 4, 1823, Jefferson County, Alabama. Died: May 8, 1885, Van Zandt County, Texas. Married: Robert McClellen, Sr. Children: Mary M., Sarah Jane, Susan, and Martha E. Father: Unknown Knox. Mother: Unknown. Comments: After her husband's death, Elizabeth McClellen came to Van Zandt County with two of her children and several other relatives. She lived with her brother-in-law, Andrew Jackson McClellen, until her death. Source: *Texan Telephone,* May 16, 1885.

McClellen, Frances Rachel "Fannie"

Born: March 10, 1849, Calhoun County, Alabama. Died: May 5, 1917, Van Zandt County, Texas. Married: Robert McClellen, Jr., September 4, 1868, Alabama. Children: Robert W., Mary A., Edgar May, Thomas A., T. Oscar, Annie V., Connie V., Sophronia A., William F., and Ollie. Father: A. L. Bowden, Georgia. Mother: Mary Bowden, South Carolina. Sources: 1860 U. S. Census, Ancestry.com.

McClellen, Infant Daughter

No dates. Father: Andrew Jackson McClellen. Mother: Ellen Adams Nolen. Source: Tombstone.

McClellen, Robert Jr.

Born: January 17, 1841, Talladega County, Alabama. Died: May 25, 1920, Van Zandt County, Texas. Married: Frances Rachel Bowden, September 10, 1868, Alabama. Children: Robert W., Mary Alabama, Thomas O., Edgar May "Edd", Annie V., Sophronia A., Florence William, and Ollie. Father: Robert McClellen. Mother: Martha W. McClellen. Military: CSA, 29th Alabama Infantry, Co. A. Occupation: Farmer. Comments: Robert McClellen came to Van Zandt County in 1872 with his mother and other relatives He farmed most of his life. When he applied for a pension for his Confederate service on July 18, 1908, he was 68 years old and totally disabled. Sources: Confederate Records; *Wills Point Chronicle,* June 3, 1920.

McDaniel, Lovie

Born: March 31, 1908, Texas. Died: February 6, 1971, Van Zandt County, Texas. Married: Wiley McDaniel, August 4, 1949. Children: Ada Lou, Julia Marie, and Vertis. Father: Taylor Shamlin. Mother: Julia Scates. Sources: Death Certificate; Vanessa Scott, Wynne Community historian.

McDavid, R.N. "Dick"

Born: January 17, 1863. Died: December 26, 1891. Father: Unknown McDavid. Mother: Unknown. Comments:

There is limited information regarding Dick McDavid other than his obituary. The *Canton Telephone* reported Dick McDavid's death as follows: "It becomes a sad duty to chronicle the death of Mr. R. N. McDavid, which occurred at the residence of Mr. J. T. McWilliams, in this city last Saturday evening. The funeral services were conducted by Rev. D. P. Cullen at the Methodist church Sunday at noon, and at 1 o'clock all that was mortal of 'Dick' McDavid was buried in the city cemetery. He leaves behind a host of friends and relatives whose heads are bowed in sorrow. The *Telephone* extends condolence to the bereaved, and would point them to Jesus if they would meet 'Dick' 'Beyond the River,' as he fell asleep in the blessed Savior. He was converted ten or fifteen years ago and united with the Baptist church. 'Peace to his bones.' J. T. McWilliams at whose residence McDaniel died was his brother-in-law having married his sister, Annie McDavid, November 13, 1877." Source: *Canton Telephone*, January 1, 1892.

McKenzie, Florence Elizabeth

Born: February 9, 1915, Van Zandt County, Texas. Died: February 9, 1942, Tarrant County, Texas. Cause of death: Intestinal obstruction. Married: Grady McKenzie, June 19, 1937. Children: Robert Nelson and Sarah Sue. Father: Sidney James McCauley, Van Zandt County, Texas. Mother: Florence Eva Prather, Van Zandt County, Texas. Sources: Death Certificate; *Canton Herald*, February 12, 1942.

McKenzie, Rena Sides

(Buried beside James E. Sides with double tombstone). Born: September 20, 1885, Kaufman County, Texas. Died: February 5, 1952, Dallas County, Texas. Cause of death: Heart disease, pneumonia. Married: (1) James Emory Sides, July 28, 1904. Children: one infant death, Jack D., W. Irvine, and Mary. (2) W. W. McKenzie. Father: W. D. Irvine. Mother: Emma Gillespie. Source: Death Certificate; *Canton Herald*, February, 1952; Ancestry.com.

McKinnon, Lettie S.

Born: January 11, 1894. Died: January 1982, Oklahoma. Married: Bryant H. McKinnon, June 16, 1912. Father: Charles P. Smith. Mother: Lula Peel. Occupation: Public stenographer. Comments: Lettie McKinnon was born into a prominent Smith family in Canton. She was the third wife of Bryant McKinnon. He was born in Alabama in 1867 and moved to Texas at the age of two. He first lived in Edom, moved to Terrell and then back to Canton in the early 1890's. He served four years as a Constable and as Tax Collector for Van Zandt County. In 1910 he helped to organize a bank at Canton and served eight years as its cashier. He owned city property in Canton and 1,020 acres of farmland where he raised cattle under the name of Sunny South Stock Farm. He is not buried in the Hillcrest Cemetery. Sources: *The Southland; U. S. Social Security Death Index, 1935-2014*; *Canton Herald,* August 16, 1951 and January 21, 1982; Ancestry.com.

McMahon, Anna Beatrice Mayne

Born: April 1, 1879, Van Zandt County, Texas. Died: April 8, 1942, Van Zandt County, Texas. Cause of death: Liver disease. Married: M. L. McMahon, December 9, 1896. Father: Wesley Horace Mayne, Hunt County, Texas

James Harvey Mills

Mary Missouri Mills

Robert Padian "Bobbie" Mills and William Samuel Mills, author of History of Van Zandt County, *published 1950*

Mother: M. J. Fowler, Van Zandt County, Texas. Comments: Anna McMahon and her husband had no children of their own, but provided a home for a niece and nephew, Clara Parks and Ray Tunnell. Sources: Death Certificate; *Canton Herald*, April 16, 1942; Eubank Funeral Home records.

McWilliams, Warren W. "Happy"

(Photo page 94) Born: December 19, 1885. Died: September 20, 1916. Cause of death: Gunshot wounds. Father: Marion L. McWilliams. Mother: Mary Ann Henderson. Comments: In September of 1916, R. E. "Bob" Parker, former Deputy Sheriff and current Constable, shot and killed Warren "Happy" McWilliams while he was eating a meal in Kasper Griser's restaurant in Canton, Texas. This is the *Canton Herald's* account of the shooting: "Warren McWilliams was shot to death by Bob Parker about 4 o'clock Wednesday evening. The shooting took place in the Griser restaurant. Three shots were fired and two took effect, one in the right side and the other just below the collar bone half way from the neck to the point of the shoulder. The shots were fired while inside the restaurant and Mr. McWilliams ran out on the gallery and sat down on a bench for a few minutes before falling to the floor. He lived a few minutes after being shot. Parker was put under arrest at once." McWilliams had grown up in Van Zandt County and for a number of years had owned and operated a tailoring and barber shop. Because of his cheerful disposition and genial hospitality, he generally answered to the name "Happy." The cause of the shooting was never really discussed, but it may have been because Happy was paying too much attention to Parker's wife. What followed the shooting and arrest of Bob Parker was one of the hardest fought criminal cases in the history of Van Zandt County. In the trials in Van Zandt County the state was represented by County Attorney Earl M. Greer and the law firm of Stanford and Sanders. The defense was represented by Wynne, Wynne and Gilmore of Wills Point. Parker was charged with murder in September 1916. In October of 1916, he was tried in the District Court of Van Zandt County and was given thirty years by the jury. Parker appealed, and the Court of Criminal Appeals reversed the judgement and sent the case back for retrial. There were two more trials of the case in the county which resulted in a hung jury in each trial. Another trial in February of 1919 resulted in a verdict of five years. Parker again appealed and the case was reversed a second time. The case was transferred to Kaufman County on a Change of Venue, and the result was the jury returned a verdict of not guilty. In the Kaufman County trial, the state was represented by M. G. Sanders of Canton; G. O. Crisp, County Attorney of Kaufman County; and Herbert Young, Assistant County Attorney of Kaufman. The defendant was represented by Wynne, Wynne & Gilmore and J. S. Orsborn. Five trials and one defendant may be a record still in Van Zandt County. Sources: *Grand Saline Sun*, August 11, 1916; May 10, 1918; and Mary 25, 1920. *Canton Herald*, September 29, 1916 and September 22, 1920; *Wills Point Chronicle*, 1918.

Medley, William P.

Born: June 22, 1874. Died: December 31, 1906. Cause of death: Paralysis. Married: Cora Yarbrough. Father: Unknown Medley. Mother: Unknown. Comments: William P. Medley was a member of Woodmen of the World Camp 1355. Source: *Wills Point Chronicle*, January 10, 1907.

Meredith, Katie P.

Born: January 21, 1880. Died: May 17, 1882. Father: A. W. Meredith. Mother: Belle Bartlett. Comments: Katie Meredith's father came to Texas in 1872 from Georgia and was a teacher in the rural schools of Van Zandt County. Her mother was from a well-known Canton family. A. W. served as District Clerk of Van Zandt County 1879-1884; and in 1885, he was appointed Sheriff. In 1886, he moved to Wills Point and was elected County Tax Collector in 1890. He also served as Mayor of Wills Point. Meredith was a Confederate soldier during the Civil War and was active in the Confederate Veterans Association. He died in Wills Point at the age of 98. Sources: Tombstone; Insert for the Van Zandt County newspapers on Confederate Veterans prepared by Linda Brown, date not known.

Meredith, Willis David

Born: January 18, 1885. Died: April 9, 1885. Father: A. W. Meredith. Mother: Belle Bartlett. Comments: See Katie P. Meredith. Source: Tombstone.

Milam, Martha Ann

Born: March 28, 1854, Mississippi. Died: July 10, 1930, Van Zandt County, Texas. Married: Willis A. Milam, 1880. Children: Ora E., Mada D., John Thomas, Susan Era, Thomas Allie, Frank W., Anna L., and Byron B. Father: James H. Hardin Jr. Mother: Unknown Smith. Sources: Death Certificate, Ancestry.com.

Milam, Willis Andy

Born: May 28, 1857, Pontotoc County, Mississippi. Died: September 24, 1933, Van Zandt County, Texas. Married: (1) Martha Cobb, 1871. (2) Martha Ann Hardin, 1880. Children: Ore E., Mada D., John Thomas, Susan Era, Thomas Allie, Frank W., Anna L., and Bryon B. Father: John Wesley Milam, South Carolina. Mother: Permelia Andrews, South Carolina. Occupation: Farmer. Sources: Death Certificate, Ancestry.com.

Mills, Cathern Ann

Born: February 2, 1875, Tuscaloosa County, Alabama. Died: July 20, 1917, Tarrant County, Texas. Father: James H. Mills. Mother: Unity Hughes. Comments: Cathern Mills came with her parents to Van Zandt County in December of 1876 when she was 1 year old. Cathern was in poor health all of her life. Her parents moved to Munday, Knox County, Texas in 1906 to try to improve her health. Later, she was taken to Fort Worth for an operation to remove gallstones and did not recover from the operation. Source: *Canton Herald*, July 27, 1917.

MILLS, CORA ALMEDA
Born: February 28, 1874, Van Zandt County, Texas. Died: September 24, 1964, Midland County, Texas. Cause of death: Heart failure. Married: Edward H. Mills, April 1, 1900. Child: Elaine. Father: John R. Martin. Mother: Mary Martin. Siblings: Mary Catherine, General Lee, and Ora C. Sources: Death Certificate, *Canton Herald* October 1, 1964.

MILLS, EDWARD HUGHES
Born: February 17, 1870, Alabama. Died: February 15, 1928, Harris County, Texas. Cause of death: Shock from accidental injuries. Married: Cora Almeda Martin, April 1, 1900. Father: James Harvey Mills. Mother: Mary M. Samuels. Occupation: Highway Engineer. Military: Spanish American War. Sources: Death Certificate; *Free State Enterprise*, February 15, 1900.

MILLS, HOMER
Born: February 7, 1901. Died: May 24, 1901. Father: Edward H. Mills. Mother: Cora A. Martin. Source: Tombstone.

MILLS, INFANT SON
Born: 1895. Died: 1895. Father: W. S. Mills. Mother: R. P. Dowdle. Source: Tombstone.

MILLS, INFANT TWIN DAUGHTERS
Born: 1916. Died: 1916. Father: W. S. Mills. Mother: R. P. Dowdle. Source: Tombstone.

MILLS, JAMES HARVEY
(Photo page 96) Born: March 12, 1844, Tuscaloosa County, Alabama. Died: February 10, 1914, Van Zandt County, Texas. Married: Mary Missouri Samuels. Children: William S., Edward Hughes, Nellie Eston, Catherine Ann, James Milton, May Virginia, Rufus E. Lee, and John Jacob. Father: James Milton Mills. Mother: Unity Hughes. Military: CSA, Cpl. Co. A. 41st Alabama Infantry. Comments: James Harvey Mills and his family moved from Alabama to Van Zandt County, Texas in the fall of 1876 and settled on land north of Canton. In 1881, he bought a farm in the Mill Creek community south of Canton and moved there to farm. He was there until 1906 when he moved to Knox County due to his daughter's illness. He returned to Canton in the fall of 1913 and died in February, 1914. He had lived in Van Zandt County for thirty years. Sources: *The History of Zandt County Texas, Vol, I*; *Canton Herald*, February 19, 1914.

MILLS, MARY MISSOURI
(Photo page 96) Born: September 28, 1849, Alabama. Died: April 30, 1929, Van Zandt County, Texas. Married: James Harvey Mills. Children: William S., Edward Hughes, Nellie Eston, Catherine Ann, James Milton, May Virginia, Rufus Lee, and John Jacob. Father: John Jacob Samuels, Virginia. Mother: Catherine Ann Lee, Alabama. Sources: Death Certificate; *The History of Van Zandt County Texas, Vol. I.*

MILLS, MAUDIE M.
Born: October 7, 1889. Died: November 1, 1890. Father: James H. Mills. Mother: Mary M. Samuels. Source: Tombstone.

MILLS, ROBERT PADIAN "BOBBIE"
(Photo page 96) Born: October 15, 1873, Carroll County, Mississippi. Died: November 13, 1947, Van Zandt County, Texas. Married: William Samuel Mills, December 27, 1892. Children: Maude Etta, Baby Son, Nellie Elizabeth, Edward Merritt, Lettie Jeanette, Mary Christine, James Irby, Verlie May, Roger Q., and William Samuel Jr. Father: Robert Padian "Bob" Dowdle, Mississippi. Mother: Eliza Jane Tyler, Mississippi. Sources: *The History of Van Zandt County Texas, Vol I*; Hilliard Funeral Home records.

MILLS, ROGER Q
Born: April 17, 1911, Texas. Died: March 26, 1939, Van Zandt County, Texas. Single. Father: William Samuel Mills. Mother: Robert Padian "Bobbie" Dowdle. Comments: Roger Mills had severe health problems all of his life. He was living with his parents when he died. Source: Hilliard Funeral Home records.

MILLS, WILLIAM SAMUEL
(Photo page 96) Born: May 2, 1868, Alabama. Died: January 16, 1950, Dallas County, Texas. Married: Robert Padian "Bobbie" Dowdle, December 27, 1892. Children: Maude Etta, baby son, infant twins, Nellie Elizabeth, Edward Merritt, Lettie Jeanette, Mary Christine, James Irby, Verlie May, Roger Q., and William Samuel Jr. Father: James Harvey Mills, Tuscaloosa County, Alabama. Mother: Mary M. Samuels, Alabama. Occupation: Teacher, County official. Comments: W. S. Mills was a prominent figure in Van Zandt County for many years. He moved with his family from Alabama in the fall of 1879 and settled on land between Canton and Edgewood. Later the family moved closer to Canton where he attended school. He obtained his teaching certificate about 1891 and started teaching at Red Mill. Over the years, he taught at Myrtle Springs, Jackson, Edom, Union Hill, Mill Creek, Mt. Pisgah, Landmark, and Lone Star schools. Wentworth School was his last teaching assignment before his retirement after 43 years. W. S. also ventured into politics serving as Van Zandt County District Clerk from 1925 through 1928 and as County Surveyor

Berry Alvie Mitchell *served as a rural mail carrier in Van Zandt County for thirty-eight years, one of the most popular carriers in the history of the county. He also established Mitchell Hatchery, providing chickens to rural customers. His funeral was attended by hundreds, and his tombstone is inscribed: "Uncle Berry was loved by all who knew him."*

from 1935 to 1946. W. S.'s wife died in November, 1947; and he devoted the next two years writing Mill's *History of Van Zandt County*. The book was published after his death later that year. It was the most comprehensive history of Van Zandt County. Sources: *The History of Van Zandt County Texas, Vol I; Canton Herald*, May 5, 1938 and January 7, 1943; Hilliard Funeral Home records.

Mitchell, Alice Victoria
Born: June 16, 1872, Van Zandt County, Texas. Died: August 8, 1951, Van Zandt County, Texas. Cause of death: Stroke. Married: Willis Bunyon Mitchell, 1894. Children: Nina C., Arthur Graves, and Lorine. Father: J. F. Samples, Georgia. Mother: Nancy James. Comments: Alice Mitchell's husband died in 1902. Sources: Death Certificate, Ancestry.com.

Mitchell, Amy Eliza
Born: January 4, 1839, Calhoun County, Alabama. Died: October 30, 1874, Van Zandt County, Texas. Married: Marshal E. Mitchell, December 13, 1860, Alabama. Children: James Glover, Thomas Jefferson, Laura F. "Fannie," and Wiley W. Father: Thomas Jefferson Downing. Mother: Charity Mira Autry. Siblings: Elijah Berryman, Arch, Charity Mira, and Giles L. Sources: Ancestry.com, Find A Grave.

Mitchell, Baby Girl
Born: October 6, 1974. Died: October 7, 1974. Father: Charles Leon Mitchell. Mother: Suzanne Fitzgerald. Source: Eubank Funeral Home records.

Mitchell, Berry Alvie
Born: July 26, 1876, Van Zandt County, Texas. Died: January 8, 1950, Van Zandt County, Texas. Married: (1) Nancy Elizabeth Parsons, November 8, 1896. Children: Chester Arthur, Gladys Valera, Lois, Bessie, B. A. Jr., and William B. (2) Sarah Katherine Williams, April 8, 1920. Children: Dr. Jack A. and H. Judd. Father: Rev. Newton Mitchell, Alabama. Mother: Sarah Ann Wright, Monroe County, Georgia. Siblings: Andrew, Bunyon, Docie, Callie, Paralee, Elizabeth, Necie, Joseph, Arabelle, and Leth. Occupation: Rural mail carrier; owner, Mitchell Hatchery. Comments: Berry Mitchell was one of the more popular rural mail carriers in the history of Van Zandt Country. . He retired in 1941 after thirty-eight years of service. He also established Mitchell Hatchery, providing chickens to rural customers. Berry loved to sing and attended many Sacred Harp and Progressive Singing Conventions all over Texas. He also was interested in the War effort and was Chairman of the Rationing Board. At his death, hundreds of people attended his funeral. Sources: *Canton Herald*, January 12, 1950; *Van Zandt County Texas Biographies, 1848-1991*; Eubank Funeral Home records.

Mitchell, Kevon Lamont
Born: 2001. Died: 2001. Father: Unknown Mitchell. Mother: Unknown. Source: Metal grave marker.

Mitchell, Mary M.
Born: December 18, 1872. Died: October 12, 1873. Father: Newton Mitchel. Mother: Sarah Ann Wright. Source: Tombstone.

Mitchell, Nancy Elizabeth "Nannie"
Born: January 23, 1880. Died: February 2, 1919. Married: Berry Alvie Mitchell, November 8, 1896. Children: Chester Arthur, Gladys Valera, Lois, Bessie, B. A. Jr., and William B. Father: Lewis Manuel Parsons. Mother:

William Herbert Morrison and Elsie Josephine Morrison

Sarah Colon Cox. Source: *Canton Herald*, February 7, 1919.

MITCHELL, SARAH KATHERINE
Born: October 14, 1884, Parker County, Texas. Died: June 21, 1955, Van Zandt County, Texas. Cause of death: Cancer. Married: Berry Alvie Mitchell, April 8, 1920. Children: Dr. Jack Andrews and H. Judd. Father: John Franklin Williams. Mother: Mary Beatrice Toland. Occupation: Home Demonstration Agent for Van Zandt County, Texas. Sources: Death Certificate, Eubank Funeral Home records, Ancestry.com.

MITCHELL, WILLIAM B. "BRIAN"
Born: March 14, 1910, Van Zandt County, Texas. Died: September 4, 1986, Los Angeles County, California. Father: Berry A. Mitchell. Mother: Nancy Parsons. Siblings: Chester Arthur, Gladys, Valera, Lois, Bessie, and B. A. Jr. Occupation: North American Aviation, Broadway Department Stores. Comments: William B. Mitchell's parents were lifelong residents of Van Zandt County. He graduated from Canton High School and attended North Texas and Texas A&M Universities. He moved to California during WWII and was employed by North American Aviation and the Broadway Department Stores. William was a writer and a painter. He won many awards for his breeding of cockatiels and canaries. Sources: *Canton Herald*, September 24, 1986; *Van Zandt County Texas Biographies, 1848-1991*.

MITCHELL, WILLIS BUNYAN
Born: 1870, Cherokee County, Texas. Died: 1902, Van Zandt County, Texas. Cause of death: Suicide. Married: Alice Victoria Samples, 1894. Children: Nina C., Arthur Graves, and Lorine. Father: Newton Mitchell, Alabama. Mother: Sarah Ann Wright, Georgia. Siblings: Andrew, Docia, Callie, Paralee, Elizabeth, Necie, Joseph, Arabelle, Letha, and Berry. Comments: The *Wills Point Chronicle* reported his death as follows: "Last Thursday morning W. B. Mitchell of this place was found locked in his room and his throat cut, his windpipe having been nearly severed. The work was done with a pocket knife and it is supposed that the deed was committed by himself while in a state of temporary mental aberration, caused by years of physical suffering. He has worked in the store of G. W. Tull for many years and early Thursday morning he came down to the store as was his custom to open up. His wife and children were away from home—and he had been taking his meals at Mrs. Day's hotel. After opening the store and making a few sales, he told Mr. Abbe, who works in the store with him—that he was not feeling well and would go home and attend to feeding his stock. He remained away so long that W. N. Tull became alarmed and went to his residence to see about him. He forced an entrance to the house and found Mitchell on the bed with the wound as described above." He lived about seven weeks and died from his wounds. Sources: *Wills Point Chronicle*, October 2, 1902 and November 21, 1902; Ancestry.com.

MONROE, JEFFERSON DAVIS "JEFF"
Born: December 21, 1860, Newton County, Mississippi. Died: 1944, Van Zandt County, Texas. Married: Mollie Atkins, September 24, 1887, Mississippi. Father: James Joseph Monroe. Mother: Blanche Narcissa Kelly. Siblings: Napoleon Bonaparte, John Marshall, James Polk, Sarah Joanne, William S., Robert B., Caroline , Blanche Narcissa, Juliette Drinkwater, Barney Archibald Sr., and Joseph Storey. Comments: The Monroe's came from Mississippi and settled in various communities. They married into prominent families in Van Zandt County. Jeff Monroe's sister, Juliette Drinkwater Monroe, married Willis J. Hale, who became the largest producer of ribbon cane syrup in East Texas and was known for the quality of his syrup all over the Texas and the United States. Barney Archibald Monroe was somewhat of a character, but was well known for the quality of his farming methods. Sources: Select Marriage Index, 1837-1865, T*he History of Van Zandt County*, Ancestry.com.

MOORE, ARLENE F.
Born: December 28, 1892, Van Zandt County, Texas. Died: September 14, 1985, Dallas County, Texas. Married: Horace Erskin Moore. Father: Unknown Ford. Mother: Unknown. Occupation: Sales clerk, Sanger Harris and Nardis Department Stores. Source: *Canton Herald*, September 19, 1985.

MOORE, BERTHA IMA
Born: July 31, 1893, Maryland. Died: October 11, 1964, Dallas County, Texas. Cause of death: Coma. Married:

Dee Otis Moore. Father: Arthur Bomberger. Mother: Francis Bomberger. Source: Death Certificate.

Moore, Dee Otis
Born: December 27, 1878. Died: January 29, 1935. Cause of death: Pneumonia. Married: Bertha I. Bomberger. Father: Napoleon Moore. Mother: Mary Bottoms. Military: U.S. Army, 31 years, officer, retired. Sources: Death Certificate; *Grand Saline Sun*, January 31, 1935.

Moore, Horace Erskin
Born: August 28, 1892, Tennessee. Died: June 15, 1962, Dallas County, Texas. Married: Arlene Ford, March 6, 1918. Father: Hugh Moore. Mother: Mary Powell. Sources: *Canton Herald*, June 21, 1962; Eubank Funeral Home records.

Moore, James Elmer "Jimmie"
Born: January 6, 1924, Virginia. Died: January 11, 1981, Dallas County, Texas. Cause of death: Lung cancer. Divorced. Father: Dee Otis Moore. Mother: Bertha Bomberger. Military: WWII, Korea, U. S. Navy. Sources: Death Certificate; *Canton Herald*, January 15, 1981.

Moore, John Franklin "Johnny"
Born: January 6, 1924, Amhurst County, Virginia. Died: April 27, 1933, Van Zandt County, Texas. Cause of death: Hit by automobile. Father: Dee Otis Moore. Mother: Bertha I. Bomberger. Source: Death Certificate.

Moore, William C.
Born: August 26, 1919, Maryland. Died: December 5, 1983, Texas. Married: Mary L. Moore. Father: Dee Otis Moore. Mother: Bertha I. Bomberger. Source: 1930, 1940 U. S. Census.

Morris, Alford Lee
Born: February 24, 1956. Died: June 3, 1985. Father: Maston A. Morris. Mother: Myrtle Treva Mayne. Occupation: Brookshire Grocery Store, clerk. Military: Pvt., U. S. Army. Source: *Canton Herald*, June 6, 1985.

Morris, Jettie Pearl
Born: December 12, 1922. Died: February 7, 1940. Single. Father: Maston L. Morris. Mother: Mary Bussey. Source: Eubank Funeral Home records.

Morris, Mary Ola
Born: October 13, 1890, Dallas County, Texas. Died: June 25, 1981, Dallas County, Texas. Cause of death: Heart disease. Married: Maston L. Morris, December 3, 1907. Children: Hubert Leslie, Julius Edgar, Alma, Maston Alfred, and Emogene. Father: Willie Bussey. Mother: Hanna Duretta Francis. Comments: Mary Morris spent her early life in Van Zandt County, but resided in Dallas County for the last thirty years of her life. Sources: Death Certificate; 1920, 1930 U. S. Census; *Canton Herald*, July 2, 1981.

Morris, Maston Alford "Buster"
Born: February 17, 1919, Van Zandt County, Texas. Died: August 25, 2000, Van Zandt County, Texas. Married: Myrtle Trava Mayne, May 4, 1942. Children: Phillip, Alford, Annie Ruth, Trena, Shirley, and Doris. Father: Maston Luther Morris. Mother: Mary Ola Bussey. Military: WWII, PFC, US Army, Purple Heart. Source: Find A Grave.

Morris, Maston Luther
Born: March 17, 1886, Texas. Died: April 18, 1950, Van Zandt County, Texas. Cause of death: Automobile accident. Married: Mary Ola Bussey, December 3, 1907. Children: Hubert Leslie, Julius Edgar, Alma, Maston Alfred, and Emogene. Father: George W. Morris. Mother: Melinda J. Coffee. Occupation: Farming. Source: Death Certificate.

Morris, Myrtle Trava
Born: February 28, 1921, Van Zandt County, Texas. Died: August 28, 1997, Smith County, Texas. Married: Maston Alford Morris, May 4, 1942. Children: Alfred, Phillip, Anna, Trena, Shirley, and Doris. Father: Elmer Burnell Mayne. Mother: Minnie Bell Olliver. Comments: Myrtle Morris was born in the Colfax Community of Van Zandt County and graduated from Van High School. She moved to Dallas to live for thirty years before returning to the Colfax community. Source: *Van Zandt News*, August 31, 1997.

Morrison, Elsie Josephine
Born: December 5, 1887, Texas. Died: April 28, 1981, Brazoria County, Texas. Cause of death: Heart disease. Married: William Herbert Morrison, November 5, 1911. Father: Curran Preston Paschall. Mother: Mary Elizabeth "Mollie" Norman. Source: Death Certificate.

Morrison, William Herbert
Born: February 7, 1886, Van Zandt County, Texas. Died: March 17, 1952, Van Zandt County, Texas. Cause of death: Heart disease. Married: Elsie Josephine Paschall, November 5, 1911. Father: William Louis Morrison, Texas. Mother: Mary Ellen Clardy Carr, Texas. Occupation: CPA, Van Zandt County Tax Assessor-Collector 1919-1922. Comments: William Morrison was the Mineral Evaluation Officer for Van Zandt County. He served as a member of the Board of Stewards and as Financial Secretary for the Canton United Methodist Church. William also served as City and School Tax Collector and was the County Democratic Chairman for a number of years. Sources: Death Certificate; *The Dallas Morning News*, March 20, 1952; *Grand Saline Sun*, March 27, 1952; Eubank Funeral Home records.

Morrissey, James Fair
Born: December 15, 1872, Connecticut. Died: March 15, 1948, Kaufman County, Texas. Cause of death: Automobile accident. Married: Julia Francis Canterbury. Father: William Morrissey, Connecticut. Mother: Katherine Fair, Canada. Occupation: Oil Well Supply Dealer. Source: Death Certificate, *Canton Herald*, March 18, 1948.

N

Nash, Miranda Jane Tracy
Born: June 20, 1834, New York, New York. Died: June, 1911, Van Zandt County, Texas. Married: George Munson Nash. Children: Eva, Alice, Frank, and Floyd. Father: John Long. Mother: Annie Glinn. Comments: Miranda Jane Nash came with her family from New York State in 1886. Their daughter, Alice, married A. R. Maume. Alice was the mother of Mamie Maume, who was the owner of the noted Dixie Hotel in Canton, Texas. After Miranda's death, her husband moved to Lincoln, Arkansas to live with his son, Frank. He died there on March 23, 1922 at the age of 89. Sources: 1900 U. S. Census; *Canton Herald*, April 4, 1922; Ancestry.com

Jessie Riley Nolen and Albert Sidney "Mr. Sid" Nolen

Neely, Altha
Born: May 1, 1908. Died: May 1, 1908. Father: Samuel A. Neely. Mother: Ivy Jane Long. Source: Tombstone.

Neely, Alvia Lee
Born: August 12, 1919. Died: August 12, 1919. Father: Samuel A. Neely. Mother: Ivy Jane Long. Source: Tombstone.

Neely, Ivy Jane
Born: November 7, 1888, Kaufman County, Texas. Died: February 12, 1949, Tarrant County, Texas. Cause of death: Spinal tuberculosis. Married: Samuel Acie Neely, November 16, 1903. Children: Alton N., William A., James, Alvia Lee, and Altha. Father: John Long, Kaufman County, Texas. Mother: Annie Glinn, Kaufman County, Texas. Source: Death Certificate.

Neely, James Abraham
Born: July 6, 1928, Van Zandt County, Texas. Died: December 3, 1940, Kaufman County, Texas. Cause of death: Appendicitis. Father: Samuel Acie Neely, Leon County, Texas. Mother: Ivy Jane Long, Kaufman County, Texas. Sources: Death Certificate, Tombstone.

Neely Lela Roberta
Born: July 7, 1861, Alabama. Died: December 18, 1902, Van Zandt County, Texas. Cause of death: Childbirth. Married: William C. Neely, 1879. Children: Lela Bell, Samuel Acie, Clara Elizabeth, Lillie, Linnie, and Sophia. Father: Dr. William Whitlock. Mother: unknown. Comments: Lela Neely died at the birth of Sophia. Sources: *The History of Van Zandt County, Texas, Vol. I*, Ancestry.com.

Neely, Samuel Acie
Born: September 1, 1883, Leon County, Texas. Died: November 27, 1980, Smith County, Texas. Married: (1) Ivy Jane Long, November 16, 1903. (2) Mrs. Rosella Gwinn, May 28, 1949. Children: Avis, Annie, Acie, Alton, Albert, Aubrey, Alenia, and three deceased. Father: William Carroll Neely. Mother: Lela Roberta Whitlock. Occupation: Farmer. Comments: Samuel Neely came to Van Zandt County in 1894 at the age of 9 and spent most of his life in the Willow Springs community. He was the father of ten children, seven who survived him. Sources: *The History of Van Zandt County, Vol. I*; *Marriage Records, Van Zandt County, Texas, 1848-1909, 1909-1931, 1931 1950*; *Canton Herald*, December 4, 1980.

Neely, William Carroll
Born: April 4, 1850, Lafayette County, Arkansas. Died: December 18, 1924, Cherokee County, Texas. Married: Lela Roberta Whitlock, 1879. Children: Lela Bell, Samuel Acie, Clara Elizabeth, Lillie, Linnie, and Sophia. Father: Fleming Ridley Neely. Mother: Eliza Williams. Occupation: Farmer. Comments: William Neely lived in

America Emaline "Emma" Norman and Jacob A. "Jake" Norman

Arkansas, Louisiana, and Angelina and Leon Counties, Texas prior to moving to Van Zandt County in 1894. They settled in the Willow Springs community where they made their home for twenty-five years. His wife died at the birth of their youngest child, Sophia. Sophia died at the age of 16. Sources: *The History of Van Zandt County, Vol. I*; *Canton Herald*, December 26, 1924; Ancestry.com.

NELSON, BABY GIRL
Born: February 10, 1974. Died: February 16, 1974. Mother: Virginia Nelson. Source: Eubank Funeral Home records.

NELSON, BERNICE SCATES
Born: April 24, 1928. Died: March 16, 1970. Married: Johnny B. Nelson. Father: Pecos Scates. Mother: Lucille Williams. Source: Eubank Funeral Home records.

NELSON, VIRGINIA LOIS
Born: February 26, 1954, Van Zandt County, Texas. Died: June 28, 2009, Van Zandt County, Texas. Single. Child: Juaniita Nelson. Father: Johnny B. Nelson. Mother: Bernice Scates. Occupation: Seamstress, Malouf's Company. Surviving siblings: Johnny Ray, Melvin Dewayne, Hazel, and Norma. Sources: *Tyler Morning Telegraph*, July 4, 2009; Hilliard Funeral Home records.

NICHOLS, BIRDIE OLETA BARTLETT
Born: September 11, 1920, Van Zandt County, Texas. Died: September 1, 1997, Dallas County, Texas. Married: D. W. Nichols, August 4, 1940. Children: Jeanie, Francis Joanne, and Janice. Father: Samuel Lusk Bartlett. Mother: Lillie Mae Bodine. Comments: D. W. and Oleta Nichols lived in Canton and Greenville prior to moving to Cherokee Village, Arkansas in 1972. They were living there when Oleta died. She was a member of the Daughters of the American Revolution and the National Society of Magna Carta. Sources: *Van Zandt News*, September 7, 1997; Ancestry.com.

NICHOLS, D.W.
Born: May 18, 1918, Van Zandt County, Texas. Died: October 10, 2008, Dallas County, Texas. Married: Oleta Bartlett, August 4, 1940. Children: Francis Joanne, Janice Oleta, and Jeanne. Father: William Jessie "Willie" Nichols. Mother: Daisy Louella Kelly. Occupation: Temco in Grand Prairie; E-Systems in Greenville, Texas. Military: WWII, US Army. Sources: *Van Zandt News*, October 26, 2008; Ancestry.com.

NICHOLS, DAISY LOUELLA
Born: October 2, 1894, Georgia. Died: September 5, 1977, Van Zandt County, Texas. Cause of death: Heart disease. Married: William Jessie Nichols. Child: D. W. Father: D. S. Kelly. Mother: Nora Smith. Comments: Daisy Nichols had lived in Canton for sixty years at the time of her death. Sources: Death Certificate; *Canton Herald*, September 8, 1977.

NICHOLS, JEANIE
Born: November 12, 1941. Died: February 9, 2015. Father: D. W. Nichols. Mother: Bertie Oleta Bartlett. Siblings: Francis Joanne and Janice. Source: Ancestry.com.

NICHOLS, WILLIAM JESSE "WILLIE"
Born: June 5, 1891, Texas. Died: October 24, 1974, Van Zandt County, Texas. Married: Daisy L. Kelly. Father: Will Warren Nichols. Mother: Mary Sue Cooper. Occupation: Farmer. Source: Death Certificate.

NOLEN, ALBERT SIDNEY "MR. SID"
Born: April 21, 1870, Smith County, Texas. Died: December 21, 1941 Van Zandt County, Texas. Married: Jessie Love Riley, November 18, 1908. Father: Albert A. Nolen. Mother: Arabella Elizabeth Baskin. Siblings: George Tate and Oscar Lee. Occupation: Drugstore owner. Comments: Sid Nolen came to Van Zandt County when he was 2 years old. In 1902, Sid and his brother, Tate, purchased a drug business from D. F. Clark. The business, operating as Nolen Brothers Drugs, was located on the west side of the Canton square. The partnership lasted until Tate's death in 1936. Sid then operated it alone until his death in 1941. The Nolen Brothers became one of the more prominent and popular families in Canton. Sid's tombstone sums up his life with this inscription: "Faithful Druggist of Canton for Fifty Years." Sources: *Canton Herald*, January 1, 1942; Hilliard Funeral Home records.

NOLEN, GEORGE TATE
Born: January 15, 1875, Kaufman County, Texas. Died: February 25, 1936, Dallas County, Texas. Married: Mat-

***CLYDE AUGUSTA PEACE** was one of Van Zandt County's earliest settlers. His father, J.A. Peace, bought the blacksmith and wagon shop on the southwest corner of the Canton Square, and Clyde Peace worked there as a blacksmith. The family has been part of the Canton business community for more than 130 years, and still owns the Peace Pharmacy, which occupies part of J.A. Peace's original property on the Square.*

tie A. Clark, October 30, 1901. Father: Albert A. Nolen. Mother: Arabella Elizabeth Baskin. Siblings: Albert Sidney and Oscar Lee. Occupation: Drugstore owner. Comments: In 1902, George Tate Nolen and his brother, Sid, purchased the drug business from his father-in-law, Doc Franklin Clark. Operating as Nolen Brothers Drugs on the west side of the Canton square, the two brothers became fixtures in the Canton business community. The partnership lasted until Tate's death in 1936. Sid continued to operate as sole owner of the business until his death in 1941. Sources: *Canton Herald*, January 1, 1942; Ancestry.com.

NOLEN, JESSIE RILEY

(Photos page 102) Born: January 16, 1876, Van Zandt County, Texas. Died: August 24, 1966, Smith County, Texas. Married: Albert Sidney Nolen, November 18, 1908. Father: David Love Riley, Jr. Mother: Mary C. Hobbs. Siblings: Belle, James T., Claude F., Lydia Colon, Mary Daisy, David Thompson, and Jay Holt. Comments: Jessie Nolen had been a member of the First Baptist Church at Canton for seventy-eight years. She had no children and donated her real estate and properties to the Baptist Foundation—half to the East Texas Baptist College in Marshall and half to Mary Hardin Baylor College in Belton, Texas. Sources: *Canton Herald*, September 1, 1966; Eubank Funeral Home records; Find A Grave.

NOLEN, MATTIE A.

Born: July 15, 1880. Died: October 8, 1925. Married: George Tate Nolen, October 30, 1901. Father: Doc Franklin Clark. Mother: Fannie Aurelia McCurley. Siblings: Percy R., Mattie, and Loy. Comments: Mattie Nolen assisted her husband in Nolen Brothers Drugs. Sources: *Canton Herald*, October 16, 1925; Ancestry.com.

NOLEN, OSCAR LEE

Born: 1868, Smith County, Texas. Died: 1924, Van Zandt County, Texas. Married: Bettie Matthews, September 14, 1890. Children: Russell, Sid, Mary, and Imogene. Father: Albert A. Nolen. Mother: Arabella Elizabeth Baskin. Siblings: Albert Sidney and George Tate. Occupation: Owner, Nolen Hardware Company. Comments: Lee Nolen was reared in Canton along with his brothers, Sid and Tate. He moved to Canadian, Texas and established Nolen Hardware Company. He became ill and returned to Canton to be treated by Canton and Dallas doctors. He died in Canton from his illness. Source: *Wills Point Chronicle*, August 21, 1924; *Van Zandt County Marriage Records 1848-1909.*

NORMAN, AMERICA EMALINE "EMMA"

*(Photos page 103)*Born: November 19, 1876, Stoddard County, Missouri. Died: September 9, 1952, Dallas County, Texas. Cause of death: Heart disease. Married: Jacob A. Norman, August 20, 1891, Missouri. Children: David, Walker, and Mrs. A. A. Brown. Father: Jesse William Ballard, Missouri. Mother: Samantha Oglesby Stanbery Price. Comments: America Norman's mother married Nathaniel Stanbery, Jesse Ballard, and William R. Price. America came to Van Zandt County in 1901. She later lived in Hunt and Dallas Counties. Sources: Death Certificate; *Canton Herald*, September 25, 1952; Find A Grave.

NORMAN, JACOB A. "JAKE"

(Photos page 103) Born: July 12, 1867, Stoddard County, Missouri. Died: November 9, 1944, Kaufman County, Texas. Cause of death: Lung disease. Married: America Emaline Ballard. Father: William Norman, Illinois. Mother: Sara Cox, Illinois. Occupation: Farmer. Comments: The Norman's moved from Missouri to Van Zandt County in 1901 and settled near Grand Saline, Texas The

family later moved to the Wallace Community. Sources: Death Certificate, Find A Grave.

Nunnally, Sarah Tull
Born: December 15, 1872. Died: May 7, 1904. Married: Joseph Guy Nunnally, February 12, 1890. Father. George Washington Tull. Mother: Mary Jane "Mollie" Cowan. Siblings: Romilda, George L., Thomas G., William N., Walter H., Lula, Noma, Bertie, Allie, Estelle, and Lillian. Sources: *Wills Point Chronicle*, May 12, 1904; Ancestry.com.

O

Ogletree, Sylvia Shuttles
Born: October 12, 1928, Dallas County Texas. Died: July 5, 2016, Van Zandt County, Texas. Married: (1) Unknown Slaughter. Children: John, Pat, and Marianne. (2) Terrell Ogletree. Father: Robert Hall. Mother: Lila Cox. Occupation: Nurse, art teacher. Comments: Sylvia Ogletree was the granddaughter of Marion Love and Millie Youngblood Cox. The Cox and Youngblood families were pioneer settlers of the Martins Mill area of Van Zandt County. Marion Cox was a successful Canton doctor and businessman. He died in 1931, and his wife died in 1956. Sylvia's husband, Terrell Ogletree, died in 1992 and is buried in Haven of Memories Cemetery in Canton, Texas. Sylvia worked as a nurse and taught art therapy to patients at Terrell State Hospital. Source: Eubank Funeral Home records.

Overturf, Effa Ann
Born: November 27, 1849, Arkansas. Died: April 1, 1934, Van Zandt County, Texas. Cause of death: Bronchitis. Married: William Ira Overturf. Father: James Duncan Patterson, Sr., Arkansas. Mother: Lucretia Green. Source: Death Certificate, Ancestry.com.

Overturf, Infant Daughter
Born: July 25, 1915. Died: July 25, 1915. Father: Lee H. Overturf. Mother: Sallie L. Travis. Source: Wills Point Chronicle, August 5, 1915.

Overturf, William Ira
Born: May 26, 1866, Illinois. Died: March 17, 1934, Van Zandt County, Texas. Cause of death: Measles, double pneumonia. Married: Effa Ann Patterson. Father: Benjamin Franklin Overturf, Sr. Mother: Susanna "Annie" Hammonds. Occupation: Farmer. Comments: William Overturf had lived in Van Zandt County for thirty years prior to his death. Sources: Death Certificate; *Canton Herald*, March 23, 1934.

Owens, David
Born: 1892. Death: Death date broken off tombstone. Father: J. I. Owens. Mother: C. L. Owens. Source: Tombstone.

Owens, Laura Virginia
Born: November 17, 1847. Died: January 21, 1902. Married: George Lott Owens. Children: Fred Patterson, William L., Augustus G., John, Horace W., and Samuel Roy. Father: J. W. Robbins. Mother: Francis Robbins. Sources: Ancestry.com, Find A Grave.

Owens, Lucille
Born: Unknown. Died: Unknown. Father: Unknown. Mother: Unknown. Source: Tombstone.

Owens, Mytra
Born: Unknown. Died: Unknown. Father: Unknown. Mother: Unknown. Source: Tombstone.

P

Parker, Eugene M.
Born: July 17, 1921. Died: November 24, 1923. Father: M. J. Parker. Mother: Devera E. Parker. Source: Tombstone.

Parker, M.J.
Born: March 23, 1856. Died: August 29, 1875. Married: Andrew D. Parker, November 10, 1874. Father: Unknown Mathis. Mother: Unknown. Sources: Tombstone, *Marriage Records, Van Zandt County, Texas, 1848-1909.*

Paschall, Mary Mollie
Born: September 10, 1861, Texas. Died: September 22, 1900, Van Zandt County, Texas. Married: William James Paschall, January 22, 1882. Father: Mastin M. Chappell. Mother: Jane Williams. Sources: *Wills Point Chronicle, September 27, 1900*; Ancestry.com.

Paschall, William James
Born: Unknown. Died: Unknown. Married: Mary Chappell, January 22, 1882. Father: Unknown Paschall. Mother: Unknown. Source: Footstone only.

Patrick, Annie
Born: December 4, 1886. Died: December 27, 1901. Married: William H. Patrick, December 24, 1899. Father: John Henry Tyson. Mother: Phoebe Jane Sanger. Siblings: Mamie L., Caroline Francis, and Spencer. Comments: William Patrick and Annie Tyson were married only two years when she died. William married again four

months later to Ida Watson, April 6, 1902. Sources: *Free State Enterprise*, January 2, 1902; J. M. Hadley, Family historian; Find A Grave.

Patrick, Baby
Comments: There is a broken tombstone with no dates. The grave is next to Annie Patrick.

Patrick, Mattie Alma
Born: November 1, 1882, Mississippi. Died: April 7, 1949, Dallas County, Texas. Cause of death: Pneumonia. Married: Thomas Jefferson Patrick, November 27, 1898. Children: Jeffie, Dewight, Loy Dean, Annie, Lorine, and Louella. Father: James A. Norris. Mother: Susan Francis Norris. Sources: Death Certificate, Ancestry.com.

Patrick, Naomia Lucille
Born: September 17, 1912, Texas. Died: January 14, 1977, Van Zandt County, Texas. Married: Virgil Avery Patrick. Children: Gary, Ronnie, Pat, and Avis. Father: James Byron Hendley. Mother: Naomia Brown. Sources: Death Certificate; *Canton Herald*, January 20, 1977.

Patrick, Thomas Jefferson
Born: May 25, 1879, Van Zandt County, Texas. Died: March 17, 1948, Dallas County, Texas. Cause of death: Heart disease. Married: Mattie A. Norris, November 27, 1898. Children: Jeffie, Dewight, Loy Dean, Annie, Lorine, Louella, and Virgil Avery. Father: Erasmus Patrick. Mother: Lucy Dewsianberry. Occupation: Farmer. Comments: Thomas Patrick had lived in Van Zandt County for forty-three years at the time of his death. Sources: Death Certificate; *Canton Herald*, March 25, 1948; Ancestry.com.

Patrick, Virgil Avery
Born: June 9, 1912. Died: August 25, 1970. Cause of death: Heart disease. Married: Naomia Lucille Hendley. Children: Gary, Ronnie, Pat, and Avis. Father: Thomas J. Patrick. Mother: Mattie A. Norris. Occupation: Printing press operator. Source: Death Certificate.

Patterson, Elizabeth
Born: October 16, 1830. Died: April 30, 1899. Father: Duncan P. Patterson. Mother: Lucretia Green. Source: Ancestry.com.

Patterson, Francis "Frannie"
Born: September 2, 1848. Died: March 30, 1864. Father: M. K. Patterson. Mother: Lucinda unknown. Siblings: Clary M., Mary, Sarah, David, and Nancy. Comments: The 1860 census lists Francis Patterson, age 11, living with Robert and Mary Doyle in Van Zandt County. Their relationship is unknown. Source: 1860 U. S. Census.

Patterson, James Duncan
Born: June 10, 1840, Louisiana. Died: December 26, 1915, Van Zandt County, Texas. Father: Duncan P. Patterson Mother: Lucretia Green. Military: CSA, Ark. Inf. Co. K. 2 Regt. Occupation: Farmer. Comments: James Patterson came to Van Zandt County about 1880 from Claiborne Parish, Louisiana and was a farmer. He died at the age of 77 while living with his sister, Mrs. Elbert Travis. He had lived in the same community for forty years. Source: *Canton Herald*, December 31, 1915.

Patterson, Lucretia
Born: April 27, 1812, Mississippi. Died: September 22, 1887. Married: Duncan P. Patterson. Children: Neil B., M. C., James D., William Franklin, Effa Ann, and Martha Ann. Father: Unknown Green. Mother: Unknown. Sources: U. S. 1870 Census, Ancestry.com.

Patterson, Neill B.
Born: January 15, 1833. Died: December 27, 1891. Father: Duncan P. Patterson. Mother: Lucretia Green. Source: *Canton Telephone*, January 1, 1892.

Paul, Emmett David
Born: April 25, 1892, Lamar County, Texas. Died: March 16, 1971, Dallas County, Texas. Married: Eva Joe Hutchinson. Father: James W. Paul. Mother: Mary Scott. Occupation: Farmer. Source: Death Certificate.

Paul, Eva Joe
Born: June 1, 1895, Archer County, Texas. Died: November 6, 1921, Van Zandt County, Texas. Married: Emmett David Paul. Father: Frank G. Hutchinson. Mother: Susan Gibson, Tennessee. Occupation: School teacher. Sources: 1900 U. S. Census; *Canton Herald*, November 11, 1921; Find A Grave.

Paul, James Winston
Born: June 8, 1861, Kentucky. Died: May 1, 1929. Married: Mary Jane Scott, 1881. Father: Alex Paul. Mother: Nancy Paulley. Source: Ancestry.com.

Paul, Mary Jane
Born: December 19, 1855, Kentucky. Died: January 8, 1929, Van Zandt County, Texas. Married: James Winston Paul, 1881. Father: Watson Scott. Mother: Harriet Scott. Sources: Death Certificate, 1870 U. S. Census.

Payne Ruth
Born: January 14, 1898, Van Zandt County, Texas. Died: September 21, 1941, Hopkins County, Texas. Cause of death: Heart disease. Married: William Leroy Payne. Father: Kasper George Griser, Germany. Mother: Gussie May Mullins, Alabama. Source: Death Certificate.

Josephine "Josie" Penny *William Robert "Billy" Phillips*

PAYNE, WILLIAM LEROY
Born: September 21, 1897. Died: October 12, 1946. Married: Ruth Griser. Father: Roscoe Miller Payne. Mother: Lula Ellen Holt. Source: Ancestry.com.

PEACE, ADA
Born: 1857. Died: 1918. Married: J. A. Peace, December 17, 1874. Father: J. R. Higginbotham. Mother: Elizabeth Abigail Dulaney. Source: *Canton Herald*, June 14, 1918.

PEACE, CLYDE AUGUSTA
Born: May 21, 1881, Texas. Died: April 19, 1959, Van Zandt County, Texas. Cause of death: Stroke. Married: Fannie Starnes, 1902. Children: James, Ada Lou, Nancy Ann, Mary Virginia, Kathryn, Marion, Margaret, and Little Clyde. Father: J. A. Peace. Mother: Ada Higginbotham. Occupations: Blacksmith, garage owner. Comments: The Peace family were early Van Zandt County settlers. In November of 1885, J. A. Peace bought the blacksmith and wagon shop on the southwest corner of the Canton square from W. H. Ballard. The Peace family has been a part of the Canton business community for over 130 years. Members of the family also owned various other businesses such as saloons and hotels in Canton and Wills Point. Their remaining business is the Peace Pharmacy in Canton which occupies part of the original property. Sources: Death Certificate; Sylvia Rodriquez, Peace Family historian.

PEACE, ETTIE L.
Born: August 14, 1884. Died: August 14, 1884. Father: Nathaniel Ennis Vinson Peace, Jr. Mother: Romilda Tull. Source: Tombstone.

PEACE, EVERETT
Born: April 14, 1887. Died: September 23, 1887. Father: Nathaniel Ennis Vinson Peace, Jr. Mother: Romilda Tull. Comments: Everett Peace's father is buried in White Rose Cemetery in *Wills Point*, Texas. Source: Tombstone.

PEACE, FANNIE
Born: July 1, 1885, Texas. Died: February 8, 1971, Henderson County, Texas. Cause of death: Paralysis. Married: Clyde A. Peace, 1902. Children: James, Ada Lou, Nancy Ann, Mary Virginia, Kathryn, Marion, Margaret, and Little Clyde. Father: John A. Starnes. Mother: Nancy Ann Orsborn. Sources: Death Certificate; *Canton Herald*, February 11, 1971.

PEACE, LITTLE CLYDE
Born: October 23, 1905. Died: September, 1906. Father: Clyde A. Peace. Mother: Fannie Starnes. Source: Tombstone.

PENNY, INFANT TWIN 1
Born: September 27, 1903. Died: September 27, 1903. Father: Samuel Barney Penny. Mother: Josephine (Josie) Branson. Comments: Mother and twins died in childbirth. Source: Mother's tombstone.

PENNY, INFANT TWIN 2
Born: September 27, 1903. Died: September 27, 1903. Father: Samuel Barney Penny. Mother: Josephine (Josie) Branson. Comments: Mother and twins died in childbirth. Source: Mother's tombstone.

PENNY, JOSEPHINE "JOSIE"
Born: November 10, 1881, Van Zandt County, Texas. Died: September 27, 1903, Van Zandt County, Texas. Cause of death: Childbirth complications. Married: Samuel Barney Penny, November 6, 1900. Father: James B. Branson, Kentucky. Mother: Dora Alice Bell, Texas. Siblings: William, Jim, Nettie, Wesley B., Hattie May, Bertha, and Ida Rebecca. Comments: Josie Branson and Sam Penny went to Wills Point to get married. Elder W. A. Neal married them while they were sitting in their buggy. After Josie's death, her husband left Texas and joined the Army. He later married Hattie May Rainwater and moved to Oregon. Sam died August 4, 1941 and is buried in Ereka Cemetery and Mausoleum, Newport, Lincoln County, Oregon. Josie's father, mother, sister, and brother are buried at Hillcrest. Sources: *Wills Point Chronicle*, November 8, 1900 and October 15, 1903; Find A Grave.

PERRY, BAKE
Born: May 12, 1845, Alabama. Died: April 23, 1911, Van Zandt County, Texas. Married: Sarah Jane McClellan, February 2, 1869, Alabama. Children: Ida May, Howard, Dora Effie, and Anna Blanche. Occupation: Farmer, cotton gin owner. Comments: The Perry's came into Texas sometime after the Civil War; and by 1876, Bake Perry was in Van Zandt County. He built his house there,

Jessie James "Jim" Rascoe and June Julia Rascoe

Eva Jewell Ratzlaff *Maudella Rice*

farmed, and raised his children. In 1889, he bought 100 acres of land and moved near Canton. He also owned a horse-drawn cotton gin. Sources: *Van Zandt County Texas History Book, Vol 1*; *Grand Saline Sun*, April 20, 1911; Ancestry.com.

PERRY, HOWARD CARNELUS
Born: August 26, 1897, Tennessee. Died: July 2, 1964, Van Zandt County, Texas. Cause of death: Heart disease. Married: Unknown. Child: Lottie Fay. Father: Sam Perry. Mother: Lizzie Malone. Occupation: Produce dealer. Military: WWI, PVT C0. D 168 Inf. Sources: Death Certificate; *Canton Herald*, July 9, 1964.

PERRY, SARAH JANE
Born: August 20, 1848, Alabama. Died: December 30, 1941, Van Zandt County, Texas. Married: Bake Perry, February 2, 1869. Children: Howard, Ida May, Dora Effie, and Anna Blanche. Father: Robert McClellen, Alabama. Mother: Elizabeth Knox, Alabama. Sources: Death Certificate; *Van Zandt County Texas History Book Vol. 1*; Hilliard Funeral Home records.

PETTY, NANCY ALICE
Born: April 27, 1864, Van Zandt County, Texas. Died: January 14, 1930, Dallas County, Texas. Cause of death: Bright's disease. Married: S. Jefferson Petty, February 26, 1893. Father: Richard Williams, Tennessee. Mother: Rebecca Christman, Mississippi. Sources: Death Certificate; *Marriage Records Van Zandt County, Texas, 1848-1909*; *Canton Herald*, January 17, 1930.

PETTY, S. JEFFERSON "JEFF"
Born: January 10, 1860. Died: May 16, 1916. Married: Nancy Alice Williams, February 26, 1893. Child: Nona. Father: William Petty. Mother: Elizabeth Petty. Comments: J. S. Petty moved to Canton from Smith County in 1884 and lived there until his death. He was a deacon of the Canton Baptist Church and a Mason. Sources: 1870 U. S. Census; *Canton Herald*, May 19, 1916; Ancestry.com.

PETTY, SARAH E.
Born: June, 1844. Died: October 8, 1896. Married: W. F. Petty. Father: Unknown. Mother: Unknown. Comments: After Sarah Petty's death, her husband married Mrs. Mattie Sands, August 31, 1902. Source: Tombstone, *Marriage Records of Van Zandt County, 1848-1909.*

PETTY, VELMA R.
Born: January 7, 1894. Died: June 25, 1896. Father: S. Jefferson Petty. Mother: Nancy Alice Williams. Source: Tombstone.

PHILLIPS, ALICE "ALLIE"
Born: 1873 (Tombstone date is incorrect.) Died: March 9, 1920, Van Zandt County, Texas. Cause of death: Influenza. Married: (1) Moses Claybourne Bateman, November 3, 1891. Divorced: November 18, 1892. (2) John W. Phillips, January 4, 1893. Children: Vernon Lee Chaney, Rosa, Bertha Lee, Dora M., Ida Estell, William Walter, John Henry, Lovie, Orville, James Edward, and J. B. Father: Thomas W. Chaney. Mother: Mary M. McClellen. Sources: Death Certificate; *Divorce Records of Van Zandt*

County; Kitty Wheeler, Chaney Family historian; Find A Grave.

PHILLIPS, HENRY LEE
Born: July 21, 1930, Van Zandt County, Texas. Died: December 20, 1940, Kaufman County, Texas. Cause of death: Pneumonia. Father: John Henry Phillips. Mother: Maudie Lee Thompson. Siblings: Horace Ben and Ella Ruth. Source: Hilliard Funeral Home records.

PHILLIPS, INFANT SON
Born: March 26, 1960. Died: March 26, 1960. Father: William Robert Phillips. Mother: Elizabeth Ann Rasco. Source: Hilliard Funeral Home records.

PHILLIPS, JOHN HENRY "BOOSE"
Born: March 28, 1905. Died: October 21, 1969. Married: Maudie Lee Thompson, January 2, 1926. Children: Horace Ben, Henry Lee, and Ella Ruth. Father: John Walter Phillips. Mother: Alice Chaney Bateman. Siblings: Bertha, Dora M., Ida Estell, Walter William "Buck," Vernon Lee Chaney, Orville, James Edward, and J.B. Source: Ancestry.com.

PHILLIPS, JOHN WALTER
Born: June 20, 1869, Alabama. Died: August 30, 1938, Van Zandt County, Texas. Cause of death: Bright's disease. Married: (1) Alice Chaney Bateman, January 4, 1893. Children: Rosy, Bertha, Dora S., Ada Estell, Walter William "Buck," John Henry "Boose," Lovie, Orville, James Edward, and J.B. (2) Mrs. Maggie L. Ballow (Blue) Davenport Treadway, April 3, 1923. Father: John William Phillips. Mother: Edna Hunt. Occupation: Farmer. Sources: Death Certificate; *Canton Herald*, September 1, 1938; Kitty Wheeler, Chaney Family historian.

PHILLIPS, MAUDIE LEE
Born: June 28, 1906, Mississippi. Died: December 24, 1976, Van Zandt County, Texas. Cause of death: Heart disease. Married: John Henry Phillips, January 2, 1926. Children: Henry Lee, Ella Ruth, and Horace Ben. Father: Doyle Thompson. Mother: Annie Belle Prichard. Sources: Death Certificate; 1930 U. S. Census; *Canton Herald*, January 6, 1977.

PHILLIPS, WILLIAM ROBERT "BILLY"
(Photo page 107) Born: July 18, 1935, Montgomery County, Arkansas. Died: February 17, 2013, Van Zandt County, Texas. Married: Elizabeth Ann Rasco. Children: William Robert II, Jillinda, and Infant Son. Father: Lee Roy Diffie. Mother: Minnie Lee Johnson Phillips. Occupation: Truck driver. Military: Korea, U. S. Army, SPC, Disabled veteran. Comments: Billy Phillips drove a truck for thirty-seven years covering three million miles without an accident or a ticket. He drove the last twenty-one years for Texas Oklahoma Express. He was a truck rodeo champion with many trophies. Source: *Van Zandt News*, February 24, 2013.

PICKENS, JARVIS EUGENE
Born: January 6, 1954, Van Zandt Co., Texas. Died: May 12, 2017, Tyler, Texas. Never married. Father: Jarvis Lee Pickens. Mother: Nettie LaVesta Potts. Siblings: Charles, Eddie Wayne, Barry, Eric, Carol, Janice, Sharon Loresa, Rita, and LaVesta. Source: Eubank Funeral Home records.

PITTMAN, JOHN M.
Born: March 16, 1879, Kentucky. Died: July 3, 1943, Van Zandt County, Texas. Married: Maggie Waldon, November 4, 1906. Father: Newton W. Pittman, Kentucky. Mother: Sarah Ellen Scott, Texas. Occupation: Farmer. Sources: Death Certificate, Ancestry.com.

PITTMAN, SARAH E.
Born: November 13, 1861. Died: February 17, 1929. Married: Newton W. Pittman. Father: Henry C. Scott. Mother: Mary Scott. Source: Ancestry.com.

PRESTLEY, RUFUS
Born: August 18, 1888. Died: April 9, 1937. Married: Linnie Prestley. Father: J. S. Prestley. Mother: Ann Mathes. Military: WWI, TX Pvt. 1st Bn. 165 Depot Brigade. Source: Eubank Funeral Home records.

PRIER, MARGARET
Born: ca. 1811. Died: November 7, 1889. Married: Unknown Prier. Children: William C. Father: Unknown. Mother: Unknown. Source: Tombstone.

PRIER, MARY A.
Born: September 9, 1842, Alabama. Died: February 16, 1923, Van Zandt County, Texas. Married: William C. Prier, December 31, 1858, Rusk County, Texas. Father: Unknown Edington. Mother: Unknown. Comments: The *Wills Point Chronicle* reported Mary Prier's death as follows: "Mrs. Prior was born in Alabama September 9, 1842, and came to Texas in the early 1850s with her parents, who settled in Rusk County. She was married to Wm. C. Prior December 31, 1858, both moving to Van Zandt County soon after the Civil War, locating in the Moore community, six miles east of Canton. They moved to Myrtle Springs in 1893, where each resided until death, the husband dying November 21, 1909. She is survived by one sister, Mrs. N. A. Ledbetter, who has made her home with deceased for the past eight or ten years. Two nephews also are living, J. O. Edington of Grapeland, Texas and Harvey Thompson." Mary assisted her husband in the mercantile business in Myrtle Springs. Source: *Wills Point Chronicle*, February 22, 1923.

PRIER, WILLIAM CATS
Born: January 1, 1836, Mississippi. Died: November 21, 1909, Van Zandt County, Texas. Married: Mary A. Edington, December 20, 1858, Rusk County, Texas. Father: Unknown Prier. Mother: Mary A. Unknown. Occupation; Mercantile businessman. Military: CSA, Company F., 17th Texas Cavalry, Wounded in War. Comments: W. C. Prier and his family came to Texas in 1852 and settled in Rusk County near Henderson. In 1885, he moved to Van Zandt County and resided five miles east of Canton. In 1893, he moved to Myrtle Springs and embarked in the mercantile business, which he conducted until his death. The *Wills Point Chronicle* reported his death as follows: "DIED WHILE PRAYING. Sunday morning at 11:30 o'clock, W. C. Prier of Myrtle Springs died suddenly from heart failure while leading prayer at the Blue Springs Baptist Church. Mr. Prior had been in bad health for some time but appeared to be in as good spirits as usual Sunday morning when he drove to the church at Blue Springs of which he is a member, for the regular Sunday services. After a prayer and a song, Mr. Prier was engaged in the second prayer of the services when he fell over in the arms of S. M. Wright, who was near, and almost immediately expired. The only surviving relative is his aged widow." Source: *Wills Point Chronicle,* November 25, 1909.

PRIESLEY, INFANT
Born: February 13, 1880. Died: February 13, 1880. Father: J. S. Priesley. Mother: Ann Mathes. Source: Tombstone.

PRIESLEY, J.S.
Born: December 29, 1851 (a slave). Died: March 10, 1891. Married: Ann Mathes, March 4, 1877. Comments: J. S. Priesley was born a slave. His parents are not known. His wife was the daughter of Tom Mathes, one of the original settlers of the Wynne Community adjacent to Canton, Texas. She married Edmond Wynne May 10, 1896 as his third wife. Edmond Wynne was the namesake of the Wynne community. Ann died June 24, 1930. Sources: *Marriage Records 1848-1909 Van Zandt County*; Vanessa Scott, Wynne Community historian.

PRUIETT, MYRTLE DELILAH
Born: July 29, 1911, Van Zandt County, Texas. Died: February 13, 1950, Dallas County, Texas. Cause of death: Gangrene. Married: Walter Pruiett, June 28, 1924. Father: Edward Wilson Driver. Mother: Mary William Azie. Sources: Death Certificate; *The Dallas Morning News*, February 16, 1950; Eubank Funeral Home records.

PURKEY, LILLIE BELLE
Born: August 28, 1920, Van Zandt County, Texas. Died: February 25, 1990, Smith County, Texas. Married Unknown Purkey. Father: John E. Brewer. Mother: Lelia B. Mack. Occupation: Vocational nurse. Comments: Lillie Belle Purkey's death was reported in the *Van Zandt News* as follows: "She was born August 28, 1920 at Canton. She was a member of the Bethel Pentecostal Church in Dallas. She was a retired vocational nurse who spent most of her life in the Canton and Dallas areas. Survivors include three brothers, William G. Brewer, Mineola, Lee G. Brewer, Fort Worth, G. W. Brewer, Warrington, Oregon." Sources: 1930 U. S. Census; *Van Zandt News*, March 4, 1990.

PYRON, ELIZABETH ANN
Born: February 9, 1835, Lowndes County, Mississippi. Died: July 15, 1890, Van Zandt County, Texas. Married: Eli Pyron, ca 1855. Child: Elizabeth Candress. Father: Allen Dowdle. Mother: Elizabeth Love. Comments: Annie Pyron's husband joined the Confederate Army and served as a Private. He was killed at the Battle of Stones River, Murfreesboro, Tennessee. In the mid 1880's, the Pyrons, Robinsons and Dowdles families moved to Van Zandt County; and the Pyrons and Dowdles settled in the Walton Community. Before 1890 the Pryron's and Dowdles families moved to Canton and lived in the C. A. Wortham Hotel. The hotel was owned by Charles Allen Wortham who had married Elizabeth Candress Pyron prior to moving to Texas. Annie died shortly after moving to Canton. Sources: Ancestry.com; "Some Foster/

RANDALL ELIJAH RICHARDS *received his Bachelor's and Master's degrees from East Texas State Teachers College in Commerce, Texas, and spent twenty-four years in the teaching profession, including seventeen years in Van Zandt County. In addition to teaching in the classroom, Richards served as a football coach, high-school principal, and superintendent.*

Dowdle/Mills Family Memories" by Jean Foster Dove Published in *Our Heritage*, February, 1992.

R

RAGLIN, BABY
Born: Unknown. Died: 1955. Father: Unknown Raglin. Mother: Unknown. Source: Tombstone.

RASCO, ALTON M. "JACK"
Born: October 15, 1913, Van Zandt County, Texas. Died: November 24, 1995, Van Zandt County, Texas. Married: Minnie Belle Tull, August 12, 1935. Child: Elizabeth. Father: Jessie Frank Rasco. Mother: Mary Elizabeth Todd. Occupation: Director of Transportation Canton Public Schools forty-two years; volunteer fireman for Canton Fire Department sixty-five years; Plaza Theater Canton, Texas part-time for forty-six years. Source: Elizabeth Rasco Phillips, Rasco Family historian.

RASCO, FRANK MONROE
Born: March 27, 1884. Died: December 1, 1946. Married: Mary Elizabeth Todd, June 20, 1906. Children: Mrs. Lloyd Groves, Alton, and Mrs. Fred Callahan. Father: Jessie Frank Rasco. Mother: Mattie D. Willis. Occupation: Canton businessman. Sources: *Canton Herald*, December 5, 1946; *Wills Point Chronicle*, December 6, 1946; Hilliard Funeral Home records.

RASCO, MARY ELIZABETH "LIZZIE"
Born: November 1, 1887, Van Zandt County, Texas. Died: October 10, 1975, Van Zandt County, Texas. Cause of death: Natural causes. Married: Frank Monroe Rasco, June 20, 1906. Father: Charlie S. Todd. Mother: Tennessee "Ginnie" Jeter. Source: Death Certificate.

RASCO, MINNIE BELL
Born: July 5, 1917. Died: August 9, 2005. Married: Alton M. "Jack" Rasco, August 12, 1935. Child: Elizabeth. Father: Benjamin Franklin Tull. Mother: Willie Bell Green. Source: Elizabeth Rasco Phillips, Rasco Family historian.

RASCOE, JESSIE JAMES "JIM" "DADDY JIM"
(Photo page 108) Born: April 22, 1882. Died: July 7, 1933, Smith County, Texas. Cause of death: Automobile accident. Married: June Julia Oakley, December 24, 1900.

Daniel D. Richardson and a Socialist encampment held on his land in Van Zandt County.

***DANIEL D. RICHARDSON** and his family came to Van Zandt County in 1869, settling in Corinth. Later, the family moved to a Socialist Community adjacent to Grand Saline, where the Texas Socialist Party was headquartered. Some of the largest Socialist encampments in the United States were later held at a park owned by Richardson. He was a farmer but also was involved in the mill and gin business for twelve years. In 1898, he was ordained as a Baptist minister and spent eighteen years in pastoral work in Van Zandt County. In 1933, Richardson was elected to the Texas Legislature as a Democrat and served two terms.*

Bird Riley and David Thompson "Tom" Riley *played a significant role in the commerce of Canton in the twentieth century.* **Bird Riley** *was the first woman in Van Zandt County to become a Registered Pharmacist and work in that profession, receiving her A.B. degree with Highest Honors from Patton Seminary in Dallas, Texas. Five years after beginning her pharmacy career, she ran for the office of County Clerk of Van Zandt County, the first woman to seek a public office in the county. In 1911, she formed the Riley-Richardson Dry Goods Company with* **Tom Riley**, *whom she married two years later. The Riley-Richardson Dry Goods Company was in business for more than sixty years at the same location on the Canton square.*

David Thompson "Tom" Riley

Child: Eva Jim. Father: Jessie Frank Rascoe. Mother: Mattie D. Willis. Comments: Jim Rascoe was fatally injured when the truck he was driving collided with a Pierce Arrow driven by Pete P. Hoffman, a Tyler oil man on the Dixie Highway (Highway 64). Jim was carrying about 1,000 gallons of gasoline which pinned him to the dash of his truck. He was taken to a hospital in Tyler where he died. Jim was extremely well liked. He had spent most of his life in Canton, and the funeral was attended by an overflow crowd at the church. Sources: *Canton Herald*, July 1933; Elizabeth Rasco Phillips, Rasco Family historian.

Rascoe, June Julia Oakley
(Photo page 108) Born: January 17, 1886, Fulton County, Georgia. Died: February 10, 1971, Van Zandt County, Texas. Married: Jessie James "Jim" Rascoe, December 24, 1900. Child: Eva Jim. Father: John Dennis Christopher Oakley. Mother: Martha A. Hobbs. Source: Ancestry.com.

Ratzlaff, Eva Jewell Green
(Photo page 108) Born: January 8, 1923, Cherokee County, Texas. Died: June 30, 2010, Travis County, Texas. Married: (1) Wilbur Johnson. Children: David Keith, Craig Steven, and Wilbur Doyle. (2) Vernon Ratzlaff. Father: John Wesley Green. Mother: Mattie Victoria Terrell. Occupation: Legal secretary. Comments: Jewell Ratzlaff was reared in Corsicana, Texas and worked as a legal secretary until her retirement in 1983. Jewell's sister, Cathaleen Hilliard, is also buried in Hillcrest Cemetery. Source: *Van Zandt News*, July 11, 2010.

Ray, William J.
Born: December 5, 1860, Tennessee. Died: September 7, 1902, Van Zandt County, Texas. Married: Elizabeth Unknown, 1887. Children: Barton L., Katie, Arthur, Nancy, and Elizabeth M. Father: George W. Ray, Illinois. Mother: Nancy S. Ray, Tennessee. Sources: 1880, 1900 U. S. Census.

Read, Lennis H.
Born: September 22, 1886. Died: March 8, 1917. Father: Unknown Read. Mother: Unknown. Source: Tombstone.

Redmon, Harold
Born: June 29, 1911, Missouri. Died: June 7, 1979, Dallas County, Texas. Cause of death: Cancer. Married: Mary Katherine Unknown. Father: Frederick E. Redmon. Mother: Grace D. Freemeyer. Occupation: Correctional officer, Federal Prison, Missouri. Military: WWII, Captain US Army. Source: Death Certificate.

Reese, Infant Son
Born: July 16, 1894. Died: July 16, 1894. Father: F. Jeff Reese. Mother: Mary E. Thompson. Source: Tombstone.

David Love Riley, Jr. *worked as a farmer before being appointed Sheriff of Van Zandt County in 1871. He moved to Canton in 1878 where he opened a drugstore and then, after selling the drugstore, a general merchandise store, D.L. Riley, Co. When his son joined him in the business, they changed the name to D.L. Riley & Son. He operated a business in Canton for thirty-one years, and it was the second oldest firm in Canton when it was sold. In addition to his business and farming operations, he was appointed Postmaster at Canton in 1878, serving four years under the administration of President Rutherford B. Hayes. Riley was so beloved in the community that all stores, businesses, and public schools were closed for his funeral.*

Reese, Infant Son
Born: 1895. Died: 1895. Father: F. Jeff Reese. Mother: Mary E. Thompson. Source: Tombstone.

Reese, Mary E.
Born: November 1, 1872. Died: November 10, 1895. Married: F. Jeff Reece, November 15, 1893. Father: William D. Thompson. Mother: Leah E. Walters. Sources: Tombstone; *Marriage Records Van Zandt County, Texas 1848-1909*; *Wills Point Chronicle,* November 14, 1895; Ancestry.com.

Reese, Walter
Born: February 3, 1886. Died: August 19, 1889. Father: William Reese. Mother: Sallie Riley. Comments: At Walter Reese's death the *Canton Telephone* published the following: "In memory of Little Walter Reese. Dear little Walter is gone to rest, To reign with God forever blest; His little tongue will always praise, A Saviors love, redeeming grace. Far from a world of sin and strife, He now enjoys a heavenly life." Sources: *Canton Telephone,* August 23, 1889; Tombstone.

Reid, F. Z.
Born: August 12, 1866. Died: September 8, 1894. Father: Unknown Reid. Mother: Unknown. Source: Tombstone.

Reid, Luvena A.
Born: August 12, 1866. Died: September 8, 1891. Father: Unknown Reid. Mother: Unknown. Source: Tombstone.

Reid, Unknown
Born: March 28, 1841. Died: August 13, 1907. Comments: Tombstone is broken. Source: Tombstone.

Rhodes, Agatha Mae
Born: March 24, 1912, Texas. Died: March 24, 1983, Van Zandt County, Texas. Married: (1) Earl Clinton Chapman. Died: June 27, 1944. (2) Unknown Rhodes. Father: Jessie Hickman Moody. Mother: Ellen Levina Cummings. Sources: 1930 U. S. Census, Texas Death Index, Ancestry.com.

Rice, Maudella
(Photo page 108) Born: June 15, 1896, Van Zandt County, Texas. Died: June 2, 1969, Van Zandt County, Texas. Married: Archie Blaine Rice. Father: Walter Smith. Mother: Lannie Bell Wynne. Siblings: Henry Hawthorn, Leta Bell, Zeffie Telaska, Nona Ethelene, and Elvis Franklin. Source: Vanessa Scott, Wynne Community historian.

Richards, Randall Elijah
Born: August 5, 1910, Van Zandt County, Texas. Died: April 4, 1952, Van Zandt County, Texas. Cause of death: Heart disease. Married: Ruby Norene Groves, May 17, 1932. Father: G. B. Richards. Mother: Corrie Hubbard. Occupation: School teacher, principal, superintendent. Comments: Randall Richards graduated from Wills Point High School and received his BS and MS degrees from East Texas State Teachers College in Commerce, Texas. He spent twenty-four years in the teaching profession with seventeen of those years in Van Zandt County. Randall was the high school principal and football coach in Wills Point. He then moved to Dangerfield, Texas where he was high school principal 1945-46 and then superintendent until his death in 1952. Sources: Death Certificate; *Canton Herald*, April 17, 1952.

Richards, Ruby Norene "Nonnie"
Born: May 31, 1912, Van Zandt County, Texas. Died: August 30, 2003, Montgomery County, Texas. Married:

Claude Franklin Riley and Lina Hardy Riley

(1) Randall E. Richards, May 17, 1932. (2) Tom McGill. Father: Carlos Alonzo Groves. Mother: Ida Mae Beard. Source: Eubank Funeral Home records.

Richardson, Daniel D.

(photo page 111) Born: December 11, 1859, Rockdale County, Georgia. Died: December 17, 1942, Van Zandt County, Texas. Married: Emily "Emma" Belsora Rose, June 8, 1882. Children: Eva Gladys, Maggie M., and Zeola Cloe. Father: James B Richardson, South Carolina. Mother: Lucretia E. New. Siblings: E. L., Luvina Luce, and Emma Jane. Occupation: Farmer, ginner, Baptist minister, State Representative. Comments: Dan Richardson and his family came to Van Zandt County in 1869. They settled in the Corinth community south of Grand Saline. Later, the family moved to Rhodesburg, a Socialist community, adjacent to Grand Saline, Texas. Politically, Dan was a Socialist. The headquarters for the Texas Socialist Party was located in Grand Saline. Some of the largest Socialist encampments in the United States were held at Richardson Park which was owned by Dan. He was a farmer, but also engaged in the mill and gin business for twelve years. In 1898, he was ordained as a Baptist minister and spent eighteen years in pastoral work in Van Zandt County. In 1933, Dan was elected to the Texas Legislature as a Democrat and served two terms. His last years were spent living with his daughter, Gladys, and son-in-law, George Homer Hilliard, in Canton. Sources: *The Southland, 1903*; *Van Zandt County Texas Biographies, 1848-1991*; *Canton Herald*, December 24, 1942; Hilliard Funeral Home records.

Richardson, Elisha Levi "Lit"

Born: July 10, 1848, Rockdale County, Georgia. Died: June 16, 1910, Van Zandt County, Texas. Married: Mary Eliza Powell, September 23, 1879. Children: Bird, Carrie, and Maurice. Father: James B. Richardson, South Carolina. Mother: Lucretia E. New. Occupation: School teacher, druggist, County Clerk 1893-1894. Comments: Lit Richardson and his wife moved to Canton in 1892 from Martin's Mill. They built a house on Buffalo Street where they lived for many years. His daughters married brothers. Bird married Tom Riley, and Carrie married his brother, Jay. Both were sons of D. L. Riley, an early-day Sheriff of Van Zandt County and a prominent Canton businessman. Sources: *Van Zandt County, Texas Biographies 1848-1991*; *Grand Saline Sun*, June 23, 1910.

Richardson, Emily Belsora "Emma"

Born: October 21, 1855, Tennessee. Died: May 17, 1943, Van Zandt County, Texas. Married: Daniel D. Richardson, June 8, 1882. Children: Eva Gladys, Maggie M., and Zeola Cloe. Father: Milo G. Rose, North Carolina. Mother: Margaret J. Lock. Comments: Dan and Emma Richardson had three children. Maggie died young, Zeola Cloe was burned to death at the age of 16, and Eva Gladys married George Homer Hilliard. Sources: Hilliard Funeral Home records, Rose Family Bible.

Richardson, Mary Elizabeth "Eliza"

Born: March 12, 1852, Carroll County, Alabama. Died: June 7, 1925, Van Zandt County, Texas. Married: Elisha Levi "Lit" Richardson, September 23, 1879. Children: Bird, Carrie, and Maurice. Father: James Jackson Powell, North Carolina. Mother: Amelia Corley. Comments: Mary Richardson came to Van Zandt County in 1875. She was from a family of ten children. She outlived all of her siblings with the exception of one brother, William O. Powell. Sources: 1860 U S. Census; *Wills Point Chronicle*, June 18, 1925; Ancestry.com.

Riley, Bird Richardson

Born: October 22, 1882, Van Zandt County, Texas. Died: September 5, 1968, Van Zandt County, Texas. Cause of death: Automobile accident. Married: David Thompson "Tom" Riley, April 28, 1913. Father: Elisha L. Richardson. Mother: Mary Elizabeth Powell. Occupation: Registered Pharmacist, Partner in Riley-Richardson Dry Goods Store. Comments: Bird Riley attended local schools. In 1902 she graduated from Patton Seminary in Dallas, Texas. She received an A. B. Degree with Highest Honors. She was the first woman in Van Zandt County to become a Registered Pharmacist and to work in that profession. In April of 1908, after working as a pharmacist for five years, she entered politics by running for the office of County Clerk of Van Zandt County—the first female to seek a public office in the county. On October 6, 1911, Bird and Tom Riley formed the Riley-Richardson Dry Goods Company partnership, operating a dry goods store on the north side of the Canton square. Two years later they were married. In 1892, the Richardson family built a frame house on Buffalo Street in Canton. In 1910 Bird's father died; and by 1925, her mother had died leaving the home place to her. Bird and Tom had the old house demolished in 1926 and built one of the most modern homes in Canton. The house remains today, but is no longer owned by the Riley family. On September 5, 1968, the car in which Bird was riding was involved in a collision with a truck about five miles west of Wills Point; and she was killed at the age of 86. Sources: *Grand Saline Sun*, April 2, 1908 and November 16, 1911; *Wills Point Chronicle*, May 1, 1913; *Canton Herald*, October 3, 1968 and May 2, 1970; "The Red Brick House," by Martha Heard, a member of the Van Zandt County Genealogical Society.

RILEY, CHARLES PENDLETON "CHARLIE"
Born: November 12, 1887, Van Zandt County, Texas. Died: July 20, 1970, Dallas County, Texas. Married: Elizabeth Murrie. Father: David Love Riley, Jr. Mother: Nannie Arabella Thompson. Comments: Charlie Riley worked at Higginbotham Bailey Company, Dallas, Texas for thirty years. Military: WWI, US Army Medical Corps. Source: Eubank Funeral Home records.

RILEY, CLAUDE FRANKLIN
Born: April 5, 1872, Van Zandt County, Texas. Died: May 15, 1965, Van Zandt County, Texas. Cause of death: Pneumonia. Married: Lina Hardy Neilson, April 8, 1896. Father: David Love Riley, Jr. Mother: Mary Colon Hobbs. Siblings: Belle, James T., Lydia, Jessie, Mary Daisy, David Thompson, and Jay Holt. Occupation: Postmaster of Canton, Texas. Canton businessman, farmer. Comments: Claude F. Riley graduated from Canton High School. After graduation, he worked in his father's mercantile business in Canton. In 1905 he became an insurance agent. In 1908 he moved to Dallas and worked in the insurance business until 1912. Then he moved back to Canton. From 1912-1923, he was a farmer and cattleman. He was appointed Postmaster of the Canton Post Office in 1923 and continued in that position until his retirement in 1942. He was a deacon in the First Baptist Church of Canton for seventy-one years. Sources: Death Certificate; *Texas Under Many Flags*; *Canton Herald*, May 20, 1865.

Lydia Colon Riley *Mary Daisy Riley*

RILEY, CORRIE RICHARDSON
Born: September 10, 1887, Van Zandt County, Texas. Died: November 15, 1977, Smith County, Texas. Married: Jay Holt Riley. Father: E. L. "Lit" Richardson. Mother: Elizabeth Ann Powell. Comments: Corrie Riley and her sister, Bird, married brothers Tom and Jay Riley. Source: Eubank Funeral Home records.

RILEY, DAVID LOVE, JR.
(Photo page113) Born: July 27, 1846, Talladega County, Alabama. Died: October 2, 1921, Van Zandt County, Texas. Married: (1) Mary C. Hobbs, August 26, 1866. Mary died September 11, 1879. Children: James T., Jessie Love, Mary Daisy, Claude Franklin, California Belle, Lydia, and Mrs. C. H. Matthews. (2) Nannie Thompson, October 31, 1880. Nannie Thompson Riley died October 9, 1905. Children: David Thomas, Jay H., Love, Charles, Mamie, and Russell Steele. Father: David Love Riley, Sr. "Love." Mother: Mary Colon Sides. Occupation: Farmer, County Sheriff, drugstore owner, merchant, Postmaster. Military: CSA, Pvt. 33rd Texas Cavalry. Co. B. Comments: David Love Riley's family came to Van Zandt County and settled in the Cream Level community near Martin's Mill on November 26, 1850. He attended private subscription schools. After the Civil War, he returned to the farm at Martin's Mill. In 1871, he was appointed Sheriff of Van Zandt County and served two years. In 1878, he moved to Canton and opened a drugstore. He sold the drugstore in 1880 and opened a general merchandise store operating as D. L. Riley Co. This business was one of the more successful in Van Zandt County during that era, with a volume of over $50,000 per year. His son joined him in the business and they operated as D. L. Riley & Son. In 1909, they sold their merchandise stock to M. D. Hale. (There is some confusion here about the business as reported in different dated news reports. The March 29, 1906 edition of the *Wills Point Chronicle* reported that the D. L. Riley Co. failed March 27, 1906 and filed a Deed of Trust in the County Clerk's office naming J. T. Todd as assignee with liabilities of $11, 535.) David had operated a business in Canton for thirty-one years, and it was the second oldest firm in Canton when it was sold. In addition to his business and farming operations, David was appointed Postmaster at Canton in 1878 and served four years under the administration of President Rutherford B. Hayes. After his business career, he moved back to his farm and lived there until his death. As a show of respect, all stores, businesses, and the public schools were closed for his funeral. Sources: *Canton Telephone*, August 14, 1891; *The Southland*; *Wills Point Chronicle*, March 29,

George Edward "Ed" Rosinbaum *was a lawyer elected Van Zandt County Attorney at age 26. He served one term in that position. Over the next few years, for reasons that were never clear, an animosity developed between him and fellow Canton townsman and saloon owner Isaac Henry Smelser. One night, a fight broke out between the two. Smelser fought with a whiskey bottle and baseball bat, getting the best of Rosinbaum, who left the bar mortified and telling his friends he wanted to kill Smelser. Aware of these threats, Smelser was prepared and shot Rosinbaum dead when he came after Smelser on the afternoon of February 8, 1889. Ten months later, Smelser went on trial. The jury deliberated for seven minutes before aquitting Smelser of murder.*

1906 and October 13, 1921; *Grand Saline Sun*, March 3, 1910; *Canton Herald*, October 1921.

Riley, David Thompson "Tom"
(Photo page 112) Born: July 31, 1881, Van Zandt County, Texas. Died: April 26, 1970, Van Zandt Count, Texas. Married: Bird Richardson, April 28, 1913. Father: David Love Riley, Jr. Mother: Nannie A. Thompson. Occupation: Mercantile store owner. Comments: Early in his career Tom Riley worked for his father in D. L. Riley & Son, a dry goods and general merchandise store in Canton. On October 6, 1911, Tom Riley and Bird Richardson, a local pharmacist, bought the stock of general merchandise from J. C. Marney. They continued to operate a dry goods business at the same location as Marney on the north side of the Canton Square. They named the business Riley-Richardson Dry Goods Company. In 1913, Tom and Bird were married at her uncle, Rev. D. D. Richardson's, home near Grand Saline, Texas. The Riley-Richardson Dry Goods Company was in business for more than sixty years at the same location on the Canton square. Sources: *Grand Saline Sun*, January 12, 1911 and November 16, 1911; *Wills Point Chronicle*, May 1, 1913; *Canton Herald*, May 2, 1970; Eubank Funeral Home records.

Riley, Elizabeth
Born: August 15, 1892, Hopkins County, Texas. Died: May 30, 1984, Dallas County, Texas. Married: Charles P. Riley. Father: Charles L. Murrie. Mother: Jennie Murrie. Occupation: School teacher. Comments: Elizabeth Riley taught school in Sulphur Springs and Greenville, Texas. She moved to Dallas in 1936 and lived there until her death. Source: *Van Zandt News*, June 3, 1984.

Riley, Infant Son
Born: Unknown. Died: Unknown. Father: David Love Riley, Jr. Mother: Mary C. Hobbs. Source: Foy Riley, Riley Family historian.

Riley, Jay Holt
Born: December 5, 1885, Van Zandt County, Texas. Died: August 11, 1972, Van Zandt County, Texas. Married: Corrie Richardson. Father: David Love Riley, Jr. Mother: Nannie Arrabella Thompson. Comments: Jay Holt Riley was appointed Postmaster of Canton in March, 1937 and served until March, 1954. Source: Eubanks Funeral Home records.

Riley, Lina Hardy
(Photo page 114) Born: January 29, 1872, Hardeman, Tennessee. Died: October 20, 1939, Van Zandt County, Texas. Cause of death: Apoplexy. Married: Claude Franklin Riley, April 8, 1896. Father: Joseph H. Neilson. Mother: Martha Hardy. Source: Death Certificate.

Riley, Lydia Colon
(Photo page 115) Born: July 21, 1874, Van Zandt County, Texas. Died: February 24, 1946, Van Zandt County, Texas. Cause of death: Heart disease. Married: William Edgar Riley, June 8, 1904. Children: Edgar Foy, Jesse Buckner, David Edward, and Mary Belle. Father: David Love Riley, Jr. Mother: Mary Colon Hobbs. Siblings: Belle, James T., Claude Franklin, Jessie Riley, Mary Daisy, David Thompson R, and Jay Holt. Sources: Death Certificate; Foy Riley, Riley Family historian; Ancestry.com.

Riley, Mamie Keys
Date of birth: Unknown. Date of death: Unknown. Father: David Love Riley, Jr. Mother: Nannie Thompson. Source: Foy Riley, Riley Family historian.

Riley, Mary Daisy
(Photo page 115) Born: November 16, 1877. Died: July 14, 1929. Never married. Father: David Love Riley, Jr. Mother: Mary Hobbs. Siblings: Belle, James T., Claude Franklin, Lydia Colon, Jessie, David Thomson, and Jay Holt. Sources: Tombstone, Find A Grave.

Riley, Mary Francis "Fannie"
Born: June 7, 1839, Alabama. Died: January 29, 1921, Van Zandt County, Texas. Cause of death: Heart disease. Married: Jessie Miles Riley, ca 1858. Children: G. W., J.M., W. E., and Mrs. Robertson. Father: William J. Baker, Alabama. Mother: Nancy Armstrong. Comments: The *Canton Herald* reported Mary Riley's death as follows: "Mrs. Mary F. Riley passed away Saturday afternoon, January 29, 1921, at the home of her son W. E. Riley, in Canton. Deceased was born in the state of Alabama on June 7, 1889, where she grew to young womanhood and joined the Old Beulalar Missionary Baptist church at the age of 17 years. At the age of 19, she married J. M. Riley and to this union were born seven children, three girls and four boys. She with her husband moved to Canton about twenty years ago and made their home with Ed Riley, the husband preceding her to the better world several years ago. The children surviving her are Mrs. Robertson, of Dallas, Rev. G. W. Riley, of Jackson, Miss., J. M Riley, residing in West Texas, and W. E. Riley of Canton. In addition to these many friends will regret her home-going and will join in words of condolence and sympathy for the sorrowing children. The quiet life of this good woman was pure and wholesome in its influence on those with whom she came in contact. The Herald tenders sympathy." Sources: Death Certificate; *Canton Herald*, February 4, 1921; Ancestry.com.

Riley, Nancy Arrabella "Nannie"
Born: February 26, 1851, Alabama. Died: October 9, 1905, Van Zandt County, Texas. Cause of death: Fell into a well. Married: David Love Riley, October 31, 1880. Children: David Thompson, Jay H., Love, Charles, Mamie Keys, and Russell Steel. Father: James Addison Thompson. Mother: Nancy Richey Prewitt. Comments: The *Wills Point Chronicle* explained Nannie Riley's death as follows: "The entire county was shocked Monday morning at the announcement of the tragic death of Mrs. D. L. Riley of Canton. The family arising in the morning missed her from her room and a search was instituted, resulting finally in the discovery of her body in a well some sixty feet deep. The funeral occurred at Canton Monday afternoon, the services being conducted by Rev. P. C. Shillings and attended by a very large number of sorrowing friends. Mrs. Nannie Thompson Riley was a most excellent Christian lady and loving wife and mother, and among the earliest recollections of this writer is her kindly face and gentle manners. For a year or more she has been in ill health and at times subject to mental aberration, to which latter fact was no doubt due to her untimely death." Sources: *Wills Point Chronicle*, October 12, 1905; Ancestry.com.

Riley, Russell Steel
Born: March 31, 1884. Died: October 12, 1885. Father: David Love Riley, Jr. Mother: Nannie Thompson. Source: Tombstone.

Riley, William Edgar
Born: April 2, 1873, Union County, Mississippi. Died: January 12, 1952, Van Zandt County, Texas. Cause of death: Stroke. Married: Lydia Colon "Liddie" Riley, June 8, 1904. Father: Jesse Miles Riley. Mother: Mary Francis "Fannie" Baker. Occupation: Rural mail carrier, 1913-1937, Secretary for Woodman of the World. Sources: Death Certificate; *Canton Herald*, January 17, 1952; Eubank Funeral Home records; Ancestry.com.

Roberts, Cory Lee
(Photo page 118) Born: May 21, 1984, Kaufman County, Texas. Died: October 21, 1998, Van Zandt County, Texas. Single. Father: Ronnie Roberts. Mother: Susan Hilliard. Occupation: Student. Comments: Cory Roberts was in the eighth grade at the Canton Junior High School at his death. Source: *Van Zandt News*, October 25, 1998.

Roberts, Henry Oliver
Born: May 18, 1852, Arkansas. Died: March 31, 1924, Van Zandt County, Texas. Married: (1) Caroline Dunn Roberts. Children: Samantha B., and Martha V. (2) Sarah Elizabeth Ferguson Conway Chesshir, May 14, 1876. Children: Andrew Berry, Cordelia, Oliver, John W., Thomas Ulysses, Lonnie, Nora, and Joseph Irvin. Father: Benjamin Roberts, Virginia. Mother: Winnefred Unknown. Comments: Henry Roberts lived several years in Sebastian County and Little River Counties, Arkansas prior to moving to Van Zandt County, Texas. Source: Roberts Family History, Ancestry.com.

Roberts, Mattie Jean "Jane"
Born: August 25, 1889, Cherokee County, Texas. Died: September 8, 1954, Dallas County, Texas. Married: Thomas Ulysses Roberts, October 4, 1908. Children: Geneva, Elizabeth, Mrs. F. O. Galloway, Herbert, Theodore, Thomas, and Wayne. Father: James Chesley Couch, Cherokee County, Texas. Mother: Parelee Johnson, Cherokee County, Texas. Source: Eubank Funeral Home records.

Roberts, Sarah Elizabeth
Born: August 24, 1856, Arkansas. Died: August 29, 1924, Van Zandt County, Texas. Married: Henry Oliver Roberts, May 14, 1876. Children: Samantha Belle, Martha V., Andrew Berry, Mary Cordelia, Oliver Pleasant, John W. R, Thomas Ulysses, Lonnie V., Nora, and Joseph Irwin. Father: I. B. Chesshir. Mother: N. I. Chesshir. Sources: 1860 U. S Census, Ancestry.com, Find A Grave.

Cory Lee Roberts

Roberts, Theodore Earnest
Born: May 2, 1915, Van Zandt County, Texas. Died: April 1, 1951, Van Zandt County, Texas. Cause of death: Burns. Married: Betty Jean Kennedy, March 11, 1949, Divorced. Father: Thomas U. Roberts, Texas. Mother: Mattie Jean "Jane" Couch, Texas. Military: WWII, M/Sgt. US Army. Comments: The *Canton Herald* reported Theodore Roberts' death as follows: "Funeral services were held Monday afternoon April 2, at 3 o'clock at the Baptist Church for Theodore L. Roberts, 36, who was burned beyond recognition in the charred truck near here. The body was discovered at 6:30 o'clock Sunday morning. Charges of murder have been filed before Justice of Peace C. A. Groves in Canton against Mrs. Lila Lewellyn and her son-in-law, Roscoe Tennison. Roberts had argued with the suspects before he had left their house. His truck had run into a ditch and an analysis of the body revealed that he was still alive before he was burned to death." An indictment of murder (against the advice of the District Attorney) was brought against the suspects in June, 1951. Lewellen family members explained that the suspects were cleared of all charges. Sources: Death Certificate; *Marriage Records of Van Zandt County 1931-1950*; *Canton Herald*, April 5, 1951 and June 7, 1951; Hilliard Funeral Home records; Lewellen Family member interview.

Grady Lee Rushing and Ruby D. Rushing

Roberts, Thomas Ulysses
Born: October 3, 1884, Rains County, Texas. Died: June 16, 1958, Kaufman County, Texas. Married: Mattie Jane Couch, October 4, 1908. Children: Geneva, Elizabeth, Mrs. F. O. Galloway, Herbert, Theodore, Thomas, and Wayne. Father: Henry Oliver Roberts. Mother: Sarah Elizabeth Ferguson. Sources: *Texas Deaths 1890-1976*, Ancestry.com.

Robertson, Elsie Marie
Born: June 2, 1923, Texas. Died: August 14, 1973, Dallas County, Texas. Cause of death: Stroke. Married: John Porter Robertson. Father: Henry Fisher Blackwell, II. Mother: Lillie Leona Youngblood. Comments: The Blackwell House built in June and July of 1887 by Elsie Marie Robertson's father is the oldest surviving house in Canton. Sources: Death Certificate, Eubank Funeral Home records.

Robertson, Irena
Born: March 2, 1816, Mississippi. Died: November 2, 1887, Van Zandt County, Texas. Married: Thomas E. Robertson, ca 1839. Father: Unknown. Mother: Unknown. Comments: Thomas E. and Irena Robertson had ten children in twenty-one years. Irena was in Dallas County, Texas in 1870 and died in Canton, Texas. Sources: 1870 U. S. Census, Ancestry.com.

ROBERTSON, JOHN PORTER

Born: May 21, 1910, Hunt County, Texas. Died: April 4, 1992, Van Zandt County, Texas. Married: Elsie Marie Blackwell. Father: John P. Robertson, Sr. Mother: Mamie Cullam Fugate. Military: WWII, US Army. Comments: John Robertson grew up in Van Zandt County and moved back to the county after his discharge from the Army in 1945. Sources: *Van Zandt News*, April 12, 1992; Ancestry.com.

ROBERTSON, THOMAS E.

Born: January 1, 1802, South Carolina. Died: June 16, 1891, Dallas County, Texas. Married: Irena Box, ca 1839. Father: John Robertson. Mother: Mary Parker. Comments: Thomas Robertson moved to Newton County, Mississippi by the 1830's when he married. They had ten children together in Mississippi before moving to Dallas, Texas before 1870. After his death, he was brought back to Canton to be buried beside Irena in Hillcrest Cemetery. Sources: 1870 U. S. Census, Ancestry.com.

ROBINSON, MINNIE

Born: January 28, 1879, Texas. Died: March 17, 1971, Van Zandt County, Texas. Cause of death: Stroke. Single. Father: C. F. "Lum" Robinson. Mother: Melessie Koen. Comments: Minnie Robinson's father served as Van Zandt County Treasurer from 1911-1922. Source: Death Certificate.

RODGERS, EDNA MAE

Born: May 5, 1880, Van Zandt County, Texas. Died: July 8, 1967, Smith County, Texas. Married: William Brown Rodgers, July 18, 1907. Father: Will Russell. Mother: Margaret Ann Weir. Source: Eubank Funeral Home records.

RODGERS, WILLIAM BROWN

Born: November 13, 1873, Buncombe County, North Carolina. Died: August 7, 1950, Van Zandt County, Texas. Married: Edna Mae Russell, July 18, 1907. Father: James William Rodgers. Mother: Jane T. Long. Occupation: Bank clerk. Sources: Death Certificate; *Canton Herald*, August 10, 1950; Eubank Funeral Home records; Ancestry.com.

ROGERS, J. E.

Born: April 12, 1884. Died: August 22, 1889. Father: H. E. Rogers. Mother: M. E. Rogers. Source: Tombstone.

ROSEMAND, ANNIE LEE

Born: August 18, 1903, Jackson County, Alabama. Died: December 11, 1928. Married: Jessie Rosemand, November 9, 1921. Father: Robert Lee Knowles. Mother: Betty Elizabeth Felts Baker. Source: Ancestry.com.

ROSINBAUM, GEORGE EDWARD "ED"

Born: October 19, 1856, Smith County, Texas. Died: February 8, 1889, Kaufman County, Texas. Cause of death: Gunshot wounds. Married: Ella Virginia Davis, November 24, 1881, Trinity County, Texas. Child: Georgia Ann. Father: George Rosinbaum, Sr. Mother: Mary Theresa "Mariah" Foster. Occupation: Lawyer, County Attorney. Comments: George "Ed" Rosinbaum Jr. and George Rosinbaum Sr. both met tragic deaths. George, Sr. is included in this narrative because he was important in Van Zandt County's early history. Ed was born in Smith County, Texas while his father was serving as District Attorney. His father was born in Virginia; but very early the family became part of a German community in Wythe County, Virginia. George, Sr., as a young man, wanted to be a lawyer. Instead of reading law with a local lawyer as was the custom in those early days, he chose to study at Emory and Henry College in Virginia. After graduation, he practiced law at Floyd, Virginia for a short time. While living there, he married and moved to Van Zandt County, Texas in the early 1850's. He was elected District Attorney of the 9th Judicial District, August 4, 1856 and served until 1860. He was opposed to Texas' breaking away from the United States and became a strict Unionist which put him in direct conflict with the local Confederates. In 1862, Camp Ford in Tyler, Texas was established as a Confederate training camp; but in August of 1863, its use was shifted to a Union prisoner of war stockade. As more Union prisoners arrived, there were not enough guards to effectively control them which created a crisis of management. In late October, 1863, a Confederate guard, Frank Smith, killed a Union prisoner for straying across a boundary line. The prisoners threatened to break out and burn Tyler if Smith were not punished. At the same time, three local Unionists, George and William Whitmore, and George Rosinbaum were suspected of conspiring with the POWs to facilitate their escape. The plot was discovered, and the Unionists were arrested. George and William Whitmore were eventually released, but George Rosenbaum drops from the records in early 1865. Was he murdered? Some of his family believe so. Mariah raised the children alone until December 9th 1868 when she married Richard Wells, an old friend from Virginia. George, Sr., and Mariah had two children other than George, Jr.,—Georgia Ann who married J. M. Morrison and Sallie who married John Henry Engledow. Both are buried in Hillcrest Cemetery. Ed was reared by his mother and Richard Wells in Van Zandt County. He became a lawyer; and at the age of 26, he was elected County Attorney and served one term. Not much is known about his activities in Canton for the next few years. However, there seems to have developed an animosity between himself and fellow Canton townsman, Isaac Henry Smelser. Smelser had been in Canton for some time and owned the White Elephant Saloon. He was also a partner with J. F. Samples in Smelser & Samples dealers in family groceries and with T. J. Foster in a wine and liquor business. Both men were influential in the early Canton business community. In 1886, Lawndale, a boomtown sprang up along the Van Zandt and Kaufman county line. As many

Historical Marker
Morgan Gurley Sanders

The Van Zandt County Historical Commission dedicated a Historical Marker in honor of Morgan Gurley Sanders on August 13, 2011. Located in Ben Wheeler on FM 858 just west of Highway 64, the Marker reads as follows:

Legislator Morgan Gurley Sanders was born near Ben Wheeler. He published newspapers, worked as Journal Clerk of the State Senate and was admitted to the State Bar of Texas before winning a seat in the State Legislature. His public service as a Democratic politician included terms as a state legislator (1903-07), Van Zandt County Attorney (1911-15), District Attorney (1915-17) and U.S. Congressman (1921-39); he also continued to practice law. In 1931, Speaker of the House John Nance Garner appointed Sanders to his previous position on the powerful Ways and Means Committee. Sanders lost his seat in a 1938 election. Twice widowed and married three times, he remained active in Van Zandt County until his death in 1956.

as 20 businesses were gathered there in a very short time. I. H. Smelser opened a saloon. Rosinbaum and Smelser got into a fight—Smelser using a whisky bottle and a baseball bat, Rosinbaum using his knife. Smelser got the best of the fight, and Rosinbaum left the saloon mortified over losing and made threats about Smelser to his friends. Smelser was notified of Rosinbaum's threats and he prepared himself. One afternoon, Rosinbaum came into Smelser's saloon saying he intended to kill him. As he advanced on him, however, Smelser shot and killed Rosinbaum. Smelser went to trial in December of 1889 in the District Court at Kaufman and was acquitted of murder. The jury was only out seven minutes determining their verdict. Sources: *Texas Telephone*, February 15, 1889; *Wills Point Chronicle*, March 7, 1889; *Canton Telephone*, December, 13, 1889 and December 20, 1889; Lisa Pierce, Rosinbaum Family historian; Ancestry.com.

Ross, Clinton "Clint"
Born: October 24, 1896, Arkansas. Died: December 20, 1980, Smith County, Texas. Married: Lillian C. Shivers, January 8, 1939. Child: Paula Jean. Father: John William Ross, Grant County, Arkansas. Mother: Martha Onia Lites. Occupation: Business owner, Mayor of Canton 1967-1971. Military: WWI, US Army. Source: *Canton Herald*, January 1, 1981.

Ross John William
Born: December 20, 1874, Grant County, Arkansas. Died: May 16, 1922, Fannin County, Texas. Married: Martha Onia Lites. Father: William H. Ross. Mother: Mary L. Taylor. Source: Ancestry.com.

Ross, L.V.
Born: May 5, 1919, Texas. Died: March 8, 1968, Van Zandt County, Texas. Cause of death: Stroke. Divorced. Father: Richard Ross. Mother: Lessie Mae Ross. Occupation: Construction worker. Sources: Death Certificate, 1940 U. S. Census.

Ross, Lillian C.
Born: June 23, 1912. Died: October 9, 2001. Married: Clinton Ross, January 8, 1939. Child: Paula Jean. Father: George R. Shivers. Mother: Nora C. Unknown. Sources: 1930, 1940 U. S. Census; U. S. Social Security Death Index.

Ross, Martha Onia
Born: September 7, 1874, Arkansas. Died: January 8, 1948, Arkansas. Married: John William Ross, 1896. Father: Caleb Lites. Mother: Louisa Ionia Mitchell Purnell. Sources: *Canton Herald*, January 15, 1948; Ancestry.com.

Roundtree, Elizabeth Grace
Born: March 24, 1958, Dallas County, Texas. Died: July 6, 1979, Dallas County, Texas. Never married. Father: Wesley Leon Roundtree. Mother: Carmen Hernandez. Comments: Elizabeth Roundtree died suddenly while residing in a Canton nursing home. Sources: Death Certificate, Eubank Funeral Home records.

Rusek, Madge Lantrip
Born: October 27, 1910, Mississippi. Died: April 2, 1926, Van Zandt County, Texas. Married: Joe Rusek, December 26, 1925. Father: J. Frank Lantrip. Mother: Fannie Brasher. Comments: Madge Lantrip was 16 when she married. She had been married a little over three months when she became ill with tonsillitis and died. Madge's husband later married Annie Irene Peden. He died in 1982 and is buried in Laurel Land Memorial Park, Dallas, Texas. Sources: 1920 U. S. Census; *Wills Point Chronicle*, April 29, 1926; Ancestry.com.

Rushing, Grady Lee
(Photo, page 118) Born: November 17, 1907. Died: August 4, 1989. Married: Ruby D. Staley, October 23, 1927. Father: Elie Edward Rushing. Mother: Jennie Magnolia Davidson. Child: Billy Jack. Occupation: Road construction. Siblings: Ira, infant Rushing, and Jennie Agnes. Comments: Grady Lee Rushing worked for Van Zandt County, Precinct 1. Sources: *Van Zandt News*, August 13, 1989; Find A Grave.

Rushing, Ruby D.
(Photo, page 118) Born: July 8, 1908, Van Zandt County, Texas. Died: February 14, 2002, Van Zandt County Texas. Married: Grady Lee Rushing, October 23, 1927. Father: John Franklin Staley. Mother: Florence Leila Bailey. Siblings: Maggie Lee, Mattie Oler, Jessie James, Carrie Lenora, Willie Raymond, Oddie Franklin, Lillie May, Essie Anise, Ruthy B.,(twin of Ruby's who died at birth), Elsie Carmon, and Ellie Gladis. Comments: Ruby Rushing's parents came from Davidson County, North Carolina ca 1885 and settled in the Starr community of Van Zandt County, Texas. She grew up in that community. Sources: *Van Zandt County Biographies, 1848-1991*; Hilliard Funeral Home records; Find A Grave.

Russell, James L.
Born: October 22, 1852. Died: April 27, 1887. Father: David Russell. Mother: Phoeby Unknown. Comments: James Russell's parents came to Texas about 1850 and to Van Zandt County by 1854. His father was a farmer and was involved in the early development of Van Zandt County. He died in 1893. James' parents are buried in unmarked graves in Hillcrest Cemetery. Sources: 1870 United States Census; Ancestry.com.

Russell, Jessie
Born: December 15, 1876, Van Zandt County, Texas. Died: November 9, 1910, Roosevelt County, New Mexico. Cause of death: Tuberculosis. Married: Dr. Ike D. Russell, December 29, 1892. Father: Dr. James L. Matthews, Georgia. Mother: Georgia Matthews. Comments: Jessie Russell was born in the Scott Community and lived most of her life in Van Zandt County. After their marriage, they resided in Edgewood and Small. Seeking a cure for her tuberculosis, the family moved to Roswell, Petrolia, and Portales, New Mexico where she died. Sources: 1870, 1880, 1900 U. S. Census; *Wills Point Chronicle*, November 17, 1910.

Russell, Leila
Born: ca 1885. Died: June 3, 1887. Father: J. Gordon Russell. Mother: Jennie Matthews. Source: Tombstone.

Russell, Mary C.
Born: October 3, 1888. Died: August 9, 1889. Father: J. Gordon Russell. Mother: Jennie Mathews. Comments: Mary Russell's father had at least two children buried in the Hillcrest Cemetery: Mary and Leila. Gordon was a lawyer and became one of the more accomplished individuals to live in Canton. He came to Canton from Georgia in 1879, was elected County Judge in 1884, and District Attorney of the Seventh Judicial District of Texas in 1892. He moved to Smith County in 1895; and in 1896 he was elected District Judge of the Seventh Judicial District of Texas, and U. S. Congressman in 1902. He was appointed a Federal Judge of the United States District Court for the Eastern District of Texas by President Taft in 1910, and served until his death September 14, 1919, in Kerrville, Texas. Sources: Tombstone; *Canton Telephone*, August 16, 1889; *Wills Point Chronicle*, June 2, 1910; Wikipedia.com.

S

Sambel, Walter William
Born: January 9, 1922, New York, New York. Died: February 20, 1977, Tarrant County, Texas. Cause of death: Gunshot wound. Married: Doris Mae Unknown. Father: Joseph Sambel. Mother: Ann Elizabeth Mietke.

Children: Ronald Joseph, Walter, Elana, Patricia, John, Ann, and Susan. Occupation: Materials analyst. Military: WWII Sgt. U S Marine Corps. Sources: Death Certificate; Ancestry.com; *Canton Herald*, February 1973.

SAMPLES, JESSE F.

Born: November 13, 1841, Forsyth County, Georgia. Died: August 7, 1889, Van Zandt County, Texas. Cause of death: Consumption (T. B.). Married: (1) Nancy Jane Grimes, 1858, Georgia. Died: December 21, 1874. Children: Evaline Caroline, Georgia Ann, and Alice Victoria. (2) Nancy Jane Jackson, July 14, 1875, Van Zandt County, Texas. Children: Mary Lou, Martha Arletha, Nancy A., Jettie, Jesse H., and Rosa Dell. Father: Jesse B. Samples. Mother: Phoebe Fincher. Siblings: Judge Valentine, William, John G., Nancy Elizabeth, and Arminta. Occupation: Farmer, grocer. Military: CSA, Warsaw Rebels, Co E., Georgia Infantry. Comments: Jesse Samples came to Texas in 1866. He farmed in Van Zandt County until he moved to Canton in 1880 to enter the merchandising business. He and his partner, I. H. Smelser operated a grocery store in 1885. Later, he became the sole owner, operating as J. F. Samples dealer in first-class family groceries. After his death, his widow married W. S. Sherman. She died in 1899 and is buried beside Jesse with the name "Samples." Sources: 1880 U.S. Census; *Canton Telephone*, August 23, 1889; Ancestry.com, Find A Grave.

SAMPLES, JESSE H.

Born: January 31, 1883, Van Zandt County, Texas. Died: November 23, 1909, Dallas County, Texas. Cause of death: Gunshot wounds. Married: Ella Mae Barnes, December 11, 1903. Father: Jesse F. Samples. Mother: Nancy Jane Jackson. Occupation: Painter and paper hanger. Comments: Jesse H. Samples was reared in Canton, Texas, but had been living and working in Dallas for several years. He was squirrel hunting near Edgewood with Chester Eaton and James Jones. One of his companions accidently shot him in the left side of the face with bird shot which completely destroyed the left eye. Some of the shot entered the brain through the eye socket and resulted in total paralysis in his right side. He was carried to a Dallas hospital where he died two days later. His father had been a prominent businessman in Canton during its early years. Jesse was only 26 years old, married, but had no children. Source: *Wills Point Chronicle*, December 2, 1909.

SAMPLES, JETTIE

Born: December 9, 1880, Van Zandt County, Texas. Died: October 13, 1881, Van Zandt County, Texas. Father: Jesse F. Samples. Mother: Nancy Jane Jackson. Source: Ancestry.com.

SAMPLES, (SHERMAN) NANCY JANE

Born: December 14, 1856, Texas. Died: February 9, 1899, Texas. Cause of death: Pneumonia. Married: (1) Jesse F. Samples, July 14, 1875. Children: Mary Lou, Martha A., Nancy A., Jettie, Jesse H., and Rosa Dell. (2) William S. Sherman, April 15, 1894. Child: Sim. Father: John C. Jackson, Alabama. Mother: Martha Jackson. Occupation: Part owner of the Phoenix Hotel on the Canton townhouse square. Comments: Nancy Jane Jackson was the second wife of Jesse F. Samples who was a Canton businessman for several years before his death in 1889. Five years after her husband's death, she married W. S. Sherman. At her death, she was buried next to her first husband under the Samples name. She left a will bequeathing her property as follows; "First, I direct that my body be decently interred and done in a manner corresponding with my estate and situation in life. Second, I give and bequeath to my beloved children, Sim Sherman, Letha Ward, Rena Evans, Jesse Samples, Mamie Samples and Della Samples, all my estate, real, personal, and mixed in equal shares. Third, I will that two hundred dollars being an undivided interest in the Phoenix Hotel situated in Canton, Van Zandt County, Texas, being paid to my three children, Jesse Samples, Mamie Samples, and Della Samples, the same being the amount of their money invested in said property and the remainder of said hotel being equally divided among my children as set out in the second paragraph of this will." Sources: 1860 U. S. Census; *Free State Enterprise*, February 16, 1899; Ancestry.com; Find A Grave.

SANDERS, CLAUD H.

Born: July 27, 1884, Van Zandt County, Texas. Died: January 2, 1967, Smith County, Texas. Never Married. Father: Jefferson H. Sanders. Mother: Sara Jane Jones. Occupation: Farmer. Source: Death Certificate.

SANDERS, CORA ISABELLE

Born: October 14, 1874. Died: May 18, 1888. Father: Jefferson H. Sanders. Mother: Sara Jane Jones. Source: Tombstone.

SANDERS, FLORENCE W.

Born: March 25, 1891, Harrison County, Texas. Died: December 5, 1977, Smith County, Texas. Married: (1) Robert Campbell Martin, January 25, 1910. Children: Florence Eleanor, Robert Campbell Jr., William T., and Frank Littlejohn. (2) Morgan Gurley Sanders, January 10, 1942. Father: Robert Wren. Mother: Alzaeda Eleanor Mullen. Sources: Death Certificate, Ancestry.com.

SANDERS, HENRY

Born: September 6, 1870. Died: October 2, 1889. Father: Jefferson H. Sanders. Mother: Sara Jane Jones. Source: Tombstone.

SANDERS, JAMES E.

Born: January 7, 1880. Died: October 24, 1882. Father: Jefferson H. Sanders. Mother: Sara Jane Jones. Source: Tombstone.

Angus Truett Seale

Buck Shannon

Taylor Shamlin

Oscar Shamlin, Sr.

SANDERS, JEFFERSON H.

Born: June 1846, Tallapoosa County, Alabama. Died: September 28, 1923, Van Zandt County, Texas. (Tombstone death date: 1924, newspaper obituary death date: 1923). Married: Sara Jane Jones Wyatt, December 24, 1866, Newton County, Mississippi. Children: Charlie, Emma E., Henry B., Thomas H., Cora Isabelle, Joseph Lee, James E., and Claud H. Father: Robert Sanders. Mother: Sarah Ann Phillips. Occupation: Farmer. Military: CSA, MS Calvary Co. F. Comments: Jefferson Sanders' wife's first husband was Riley Battle Wyatt, a Civil War soldier who died in a Union Prisoner of War Camp in Indiana February 5, 1865. They had one child, Charles. He came to Texas with his mother and died in 1896. He is buried in the Hillcrest Cemetery. Jefferson Sanders and his family came from Mississippi to Van Zandt County in 1877 and remained there for forty-five years. He settled in Edom, then moved to a farm near Canton, then moved to Canton in 1902. Sources: *Wills Point Chronicle*, October 4, 1923; Ancestry.com; Find A Grave.

SANDERS, MORGAN GURLEY

(Photo, page 120) Born: July 14, 1878, Van Zandt County, Texas. Died: January 7, 1956, Navarro County, Texas. Married: (1) Jessie Irene Cox, September 30, 1896. Child: Gurley H. (2) Noma Louisa Tull, February 19, 1905. (3) Florence Wren Martin, January 1942. Father: Levi Lindsey Sanders. Mother: Sarah Francis Smith. Occupation: Lawyer, politician. Comments: Morgan Gurley Sanders, one of the more successful politicians to ever come out of Van Zandt County, Texas, was born on a farm near Ben Wheeler, Texas. He attended county schools until 1892 when he moved with his family to Ben Wheeler and entered the Alamo Institute. This school was considered the top school in Van Zandt County. Morgan was an excellent student, graduating in the top of his class in 1895 at the age of 16. After graduation, he taught in the public schools for a little more than two years before entering the newspaper business. He established the *Ben Wheeler Headlight*, a weekly newspaper, then moved to Canton, Texas to publish the *Free State Enterprise*, another weekly newspaper. He later became Journal Clerk of the State Senate and studied law at the University of Texas at night and when the Senate was not in session. He became a lawyer and began his career in politics. His public service of twenty-eight years as a Democratic politician included terms as a State Legislator (1903-07), Van Zandt County Attorney (1911-15), District Attorney (1915-17), and U. S. Congressman (1921-39). In 1931, Speaker of the House, John Nance Garner, appointed Morgan to his previous position on the powerful Ways and Means Committee. When he was defeated for office in 1938, he quietly returned to Van Zandt County and practiced law until his death in 1956 at the age of 77. Source: Texas Historical Commission Marker Application.

SANDERS, NOMA LOUISA

Born: February 4, 1881, Van Zandt County, Texas. Died: December 3, 1932, Bell County, Texas. Married: Morgan G. Sanders, February 19, 1905. Father: George Washington Tull. Mother: Mollie Cowen. Comments: Noma Tull Sanders was born and reared in Canton, Texas. Her parents were pioneer settlers of Van Zandt County. She graduated from the local high school and Baylor College at Belton, Texas. She had further schooling at Bascobal College in Nashville, Tennessee. Noma's husband became one of the more successful politicians to come from Van Zandt County, including eighteen years as a U. S. Congressman. She spent her life in Canton, except when in college or with her husband in Washington D. C. when Congress was in session. She had surgery at Scott and

Douglas Shaw, Sr.

Lonnell Shaw

Madelene "Mayde" Shaw

Henry Hawthorne Smith

White Hospital in Temple, Texas and lived several weeks before an unexpected death. Sources: Death Certificate; *Canton Herald*, December 9, 1932.

SANDERS, PAULINE B.
Born: February 25, 1907, Wood County, Texas. Died: June 3, 1951, Dallas County, Texas. Cause of death: Meningitis. Married: Lonnie E. Sanders. Father: Isaac Bowman. Mother: Ethel Presley. Occupation: Cook. Source: Death Certificate.

SANDERS, SARAH JANE
Born: 1846, Green County, Alabama. Died: February 5, 1930, Van Zandt County, Texas. Married: (1) Riley Battles Wyatt. Child: Charlie. Riley had a daughter, Nancy, Deliah, from a previous marriage. She was adopted by a Gibbs family. (2) Jefferson H. Sanders, December 24, 1866. Children: Emma E, Henry B, Thomas H., Cora Isabelle, Joseph Lee, James E., and Claud. Father: Unknown Jones. Mother: Unknown. Comments: Sara Jane Jones married Riley Battles Wyatt in Newton County, Mississippi. Riley joined the Confederate Army February 24, 1862 at Meridian, Mississippi at the age of 30. He served as a Private in Co. I, 36 Reg't Mississippi Volunteers. On December 20, 1863, he appeared on a list of prisoners from the battles of Vicksburg and Port Hudson paroled and exchanged. He rejoined his unit and was captured again near Marietta, Georgia on June 19, 1864. He was forwarded from Military Prison, Louisville, Kentucky to Camp Morton, Indiana on June 27, 1864. He died in prison on February 5, 1865. Charley Wyatt came to Texas with his mother, died January 31, 1896 and is buried in Hillcrest Cemetery. Sources: Confederate Pension Records; Confederate Soldiers Service Records; *Canton Herald*, February 14, 1930; Find A Grave.

SANSOM, GEORGE I.
Born: April 16, 1871. Died: August 6, 1882. Father: W. C. Sansom. Mother: L. B. Sansom. Source: Tombstone.

SCATES, JERRY
Born: December 11, 1893. Died: April 8, 1948. Cause of death: Heart disease. Married: Minnie Bell, December 6, 1922. Father: Sam S. Scates. Mother: Angeline Johnson. Siblings: Prena, Martin, Bob, and Riley. Military: WWI, PVT US Army. Sources: 1900 U. S. Census, Death Certificate, Ancestry.com.

SEALE, ANGUS TRUETT
(Photo, page 123) Born: June 20, 1917, Van Zandt County, Texas. Died: April 20, 2009, Smith County, Texas. Married: Lavinia Hubbard, December 26, 1936. Children: Truett, Dan, Paulette, Ron, and Pam. Father: Henry Jones Seale. Mother: Susan Era Milam. Occupation: Farmer, rancher. Sources: *Canton Herald*, April 2009; Eubank Funeral Home records.

SEALE, CLARA LAVINIA
Born: February 9, 1917, Van Zandt County, Texas. Died: April 6, 2001, Van Zandt County, Texas. Married: Angus Truett Seale, December 26, 1936. Children: Truett, Dan, Paulette, Ron, and Pam. Father: Albert J. Hubbard. Mother: Amelia Williams. Siblings: Bob, Dan, Al, Edith, Doris, and Ila. Comments: Lavinia Seale was a life-long resident of Van Zandt County and a graduate of Canton High School in 1935. Her hobbies included being a seamstress, quilting and cooking. Lavinia was famous for her cooking and especially for her sweet potato pie. Her potato pie won a Blue Ribbon at the Van Zandt County Fair. Sources: 1940 U. S. Census; U. S. Social Security Death Index; *Canton Herald*, April 12, 2001.

Seale, Henry Jones
Born: November 27, 1882, Pontotoc County, Mississippi. Died: August 20, 1976, Smith County, Texas. Cause of death: Heart disease. Married: Susan Era Milam, December 26, 1903. Father: Eli Jones Seale. Mother: Lizzie Hardin. Occupation: Farmer. Sources: Death Certificate, Eubank Funeral Home records.

Seale, Susan Era
Born: September 1, 1885, Mississippi. Died: May 15, 1959, Smith County, Texas. Cause of death: Heart disease. Married: Henry Jones Seale, December 26, 1903. Father: Willis A. Milam. Mother: Martha A. Hardin. Siblings: Ora A., Mada Docia, John Thomas, Willis Frank, Anna Lou, and Byron Onyx. Sources: Death Certificate, Eubank Funeral Home records, Find A Grave.

Shamlin, Evelyn
Born: December 3, 1907, Smith County, Texas. Died: April 21, 1955, Van Zandt County, Texas. Married: Napoleon Shamlin, June 3, 1939. Father: Manuel Greer, Harrison County, Texas. Mother: Pauline Nolan, Harrison County, Texas. Source: Eubank Funeral Home records.

Shamlin, Napoleon
Born: November 26, 1902, Van Zandt County, Texas. Died: January 13 (11), 1964, Van Zandt County, Texas. Cause of death: Heart disease. Married: (1) Janie Fitzgerald, September 7, 1925. (2) Evelyn Greer, June 3, 1939. Father: Taylor Shamlin. Mother: Julia Scates. Occupation: Laborer. Source: Death Certificate.

Shamlin, Oscar, Sr.
(Photo, page 123) Born: January 21, 1906, Texas. Died: August 22, 1966, Dallas County, Texas. Cause of death: Aneurism. Married: Rosa Riggs, February 5, 1927. Children: Oscar, Jr. and Lennell. Father: Taylor Shamlin. Mother: Julie Scates. Occupation: Farmer. Sources: Death Certificate; *Canton Herald*, September 1, 1966.

Shamlin, Taylor
(Photo, page 123) Born: December 1, 1866, Van Zandt County, Texas. Died: March 2, 1949, Van Zandt County, Texas. Married: Julia Scates, November 6, 1892. Children: Rufus, Sadie, Malcolm, Napoleon, R. B., Oscar, Lovie, Sandy, Jack Porter, Ida S., and Leonard (Sonny). Father: Alfred Shamlin, Louisiana. Mother: Mandela Nice, Georgia. Occupation: Farmer. Sources: Death Certificate; *Canton Herald*, March 10, 1949; Eubank Funeral Home records; Ancestry.com.

Shamlin, Willie Mae
Born: July 19, 1910, Van Zandt County, Texas. Died: December 11, 1980, Van Zandt County, Texas. Married: R. B. Shamlin, February 26, 1938. Children: Marguerite and Helen. Father: Nelson Brown. Mother: Mary Stephens. Siblings: Easter, Eddie, R. C., Andy, and Roscoe. Sources: 1920 U. S. Census; *Van Zandt News*, December 18, 1980.

Shannon, Buck
(Photo, page 123) Born: 1892. Died: 1979. Married: Mrs. Lucy Ann Vernon, December 16, 1922. Father: T. Shannon. Mother: Ellen Bradley. Military: U.S. Army WWI Co C 332nd Division, Service Bn QMC. Sources: *Marriage Records, Van Zandt County Texas, 1909-1931*; Ancestry.com.

Shannon, Edmond Davis
Born: ca 1866, Mississippi. Died: September 11, 1948. Father: Earl Shannon. Mother: Lucy Shannon. Occupation: Servant. Sources: 1870, 1900 U. S. Census; Eubank Funeral Home records.

Shannon, Lucy Ann
Born: August 15, 1895, Texas. Died: February 10, 1974, Kaufman County, Texas. Cause of death: Heart disease. Married: (1) Unknown Vernon. (2) Buck Shannon. Father: John Taylor. Mother: Rosie Taylor. Source: Death Certificate.

Shaw, Dave
Born: July 29, 1928, Van Zandt County, Texas. Died: March 22, 1956, Los Angeles County, California. Father: Douglas Shaw, Sr. Mother: Madelene "Mayde" Hambrick. Siblings: Lonnell and Claudia Faye. Military: WWII, TX TA US Navy. Sources: Veterans' Affairs Headstone Application, Eubank Funeral Home records, Ancestry.com.

Shaw, Donnel
Born: September 7, 1955, Van Zandt County, Texas. Died: January 2, 1996, Dallas County, Texas. Father: Lonnell Shaw. Mother: Ivy Ruth Batiste. Military: Pvt. US Marine Corp. Source: Ancestry.com.

Shaw, Douglas, Jr.
Born: February 5, 1917, Van Zandt County, Texas. Died: April 26, 1978, Dallas County, Texas. Cause of death: Stroke. Never married. Father: Douglas Shaw, Sr. Mother: Madelene "Mayde" Hambrick. Military: WWII, PFC US Army. Source: Death Certificate.

Shaw, Douglas, Sr.
Born: March 6, 1882. Died: February 28, 1971. Married: (1) Mrs. Edna Bunton, April 14, 1909. Divorce: Granted October 20, 1913. (2) Madelene "Mayde" Hambrick. Children: Geneva, Douglas, Jr., Edward, Dave, Lonnell, and Claudia Faye. Father: Unknown Shaw. Mother: Ellen Bradley. Sources: WWII Draft Card, Ancestry.com.

BERRY SMITH *was born into slavery in Cass County, Georgia and moved to Van Zandt County as a free man in 1890. "Uncle Berry," as he was called, was described in town to be a man who stood up for what was right and fought against what was wrong. At his death in 1919, he left a wife, seven children, nine grandchildren, and two great-grandchildren.*

SHAW, LONNELL
(Photo, page 124) Born: July 20, 1935. Died: May 14, 1991. Married: Ivy Ruth Batiste. Children: Don, Gregory, Troy, Gary, Connie, and Camille. Father: Douglas Shaw, Sr. Mother: Madelene "Mayde" Hambrick. Occupation: Jones Service Station. Sources: 1940 U. S. Census; *Van Zandt News,* May 19, 1991; Ancestry.com.

SHAW, MADELENE "MAYDE"
(Photo, page 124 Born: March 11, 1897, Van Zandt County, Texas. Died: May 21, 1991, Van Zandt County, Texas. Married: Douglas Shaw, Sr. Children: Dave, Catherine, Claudia Faye, Lonnell, and Douglas Jr. Father: William Hambrick. Mother: Catharine Hambrick. Comments: Mayde Shaw lived in the Canton, Texas area most of her life. She was a member of the New Hope Baptist Church in the Wynne Community and the Eastern Star. Sources: *Van Zandt News,* May 26, 1991; Ancestry.com.

SHERMAN, DADA
Born: September 10, 1882. Died: September 21, 1884. Father: W. S. Sherman. Mother: L. A. Sherman. Source: Tombstone.

SHETTLES, JOHN E.
Born: November 23, 1823, South Carolina. Died: November 21, 1902, Van Zandt County, Texas. Married: Rebecca Jane Buchanan, December 28, 1857. Children: Joseph S., Mary Alice, and George Robert "Bob." Father: David M. Shettles. Mother: Sarah "Sallie" Nixon. Source: Ancestry.com.

SHETTLES, JOSEPH S.
Born: January 7, 1869, Mississippi. Died: August 7, 1921. Married: Nancy E. "Nannie" Foster, May 13, 1901. Father: John E. Shettles. Mother: Rebecca Jane Buchanan. Source: Ancestry.com.

SHETTLES, NANCY E.
Born: September 3, 1881, Mississippi. Died: November 30, 1961, Van Zandt County, Texas. Cause of death: Heart disease. Married: Joseph S. Shettles, May 13, 1901. Father: Willis (William) Foster. Mother: Mollie Foster. Sources: Death Certificate, 1900 U. S. Census, Newman Brothers Funeral Home records.

SHIPP, GOLDIE JEWELL
Born: October 8, 1920, Denton County, Texas. Died: August 6, 1993, Van Zandt County, Texas. Married: Richard Dorman Shipp. Child: Dorman Nelson. Father: Andrew Jackson Davis. Mother: Lulu Davis. Source: Ancestry.com.

SHIPP, RICHARD DORMAN
Born: February 2, 1907, Arkansas. Died: May 9, 1983, Van Zandt County, Texas. Married: Goldie Jewel Davis. Child: Dorman Nelson. Father: John Henry Shipp. Mother: Mable Gordon. Sources: Ancestry.com, Find A Grave.

SHIVERS, JOHN WILLIAM
Born: May 6, 1910. Died: August 18, 1972. Married: Mary Lou "Mickey" Ross. Father: G. A. Shivers. Mother: Nora Cleo Gray. Sources: *Canton Herald,* August 24, 1972; Find A Grave.

SHIVERS, MARY LOU "MICKEY"
Born: November 22, 1912, Jefferson County, Arkansas. Died: April 6, 1998, Gregg County, Texas. Married: John William Shivers. Father: John William Ross. Mother: Martha Onia Lites. Comments: Mickey Shivers was a Van Zandt County resident for many years. She was a member of the First Baptist Church and was a long-term employee at the Ben Franklin Variety Store in Canton. Sources: *Canton Herald*, April 9, 1998; *Van Zandt News,* April 12, 1998.

SIDES, BILLY GENE
Born: November 14, 1925, Van Zandt County, Texas. Died: March 14, 1951, Van Zandt County, Texas. Cause of death: Airplane crash. Single. Father: Henry Monroe Sides. Mother: Minnie Lee McClellen. Military: WWII US Navy. Comments: The *Canton Herald* reported Billy Gene Sides' death as follows: "At about 3 o'clock on the afternoon of March 14, 1951, B. T. Sanders, Jr. and Billy Gene Sides, both graduates of Canton High School, had

Charles Pinkney Smith, MD, "Dr. C.P." *was educated in the common schools of Georgia and later attended Charm Wood Institute, Tyler, Texas. He began the study of medicine under Dr. E. Jones on January 12, 1880, and earned his degree from the American Medical College of St. Louis, Missouri. After graduation, he came to Van Zandt County where he established his medical practice. Dr. C.P. practiced medicine for thirty-five years and was a highly respected citizen of Canton.*

obtained an airplane from a flying service in Grand Saline and were about one and a half miles east of Canton when the plane crashed killing both of them. The plane was dual control so it was never determined who the pilot was at the time of the crash." Sources: Death Certificate; *Canton Herald*, March 22, 1951.

Sides, Effie Letitia
Born: February 24, 1879, Van Zandt County, Texas. Died: January 11, 1938, Smith County, Texas. Cause of death: Cancer. Married: Walter Lee Sides. Children: Julia Paralee, Stella M., Bonnie, Azle A., Kelly Hobbs, Audra Geroline, Lela Bell, Walter Love, and James C. Father: Jordon W. Hobbs. Mother: Paralee Walters. Sources: Death Certificate; *Canton Herald*, January 13, 1938; Quana Barber, Sides Family historian.

Sides, Floy E.
Born: 1874. Died: August 12, 1898. Married: Lewis H. Sides, October 12, 1893. Father: Unknown Petty. Mother: Unknown. Source: Tombstone.

Sides, Henry Monroe
Born: December 31, 1888, Texas. Died: January 3, 1961, Van Zandt County, Texas. Cause of death: Lung cancer. Married: Minnie Lee McClellan. Children: Inez and Billy Gene. Father: William A. Sides. Mother: Sarah Ruth Dean. Occupation: Farmer. Sources: Death Certificate, Eubank Funeral Home records.

Sides, James Love
Born: September 13, 1907, Henderson County, Texas. Died: October 20, 1930, Kaufman County, Texas. Cause of death: Automobile accident. Married: Unknown, 1928. Father: John Emory Sides. Mother: Rena Irvine. Occupation: Installed and equipped radios. Siblings: Jack, W. Irvine, and Mary Bell. Comments: James Love Sides had just recently moved to Houston from Dallas where he was working installing and equipping radios. He was en route from Dallas to Canton when he hit a soft spot in the road, wrecked his automobile, and was killed. His body was brought to Canton, Texas where an impressive service was held at the Methodist church. U.S. Congressman Morgan Sanders was one of the speakers. Source: *Canton Herald*, October 24, 1930.

Sides, John Emory
Born: February 22, 1873, Van Zandt County, Texas. Died: August 12, 1941, Kaufman County, Texas. Cause of death: Heart disease. Married: (1) Virdie Youngblood, March 8, 1899. (2) Rena Irvine, July 28, 1904. Children: James Love, Jack, W. Irvine, and Mary Bell. Father: William A. Sides. Mother: Susan Parker. Occupation: Livestock dealer. Sources: Death Certificate; *Canton Herald*, August 14, 1941; Quana Barber, Sides Family historian.

Sides, Katie
Born: January 17, 1903, Texas. Died: March 1, 1999. Married: Lewis Lamar Sides, February 14, 1926. Children: Marvonne and Gloria. Father: Charles E. Harris. Mother: Minnie E. Harris. Occupation: Manager of claims, Fireman's Fund Insurance. Sources: 1910 U. S. Census; *Van Zandt News*, March 7, 1999.

Sides, Lewis H. "Lude"
Born: January 14, 1870, Van Zandt County, Texas. Died: April 5, 1920, Van Zandt County, Texas. Married: (1) Floy E. Petty, October 12, 1893. Died: August 12, 1898. (2) Lula L. Starnes, November 24, 1901. Children: Avis, Jack, and Lamar. Father: William A. Sides. Mother: Susan Parker. Occupation: Deputy Sheriff. Comments: Lude Sides worked as a Van Zandt County Deputy Sheriff under Sheriff John R. Kellis. Sources: *Canton Herald*, April 9, 1920; Quana Barber, Sides Family historian.

SIDES, LEWIS LAMAR
Born: January 9, 1897, Van Zandt County, Texas. Died: March 5, 1952, Galveston County, Texas. Married: Kate Harris, February 14, 1926. Children: Marvonne and Gloria. Father: Louis H. "Lude" Sides. Mother: Floy E. Petty. Occupation: Banker. Comments: Lamar Sides worked at the First National Bank in Canton for thirty-six years. He was a cashier and Vice President. Sources: *Canton Herald*, March 13, 1952; Eubank Funeral Home records.

SIDES, LILA BELLE
Born: December 9, 1909, Van Zandt County, Texas. Died: April 9, 1964, Dallas County, Texas. Cause of death: Cancer. Never married. Father: Walter L. Sides. Mother: Effie L. Hobbs. Source: Death Certificate.

SIDES, LULA L.
Born: February 1, 1879, Van Zandt County, Texas. Died: August 15, 1966, Van Zandt County, Texas. Married: Lewis H. "Lude" Sides, November 24, 1901. Children: Avis and Jack. Father: John Jacob Starnes. Mother: Nancy A. Osborn. Sources: *Canton Herald*, September 1, 1966; Eubank Funeral Home records.

SIDES, MINNIE LEE
Born: March 20, 1895, Texas. Died: September 15, 1972, Van Zandt County, Texas. Cause of death: Heart disease. Married: Henry Monroe Sides. Father: Andrew Jackson "Jack" McClellen. Mother: Ellen Adams. Sources: Death Certificate, Eubank Funeral Home records.

SIDES, STELLA M.
Born: November 19, 1899, Van Zandt County, Texas. Died: February 27, 1955, Dallas County, Texas. Cause of death: Heart disease. Single. Father: Walter Lee Sides. Mother: Effie L. Hobbs. Occupation: Bookkeeper. Source: Death Certificate.

SIDES, WALTER LEE
Born: January 18, 1878, Van Zandt County, Texas. Died: September 10, 1959, Dallas County, Texas. Cause of death: Heart disease. Married: Effie Letitia Hobbs, December 13, 1896. Children: Julia Paralee, Stella M., Bonnie S, Azle A., Kelly Hobbs, Audra Geroline, Lela Belle, Walter Love, and James C. Father: Elias Brock Sides. Mother: Sarah Elizabeth Cox. Occupation: Building contractor. Sources: Death Certificate, Sides Family History.

SIDES, WILLIAM ROY
Born: May 7, 1899, Van Zandt County, Texas. Died: August 1, 1930, Lubbock County, Texas. Married: Leola Cox. Father: Louis H. "Lude" Sides. Mother: Floy E. Petty. (Note: Possible error on tombstone. Death certificate shows the name of mother as Floy Petty. Tombstone shows Petty's death date as August 12, 1898. Tombstone for William shows he was born May 7, 1899.) Occupation: Grocery store manager. Comments: William Sides' obituary was reported as follows: "At an early age his mother passed away, after which his keeping reverted to his grandparents, then to his step mother, his father having remarried, the latter, Mrs. Lula Sides, nee Starnes, proving a mother to the young man in all that the word implies from his boyhood on up to young manhood." He was the manager of the local Piggly Wiggly grocery store for many years. Sources: Death Certificate; *Canton Herald*, August 8, 1930.

Jesse Smith

Lannie Bell Smith

SIMMONS, HENRY SCOTT
Born: January 7, 1886, Van Zandt County, Texas. Died: December 11, 1976, Van Zandt County, Texas. Married: Maude Green Mullins, January 31, 1909. Children: Avis, Lorene, Sibyl, John, Williard, and Jack. Father: John T. Simmons. Mother: Elizabeth Rowan. Sources: Eubank Funeral Home records, Ancestry.com.

SIMMONS, MAUDE GREEN
Born: February 18, 1887, Van Zandt County, Texas. Died: February 28, 1961, Van Zandt County, Texas. Cause of death: Heart disease. Married: Henry Scott Simmons, January 31, 1909. Children: Avis, Lorene, Sibyl, John, Williard, and Jack. Father: W. B. Mullins. Mother: Fannie Shriver. Source: Death Certificate.

SIMMONS, WILLIARD G.
Born: December 18, 1911, Texas. Died: April 10, 1928, Dallas County, Texas. Cause of death: Appendicitis. Single. Father: Henry Scott Simmons. Mother: Maude Green Mullins. Source: Death Certificate.

Simpson, Frances Merle
Born: August 28, 1893, Van Zandt County, Texas. Died: April 11, 1963, Smith County, Texas. Married: Jessie Pinkney Simpson. Children: Frank Foster, Jesse P, Jr. Father: Marcus Columbus Foster. Mother: Jeffie Lona Thompson. Siblings: Oscar Thompson, Bessie, Marcus Homer, Mary Mildred, Jessie Lona, and Marcus Glen. Sources: Death Certificate, Ancestry.com, Find A Grave.

Simpson, Frank Foster
Born: March 17, 1913, Van Zandt County, Texas. Died: August 5, 1924, Dallas County, Texas. Cause of death: Appendicitis. Father: Jessie P. Simpson. Mother: Frances Merle Foster. Sibling: Jessie Jr. Source: *Grand Saline Sun*, August 21, 1924.

Simpson, Jessie P., Jr.
Born: October 7, 1921, Van Zandt County, Texas. Died: March 26, 1929, Dallas County, Texas. Cause of death: Appendicitis. Single. Father: Jessie P. Simpson. Mother: Frances Merle Foster. Occupation: Student. Sibling: Frank Foster. Comments: Jessie Simpson and his brother, Frank, are buried with a double marker. Frank died from appendicitis in 1924. Source: Death Certificate.

Simpson, Jessie Pinkney, Sr.
Born: October 29, 1890, Texas. Died: April 3, 1979, Van Zandt County, Texas. Cause of death: Chronic obstructive pulmonary disease. Married: Frances Merle Foster, June 16, 1912. Children: Frank Foster and Jessie Pinkney, Jr. Father: Frank Morris Simpson. Mother: Emma E. Looney. Occupation: Morton Salt Company. Sources: Death Certificate, Ancestry.com.

Slaughter, John W.
Born: November 15, 1925, Donley County, Texas. Died: December 28, 2010, Eastland County, Texas. Married: Sylvia Ashby, 1966, divorced. Children: John, Steve, Leslie, and Patricia. Father: John Slaughter. Mother: Bess Burgess. Occupation: Jeweler. Military: WWII, US Navy. Source: *Van Zandt News*, January 9, 2011.

Slaughter, Dr. Manuel Owen "Jim"
Born: July 5, 1918, Van Zandt County, Texas. Died: May 7, 1983, Dallas County, Texas. Married: Margaret E. Warren. Father: Willie S. Slaughter. Mother: Sudie M. Slaughter. Occupation: Physician. Military: WWII, Medical Corps. Comments: Jim Slaughter's medical corps unit was the first to use whole blood instead of plasma in treating battlefield injuries. Jim received his Bachelor of Science Degree from the University of Texas, a Master's Degree from the University of Arkansas, and his MD Degree from the University of Arkansas in 1952. He had lived in Irving and Euless, Texas since 1957. He was a general practitioner. Sources: *Van Zandt News*, May 15, 1983.

Slaughter, Margaret Elizabeth Warren
Born: February 18, 1919, Colfax County, New Mexico. Died: March 15, 1983, Tarrant County, Texas. Married: Dr. Manuel O. "Jim" Slaughter. Father: William Joseph Warren. Mother: Alma Grace Henry. Sources: *Van Zandt News*, March 20, 1983; Ancestry.com.

Smith, Alonzo
Born: February 20, 1851, Panola County, Texas. Died: January 1, 1882, Van Zandt County, Texas. Married: Sallie Ann Ford. Father: Mitchell Smith. Mother: Martha Smith. Occupation: Farmer. Sources: 1860, 1870, 1880 US Census; Ancestry.com.

Smith, Annie
Born: Unknown. Died: Unknown. Father: Berry Smith. Mother: Unknown. (On same tombstone as Berry Smith.) Source: Tombstone.

Smith, Berry
Born: July 17, 1844, Cass County, Georgia (born a slave). Died: April 18, 1919, Van Zandt County, Texas. Married: (1) Lou Shelly, April 9, 1891. Divorce: Granted October 28, 1901. (2) Mary Smith, September 16, 1907. Father: Unknown Smith. Mother: Unknown. Comments: The *Canton Herald* gave this account of Berry Smith's death. "Uncle" Berry, as we knew him, was born in Cass County, Georgia, on July 17, 1842 (tombstone has 1844); moved to Texas in 1883, settling near Bonham. In 1890 he moved to Van Zandt County and made a good citizen of his race and the court records show him to have been a true and honest man and law-abiding. He stood up for the right and would fight the wrong, saying he believed men should lead a clean life and earn their bread by the sweat of their brow. He leaves a wife, and seven children, nine grandchildren and two great-grandchildren. K.M." Source: *Canton Herald*, December 26, 1919.

Smith, Charles P. Jr.
Born: January 11, 1888, Texas. Died: October 9, 1967, Dallas County, Texas. Single. Father: Dr. Charles P. Smith. Mother: Dorothy Tulula (Lula) Peel. Occupation: Certified Public Accountant. Source: Death Certificate.

Smith, Dr. Charles Pinkney, "Dr. C.P."
(Photo page 127) Born: May 3, 1856, Bibb County, Georgia. Died: November 1915, Van Zandt County, Texas. Married: Lula D. Peel, October 12, 1884. Father: John Thomas Smith. Mother: Elizabeth Richardson. Occupation: Physician. Comments: Dr. Charles Smith's parents were large planters and slave owners in Georgia before the Civil War. He was one of thirteen children. He remained in Georgia until he was 18 years old. Later he went to Florida and then to Smith County, Texas in 1877. Charles was educated in the common schools

of Georgia and later attended Charm Wood Institute, Tyler, Texas. He began the study of medicine under Dr. E. Jones on January 12, 1880. Later, he studied at the American Medical College of St. Louis, Missouri. After graduation, he came to Van Zandt County and began his practice at Owlet Green. A few years later he moved to Canton. By 1900, in addition to his home, he had acquired fifty acres of land adjoining Canton and also owned 154 acres of farm land elsewhere in Van Zandt County. He practiced medicine for thirty-five years prior to his death and was a highly respected citizen of Canton. Sources: *The Southland*; *Canton Herald*, November 26, 1915.

Smith, Dorothy Tulula "Lula"

Born: November 23, 1866, Macon County, Alabama. Died: June 13, 1954, Van Zandt County, Texas. Cause of death: Stroke. Married: Dr. Charles P. Smith, October 12, 1884. Children: Cannie, Charles P., Claudie, Lettie, Lessie, Katie May, and Dr. Edgar Eugene. Father: Dr. W. W. Peel, Georgia. Mother: Sarah Francis Jones, Georgia. Comments: Lula Smith was the widow of Dr. C. P. Smith, a Canton physician who died in 1915. She had been a resident of Canton for sixty-four years. One of her daughters Lessie, married G. W. Tull, Jr., the son of a prominent early merchant of Canton. Sources: Death Certificate; *Dallas Morning News*, June 14, 1954; Ancestry.com.

Smith, Dr. Edgar Eugene

Born: August 27, 1901, Van Zandt County, Texas. Died: August 28, 1954, Limestone County, Texas. Cause of death: Heart attack. Single. Father: Dr. C. P. Smith, Georgia. Mother: Dorothy Tulula Peel, Georgia. Occupation: Physician. Military: WWII, US. Air Force. Comments: Edgar Smith was the son of a pioneer Canton physician, C. P. Smith. He graduated from Baylor Medical College and interned there for two years. He served as an instructor at the college for several years. He established his practice in Lubbock in 1928. In May of 1939, he moved his practice to Canton and opened his office above the Palace Drug Store on the square. After serving in the U. S. Air Force in World War II, he moved his practice to Wortham, Texas. He lived there until his death. Sources: Death Certificate; *Canton Herald*, May 4, 1939; *Dallas Morning News*, August 29, 1954; Eubank Funeral Home records.

Smith, Henry Hawthorne

(Photo page 124) Born: January 17, 1899. Died: March 8, 1949. Married: Lillie B. Smith. Divorced in 1932. (2) Cleo Love, July 1, 1934. Father: Walter Smith. Mother: Lannie Bell Wynne. Siblings: Leta Bell and Zeffie Telasco. Occupation: Texas Department of Transportation. Sources: 1930 US Census, Eubank Funeral Home records.

Smith, Jesse

(Photo page 128) Born: April 22, 1868, Tennessee. Died: June 17, 1929, Van Zandt County, Texas. Cause of death: Paralysis. Married: Laular Porter, December 18, 1904. Father: John A. Smith. Mother: Isabelle Waltin. Occupation: Barber, jeweler. Source: Death Certificate.

Smith, Lannie Bell

(Photo page 128) Born: January 19, 1877. Died: May 2, 1958. Cause of death: Stroke. Married: Walter Smith, November 25, 1894. Children: Maudella, Henry Hawthorn, Leta Bell, Zeffie Telaska, Nona Ethelene, and Elvis Franklin. Father: Edmond Wynne. Mother: Martha Shaw. Source: Death Certificate.

Smith, Mary

Born: Unknown. Died: Unknown. Father: Berry Smith. Mother: Unknown. (On same tombstone as Berry Smith.) Source: Tombstone.

Charlie L. Spears

Lucius Mack Spears

Mary Jane Spears

Mary Elizabeth "Mollie" Spears and Rufus Spears

Smith, T.M.
Born: Unknown. Death: Unknown. Father: Unknown Smith. Mother: Unknown. Source: Tombstone.

Smith, Walter
Born: 1873, Smith County, Texas. Died: September 9, 1934, Van Zandt County, Texas. Cause of death: Heart disease. Married: Lannie Bell Wynne, November 25, 1894. Father: Charles Smith. Mother: Elsie Smith. Occupation: Farmer. Source: Death Certificate.

Smithart, Jackson H.
Born: October 15, 1903. Died: October 2, 1904. Father: Joe Smithart. Mother: Beulah Clark. Source: *Wills Point Chronicle*, October 13, 1904.

Snodgrass, Infant
Born: December 24, 1897. Died: December 24, 1897. Father: T. A. Snodgrass. Mother: L. F. Snodgrass. Source: Tombstone.

Snodgrass, Mary E.
Born: December 24, 1897. Died: April 16, 1898. Father: T. A. Snodgrass. Mother: L. F. Snodgrass. Source: Tombstone.

Spears, A.Z.
Born: December 27, 1904. Died: August 25, 1905. Father: Rufus B. Spears. Mother: Mary E. "Mollie." Montgomery. Source: Tombstone.

Spears, Charlie L.
Born: August 9, 1866, Georgia. Died: July 21, 1892, Van Zandt County, Texas. Married: Belle (Robertson) Jones, January 10, 1887. Children: Minnie Beatrice, Carlos L., and Mollie May. Father: Lucius Mack Spears. Mother: Mary Jane Barnes. Comments: Charlie Spears' widow married Thomas C. Davidson, September 3, 1895 and lived for sixty-four years. She is buried in the Barbee Cemetery, Erath County, Texas. Sources: *Canton Telephone*, July 22, 1892; Find A Grave.

Spears, Effie Vesta
Born: April 7, 1901. Died: November 5, 1901. Father: Rufus B. Spears. Mother: Mary E. "Mollie" Montgomery. Source: Tombstone.

Spears, Johnnie A.
Born: January 27, 1876. Died: July 21, 1893. Father: Lucius Mack Spears. Mother: Mary Jane Barnes. Comments: Johnnie Spears was ill with a very debilitating condition for a number of years. The *Canton Telephone* reported the following: "Johnnie Spears is in critical condition with rheumatism. His limbs can't be moved without very excruciating pain." Johnnie lived almost four more years with this illness before he died in 1893. Sources: *Canton Telephone*, September 6, 1889; Ancestry.com.

Spears, Laveta
Born: August 12, 1893. Died: December 10, 1894. Cause of death: Diphtheria. Father: Rufus B. Spears. Mother: Mary E. "Mollie" Montgomery. Comments: Laveta Spears was buried in the same grave as her sister, Mary Zula, who had died three days earlier from the same disease. Source: *Wills Point Chronicle*, December 13, 1894.

Spears, Lucius Mack
Born: June 19, 1835, North Carolina. Died: January 26, 1912, Van Zandt County, Texas. Married: Mary Jane Barnes. Children: Rufus B., Martha Eula, George Thomas, William L., Mary L., and Johnnie. Father: Nathaniel Spears. Mother: Jane G. (Jincy) Taylor. Occupation: Farmer, hotel owner, restaurant owner. Military: CSA, 28th TX. Cavalry, Co. E mechanic. Comments: L. M. Spears came to Texas in 1859 and served in the Civil War. After the War, he moved back to Georgia and lived there for six years before returning to Rusk County, Texas. He then moved to Garden Valley in Van Zandt County and from there to Canton in the early 1880's. He lived in Canton and Grand Saline for 28 years before he died. He engaged in various businesses. In September, 1887, he purchased the Star Restaurant on the Canton square and later owned a hotel. He was a Mason for 42 years and a member of the Methodist Church for 46 years. In his declining years he lived with his son, R. B. Spears, until his death. Sources: 1880 U. S. Census; *Canton Telephone*, September 16, 1887; *Wills Point Chronicle*, February 1, 1912; Find A Grave.

Spears, Mary Elizabeth "Mollie"
Born: March 18, 1870, Texas. Died: October 19, 1961, Van Zandt County, Texas. Cause of death: Heart disease. Married: Rufus B. Spears, September 3, 1889. Children: Iphis, Mary Zulalee, Laveta, M. J, Mollie Donnie , Effie Vesta, R. B., and A. Z. Father: Dr. Jim Montgomery. Mother: Mary Elizabeth Wilborn. Comments: The *Canton Telephone* announced that R. B Spears and Miss Mollie Montgomery were married at the residence of H. Morris, two miles east of town (Canton) Monday night. Mollie was 19 and Rufus was 29. They had eloped and were married. The marriage lasted for thirty-two years, ending at Rufus' death in 1921. Mollie's mother was a teacher and died less than a year after Mollie was born. Mollie's father, a doctor, practiced in Garden Valley. He had five brothers, and they were all doctors. Mollie outlived Rufus by forty years, and seven children tragically died during their marriage. Sources: Death Certificate; *Canton Telephone*, September 6, 1889; "Nannie Spears and Grandpa Spears" by Maudie Bailey Spears.

Judge John S. Spinks, Sr. *was the longest serving County Judge in Van Zandt County history. He was elected County Judge in 1882 and served intermittently until his death in 1910 for a total of almost fifteen years, during which he was in charge of carrying out the state's guidelines in the development of the rural school system in Van Zandt County. He was also a Mason, a member of the Canton Lodge 141, and a Knights Templar in Wills Point, Texas.*

Spears, Mary Jane

(Photo, page 130) Born: March 12, 1841. Died: November 5, 1898. Married: Lucius Mack Spears. Children: William L., Rufus B., Charlie L., Martha Eula, George T., Johnnie A., and Mary L. Father: Woodard Barnes. Mother: Mary "Polly" Boykin. Source: Ancestry.com.

Spears, Mary Zulalee

Born: November 5, 1891, Van Zandt County, Texas. Died: December 7, 1894, Van Zandt County, Texas. Father: Rufus B. Spears. Mother: Mary E. "Mollie" Montgomery. Comments: Tragedy struck Rufus and Mollie Spears' family. On November 5, 1894, their daughter, Mary Zula, became ill with diphtheria and died within a few hours. Her sister, Laveta, was critically ill with the same disease, and she died two days later. On December 10, 1894 the two sisters were buried in the same grave. Source: *Wills Point Chronicle,* December 13, 1894.

Spears, Mollie Donnie

Born: April 19, 1899. Died: August 28, 1904. Father Rufus B. Spears. Mother: Mary E. "Mollie" Montgomery. Source: Tombstone.

Spears, R.B.

Born: September 15, 1902. Died: July 14, 1920. Single. Father: Rufus B. Spears. Mother: Mary E. "Mollie" Montgomery. Comments: R. B. Spears was almost 18 when she died. She was one of six children of Rufus and Mollie Spears who died before adulthood. Her brother, Iphis, was thrown from a horse resulting in his death when he was 29 years old. Source: "Nannie Spears and Grandpa Spears" by Maudie Bailey Spears.

Spears, Rufus B.

(Photo page 130) Born: January 12, 1860. Died: February 6, 1921. Married: Mary E. "Mollie" Montgomery, September 3, 1889. Children: Iphis, Mary Zulalee, Laveta, M. J., Mollie Donnie, Effie Vesta, R. B., and A. Z. Father: Lucius Mack Spears. Mother: Mary Jane Barnes. Occupation: Livestock trader, farmer. Comments: In 1893 Rufus and Mollie Spears bought a 200-acre farm on the Saline Creek from the heirs of the first settler in the area, David Jackson Strickland. In 1903 the Spears sold this farm to William Jordan and his family, and the Spears family moved to Grand Saline. Rufus worked for a hardware company for a time and then went to work for Salt City Company, selling general merchandise. He started buying lots at Rhodesburg, a Socialist community. He eventually bought the "Kuykendall House," built by Rev. Kuykendall to house teachers and students for the local teacher training college that had closed. Mollie and Rufus put down their roots and lived in this two-story, eleven room house for the rest of their lives. The Spears had eight children. Six children died by the age of 18. One son, Iphis, fell off a horse at the age of 29 and broke his neck. M. J. Spears was the only surviving child, and he died at the age of 80. In his later years, Rufus worked for a monument company. During that time he placed tombstones on his children's graves who were buried at Hillcrest Cemetery. These gravestones are still there. Rufus died from cancer in 1921. Mollie lived for forty more years. Sources: *Canton Herald*, February 18, 1921; "Nannie Spears and Grandpa Spears" by Maudie Baily Spears.

Spinks, Angus Thompson

Born: 1895, Van Zandt County, Texas. Died: 1939, Oklahoma. Married: Gladys Belle Lewis, June 20, 1928. Father: John S. Spinks, Sr. Mother: Zollie T.

Claud L. "Judge" Stanford and Georgia Hassell Stanford

CLAUD LEONIDAS "C.L." STANFORD *graduated from Canton High School in 1936, North Texas Agricultural College in 1939, and the University of Texas Law School in 1942. While serving as a Captain in WWII, he was awarded a Purple Heart and three Bronze Battle Stars. During the Korean War, he served in Counter-Intelligence. C.L. practiced law in Canton for fifty-eight years and was active in civic organizations, serving as president of the Canton ISD Board for fourteen years. He was selected as "Canton Man of the Year" in 1968.*

Thompson. Occupation: Oil field worker. Source: 1930 U.S. Census.

SPINKS, ELIZABETH Z.
Born: March 4, 1901. Died: February 24, 1982. Father: John S. Spinks. Mother: Zollie T. Thompson. Occupation: Assistant treasurer, Mercantile Security Life Insurance Co. Comments: Elizabeth Spinks lived in the Dallas area for fifty-two years. She moved to Canton in 1977. Her father, John S. Spinks, was the longest-serving County Judge in Van Zandt County history. Source: *Canton Herald*, March 4, 1982.

SPINKS, GLADYS BELLE
Born: August 2, 1901, Collin County, Texas. Died: March 13, 1978, Seminole County, Oklahoma. Married: August T. Spinks. Father: Edd Lewis. Mother: Stella Lewis. Sources: 1920 U. S. Census, Eubank Funeral Home records, Ancestry.com.

SPINKS, JOHN S., JR.
Born: June 13, 1890, Van Zandt County, Texas. Died: June 4, 1942, San Francisco County, California. Single. Father: John S. Spinks, Sr. Mother: Zollie Thompson. Occupation: Truck driver. Comments: John Spinks' father was the longest-serving County Judge in Van Zandt County history. Sources: 1940 U. S. Census, California Death Index.

SPINKS, JOHN S., SR., "JUDGE"
Born: April 5, 1853, Marshall County, Mississippi. Died: March 6, 1910, Van Zandt County, Texas. Cause of death: Cirrhosis of the liver. Married: Zollie Thompson, November 25, 1886. Children: William B., Blanche, John S. Jr., Agnes T., and Zollie Elizabeth. Father: William B. Spinks, North Carolina. Mother: Susan Searcy Paynne, Mississippi. Occupation: Lawyer, County Judge. Comments: John S. Spinks was the longest serving County Judge in Van Zandt County history. When he was 10

Clarence "Ted" Stanberry

Dr. William J. Stanford

Cameron Spencer Starnes, Sr.

Daisy Lucille Starnes

years old, his family moved from Mississippi to Arkansas. At the age of 19, he was teaching school in Pulaski County, Arkansas. John moved to Rusk County, Texas in 1875. He moved to Canton in 1878 where he resided for the rest of his life. He was elected County Judge in 1882 and served intermittently until his death on March 6, 1910 for a total of almost 15 years. Besides being a County Judge, John was a well-known Democratic politician in East Texas. The *Wills Point Chronicle* described John as follows: "He was a man of unusual ability and easily one of the best-read men and most entertaining and fluent speakers in the county." As Judge, he led the county through a growing period of the 1880's, 1890's and into the first decade of the 1900's. As County Judge, he was in charge of carrying out the state's guidelines in the development of the rural school system in Van Zandt County. In 1884 Spinks appointed W. L. Haynes, G. W. Goodwin, and R. S. Jones to seek out and buy land for a pauper's farm. This was completed in 1885 when 339 acres were purchased in the James Douthit Survey. John was a prominent Mason, a member of the Canton Lodge 141, and a Knights Templar in Wills Point, Texas. He had a large funeral at the Methodist Church. He was buried in the family plot at the Canton City Cemetery (Hillcrest). Sources: Death Certificate; *Wills Point Chronicle*, December 16, 1897; *Grand Saline Sun*, March 10, 1910.

Spinks, Zollie T.

Born: February 20, 1862. Died: September 26, 1909. Cause of death: Spider bite. Married: John S. Spinks, Sr., November 25, 1886. Children: William B., Blanche, John S., Jr., Angus Thompson, and Zollie Elizabeth. Father: Angus Joseph Thompson. Mother: Mary Wells. Comments: Zollie Spinks had been bitten on the foot by a spider a few weeks before she died. The *Grand Saline Sun* reported her final hours as follows: "She was thought to be doing ok, but at 11 o'clock Sunday, her husband, Judge John S. Spinks, heard her struggling for breath and she died before medical aid could be secured." She and her husband were prominent citizens of Canton. He was a lawyer and served as Van Zandt County Judge for almost fifteen years. Sources: *Grand Saline Sun*, September 30, 1909; Ancestry.com.

Springer, Infant Son

Born: 1936. Died: 1936. Father: Owen Springer. Mother: Ruth Yantis. Comments: He was the only child of Owen and Ruth Yantis Springer. Source: *Canton Herald*, January 27, 1949 (Father's obituary).

Springer, Owen

Born: May 5, 1903, Van Zandt County, Texas. Died: January 21, 1949, Dallas County, Texas. Married: Ruth Yantis, June 12, 1932. Father: Robert L. Springer, Lee County, Mississippi. Mother: Nina Allen, McIntosh County, Oklahoma. Occupation: Druggist. Comments: Owen Springer was born in Grand Saline, Texas and moved to Canton to enter the drug business with J. T. Beard. J. T. Beard retired from the business in 1937 due to ill health. The partnership of Owen Springer and Sam Beard was then formed and lasted until Springer's death. Owen's wife was the daughter of Judge T. R. Yantis. They had one child who died as an infant. Owen was a very popular businessman. The *Canton Herald* reported his death as follows: "The esteem in which Owen was held by his friends in Canton and many other Towns was shown by one of the largest floral offerings in the history of the town and by the crowd of people filling the auditorium to overflowing." Sources: Death Certificate; *Canton Herald*, January 27, 1949.

Staley, Lottie Marie

Born: August 26, 1921. Died: June 27, 1999. Single. Father: Willie Raymond "Wid" Staley. Mother: Vergie Ina

Reynolds. Sibling: Arlie. Comments: Marie Staley was a lifelong resident of Van Zandt County living in the Oakland and Wentworth communities. She was a member of the Oakland Baptist Church and Canton Rebekah Lodge No. 277. She was survived by her brother. Source: *Canton Herald*, July 4, 1999.

Staley, Vergie Ina

Born: February 18, 1902, Kaufman County, Texas. Died: March 11, 1990. Married: Willie Raymond "Wid" Staley, October 19, 1919. Children: Arlie Lee and Lottie Marie. Father: Jesse W. Reynolds. Mother: Mattie Reynolds. Comments: Virgie Staley was a member of the Oak Grove Baptist Church in Canton, Texas. Source: *Van Zandt News*, March 18, 1990.

Staley, Willie Raymond "Wid"

Born: February 4, 1898, Van Zandt County, Texas. Died: April 2, 1980, Kaufman County, Texas. Married: Vergie Ina Reynolds, October 19, 1919. Children: Arlie Lee and Lottie Marie. Father: John Franklin Staley. Mother: Florence Bailey. Siblings: Jesse James, Carrie Lenora, Oddie Franklin, Essie Anise, Ruby D., Ruthie B., Maggie Lee, Mattie Oler, May, Elsie Carmon, and Ellie Gladys. Occupation: Farmer. Comments: The Staley family came from North Carolina and settled in Texas in 1885. Wid Staley spent most of his life farming in the Starr and Wentworth communities. His daughter, Lottie, never married and Arlie had only girls. The Staley name will end with Arlie. Sources: *Canton Herald*, April 10, 1980; *Van Zandt County Histories and Biographies Volume II.*

Stanberry, Clarence Teddy "Ted"

Born: February 2, 1905, Van Zandt County, Texas. Died: April 23, 1964, Van Zandt County, Texas. Married: Lillie May Staley, August 24, 1923. Children: Ruby and Jo Ann. Father: Van Buren Stanberry. Mother: Mary Emeline Mandy Aliminta Bond. Siblings: Samantha Jane, America Emeline, Thomas Marion, John Robert, James Albert, George Elbert, Laura May, Effie Lee, Eunice Edna, Iva Myrtle, Winnie S., Clyde Dick, Homer William, and Carl Clifford (Pat). Occupation: Texas Department of Transportation. Sources: Death Certificate; *Canton Herald*, April 30, 1964; Find A Grave.

Stanberry, Lillie Mae

Born: August 4, 1902, Van Zandt County, Texas. Died: September 2, 1977, Van Zandt County, Texas. Married: Clarence Teddy Stanberry, August 24, 1923. Children: Ruby and Jo Ann. Father: John Franklin Staley. Mother: Florence Leila Bailey. Siblings: Jesse James, Carrie Lenora, William Raymond, Oddie Franklin, Essie Annis, Ruby D., and Ruthie B. Sources: *Canton Herald*, September 8, 1977; Find A Grave.

Stanford, Claud L., Sr. "Judge"

(Photo page 133) Born: March 14, 1871, Henry County, Alabama. Died: October 21, 1924, Van Zandt County, Texas. Married: Georgia H. Chandler, December 25, 1892. Children: Roxie M., Paul Horace, Dealva K., Raymond, Eric, Geraldine, and C. L., Jr. Father: Dr. William J. Stanford. Mother: Martha Jane Guilford. Occupation: Lawyer, County Judge. Comments: Claud Stanford came to Van Zandt County with his family in 1884. He was admitted to the bar in 1895. He practiced law in Grand Saline until 1900. He moved to Canton and began a partnership with R. M. Lively. This partnership lasted for almost 15 years. In 1910, Claud was elected County Judge and served two terms. At the end of his term, he formed a law partnership with his son, Raymond, and Morgan G. Sanders. When Raymond moved to Dallas to practice

In 1869, **David Jackson "Jack" Strickland** *and his wife* **Mary A. "Polly" Austin Strickland** *became the first settlers along the Saline Creek in Van Zandt County. He purchased 200 acres of farmland, which later became the Wentworth and Oakland communities. He was involved in the formation of local schools and the early politics in the county.*

law, W. E. West joined the law firm; and this partnership lasted until Claud's death in 1924. Sources: *Canton Herald*, October 1924 and January 16, 1925; *Wills Point Chronicle*, October 23, 1924.

STANFORD, CLAUD LEONIDAS JR. "C.L."

Born: April 3, 1919, Van Zandt County, Texas. Died: October 8, 2000, Smith County, Texas. Married: Kathleen Mildred Jackson. Children: Ann, Elaine, Julia, and Carol. Father: Claud L. Stanford, Sr. Mother: Georgia H. Chandler. Occupation: Lawyer. Military: WWII, Korea, US Army Captain. Comments: C. L. Stanford graduated from Canton High School in 1936, North Texas Agricultural College in 1939, and the University of Texas Law School in 1942. During his military service, he was awarded a Purple Heart and three Bronze Battle Stars. He was recalled and served in Counter-Intelligence from 1951-52 during the Korean War. C. L. practiced law in Canton for fifty-eight years and was active in civic organizations serving as president of the Canton ISD Board for fourteen years. He was selected as "Canton Man of the Year" in 1968. Sources: *Canton Herald*, July 12, 1945 and October 12, 2000.

STANFORD, DEALVA K. "DEE"

Born: September 7, 1904, Texas. Died: March 15, 1972, Van Zandt County, Texas. Cause of death: Colon cancer. Single. Father: Claude Leonidas Stanford. Mother: Georgia H. Chandler. Sources: Death Certificate, Eubank Funeral Home records.

STANFORD, GEORGIA HASSELL

(Photo page 133) Born: December 23, 1873, Van Zandt County, Texas. Died: July 1, 1961, Van Zandt County, Texas. Cause of death: Heart disease. Married: Claud L. Stanford, December 25, 1892. Children: Eric, Paul, Roxie, Dealva K., Raymond, Dely Geraldine, and C. L. Father: John Crawford Chandler. Mother: Ruth Ann Clough. Source: Death Certificate.

STANFORD, ROXIE MATTIE

Born: September 6, 1896, Van Zandt County, Texas. Died: December 22, 1978, Van Zandt County, Texas. Cause of death: Natural causes. Single. Father: Claud L. Stanford. Mother: Georgia H. Chandler. Occupation: School teacher. Sources: Death Certificate, Hilliard Funeral Home records.

STANFORD, DR. WILLIAM JONATHAN

(Photo page 134) Born: September 3, 1834, North Carolina. Died: June 11, 1911, Van Zandt County, Texas. Cause of Death: Cancer of the larynx. Married: (1) Martha J Guilford, May 26, 1858. (2) Mrs. L.L. Stringer Hollifield, November 26, 1899. Divorced: April 11, 1901. Father: Thomas Jefferson Stanford, Duplin County, North Carolina. Mother: Dorothy McGee. Occupation: Physician. Military: CSA, Captain Assistant Staff Surgeon, 39th Alabama Reg. 2nd Division of Polk's Corps, Army of Tennessee. Comments: William Stanford moved with his parents to Georgia and later to Henry County, Alabama. He graduated from medical school at the University of Nashville, Tennessee in 1858 and served during the Civil War. After the War, William practiced medicine in Alabama until 1884 when he and his family moved to Van Zandt County. He continued his medical practice until his death. He and his wife had eleven children. Claud L. Stanford and Ada Hightower were the only children who settled in Van Zandt County. Sources: *Biographical Sketch of William J. Stanford* by C. L. Stanford of Canton, publication date unknown; *Grand Saline Sun*, June 15, 1911.

Allen C. Strickland

Margaret Ann "Tibbie" Strickland

Alma Rivers (Cole) Sumner

Judy Taylor

Staples, Isiah Rayshaun
Born: 2004. Died: 2004. Father: Unknown Staples. Mother: Unknown. Source: Tombstone.

Starnes, Cameron Spencer, Sr.
(Photo page 134) Born: April 17, 1878, Fannin County, Texas. Died: December 18, 1949, Dallas County, Texas. Cause of death: Pneumonia. Married: Daisy Lucille Coleman, February 8, 1903. Children: William, Cameron, Jasper, Lucy, Rena, Marie, and Rachel. Father: John Starnes, Texas. Mother: Mary Elizabeth Starnes. Occupation: Banker. Comments: In 1902 Cameron Spencer began his career as an Assistant in the Van Zandt County Clerk's office in Canton, Texas. He held that position for two years. In 1904, he entered the banking business as an Assistant Cashier of the Van Zandt County National Bank in Wills Point. Sources: Death Certificate; *Wills Point Chronicle*, November 8, 1904; *Canton Herald*, December 23, 1949.

Starnes, Daisy Lucille
(Photo page 134) Born: May 4, 1884, Van Zandt County, Texas. Died: August 15, 1969, Tarrant County, Texas. Married: Cameron Spencer Starnes, February 8, 1903. Children: William, Cameron, Jasper, Lucy, Rena, Marie, and Rachel. Father: William D. Coleman. Mother: Serena Rachel Copeland. Sources: *Dallas Morning News*, August 17, 1969; Eubank Funeral Home records.

Starnes, Johnathan Ryan (Twin)
Born: July 11, 1990. Died: July 12, 1990. Father: Weldon Shane Starnes. Mother: Patricia Addison. Source: *Van Zandt News*, July 15, 1990.

Starnes, Scott Harrison
Born: December 20, 1967, Van Zandt County, Texas. Died: December 20, 1967, Van Zandt County, Texas. Father: Weldon F. Starnes. Mother: Linda Lou Estes. Source: Death Certificate.

Starnes, Weldon Bryan (Twin)
Born: July 11, 1990. Died: July 11, 1990. Father: Weldon Shane Starnes. Mother: Patricia Addison. Source: *Van Zandt News*, July 15, 1990.

Starnes, Weldon F.
Born: August 11, 1930, Van Zandt County, Texas. Died: May 10, 1988. Married: Linda Lou Estes. Children: Kerry, Shane, Chad, Barbie, Bonnie, and Scott. Father: Dixon Barney Starnes, Jr. Mother: Cora Mae Hawkins. Occupation: Starnes Trucking Service. Military: Korea, U. S. Army Corps of Engineers. Comments: Weldon Starnes was an agent for the TexPack Express Freight Company. Source: Ancestry.com.

Staton, Mary Josephine
Born: March 15, 1856. Died: April 21, 1889. Cause of death: Heart failure. Married: William Jenkins Staton, January 9, 1877. Children: Nora Lee, George Damaron IV, Thomas Smeltzer, and James H. Father: Unknown Morris. Mother: Unknown. Comments: Mary Staton's husband was born in 1855 in Blount County, Alabama. He came to Van Zandt County about 1870. In 1877, it is believed that Mary Josephine's parents died on their way to Texas or shortly thereafter in Smith County. She and her brothers were left as orphans. The children were reared by a Mr. Stone who lived in Van Zandt County. After Mary's death, her husband married a widow, Louise Burks, who helped rear his children. In 1903 William Staton moved his family to Grand Saline, Texas where he and four other men opened the Salt City Company. This company became one of the more prominent businesses in Grand Saline. William Staton died on April 3, 1929 and is buried in the Woodside Cemetery at Grand Saline. Sources: *Van Zandt County History Book, Volume I*; *Canton Telephone*, April 26, 1889; Ancestry.com.

Steed, Florence
Born: April 25, 1885, Van Zandt County, Texas. Died: October 15, 1944, Dallas County, Texas. Cause of death: Heart disease. Married: Walter Lee Steed, November 2, 1902. Father: Jesse L. Taylor, Alabama. Mother: Emma A. Murray, Van Zandt County, Texas. Source: Death Certificate.

Steed, Walter Lee
Born: December 26, 1882, Smith County, Texas. Died: September 22, 1949, Van Zandt County, Texas. Cause of death: Drowning. Married: (1) Florence Taylor, November 2, 1902. (2) Mrs. Lexie Sides, 1946. Father: Dr. Leonard Marbury Steed, Tennessee. Mother: Mary Frances Scott, Texas. Occupation: Banker, County Clerk, County Judge. Comments: Lee Steed received his education in Smith and Van Zandt County public schools. He taught school five years in Van Zandt County. Later, he was engaged in the mercantile business at Myrtle Springs and Edgewood, Texas for about 10 years. In 1916 he was elected County Clerk of Van Zandt County and served two terms. In 1922, he joined the First National Bank of Canton. In 1925 he became Vice President and served in this position for over 20 years. He was very active politically with the local Democratic Party. He served as County Chairman and as a Delegate to the State Democratic Conventions. He was also a City Councilman and a member of the Canton School Board for several years. Walter was elected County Judge of Van Zandt County and served from 1946-1948. At his death, he was Executive Vice President and Cashier of the First State Bank in Van, Texas. On September 22, 1949, Walter drowned while he was fishing in a lake on his farm. When he failed to return home on time, the family went to the lake and found his body in the water. Sources: *Texas Democracy*,

Helen Mae Tawater and Noah Franklin "Frank" Tawater

1937, Vol 1; *Canton Herald*, September 29, 1949; Hilliard Funeral Home records.

STEPHENS, WILLIAM H.

Born: December 24, 1813, Tennessee. Died: June 29, 1885, Van Zandt County, Texas. Cause of death: Gunshot wounds. Married: Nancy McEacharn. Comments: The *Galveston Daily News* reported William H. Stephens' death as follows: "W. H. Stephens, a man about 72 years, living the life of a recluse, a few miles from Canton, in Van Zandt County, was found dead on his place today. He seems to have been shot with a pistol. It is thought by some he committed suicide. Stephens had a difficulty with an individual about a month ago, in which a pistol and shotgun were used, but no one was hurt. He said at that time that he expected to be killed. The old man had some money, but no family or relations living in this country. Full particulars cannot be given yet." Van Zandt County Probate Records show a will signed by W. H. Stephens dated May 28, 1885, filed July 11, 1885 bequeathing a 50 acre farm and all of his personal goods to the law firm of C. B. Kilgore and R. M. Lively. No survivors were listed in his will. Sources: 1860 U. S. Census; Van Zandt County Probate Records; *Galveston Daily News*, July 1, 1885.

STRICKLAND, ALLEN C.

(Photo page 136) Born: August 11, 1859, Georgia. Died: November 17, 1881, Van Zandt County, Texas. Single. Father: David Jackson Strickland, Georgia. Mother: Mary A. "Polly" Austin, Georgia. Siblings: Nancy Jane, Solomon J., Susan N., Gideon S., Michael J., Martha A., John Washington, and William N. Comments: Allen Strickland and his father died one week apart from an unknown illness. Source: *Van Zandt County Texas Histories and Biographies 1848-1991, Vol. 2.*

STRICKLAND, DAVID JACKSON "JACK"

(Photo page 135) Born: June 1825, Georgia. Died: November 25, 1881, Van Zandt County, Texas. Married: Mary A. "Polly" Austin. Children: Nancy Jane, Solomon J., Susan N., Gideon S., Michael J., Martha A., Allen C., John Washington, and Willian N. Father: Unknown Strickland. Mother: Unknown. Comments: Jack moved his family from Cobb County, Georgia about 1860 and settled in Wood County, Texas. He resided there until 1866 when he moved to Van Zandt County. On December 27, 1869 Jack purchased 200 acres of land from Daniel Hallman and became the first to settle along the Saline Creek. This later became the Wentworth and Oakland communities. He was a farmer in Georgia and Van Zandt County. In aggregate, Jack and his heirs accumulated almost 1,000 acres of land, all in Van Zandt County. He was also involved in his community, both in the formation of local schools and the early politics of the county. He was a member of the group who marched on Wills Point in the County Seat War of 1877. In November of 1881, Jack and his son, Allen, died within a week of each other from an unknown disease. Source: *Van Zandt County, Texas Histories and Biographies 1848-1991, Vol. 2.*

STRICKLAND, INFANT BOY

Born: October 6, 1875. Died: October 6, 1875. Father: Gideon S. Strickland. Mother: Margaret A. Manning. Sibling: Walter L. Source: Tombstone.

STRICKLAND, MARGARET ANN "TIBBIE"

(Photo page 136) Born: July 7, 1852, Pendleton County, Kentucky. Died: September 21, 1878, Van Zandt County, Texas. Married: Gideon S. Strickland, ca 1873. Children: Infant born dead and Walter L. Father: James Milo Manning, Pennsylvania. Mother: Martha Gresham, Vermont. Comments: The Manning family came to Van Zandt County in 1858 and was a prominent part of the development of Canton and Van Zandt County. After Tibbie died, her husband married Jo Ann Tyler on March 11, 1880 and lived another fifty years in the Starr and Wentworth communities of Van Zandt County. She is buried next to her parents. Source: *Van Zandt County Texas Histories and Biographies, 1848-1991.*

STRICKLAND, MARY A. "POLLY"

(Photo page 135) Born: 1826, Georgia. Died: October 18, 1888. Married: David Jackson Strickland. Father: Michael Austin, Sr. Mother: Narcyssa Austin. Children: Nancy Jane, Solomon J., Susan N., Gideon S., Michael J., Martha A., Allen C., John Washington, and William N. Comments: Polly Austin and her husband moved to Wood County, Texas about 1860 and resided there until 1866 when the family moved to Van Zandt County. Polly's relative, Mariah Alcey "Lizzy" Austin, married S. P. Compton, and they are buried Hillcrest Cemetery in unmarked graves. Sources: *Van Zandt County Texas Biog-*

raphies, 1848-1991, Vol. 2; *Canton Telephone*, October 19, 1888; Ancestry.com.

Stuart, Lucinda C.
Born: November 17, 1839. Died: December 10, 1893. Cause of death: Pneumonia. Married: J. J. Stuart. Children: Minnie R., W. J., and Buck. Father: Unknown. Mother: Unknown. Occupation: School teacher. Comments: Lucinda's daughter, Minnie, married W. O. Williams, a well- known physician in the 1880's and 1890's in Van Zandt County. Lucinda was teaching at China Grove when she died. Source: *Canton Telephone*, December 15, 1893.

Sullivan, William Adolphus "Dot"
Born: April 13, 1855, Louisiana. Died: August 21, 1899, Van Zandt County, Texas. Married: Sallie Ann Ford. Father: Alexander Sullivan. Mother: Mary Ann McRae. Sources: 1880 U. S. Census; *Free State Enterprise*, August 24, 1899; Find A Grave.

Sumner, (Cole) Alma Rivers
(Photo page 136) (Married name Cole. Buried under Sumner). Born: June 16, 1898, West Homes County, Mississippi. Died: February 19, 1980, Texas. Married: (1) Leonard Grady Sumner. Children: Duward Franklin and Juanita. (2) William E. Cole, 1925. Father: Allen C. White. Mother: Clara Arminta Rosamond. Comments: Alma Cole's first husband died from smallpox in 1918. Her son was an Air Force pilot during WWII, and he was the most decorated serviceman from Van Zandt County. He died in a plane crash in 1946 and is buried in the National Cemetery in Arlington, Texas. Source: Nell Deets Walker, Sumner Family Historian.

Sumner, Benjamin Franklin "Ben"
Born: December 2, 1870, Arkansas. Died: May 25, 1923, Dallas County, Texas. (Tombstone reflects death date, May 25, newspaper obituary reflects April 1, death date.)Married: (1) Julie Baker, January 1, 1893. Children: Leonard Grady, Bonnie Lewis, and Bertha Orene. (2) Mary Emma Baker, January 5, 1899. Children: Ben, Homer Lafayette, James M., Ruby L., Connie P., Oman, Thelma, Female Sumner, Theo Lala, and Thelma Inez. Father: Monroe Lafayette "Fate" Sumner. Mother: Martha Jane Burns. Source: 1880 U. S. Census, *Canton Herald*, March 30, 1923; *Wills Point Chronicle*, April 5, 1923; Ancestry.com; Find A Grave.

Sumner, Bonnie Lewis
Born: September 24, 1895, Van Zandt County, Texas. Died: November 12, 1963, Dallas County, Texas. Cause of death: Cancer. Married: Mary Jeanette "Nettie" Riley, November 20, 1914. Children: Waymon, Laymon, Agnes, and Harold Lavon. Father: Benjamin Franklin Sumner. Mother: Julie Baker. Occupation: Texas Department of Transportation. Sources: Death Certificate; *Canton Herald*, November 14, 1963; Eubank Funeral Home records.

Sumner, Estelle
Born: September 14, 1903, Van Zandt County, Texas. Died: October 11, 1940, Dallas County, Texas. Cause of death: Brain tumor. Married: Homer L. Sumner, December 19, 1924. Children: Emogene and H. L., Jr. Father: A. J. McCarty. Mother: Mary E. McCaffity. Occupation: Works Progress Administration. Comments: Estelle Sumner was the Community Recreational Supervisor for the W. P. A. during the 1930's. Sources: Death Certificate; *Canton Herald*, October 17, 1940; Eubank Funeral Home records.

Sumner, Homer L.
Born: October 3, 1899, Van Zandt County, Texas. Died: June 20, 1946, Van Zandt County, Texas. Cause of death: Tuberculosis. Married: Estelle McCarty, December 19, 1924. Children: H. L. and Mrs. W. R. Allen. Father: Benjamin Franklin Sumner. Mother: Mary Emma Baker. Occupation: Stock Trader. Source: Eubank Funeral Home records.

Sumner, Laymon Lewis
Born: July 3, 1916, Van Zandt County, Texas. Died: April 17, 1986, Smith County, Texas. Divorced. Children: Bonnie Lewis and Laymon Odell. Father: Bonnie L. Sumner. Mother: Mary Jeanette Riley. Occupation: Texas. Military: WWII, PFC U. S. Marine Corp. Source: Death Certificate; 1940 U. S. Census; *Canton Herald*, April 24, 1986.

Sumner, Leonard Grady
Born: December 11, 1894. Died: February 8, 1918. Cause of death: Smallpox, pneumonia. Married: Alma Rivers White. Children: Duward and Juanita. Father: Benjamin Franklin Sumner. Mother: Julie Baker. Occupation: Farmer. Comments: After Leonard Sumner's death, his widow married William Cole in 1925. Sources: *Canton Herald*, February 15, 1918; Nell Deets Walker, Sumner Family historian.

Sumner, Mary Emma
Born: June 6, 1876, Texas. Died: September 12, 1963, Tom Green County, Texas. Cause of death: Tuberculosis, pneumonia. Married: Benjamin Franklin Sumner, January 5, 1899. Children: Ben, Homer L., James M., Ruby L., Connie P., Oman, Thelma Inez, Female, and Theo Lala. Father: Thomas J. Baker. Mother: Martha A. "Nettie" Culp. Comments: Mary Sumner's sister, Julia, was married to Ben Sumner at the time Julia's death. Later, Mary Emma married her brother-in-law. Sources: Death Certificate, 1880 U. S. Census.

When **Jeptha Tolliver "Tull" Thompson** *was 13 years old, the Civil War began, and his father went to fight, leaving him as the major caretaker of his mother and sisters. Two years later, he began working for the merchant G. W. Tull, Sr., hauling freight with ox teams from Shreveport, and worked there for thirty-five years.*

Sumner, Mary Jeanette "Nettie"
Born: November 5, 1897, Van Zandt County, Texas. Died: January 5, 1964, Van Zandt County, Texas. Cause of death: Cancer. Married: Bonnie Lewis Sumner, November 29, 1914. Children: Waymon, Laymon, Agnes, and Harold Lavon. Father: Benjamin Franklin Riley. Mother: Lucille "Lucy" Ann Donohoe. Sources: Death Certificate, Eubank Funeral Home records, Ancestry.com.

Sumner, Oman
Born: January 24, 1922. Died: June 5, 1923. Cause of death: Colitis. Father: Benjamin Franklin Sumner. Mother: Mary E. Baker. Sources: Death Certificate; *Canton Herald*, June 8, 1923.

Sumner, Waymon Odell
Born: June 1, 1919. Died: June 29, 1942. Father: Bonnie Lewis Sumner. Mother: Mary Jeanette Riley. Sources: *Canton Herald*, July 9, 1942; Eubank Funeral Home records.

Sweatman, Dorothy Marie
Born: May 10, 1925, Erath County, Texas. Died: September 7, 1993, Van Zandt County, Texas. Married: Unknown Sweatman. Father: Willie Harper. Mother: Irene Powell. Occupation: Secretary. Source: *Van Zandt News*, September 12, 1993.

T

Tawater, Helen Mae
(Photo page 138) Born: December 21, 1898, Wisconsin. Died: July 26, 1996, Texas. Married: Noah Franklin Tawater, April 25, 1915. Children: Orville Clarence, Cecil, William Butler, Charlie, Mary Lee, Georgia Mae, and Lacolian. Father: William Creed Morris. Mother: Lillie Mae Walker. Comments: Helen Tawater lived another twenty-three years after her husband's death, dying at the age of 97. For most of those years, she lived alone in the old home place at the junction of Highways 17 and 1255 about a mile from downtown Canton, Texas. The house is still standing, although vacant, on the same spot where the family lived for almost sixty years. Source: *Van Zandt County Texas Histories and Biographies, 1848-1991.*

Tawater, Noah Franklin "Frank"
(Photo page 138) Born: August 15, 1889, Tarrant County, Texas. Died: January 3, 1973, Van Zandt County, Texas. Married: Helen Mae Morris, April 25, 1915. Children: Orville Clarence, Cecil, William Butler, Charlie, Mary Lee, Georgia Mae, and Lacolian. Father: Charles Tawater, Tennessee. Mother: Nancy McEligh, Tennessee. Occupation: Farmer, welder, night watchman. Comments: Frank Tawater moved from Tarrant County to Upshur County when he married in 1915. The family moved to Van Zandt County in 1923 and to Canton in 1924. They were sharecroppers until Frank went to work as a night watchman for the City of Canton in 1935. About this time, the Tawaters built a house on Highway 17 near the junction of Highways 1255 and 64. In 1942, at the beginning of World War II, the Tawaters moved to Houston where Frank worked as a welder in the shipyards. Near the end of the war, the Tawaters moved to Fort Worth where he worked at Stripling's Department Store for ten years. After his retirement, the family moved back to Canton and lived until their deaths. Sources: *Van Zandt County Texas Histories and Biographies 1848-1991*; *Canton Herald*, April 22, 1965and January 11, 1973; Eubank Funeral Home records.

Taylor, Judy
(Photo page 136) Born: September 19, 1958. Died: May 5, 2008. Married: Danny Ray Taylor. Children: Dentra, Brodrick, Danny and Ray, Jr. Father: Frank Butler. Moth-

er: Marguerite Shamlin. Sources: *Van Zandt News*, May 18, 2008; Vanessa Scott, Wynne Community historian.

Taylor, Little Nora
Born: September 15, 1889. Died: April 2, 1892. Father: Mitchel L. Taylor. Mother: Laura E. Canfield. Sources: Death Certificate of Laura Taylor, Tombstone.

Taylor, Mitchell
Born: September 10, 1859. Died: March 24, 1902, Van Zandt County, Texas. Married: Laura E. Canfield, 1882. Children: Rubie, Pearl, Lilla, Little Nora, and Mitchie. Father: Unknown Taylor. Mother: Unknown. Comments: Mitchell Taylor had been in ill health for several months prior to his death. He had been in the mercantile business prior to his illness. Woodmen of the World from several different camps conducted his funeral. The Woodmen formed one of the largest processions ever witnessed in Canton. Laura lived until 1949 and is buried in the Oak Grove Cemetery in Nacogdoches County, Texas. Sources: Death Certificate of Laura Taylor; 1900 U. S. Census; *Free State Enterprise*, March 27, 1902.

Taylor, Susan Y.
Born: October 25, 1850. Died: May 28, 1879. Married: P. Taylor, July 15, 1877. Father: Robert McClellen, Sr. Mother: Elizabeth Knox. Siblings: Mary M., Sara Jane, Martha E., and Robert Jr. Source: Find A Grave.

Teague, Hallie
Born: May 16, 1867. Died: January 18, 1908. Married: Dougan Teague. Father: Unknown. Mother: Unknown. Comments: After her death, Hallie Teague's husband married Sallie Thomas on July 3, 1908. Source: *Wills Point Chronicle*, January 23, 1908.

Teague, Infant
Birth: Unknown. Death: Unknown. Father: Dougan Teague. Mother: Hallie Teague. Source: Tombstone.

Teel, Flora Pauline
Born: September 6, 1924, Van Zandt County, Texas. Died: September 21, 1946, Van Zandt County, Texas. Cause of death: Prenatal complications. Married: Eddie Foy Teel, February 19, 1944. Child: Patricia. Father: Tommy E. Jackson, Coryell County, Texas. Mother: Johnie Haley, Coryell County, Texas. Sources: Death Certificate, Hilliard Funeral Home records.

Terry, Adde Mae
Born: September 17, 1900, Oklahoma. Died: November 18, 1973, Van Zandt County, Texas. Cause of death: Heart disease. Married: Eddie Obe Terry. Children: Eddie Ruth and Norma Jean. Father: Henry Craft. Mother: Emma Sanders. Sources: Death Certificate; *Canton Herald*, November 22, 1973.

Martha Isabella Thompson

William D. Thompson

Terry, Eddie Obe
Born: August 15, 1911, Van Zandt County, Texas. Died: October 27, 1974, Van Zandt County, Texas. Cause of death: Pancreatic cancer. Married: Adde Mae Craft. Children: Eddie Ruth and Norma Jean. Father: Enoch Ward Terry. Mother: Eva Pearl Smith Groom. Occupation: Plumber. Sources: Death Certificate; *Canton Herald*, October 31, 1974; Find A Grave.

Thames, Amos F.
Born: May 19, 1866. Died: May 5, 1904. Married: Sally Mason Longmire, January 12, 1894. Father: J. W. Thames. Mother: N. E. Temples. Source: *Wills Point Chronicle*, May 12, 1904.

Thompson, Albert
Born: Unknown. Died: 1880. Father: Unknown Thompson. Mother: Unknown. Source: Tombstone.

Thompson, Allen
Born: September 30, 1816, Williamson County, Tennessee. Died: February 19, 1883, Van Zandt County, Texas. Married: Elvira Bickerstaff, August 15, 1840, Mississippi. Children: John A., Ann E., Jeptha Tolliver "Tull", Mary Elvira, Nancy Leona, Allen F., and James P. Father: John Anderson Thompson. Mother: Elizabeth Edmonds. Siblings: Nancy E., Elizabeth, Samuel B., James Patterson, Tolliver Gideon "Tull," Abigail, Williamson Burrell, William Brown, Stephen Edmonds, Harvey M., and Thomas. Military: CSA, Cpl. 11th TX Infantry Co. I, Roberts' Regiment. Occupation: Farmer. Sources: 1860 U. S. Census, Ancestry.com.

Thompson, Anna Elizabeth
Born: October 10, 1848, Georgia. Died: February 5, 1899, Van Zandt County, Texas. Cause of death: Apoplexy. Married: (1) Richard Charles McCauley, 1872. Children: Charles Thomas "Chuck" and Sidney J. "Sid." (2) Jeptha

Tolliver "Tull" Thompson, January 13, 1884. Children: Molly and Ollie. Father: Epha Alexander. Mother: Mary A. Alexander. Comments: After Richard's death in 1881, Anna Elizabeth McCauley married Tull Thompson. He reared her two boys as if they were his own children. The boys later opened their own mercantile operation, McCauley Brothers, which became one of the more successful businesses in Canton, Texas during the early 1900's. The *Free State Enterprise* described Anna Thompson's death as follows: "Death, who knocks with equal hand at the homes of all, has been busy in his appointed work. About sundown on last Friday evening, Mrs. Anna E. Thompson, wife of Tull Thompson, was stricken with apoplexy and so intense was her suffering that she soon became unconscious and remained so till 1: 30 o'clock Sunday afternoon when her spirit took its flight to that 'Bourne from whence no traveler returns.' She was buried in the Canton City Cemetery." Sources: *Van Zandt County Histories and Biographies Volume II*; *Free State Enterprise*, February 9, 1899.

THOMPSON, CARLOS

Born: October 9, 1887, Van Zandt County, Texas. Died: August 8, 1922, Wichita County, Texas. Cause of death: Automobile accident. Single. Father: James T. Thompson. Mother: Susan Rebecca Calhoun. Comments: The *Canton Herald* gave this account of his Carlos Thompson's death: "Carlos Thompson was killed in an automobile accident at Burkburnett Sunday evening about 6 o'clock. Particulars of the incident are not known here, but it is understood that he was run down by a car on the streets of Burkburnett where he was visiting a brother. The remains were shipped to Canton for interment, arriving in Wills Point Tuesday night. The deceased was 33 years old and was not married. He is survived by his mother, Mrs. S. R. Thompson of Terrell, and the following brothers and sisters, all of whom attended the funeral in Canton Wednesday afternoon: R. B. Thompson of the Jackson Community, O. S. Thompson of Dallas, M. E. Thompson of Burkburnett, Mrs. H. Perry and Mrs. Hattie Dingler of Dallas." Sources: Death Certificate; *Canton Herald*, August 11, 1922.

THOMPSON, ELVIRA

Born: February 22, 1820, Alabama. Died: February 28, 1883, Van Zandt County, Texas. Married: Allen Thompson, August 15, 1840, Mississippi. Children: Leonia, Allen F., James P., and Tull. Father: John L. Bickerstaff. Mother: Celia Ann Hampton. Comments: Allen and Elvira Thompson were in Smith County, Texas by 1848. They moved to Van Zandt County by the 1850's and lived there for the remainder of their lives. Allen died February 19, 1883. An interesting footnote to Elvira is that she was Ben Bickerstaff's first cousin. He was a notorious outlaw operating in Northeast Texas during the Reconstruction Period of the late 1860's. Elvira's uncle, Seborn Bickerstaff, was Ben's father. Ben served in the 11th Texas Cavalry of the Confederate Army, and turned outlaw upon his release from the Army in 1865. He joined with other outlaws, Cullen Baker, Bob Lee, and Ben Griffin and preyed on Black Freedmen, Unionist, and Union Army personnel. Ben operated out of Titus County --robbing, killing, and harassing individuals who did not share his political views. He and his partner, Joe Thompson, were ambushed and killed in the streets of Alvarado, Texas, April 5, 1869 by angry citizens. It was not determined if Joe Thompson was connected to the Van Zandt County Thompsons. Sources: *The Governor's Hounds, The Texas State Police, 1870-1873*; Ancestry.com.

THOMPSON, HATTIE

Born: September 9, 1887, Van Zandt County, Texas. Died: January 25, 1955, Dallas County, Texas. Cause of death: Pneumonia. Married: Unknown. Divorced. Father: James T. Thompson. Mother: Susan Rebecca Calhoun. Source: Death Certificate.

THOMPSON, JAMES CARL "DUTCH"

Born: July 7, 1899, Madison County, Tennessee. Died: December 3, 1980, Smith County, Texas. Cause of death: Pneumonia. Married: Iva Mae Wright, February 14, 1922, Pushmataha County, Oklahoma. Child: Charles Deleon. Father: Amos Thompson. Mother: Nancy Lillie Dowdy. Occupation: Farmer. Comments: Dutch Thompson had lived in Van Zandt County from 1939 until his death. His wife died in 1999. Sources: Death Certificate; *Canton Herald*, December 11, 1980; Ancestry.com.

THOMPSON, JAMES P. "JIM"

Born: 1864. Died: December 12, 1896. (Tombstone death date of 1897 is incorrect.) Cause of death: Hunting accident. Married: Ida M. Phillips, July 15, 1886. Father: Allen Thompson. Mother: Elvira Bickerstaff. Comments: *The Dallas Morning News* reported Jim Thompson's death as follows: "Mr. Jim Thompson, who resides near Canton, in this county, accidently shot and killed himself last evening while out fishing and hunting on Sabine River about five miles north of this place (Grand Saline). His brother, Tull Thompson, came in this morning and took his remains to Canton for burial." Sources: *The Dallas Morning News*, December 13, 1896; Ancestry.com; Find A Grave.

THOMPSON, JAMES T.

Born: February 14, 1849, Georgia. Died: January 15, 1913, Van Zandt County, Texas. Married: Susan Rebecca Calhoun, July 14, 1870. Children: Thomas, Obe D., Oscar, Alice D., Robert, Bettie, Miller, Hattie, and Carlos. Father: Thomas Thompson, Georgia. Mother: Mary Thompson, Georgia. Occupation: Farmer. Sources: 1870, 1880, 1900 U. S. Census; *Texas Marriage Collection 1814-1909*; *Grand Saline Sun*, January 23, 1913; Ancestry.com.

Capt. William D. Thompson *was a local farmer who served in numerous elected positions in Van Zandt County, first as Sheriff 1883-1884. The following year, he was elected County Clerk and served in that position for eight years. He was the Democratic nominee for County Judge in 1894, but was ultimately defeated. He was then elected County Treasurer and served 1901-1902.*

Thompson, Jeptha Tolliver "Tull"
Born: March 11, 1848, Smith County, Texas. Died: April 29, 1921, Van Zandt County, Texas. Cause of death: Malaria. Married: (1) Martha I. Blair, May 9, 1872. Children: Mrs. M. C. Foster, Mrs. Mattie Farmer, Mrs. G. M. Hilliard, and Mrs. Earnest Blankinship. (2) Anna E. Alexander McCauley, January 13, 1884. Children: Infant and Mrs. Roy McFarland. (3) Ollie Durham, January 10, 1904. Children: Tull, Polk, Ruby, and Marvin. Father: Allen Thompson. Mother: Elvira Bickerstaff. Occupation: Store clerk. Comments: Tull Thompson was only 13 when the Civil War began, and his father went away to War and left him as the major caretaker of his mother and sisters. When he was about 15 years old, he began working for G. W. Tull, Sr., a merchant of Canton, hauling freight with ox teams from Shreveport. He began working in the store in 1871 and was there for about thirty-five years. He not only reared his own children, but also treated his step-children, Chuck and Sid McCauley, as if they were his own. The McCauley brothers were successful merchants in Canton for many years. Sources: *Marriage Records 1848-1909, Van Zandt County*; *Canton Herald*, May 6, 1921.

Thompson, Leah (Infant)
Born: Unknown. Died: August 29, 1904. Father: W. M. Thompson. Mother: Ora E. Milam. Source: Tombstone.

Thompson, Leah Elizabeth "Lizzie"
Born: October 12, 1844, Tennessee. Died: May 2, 1901, Van Zandt County, Texas. Married: William David Thompson, July 9, 1859, Panola County, Texas. Children: Bettie, Moses, Will, and Whit. Father: Charles Mote Walters. Mother: Mary Medford. Sources: *Texas Marriage Collection, 1814-1909*; Ancestry.com.

Thompson, Martha Isabella
(Photo page 141) Born: January 23, 1852. Died: June 21, 1883. Married: Jeptha Tolliver "Tull" Thompson, May 9, 1872. Children: Mrs. M.C. Foster, Mrs. Mattie Farmer, Mrs. G.M. Hilliard, and Mrs. Ernest Blankinship. Father: Allen Blair. Mother: Sindy Rilah Parker. Comments: Martha Thompson's parents were here before Van Zandt County was formed in 1848. Allen Blair served as County Clerk of Van Zandt County 1850-1852. Source: 1880 U. S. Census.

Thompson, Molley
Born: February 15, 1885. Died: June 21, 1886. Father: Tull Thompson. Mother: Anne E. Alexander McCauley. Source: Tombstone.

Thompson, Moses W.
Born: October 18, 1864. Died: October 9, 1883. Father: William D. Thompson. Mother: Leah "Lizzie" E. Walters. Source: Tombstone.

Thompson, Nannie
Born: May 2, 1895, Van Zandt County, Texas. Died: October 8, 1897, Van Zandt County, Texas. Father: James T. Thompson. Mother: Susan Rebecca Calhoun. Source: Tombstone.

Thompson, Obe D.
Born: February 25, 1873. Died: February 25, 1892. Father: James T. Thompson. Mother: Susan R. Calhoun. Source: 1880 U. S. Census.

Thompson, Ora E.
Born: September 8, 1880, Mississippi. Died: February 22, 1918, Kaufman County, Texas. Cause of death: Tuberculosis. Married: William M. Thompson, November 19, 1903. Children: W. M., Willie Faye, Francis, and Sara. Father: Willis A. Milam. Mother: Martha A. "Mattie" Hardin. Siblings: Mada Docia, John Thomas, Susan Era, Willis Frank, Anna Lou, and Byron O. Sources: Death Certificate, Find A Grave.

THOMPSON, RUBY IRENE
Born: December 9, 1890. Died: April 20, 1901. Father: James T. Thompson. Mother: Susan Rebecca Calhoun. Source: Tombstone.

THOMPSON, SUSAN REBECCA
Born: August 8, 1853, Mississippi. Died: May 24, 1943, Dallas County, Texas. Cause of death: Cancer. Married: James T. Thompson, July 14, 1870, Cherokee County, Texas. Children: Thomas, Obe D., Oscar, Alice D., Robert, Bettie, Miller, Hattie, and Carlos. Father: Unknown Calhoun. Mother: Mary Ann Calhoun. Sources: 1880 U. S. Census, Death Certificate.

THOMPSON, CAPT. WILLIAM D.
(Photo page 141) Born: February 11, 1839, Georgia. Died: March 13, 1903, Van Zandt County, Texas. Cause of death: Diabetes. Married: Leah Elizabeth Walters, 1859. Children: Bettie, Will, Moses, and Whit. Occupation: Farmer, county official. Military: CSA, Captain, Company G, 11th Texas Infantry. Comments: William D. Thompson moved from Georgia to Smith County, Texas in 1858. After the War, he lived in Gregg County, Texas where he joined the Baptist Church in 1876. He was farming in Van Zandt County by 1878. He was elected Sheriff of Van Zandt County serving 1883-1884. In 1885, he was elected County Clerk and served in that position for eight years. He was the Democratic nominee for County Judge in 1894, but was defeated by the Populists in a clean sweep of all the county offices for that year. He was elected County Treasurer in 1901-1902. Sources: 1900 U. S. Census; *Confederate Biography: W. D. Thompson, Texans Who Wore the Gray*; *Wills Point Chronicle*, March 19, 1903.

THOMPSON, WILLIE FAY
Born: November 22, 1912. Died: November 22, 1912. Father: W. M. Thompson. Mother: Ora E. Milam. Source: Tombstone.

THOMPSON, WILLIS MILAM
Born: November 21, 1908, Kaufman County, Texas. Died: December 25, 1932, Dallas County, Texas. Cause of death: Tuberculosis. Father: W. M. Thompson. Mother: Ora E. Milam. Siblings: Francis, Sara, and Willie Fay. Source: Death Certificate.

THOMPSON, ZORETTE
Born: December 9, 1882, Van Zandt County, Texas. Died: August 8, 1905, Van Zandt County, Texas. Father: James T. Thompson. Mother: Susan R. Calhoun. Source: *Wills Point Chronicle*, August 10, 1905.

TILLERY, N.S.
Born: Unknown. Died: Unknown. Father: Unknown Tillery. Mother: Unknown. Source: Tombstone.

TILLISON, WILLIAM PRESTON
Born: March 8, 1879, Butts County, Georgia. Died: July 7, 1954, Henderson County, Texas. Cause of death: Heart disease. Married: Fannie Alice Aldredge. Children: Alice and William Aldredge. Father: James David Tillison. Mother: Sarah Susannah Hayes. Occupation: Railroad worker. Sources: Death Certificate, Eubank Funeral Home records, Ancestry.com.

TODD, BARNEY
Born: October 1, 1886. Died: July 26, 1903, Van Zandt County, Texas. Cause of death: Lightning strike. Father: James Thomas Todd, Alabama. Mother: Emma E. Sanders, Mississippi. Comments: The *Wills Point Chronicle* reported Barney Todd's death as follows: "Barney Todd, son of Mr. and Mrs. Tom Todd of this place, was killed by lightning here Sunday evening about 1:30 o'clock. He went up in the dome of the courthouse during the rain and raised a window and was leaning out when he was struck. It is supposed that the electric bolt entered the window with a current of warm air. The building was not materially damaged. It was a sad death but one of those tragic things that cannot be helped." Sources: 1900 U. S. Census; *Wills Point Chronicle*, July 30, 1903.

TODD, EMMA EUGENE "TODDY"
Born: November 15, 1867, Newton County, Mississippi. Died: July 26, 1960, Van Zandt County, Texas. Married: James Thomas Todd, December 21, 1885. Children: James K., Janie, Thomas, Mae, Elvis, Barney, Grady, and Mrs. Homer Sides. Father: Harris (Harrison) Sanders. Mother: Sara Jane Wyatt. Sources: Death Certificate, Hilliard Funeral Home records.

TODD, HAROLD TOWLES
Born: December 24, 1901, Texas. Died: August 5, 1977, Van Zandt County, Texas. Cause of death: Automobile accident. Single. Father: William M. Todd. Mother: Eva Towles. Occupation: Import-export dealer. Comments: Harold Todd's automobile accident occurred in Grand Saline, Texas. He died at the scene and is buried in the Towles' plot. Source: Death Certificate.

TODD, HENRY GRADY "BUCK"
Born: April 27, 1896, Van Zandt County, Texas. Died: February 1, 1972, Van Zandt County, Texas. Cause of death: Heart failure. Married: Alice Phipps. Father: James Thomas Todd. Mother: Emma E. Sanders. Occupation: Mechanic. Military: WWI, TX HO CO 144 Infantry. Comments: Alice Todd is buried in White Rose Cemetery, Wills Point, Texas. Sources: Death Certificate; *Canton Herald*, February 10, 1972; Hilliard Funeral Home records.

Annie Alice Towles

James Thomas "J.T." Todd

TODD, JAMES KERNON, SR.
Born: April 7, 1887, Van Zandt County, Texas. Died: July 14, 1947, Van Zandt County, Texas. Married: Margaret "Maggie" Causey, May 30, 1917. Children: James K., Jr. and William Thomas. Father: James Thomas Todd. Mother: Emma E. Sanders. Occupation: Retail clerk. Sources: Hilliard Funeral Home records, Ancestry.com.

TODD, JAMES THOMAS "J.T."
Born: April 7, 1855. Died: July 10, 1916. Married: Emma Eugene Sanders, December 21, 1885. Children: Mrs. Homer Sides, James K., Grady, Jamie, Thomas, Mae, Elvis, and Barney. Father: Birton (Burton) B. Todd. Mother: Rebecca Elizabeth Ramsey. Siblings: B. B., W. M., Beulah, and Mrs. H. W. Wynne. Occupation: Merchant. Comments: James Todd moved from Elmore County, Alabama to Van Zandt County, Texas in 1882. He moved to Canton in 1883 and accepted a position with D. D. Thames who owned a mercantile business on the northeast corner of the Canton square. James worked for Thames until December of 1897 when the business failed due to the effects of the Panic of 1894-97. The Thames' business had assets of about $19,000 and liabilities of $10,000, and James was assigned as trustee to help settle the business affairs. He next worked for R. B. Longmire who owned a mercantile business in Canton until that business was sold. For the last ten years of his life, he owned a grocery store in Canton. On July 30, 1906, J. T. Todd donated one acre of land in the David Towns Survey to Van Zandt County to be used as a place for school purposes (Todd Hill). The school opened in the fall of 1907 and operated until 1917 when it was consolidated with the Starr school to form the Wentworth school. The *Canton Herald* gave this report of his death: "There are people who trade in Canton at this time that have traded with him (Todd) for the past thirty-three years and will not buy elsewhere articles that could be bought from the deceased. He was fair in all of his business dealings and with his fellow man and never meddled in the affairs of others." Sources: 1900 U. S. Census; *Canton Herald*, July 14, 1916; Ancestry.com.

TODD, MAE
Born: May 9, 1893, Van Zandt County, Texas. Died: January 5, 1964, Smith County, Texas. Cause of death: Pneumonia. Single. Father: James Thomas Todd. Mother: Emma E. Sanders. Siblings: Mrs. Homer Sides, J. K., Grady, Jamie, Barney, Thomas, and Elvis. Occupation: Mercantile store clerk. Comments: Mae Todd was a lifelong resident of Canton, Texas. Source: Death Certificate; *Canton Herald*, January 9, 1964.

TOWLES, ANNIE ALICE
Born: October 21, 1884, Van Zandt County, Texas. Died: May 2, 1969, Van Zandt County, Texas. Cause of death: Heart disease. Single. Father: Thomas Jefferson Towles. Mother: Nancy (Nannie) Ann Nolan. Siblings: Eva Lucille, Johnnie, infant son Towles, Howard Glenn, Minnie Merle, and Thomas Bonner. Comments: Alice Towles' family was one of the earliest and more prominent families in Canton. She never married and was known as an eccentric character who wore early 20th century clothing around town. She lived with her mother at 705 Buffalo Street in Canton until her mother died in 1925; then she lived alone until her death. Sources: Death Certificate; *Canton Herald*, May 8, 1969; Eubank Funeral Home records.

TOWLES, HOWARD GLENN
Born: February 6, 1871. Died: August 6, 1878. Father: Thomas J. Towles. Mother: Nancy (Nannie) Ann Nolan. Source: Tombstone.

TOWLES, INFANT SON
Born: Unknown. Died: Unknown. Father: Thomas J. Towles. Mother: Nancy (Nannie) Ann Nolan. Source: Tombstone.

TOWLES, JOHNNIE
Born: October 18, 1865. Died: August 15, 1869. Father: Thomas J. Towles. Mother: Nancy (Nannie) Ann Nolan. Source: Tombstone.

TOWLES, MINNIE MERLE
Born: April 5, 1873. Died: August 8, 1892. Cause of death: Congestion. Father: Thomas J. Towles. Mother: Nancy A Nolan. Siblings: Johnny, infant son, Howard Glenn, Thomas Bonner, Annie Alice, and Eva Lucille. Comments: Minnie Towles came from one of the more prominent families in Van Zandt County. She attended Trinity University, at Tehuacana, Texas in 1888-89 and had united with the Cumberian Presbyterian church at

THOMAS JEFFERSON "CAPTAIN" TOWLES *was a Canton merchant and builder and served as Van Zandt County Tax Collector. He is best known for his part in Ex parte Towles, an 1877 case whereby Towles led and won a legal battle against an election which caused the removal of the County Seat from Canton to Wills Point. This one action from Towles and the Canton citizens probably prevented Canton from slipping into a ghost town. The Texas Historical Commission has approved the application for a Historical Marker to honor Towles.*

Tehuacana. Minnie had attended the North Texas Female College, Sherman, Texas in 1890-91 and had graduated in June of 1891. The *Canton Telephone* of August 12, 1892 reported the following: "Her funeral was a sad scene—an impressive scene—and one that will never be forgotten, as the deep sympathy of the people for the heart-stricken family was attested by the tears and weeping on the part of many present on that sad occasion." Source: *Canton Telephone*, August 12, 1892.

TOWLES, NANCY ANN "NANNIE"

Born: March 5, 1843, Butts County, Georgia. (Tombstone date of 1865 is incorrect.) Died: May 3, 1925, Van Zandt County, Texas. Married: Thomas Jefferson Towles, February 14, 1864, Butts County, Georgia. Children: Annie Alice, Howard Glenn, Infant Son, Johnnie, Minnie Merle, Thomas Bonner, and Eva Lucile. Father: Richard Nolan. Mother: Nancy Ann Coleman. Siblings: Infant Child, Hartwell H., Edward Griffin, Mary, and Hilliard J. Comments: Thomas J. Towles married Nancy Ann Nolan while on furlough from the Confederate Army. By 1865, the family was living in Van Zandt County. Her family remained in Georgia. They became one of the more prominent families in Canton and Van Zandt County. Most of their children died young. There were no male members to carry on the Towles name. When Nancy died, she was one of the longest residing residents of Canton. Sources: *Grand Saline Sun*, May 7, 1925; *Canton Herald*, May 8, 1925; Ancestry.com, Find A Grave.

TOWLES, THOMAS BONNER

Born: September 6, 1876. Died: March 8, 1899. Cause of death: Meningitis. Father: Thomas J. Towles. Mother: Nancy (Nannie) Ann Nolan. Siblings: Eva Lucille, Johnnie, Infant son, Howard Glen, Minnie Merle, and Annie Alice. Comments: Bonner Towles was living in Terrell, Texas and working as a night clerk at the Harris House, a local hotel, when he acquired la grippe (flu) which developed into meningitis. The *Wills Point Chronicle* gave this account of his death: "Young Towles has been ailing several days with la grippe and last night about 10 o'clock he complained of a severe pain in his head. Dr. F. S. White prescribed for him and after remaining with him an hour or so returned home, his patient being quieted. This morning about 1 o'clock Joe Overton (a resident) was awakened by a noise overhead and on investigation it proved to be Mr. Towles, who had fallen out of his bed to the floor in an unconscious condition. He was a raving maniac and it took the united efforts of two or three men to hold him." Here is the account of his parents' reaction: "The first news of deceased's illness that reached this place (Wills Point) was telegraphed to Senator Kearby Tuesday morning about 3 o'clock announcing his serious sickness of meningitis with hardly any chance of recovery. Mr. Kearby immediately dispatched an informer to Canton to make known the sad intelligence to the parents and sisters of the dying young man. His parents, Capt. and Mrs. T. J. Towles, returned with the messenger, arriving about 9:30 o'clock a. m. A carriage with a fresh team was waiting for them and they entered it without delay and were hurriedly driven to Terrell. Their sick son never regained consciousness and after lingering in awful agony for several hours, they were bitterly grieved to witness him depart his mortal existence about midnight Tuesday evening. Remains of deceased with parents and friends were carried to Canton for internment." Sources: *Wills Point Chronicle* March 9, 1899; *Free State Enterprise*, March 9, 1899.

TOWLES, THOMAS JEFFERSON "CAPTAIN"
Born: December 29, 1843, Jones County, Georgia. Died: January 21, 1909, Van Zandt County, Texas. Married: Nancy (Nannie) Ann Nolan, February 14, 1864, Butts County, Georgia. Children: Annie Alice, Howard Glenn, infant Son, Johnnie, Minnie Merle, Thomas Bonner, and Eva Lucille. Father: William Towles. Mother: Elizabeth Jones. (The 1850 U. S. Census of Jones County, Georgia shows Thomas J. Towles, age 7, and his siblings living with Elizabeth C. McLane. Relationship not determined.) Occupation: Farmer, rancher, merchant, politician. Military: CSA, 1st Lt. Co. G. 3rd Regt., Texas Cavalry. Comments: Thomas Jefferson Towles' maternal grandfather was "Hurricane Jack" Jones. He was probably the namesake of Jones County, Georgia. Thomas' father died in 1847 when Thomas was four years old. His mother died when he was 11 years old. He came to Van Zandt County when he was 14 to live with his brother, Adam. He attended school until he was 17 when he enlisted in the Confederate Army on June 13, 1861 at Jefferson, Texas as a member of Capt. Mabrey's Company. Thomas and a friend, Robert Doyle, were the first two volunteers who went into the Confederate Army from Van Zandt County. They entered the Third Texas Regiment, commanded by Col. Greer and fought in battles in Missouri, Arkansas, Mississippi and Georgia. Towles at the age of 17 entered the Army as a Private, on May 20, 1862. At age 19, he was promoted to 2nd Lt. By January 1863 he was commanding a company of scouts for Ross' Texas Calvary Brigade, Jackson's Calvary Division, commanded by Brig. Gen. L. S. Ross. On February 14, 1864, while on an Army furlough, he married Nancy Ann Nolan in Butts County, Georgia. As Commander of Scouts, Towles became known as the "eyes and ears" of Ross' Brigade. He was wounded July 30, 1864, while in command of his Company at Newman, Georgia—his wound being a gun shot in the thigh. He was in the hospital as late as September, 1864. After the War, he returned to Van Zandt County where he became one of the more prominent and influential men in the early history of Canton. In addition to being a politician and businessman, he acquired a substantial amount of land to farm and raise stock, including a track on the Saline Creek that was identified for years as Towles Bottom. He also acquired and operated a cotton gin during the 1870's. To be eligible for any public office during Reconstruction, individuals had to sign what became known as an "Iron Clad Oath." They had to swear that they had not participated in activities against the United States. Offices became revolving doors as the elected officials failed to qualify under the strict standards. Sheriff S. Y. Carter resigned and was succeeded by T. J. Towles on January 6, 1870. He served until January 17, 1871 when he failed to qualify under the strict Reconstruction rules and had to step down. In 1871, he entered business in Canton as a liquor dealer and inn keeper. Throughout the next three decades, he owned various businesses around the Canton courthouse square. In 1875, he was elected as a Democrat from the 22nd District to the House in the 15th State Legislature and served from April 18, 1876 until January 14, 1879. In 1892 G. W. Tull was the first merchant to help build up the west side of the square with brick business buildings. In July of 1893, Thomas joined in the buildup of the town. He tore down an old wooden structure that had stood on the north side of the square for almost twenty years and replaced it with a 36' by 90' brick structure in which to operate his business. (The building still stands.) In 1882, F. W. Massey, the Van Zandt County Tax Collector, resigned and Thomas was appointed in his place. He was then elected and served in that position from 1883 until 1889. He also served in the 21st Legislature from January 8, 1889 until January 13, 1891. Towles is best known for his part in Ex parte Towles, an 1877 case whereby Towles led and won a legal battle against the election which caused the removal of the County Seat from Canton to Wills Point. This one action from Towles and the Canton citizens probably prevented Canton from slipping into a ghost town. The State Legislature had formed Canton in 1850 to serve as the County Seat of Van Zandt County, and its growth had been slow from the very beginning. After twenty-seven years, it was little more than a ramshackle little village with a courthouse. 1n 1873, the railroad missed Canton by ten miles, which shifted the shipping points to newly-formed towns along the tracks, Wills Point, Edgewood and Grand Saline. Since the railroad ran through Wills Point, the town was larger than Canton. Wills Point citizens felt that the County Seat should be moved there. In 1877, an election was held throughout the County for removal of the County Seat from Canton to Wills Point. In counting the returns of the election, three boxes were thrown out—two being from Canton—because of so-called irregularities; and Wills Point was declared the legal County Seat. The records were then removed from Canton to Wills Point. This set into action what became known as the "County Seat War." Thomas took the leadership and formed an armed force of over 300 men who moved on Wills Point with a view of taking possession of the records and returning them to Canton by any means possible. Eventually the state authorities intervened, and the records were returned without bloodshed. Thomas farmed until his death in 1909. Sources: *Confederate Military Records; Legislative Reference Library of Texas*; *The Handbook of Texas* Online; *Thomas Jefferson Towles* by Diana J. Kleiner; *Canton Telephone*, August 14, 1891 and July 21, 1892; *Wills Point Chronicle*, July 7, 1907; *Grand Saline Sun*, January 28, 1909; Find A Grave.

TRAVIS, ALLEN T.
Born: September 26, 1878. Died: October 12, 1962. Married: Lela Robison, August 2, 1903. Children: Angus, J. R., Mrs. M. B. Hill, and Mrs. Billy Deen. Father: Roland Travis. Mother: Nan Williams. Siblings: Dr. J. M., Dr. R. T., Albert, and Charles. Occupation: Farm Security Administration, Van Zandt County Tax Assessor-Collector.

Comments: Allen Travis was a member of the Van Zandt County Draft Board for a number of years, a Mason and a member of No. 141 Castillian Lodge for fifty years. Sources: *Canton Herald*, October 18, 1962; Eubank Funeral Home records.

TRAVIS, ERAN A. "ERANASLEE"
Born: October 5, 1875. Died: Unknown (broken tombstone). Father: J. Roland Travis. Mother: Nancy Jane Williams. Source: Tombstone.

TRAVIS, LELA ROBISON
Born: May 11, 1881, Texas. Died: May 25, 1940, Cherokee County, Texas. Cause of death: Heart disease. Married: Allen T. Travis, August 2, 1903. Children: Angus, J. R., Mrs. M.B. Hill, and Mrs. Billy Dean. Father: C. F. "Lum" Robison, Kentucky. Mother: Millisa Koen, Texas. Comments: The Robison family were some of the early pioneers of Van Zandt County. Lela Travis' father served fourteen years as Van Zandt County Treasurer. Sources: Death Certificate; *Canton Herald*, May 30, 1940; Eubank Funeral Home records.

TRIPP, JAMES ALFRED
Born: March 10, 1883, Benton County, Arkansas. Died: November 26, 1958, Cherokee County, Texas. Single. Father: James T. Tripp, North Carolina. Mother: Jessie Tina Gaskin, Texas. Occupation: Locomotive Engineer. Sources: 1900, 1930 U. S. Census; Eubank Funeral Home records; Ancestry.com.

TRIPP, JAMES T.
Born: June 15, 1844, North Carolina. Died: April 23, 1924, Van Zandt County, Texas. Married: Jessie T. Gaskin. Father: Hardy Tripp. Mother: Elizabeth "Betty"Slaughter. Sources: 1860, 1900 U. S. Census; Death Certificate of brother, Henry Tripp; Ancestry.com.

TUGGLE, LOVIE
Born: 1907. Died: February 2, 1967. Married: John Tuggle. Father: John Walter Phillips. Mother: Alice Chaney Bateman. Siblings: Vernon Lee, Bertha Lee, Dora M., Ida Estell, William Walter, John Henry, Orville, James Edward, and J. B. Sources: 1910, 1940 U. S. Census; *Texas Death Index 1964-1998*; *Canton Herald*, February 9, 1967; Find A Grave.

TULL, ALLIE ESTELLE
Born: August 31, 1885, Van Zandt County, Texas. Died: April 26, 1961, Dallas County, Texas. Single. Father: George Washington Tull, Sr. Mother: Mary Jane Cowan. Comments: Allie Tull was a Charter Member of the First Baptist Church of Canton. Sources: Death Certificate; *The Dallas Morning News*, April 27, 1961; Eubank Funeral Home records.

TULL, ANGELINE
Born: 1819. Died: July 22, 1878. Cause of death: Heart disease. Single. Father: Stephen Tull. Mother: Mary Martha Noble. Comments: Two Tull brothers, Thomas and G. W, moved their families from Tennessee to Van Zandt County in the late 1860's. Their mother, Martha, and sister, Angeline, stayed in Tennessee. Later, the brothers decided to move them to Van Zandt County. Thomas made the wagon trip back to Bolivar, Tennessee to get them. Martha was an invalid for thirty-four years, and Angeline never married. They lived with Thomas and G. W. until mother and daughter died. Sources: Texas State Historical Marker on G.W. Tull; Texas State Historical Marker Application researched, written, and submitted by Lawrence O. Greer.

TULL, BABY
Born: January 4, 1895. Died: September 26, 1895. Father: G. W. Tull, Sr. Mother: Mary J. Cowen. Source: Tombstone.

TULL, BERTIE
Born: March 2, 1883. Died: June 24, 1884. Father: G. W. Tull, Sr. Mother: Mary J. Cowen. Source: Tombstone.

TULL, FREDONA RUTH "DONA"
Born: January 25, 1875, Navarro County, Texas. Died: June 19, 1964, Dallas County, Texas. Cause of death: Heart disease. Married: William Newton Tull. Father: John C. Abbe. Mother: Margaret C. Waldrip. Siblings: John Luther, William Edward, and Walter H. Source: Death Certificate.

TULL, GEORGE WASHINGTON, SR. "G.W."
Born: January 4, 1827, DeKalb County, Georgia. Died: February 26, 1917, Van Zandt County, Texas. Married: (1) Sarah Moore, July 16, 1861. Child: Mrs. Ennis Peace. (2) Sarah Jane Wages, April 12, 1866. (3) Mary Jane Cowen, October 11, 1869. Children: Allie, W. N., Mary Jane, infant Tull, Bertie, Walter, G. W., Jr., Thomas, Noble N., Lula, Nona, and Lillian. Father: Stephen Tull. Mother: Mary Martha Noble. Occupation: Merchant. Military: CSA, Private Co. I. 15th Texas Calvary. Comments: The story of George Washington Tull is a reflection of the movement ever westward that contributed to the early settlement of Texas and eventually to the development of Canton and Van Zandt County. G. W. was born in Georgia, moved with his family to Alabama, then to Mississippi, and later to Hardeman County, Tennessee. He came to Texas in 1852. In 1854, he left Texas and went to the California gold fields. In November of 1858, he returned to Canton and established a liquor and mercantile business. G. W. served as a CSA Private in the Civil War. He returned to Canton after the war and went back into the mercantile business. He faced and overcame the hardships related to frontier development to establish the longest running and most successful family-owned business en-

Historical Marker
George Washington Tull, Sr. "G.W."

The Texas Historical Commission dedicated a Historical Marker in honor of George Washington Tull, Sr. The marker is located on the Canton Courthouse Square and reads as follows:

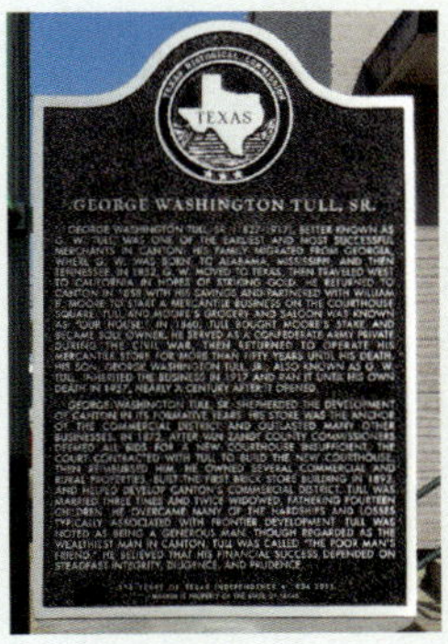

George Washington Tull, Sr. (1827-1917), better known as G.W. Tull, was one of the earliest and most successful merchants in Canton. His family migrated from Georgia, where G.W. was born, to Alabama, Mississippi, and then Tennessee. In 1852, G.W. moved to Texas, then traveled west to California in hopes of striking gold. He returned to Canton in 1858 with his savings and partnered with William B. Moore to start a mercantile business on the courthouse square. Tull and Moore's Grocery and Saloon was known as "Our House." In 1860, Tull bought Moore's stake and became sole owner. He served as a Confederate Army private during the Civil War, then returned to operate his mercantile store for more than fifty years until his death. His son, George Washington Tull, Jr., also known as G.W. Tull, inherited the business in 1917 and ran it until his own death in 1957, nearly a century after it opened. George Washington Tull, Sr. shepherded the development of Canton in its formative years. His store was the anchor of the commercial district and outlasted many other businesses. In 1872, after Van Zandt County Commissioners deemed all bids for a new courthouse insufficient, the court contracted with Tull to build the new courthouse, then reimbursed him. He owned several commercial and rural properties, built the first brick store building in 1892, and helped develop Canton's commercial district. Tull was married three times and twice widowed, fathering fourteen children. He overcame many of the hardships and losses typically associated with frontier development. Tull was noted as being a generous man. Though regarded as the wealthiest man in Canton, Tull was called "the poor man's friend." He believed that his financial success depended on steadfast integrity, diligence, and prudence.

terprise in Van Zandt County up until the time of his death. By 1890, he was regarded as the wealthiest man in Canton. He owned over 1,600 acres of farm land and had been involved in over twenty-five transactions involving land within Canton boundaries. In 1892, G. W. built the first brick building in Canton on the west side of the Canton square and this led to other business owners following his example. By the end of 1893, the west side of the courthouse square had a solid row of brick buildings. He served as the anchor of the Canton business community for fifty years. In 1917, the business passed to his son G. W., Jr., who ran it for another forty years. G. W. was married three times and was the father of fourteen children, seven of whom died before his death in 1917. Sources: *Canton Herald*, March 2, 1917; Texas State Historical Marker Application for G.W. Tull, researched, written and submitted by Lawrence Greer, May 23, 2012.

Tull, Mary Jane Cowen "Mollie"

Born: April 4, 1848, Mississippi. Died: April 11, 1938, Van Zandt County, Texas. Cause of death: Heart disease. Married: George Washington Tull, Sr., October 10, 1869. Father: P. Cowen. Mother: Martha Patsy Hardcastle. Comments: Mollie Tull was the third wife of G. W. Tull. They became one of the more prominent families in Van Zandt County history. Mollie survived her husband by twenty-one years. The *Canton Herald* published a story in which Mollie shared some of her life experiences. The paper described her as one of the oldest and best-loved characters in Van Zandt County. She and G. W. reared eleven children of their own and also reared five orphan girls. They also cared for two African-American girls. Mollie remembered the Civil War, Spanish American War, and World War I. She remembered the early Klu Klux Klan, the coming of the railroad, and the building of four county courthouses. Sources: Death Certificate; *Canton Herald*, June 10, 1927; Eubank Funeral Home records.

Tull, Mary Martha Noble

Born: April 16, 1795. Died: May 8, 1884. Married: Stephen Tull. Father: Stephen Ruff. Mother: Perinnah Smallwood. Comments: Mary Martha Tull was an invalid for thirty-four years and lived with her sons, Thomas Jefferson and G. W. until her death. Sources: G. W. Tull Texas Historical Marker Application Research, Ancestry.com.

Tull, Noble Napoleon "Polie"

Born: March 24, 1873. Died: October 13, 1888. Father: George Washington Tull, Sr. Mother: Mary Jane Cowe. Comments: The *Canton Telephone* reported Polie Tull's death as follows: "In the death of N. N. (Polie) Tull, Canton has lost one of her bright and most promising young men, the Baptist church a useful member and society one of its brightest lights. He was attending the Waco University when the sad news of his serious illness reached home. His mother, in response to a telegram, went at once to his bed-side at Waco. The next day a telegram came summoning his father to come immediately that his recovery was doubtful. Before his father had reached Waco, Polie had passed over the river of death. They returned home with him about 1 o'clock Monday morning, and his remains were interred in the city cemetery Monday evening at 4, Rev. J. C. Calhoun, pastor M. E. church south of this place, officiating. The ceremonies were solemn and impressive. The shrieks and cries and prayers of deceased relatives and friends were affecting. And there was scarcely a dry eye to be seen in the vast concourse of people. He was loved by all who knew him. It was only a short while ago that he confessed religion and united himself with the Baptist church." Source: *Canton Telephone*, October 19, 1888.

Tull, Thomas G.

Born: January 2, 1870. Died: March 6, 1878. Father: G. W. Tull, Sr. Mother: Mary J. Cowen. Source: Tombstone.

Tull, Walter H.

Born: March 20, 1877. Died: February 23, 1878. Father: G. W. Tull, Sr. Mother: Mary J. Cowen. Source: Tombstone.

Tull, William Newton

Born: May 24, 1875, Van Zandt County, Texas. Died: December 30, 1949, Dallas County, Texas. Cause of death: Heart disease. Married: Fredonia "Dona" Ruth Abbe, December 13, 1893. Father: George W. Tull, Sr. Mother: Mary J. Cowen. Occupation: Insurance agent. Sources: Death Certificate; *Marriage Records, 1848-1909 Van Zandt County, Texas.*

Tumlinson, Horace K.

Born: 1889. Died: 1892. Father: David Kaufman Tumlinson. Mother: Laura Calhoun. Source: Tombstone.

Tumlinson, Louisa

Born: April 18, 1829, Georgia. Died: December 21, 1916, Kleberg County, Texas. Married: (1) R. C. Woodall, 1848. (2) Sherd N. Mathis. (3) J. White Wood, December 24, 1868. (4) David Tumlinson, December 17, 1879. Father: James Posey. Mother: Jane Ford. Comments: Louisa Tumlinson came from Mississippi to Shelby County, Texas, in 1841. In the fall of that year, the family moved to Anderson County. Louisa married her first husband there. He died after less than three years of marriage. She married the second time about three years later also in Anderson County. The family, along with their slaves, Tom and his sisters, moved to the Cream Level community of Van Zandt County in 1858 and to Canton in the early part of 1861. Slave schedules show that Tom was valued by his owner at $1,800 with his sisters valued at somewhat less. On October 31, 1861, Sherd Mathis joined the Confederate Army as a bugler and was assigned to Co. E. 6th Texas Cavalry. He died from typhoid fever just after the noted Battle of Corinth, Mississippi in 1862. In 1868, Louisa married the third time, Captain J. White Wood, a well- known businessman in Canton. He died in Canton in 1871. She married for the fourth time a well-known and highly respected farmer, David Tumlinson. He died in 1899, and Louisa lived with her daughter, Mrs. Ida Wood Reese, until her death in Kingsville, Texas. She was the mother of five children but only her daughter, Ida, survived her. Louisa was one of the earliest pioneers of Van Zandt County and was an authority on its early history. She entered Texas when it was still a Republic and moved to Canton when it was just a little shanty town. Her slaves were freed at the end of the Civil War. Tom, who had been a slave for over 40 years, settled just north of Canton and bought a 275-acre farm. He, along with other ex-slaves

Louisa Tumlinson *was born in Georgia in 1829. In 1858, Louisa and her second husband moved with a slave named Tom and Tom's sisters to Canton. Upon the death of her second and third husbands, she married well-known Canton farmer David Tumlinson. Louisa was one of the earliest pioneers of Van Zandt County and was an authority on its early history. She entered Texas when it was still a Republic and moved to Canton when it was just a little shanty town. When the slaves owned by Louisa and her husband were freed at the end of the Civil War, Tom, who had been a slave for over forty years, took the last name "Mathes." He settled just north of Canton, buying a 275-acre farm. He, along with other ex-slaves and their descendants, developed what became the Wynne Community which still exists today. Louisa Tumlinson and Tom Mathes—slave-owner and slave—are both buried in Hillcrest Cemetery.*

and their descendants, developed what became the Wynne Community which is still in existence today. Slave and slave owner are now buried in the same cemetery. Sources: *Marriage Records of Van Zandt County 1848-1909*; *Wills Point Chronicle*, March 5, 1908; *Canton Herald*, December 23, 1916 and January 5, 1917.

Tunnell, Amphias Seaton "Amp"
Born: November 20, 1862, Smith County, Texas. Died: August 5, 1940, Van Zandt County, Texas. Cause of death: Heart disease. Married: (1) Sarah "Sallie" Rosenbaum, October 15, 1885. (2) May Petty, April 5, 1888. (3) Zorado Wallace Johnson, 1901. Father: Elisha Tunnell. Mother: Nancy Ellis. Occupation: Merchant, Deputy Sheriff, real estate agent. Comments: Amp Tunnell was born in Smith County, but came to Van Zandt County at an early age. He was operating a grocery store on the Canton Courthouse square by 1886. He later became a Van Zandt County Deputy Sheriff. After Sallie's death, he married May Petty. After her death, he married Zorado Wallace Johnson, the widow of Dr. W. G. Johnson. Amp later moved to Grand Saline where he was engaged in the real estate business. His third wife survived him by nine years. Sources: Death Certificate; *Texas Telephone*, October 24, 1885 and June 5, 1886; *Canton Telephone*, April 13, 1888; *Canton Herald*, August 8, 1940.

Tunnell, May
Born: June 9, 1868. Died: October 18, 1897. Married: Amplias S. Tunnell, April 5, 1888. Father: Unknown. Mother: Unknown. Source: *Marriage Records of Van Zandt County 1848-1909*.

Tunnell, Sarah "Sallie"
Born: January 24, 1863, Van Zandt County, Texas. Died: June 24, 1887, Van Zandt County, Texas. Married: Amphias Seaton Tunnell, October 15, 1885. Father: George Rosinbaum, Sr. Mother: Mariah Theresa Foster. Siblings: Exonia "Bettie," Harvey D., Nannie Susan, Laura Lourana, George Edward, Ella, and Georgia Ann. Comments: Sallie Tunnell's parents came to Texas from Wythe County, Virginia in the early 1850's. George, Sr., an attorney, was elected District Attorney of the 9th Judicial District of Texas August 4, 1856 and served until 1860. He was opposed to Texas' breaking away from the United States and became involved in Unionist activities. He was arrested by the Confederate Army, and no record has been found as to what happened to him. Mariah later married Richard Wells who helped rear the Rosinbaum children. Sallie's brother, Ed Rosinbaum, was killed in a saloon in Lawndale, Texas in 1889. Her husband later married twice and died in 1940 in Grand Saline, Texas. Sources: Lisa Pierce, Pierce Family historian.

Tunnell, Wilson
Born: July 13, 1906. Died: September 2, 1906. Father: F. M. Tunnell. Mother: Lora Tunnell. Source: Tombstone.

Tunnell, Zorado Johnson
Born: August 17, 1866, Van Zandt County, Texas. Died: April 4, 1949, Dallas County, Texas. Cause of death: Stroke. Married: (1) Dr. William Goodman Johnson,

November 5, 1882. Child: Minnie. (2) Amplias S. Tunnell, 1901. Father: Jesse W. Wallace. Mother: Elizabeth W. Hubbard. Comments: Zorado Tunnell's father was the namesake of the Wallace Community. Her husband practiced medicine in Canton until his death in 1893. Zorado married A. S. Tunnell in 1901. They lived in Canton and Grand Saline until his death in 1940. She then moved to Dallas to live with her daughter until her death. Sources: Death Certificate; *Canton Herald.* April 14, 1949; Eubank Funeral Home records.

TYLER, ULA LEE
Born: August 27, 1870. Died: October 23, 1870. Father: A. J. Tyler. Mother: M. J. Tyler. Source: Tombstone.

TYLER, W. J.
Born: October 29, 1876. Died: October 29, 1877. Father: Unknown Tyler. Mother: Unknown. Source: Tombstone.

TYSON, JOHN HENRY
Born: July 21, 1839, Columbia County, New York. Died: August 11, 1898, Van Zandt County, Texas. Married: Phebe Jane Sanger, September 24, 1865, New York. Children: Mary L., William H., Caroline (Carrie), Spencer Edward, Frederick Augusta, and Annie. Father: Joseph Tyson. Mother: Peggy Tyson. Military: Union Pvt. Co. M & H 1 Reg't. Massachusetts Cavalry. Comments: Comments: John and Phebe Tyson, came to Texas from Arkansas with their daughter, Carrie, and her husband William C. Dearing. They lived in the Starr Community until John's death. Pheby moved to Oklahoma to be with her children. She died there April 11, 1909 and is buried in the Blair Cemetery, Jackson County, Oklahoma. Several members of this extended family are buried in the Hillcrest Cemetery.Sources: *Freestate Enterprise*, August 18, 1898; J. M. Hadley, Tyson Family historian.

U

UTTS, ALBERT J.
Born: March 1879, Van Zandt County, Texas. Died: July 24, 1947, Van Zandt County, Texas. Cause of death: Heart disease. Single. Father: Jacob J. Utts, Pennsylvania. Mother: Martha Elizabeth Spain, Tennessee. Siblings: Martha Beth, Josephine, Allena May, Era Lucille, Johnny Walter, and Maudie D. Occupation: Farmer, rancher. Comments: The *Canton Herald* reported Albert Utts' death as follows: "Albert, as he was known by his friends, was never able to do the things that most men were to do due to an affliction which he suffered in early childhood. He was a man that did not like for everyone to know what he did but he helped many people in many different ways---He was well known in this section of the county in his efforts in improving Herford cattle. Being a farmer all of his life his efforts were devoted to the land and the improvement of it." Sources: Death Certificate; *Canton Herald*, July 31 1947; Hilliard Funeral Home records.

JACOB J. "MAJOR" UTTS *grew up on a farm in Bucks County, Pennsylvania and enlisted in the Union Army at the age of 17. In about 1874, he and his family moved to Canton, which became their home for the remainder of their lives. In 1879, he invested in the family grocery business on the Canton Courthouse Square with starting capital of $75. In addition to being a merchant, he acquired a substantial amount of land and leased it to tenant farmers. He served as Canton Postmaster for over twelve years, beginning in 1898. The Utts family was one of the more prominent families in Van Zandt County and Canton for more than fifty years.*

Utts, Allena May
Born: September 20, 1874. Died: June 17, 1883. Father: Jacob J. Utts. Mother: Martha Elizabeth Spain. Source: Tombstone.

Utts, Era Lucille
Born: March 5, 1888. Died: January 26, 1947. Married: Will Jacobs, 1921. Father: Jacob J. Utts. Mother: Martha Elizabeth Spain. Comments: The death certificate of Era Utts reflects that she was single, but there was a notice of a wedding November 1921. The article indicated that Will Jacobs, the son of Frank Jacobs, married Miss Era Utts in Myrtle Springs with W. A. T. Murry officiating. Sources: Death Certificate; Wedding notification, November 1921 (newspaper not indicated).

Utts, Jacob J. "Major"
Born: April 26, 1843, Philadelphia County, Pennsylvania. Died: August 1, 1920, Van Zandt County, Texas. Married: Martha Elizabeth Spain, March 14, 1872, Louisiana. Children: Albert, Allena May, Era Lucille, Johnie Walter, Maudie, Martha Beth, and Josephine. Father: Jacob Christian Utts. Mother: Louise Susanna School. Occupation: Farmer, merchant, postmaster. Military: U. S. Army, Pvt., First enlisted Co. F. 128th Penn. Inf., Re-enlisted Co. A, 28th Penn. Inf. Comments: Jacob J. Utts was of Dutch ancestry. He grew up on a farm in Bucks County, Pennsylvania and enlisted in the Union Army July 8, 1862 as a Private at the age of 17. He participated in the battles of South Mountain, Antietam, Chancellorsville and other smaller battles and was never wounded. After the War he drifted to Iowa, then moved south working in Dallas, Texas and Louisiana. In 1872 in Shreveport, Louisiana he married Martha E. Spain. By 1873 he and his family had moved to the Garden Valley community of Van Zandt County, Texas. About a year later, they were in Canton which became their home for the remainder of their lives. In 1879, Jacob invested in the family grocery business on the Canton Courthouse Square with a starting capital of $75. In addition to being a merchant, he acquired a substantial amount of land. Early on, he purchased a 266-acre farm in the Q. C. Nugent Survey which was close to Canton. In 1902, he purchased seven hundred acres of land along Mill Creek between Canton and Grand Saline, which now borders Highway 17. The long time reference point for this land was the Utts Bottom. Jacob did not farm the land himself, but leased it to tenant farmers. At his death, this land was passed along to his heirs who maintained a farming and ranching operation for a number of years. The grocery business was only a supplement to his farming operations, selling about $5,000 to $10,000 of goods annually. The Utts family were one of the more prominent families in Van Zandt County and Canton for more than fifty years. Jacob served as Canton Postmaster for over 12 years, starting in 1898. Martha and he had six children, the three oldest dying young. He was a staunch Republican in his political views. Sources: *1890 in Van Zandt County, Texas*; *Texan Telephone*, February 14, 1885; *Canton Telephone*, August 14, 1891; *Freestate Enterprise*, February 2, 1902; *Canton Herald*, August 6, 1920 and August 13, 1920.

Utts, Johnie Walter "Waltie"
Born: February 10, 1873. Died: July 30, 1876. Father: Jacob J. Utts. Mother: Martha Elizabeth Spain. Source: Ancestry.com.

Utts, Martha Elizabeth "Mattie"
Born: April 23, 1851, Tennessee. Died: November 6, 1908. Married: Jacob J. Utts, March 14, 1872, Louisiana. Children: Albert, Allena May, Era Lucille, Johnie Walter, Maudie, Martha Beth, and Josephine. Father: Thomas E. Spain. Mother: Nancy Smith Foster. Comments: Jacob and Mattie Utts came to Canton in the mid 1870's. They became one of the more prominent and respected families in Van Zandt County. In the fall of 1908, Mattie had an accidental fall from which she sustained a spinal cord injury. She never fully recovered. Sources: 1900 U. S. Census; *Wills Point Chronicle*, December 10, 1908; Ancestry.com.

Utts, Maudie D.
Born: May 15, 1877. Died: September 4, 1878. Father: Jacob J. Utts. Mother: Martha Elizabeth Spain. Source: Ancestry.com.

V

Valdez, Olga Lydia
Born: April 2, 1971. Died: July 7, 1971. Father: Juan Valdez. Mother: Herminia Ramirez. Source: Death Certificate.

Valentine, Azilla House
Born: November 24, 1856. Died: June 20, 1902. Married: James P. Valentine, December 6, 1876. Children: Timothy, Mary, Murray, Katherine, Clark, Hardy W., James Timothy, John Leslie, and Zilla. Father: Unknown House. Mother: Unknown. Source: *Wills Point Chronicle*, June 26, 1902.

Valentine, Carrie H.
Born: March 22, 1860, White County, Arkansas. Died: September 26, 1922, Van Zandt County, Texas. Cause of death: Dengue fever. Married: James P. Valentine, July 22, 1903. Father: Rev. Oliphant. Mother: Unknown.

***HENRY COZELLE WARD** was a young farmer who entered the U. S. Army in 1917. He was assigned to the fledgling WWI Air Unit of the Army and trained in New York and other stateside camps before being shipped overseas. He was assigned to the 361 Aero Squad based in England, and became ill and died before he could be shipped to the war zone. Although his body was initially buried in England, it was removed two years after his death and shipped home to Canton. He had a large and impressive military-style funeral led by former servicemen in uniform. He was further honored when an American Legion Post was formed in Canton and named Cozelle Ward American Legion Post 300. The Post operated for many years before it was discontinued.*

Comments: The *Canton Herald* reported Carrie Valentine's death as follows: "In the home going of Mrs. J. P. Valentine, Canton loses one of its most beloved and useful citizens. It was not our privilege to know the early life history of this Christian character. She was born at West Point, Ark. Her father, the Rev. Oliphant, one of the pioneer Methodist preachers of that section, and her life reflected the early home training that was hers in this Christian home. It was after her marriage to J. P. Valentine in 1903 that she became known to her many friends in this county. And she was there to administer to the sorrowing—Sometimes such words are life savings, but in the life of this Christian said such is not the case, for during the world war she became the little mother, to the boys of this county that went to war.—It was very fitting that she be remembered and loved by the soldier boys—and that these should serve as the active pall bearers in the funeral service. Those so acting were Hon. M. G. Sanders, Attorney, Attorney A. A. Dawson, D. B. Jones, Dr. J. K. Bateman, Dr. W. C. Herrin. All Canton mourns." Sources: 1920 U. S. Census; *Canton Herald*, October 6, 1922.

VALENTINE, CLARK

Born: 1898. Died: January 30, 1899. Age: 2 months 7 days. Father: James P. Valentine. Mother: Azilla House. Source: *Free State Enterprise*, February 2, 1899.

VALENTINE, HARDY W.

Born: August 12, 1877. Died: November 7, 1904. Father: James P. Valentine. Mother: Azilla House. Occupation: School teacher, newspaper owner. Comments: Hardy Valentine suffered from rheumatism. During the last months of his life, he was unable to move himself. He had been a school teacher and owner of the *Free State Enterprise* newspaper in Canton. He had sold the newspaper due to his health condition. Source: *Wills Point Chronicle*, November 10, 1904.

VALENTINE, JAMES P.

Born: September 27, 1855, White County, Arkansas. Died: October 3, 1930, Bexar County Texas. (Tombstone death date is incorrect.) Cause of death: Pneumonia. Married: (1) Azilla House, December 6, 1876. Children: Timothy, Zilla, Clark, John Leslie, Hardy W., Mary, Kathryne, and Murray. (2) Carrie H. Oliphant, July 22, 1903. Father: James E. Valentine, North Carolina. Mother: Mary Burrow, Arkansas. Occupation: Farmer, merchant. Comments: James Valentine moved to Van Zandt County in 1896. He farmed for one year, then moved to Canton, and started a mercantile business. For a number of years he was looked upon as one of the county's leading businessmen. After his retirement, he lived with his daughter, Kathryne Slaughter in Dallas, Texas. After James became ill, he moved to San Antonio for his health and remained until his death. Sources: Death Certificate; *Canton Herald*, October 10, 1930.

VALENTINE, JOHN LESLIE, JR.

Born: April 1918. Died: September 1918. Father: John Leslie Valentine, Sr. Mother: Wilma Davis. Source: Tombstone.

VALENTINE, JOHN LESLIE, SR.

Born: September 27, 1888, White County, Arkansas. Died: June 14, 1964, Travis County, Texas. Married: Wilma Annie Davis, August 25, 1911. Father: James P. Valentine. Mother: Azilla House. Occupation: Shoe salesman. Source: Death Certificate.

Valentine, Wilma Annie Davis

Born: February 23, 1889, Limestone County, Texas. Died: January 16, 1965, Travis County, Texas. Married: John Leslie Valentine, August 25, 1911. Father: Henry Phillips Davis. Mother: Mary Jane Cook. Sources: Death Certificate, Ancestry.com.

Valentine, Zilla

Born: July 21, 1892. White County, Arkansas. Died: September 13, 1911, Kaufman County, Texas. Cause of death: Appendicitis. Father: James P. Valentine. Mother: Azilla House. Occupation: School teacher. Comments: The *Wills Point Chronicle* reported Zilla Valentine's death as follows: "Miss Zilla Valentine was born in West Point Arkansas July 21, 1892. She moved to Canton with her father when she was four years of age, growing into young woman-hood here. She attended Kidd-Key College at Sherman for two terms and took the medal for mathematics. She attended the Sam Houston Normal for one term and secured a first grade certificate, teaching last year in the Edgewood public Schools, and she had contracted to teach this year at San Benito where her brother resides. She had had several light attacks of appendicitis and recently a severe attack. She was operated on in Terrell Tuesday, standing the operation well, but Wednesday morning she took a turn for the worse and despite all that medical skill could do the Grim Reaper claimed her as his victim." Source: *Wills Point Chronicle*, September 21, 1911.

Venable, Sarah Allyne

Born: October 6, 1911, Nolan County, Texas. Died: February 27, 1995, Van Zandt County, Texas. Married: Howard Venable. Father: John M. Pittman. Mother: Maggie Waldron. Source: *Van Zandt News*, March 5, 1995.

W

Waldrip, Seabie

Born: September 17, 1901. Died: May 13, 1911. Father: Seaborn D. Waldrip. Mother: Effie P. Youngblood. Source: *Grand Saline Sun*, May 18, 1911.

Walker, Clara Velma

Born: January 7, 1905, Warren County, Mississippi. Died: April 30, 1986, Dallas County, Texas. Married: Roy Lee Walker, November 16, 1924. Children: Robert, Ray Lee, Roy William, Earnest Lewis, and Peggy Ann. Father: Robert Lee Alford. Mother: Ella White. Siblings: Earl, Melrose, Laverne, Bob, Fynie, and Drue. Comments: Clara Walker lived in Dallas, Texas most of her adult life and worked as a volunteer in the public schools. Sources: *Canton Herald*, January 16, 1986; Eubank Funeral Home records; Nell Deets Walker, Walker Family historian.

Walker, E. A.

Born: December 22, 1839. Died: May 22, 1890. Married: W. E. Walker. Father: Unknown. Mother: Unknown. Source: Tombstone.

Walker, Francis Jeanette "Nettie"

Born: July 31, 1873, Burleson County, Texas. Died: March 24, 1948, Van Zandt County, Texas. Cause of death: Pneumonia. Married: Frank Leslie Walker, March 1, 1891. Children: Cyrus, Clyde, Lee, and Mack. Father: Dan Riley. Mother: Mary Graham. Siblings: Mattie and W. B. Sources: *Canton Herald*, March 25, 1948; Hilliard Funeral Home records.

Walker, Francis Marion "Frank"

Born: March 2, 1844. Died: October 31, 1892. Cause of death: Pneumonia. Married: Hannah Catherine Martin, February 8, 1866, Henderson County, Texas. Children: Georgia Ann and Margaret Jane. Occupation: Businessman, innkeeper. Military: CSA, 15th TX Cavalry, Jordan's Co. Comments: Frank Walker came to Texas at a young age. He lived in Henderson County and then moved to Canton. He purchased the Phoenix Hotel in May, 1888. Source: *Canton Telephone*, November 4, 1892; Find A Grave.

Walker, Frank Leslie

Born: January 19, 1866, Edgar County, Illinois. Died: March 23, 1950, Dallas County, Texas. Cause of death: Cardiovascular disease. Married: Francis Jeanette "Nettie" Riley, March 1, 1891, Hunt County, Texas. Children: Cyrus, Clyde, Lee, and Mack. Father: Unknown. Mother: Unknown. Occupation: Carpenter, home builder, cabinet maker. Comments: Frank Walker came to Texas in 1888. He moved to Van Zandt County sometime after 1910. He moved to Dallas to live with his son because of failing health. Sources: Death Certificate; Nell Deets Walker, Walker Family historian; Eubank Funeral Hone records.

Walker, Mack Gibson

Born: January 27, 1905, Hunt County, Texas. Died: May 18, 1948, Van Zandt County, Texas. Cause of death: Heart

Martha Arletha "Letha" Ward and William Henry Ward

disease. Married: Lillian Irene Pickens. Father: Frank Leslie Walker. Mother: Francis Jeanette Riley. Occupation: School bus driver. Comments: Mack Walker drove a Canton ISD bus for many years. He died from a heart attack while playing baseball in Canton. His wife, Lillian, later married Elmer Kennedy. Source: *Canton Herald*, May 20, 1948; Hilliard Funeral Home records.

WALKER, PEGGY ANN
Born: November 15, 1930. Died: January 1, 1935. Cause of death: Accident. Father: Roy Lee Walker. Mother: Clara Velma Alford. Comments: Peggy Ann Walker fell out of a moving car and received severe injuries and died. Source: Death Certificate.

WALKER, ROY LEE
Born: January 23, 1902, Van Zandt County, Texas. Died: May 27, 1969, Dallas County, Texas. Cause of death: Myelogenous Leukemia. Married: Clara Velma Alford, November 15, 1924. Children: Robert, Ray Lee, Roy William, and Earnest Lewis. Father: Frank Leslie Walker. Mother: Frances Jeanette Riley. Occupation: Mechanic. Comments: Roy Walker was a mechanic for Sears Roebuck Company for many years. Source: Death Certificate.

WALKER, SCOTTY M.
Born: 1953, Texas. Died: July 27, 2008, Tallassee County, Alabama. Married: Sharon Hindman. Children: Nick, Chris, Michael, Leah, Jessica, and Petal. Father: Frank M. Walker. Mother: Lillian Flaherty. Siblings: Tissie, Robert G., and James. Occupation: Self-employed plumber. Military: U. S. Army. Source: *Van Zandt News*, August 10, 2008.

WALLACE, J. FRANK
Born: September 3, 1883. Died: March 2, 1901. Cause of death: Congestion. Father: Isaac B. Wallace. Mother: Mary J. McCarty. Comments: Frank Wallace was planning to enter Metropolitan Business College in Dallas when he became ill and died. His parents were well known in Canton. Source: *Free State Enterprise*, March 7, 1901.

WALLACE, THOMAS W.
Born: February 13, 1888. Died: March 17, 1889. Father: Isaac B. Wallace. Mother. Mary J. McCarty. Source: *Canton Telephone*, March 22, 1889.

WALTERS (GUESS) MYRTLE MAE
Born: November 1892, Tennessee. Died: July 27, 1973, Smith County, Texas. Married: (1) Thomas J. Walters, September 3, 1927. (2) Jim Guess, 1960. Father: Henry Thomas Kennedy. Mother: Savilia Virginia Aldridge (Alldredge). Siblings: Riley, Charles, Peggy, Etta, and Annie Lou. Comments: Myrtle Walters Guess is buried next to her first husband with the name "Walters" on a double marker. Sources: Texas Death Records, 1890-1976; *Canton Herald*, August 2, 1973; Ancestry.com.

WALTERS, THOMAS JEFFERSON
Born: May 20, 1884, Smith County, Texas. Died: October 16, 1959, Smith County, Texas. Cause of death: Stroke. Married: Myrtle Mae Kennedy, September 3, 1927. Father: Olander Walters, Tennessee. Mother: Frances Emeline Beckham, Alabama. Siblings: Samuel T., Julie E., James O., Gertrude, Susie, and Charlie E. Occupation: Farmer, oil field worker. Sources: Death Certificate, 1900 U. S. Census, Ancestry.com.

Wann, Louis Homer
Born: June 8, 1912, Ellis County, Texas. Died: March 21, 1996. Married: Ruby Rae Whitaker, July 31, 1937. Children: Virginia Ann, Louis Homer, Jr., and Patsy. Father: Edward C. Wann, Alabama. Mother: Edna M. Schrader, Alabama. Siblings: Elva, Pauline, Roy, and Fay. Sources: 1920 U. S. Census, U. S. Social Security Applications and Claims Index, Ancestry.com.

Wann, Ruby Rae Whitaker
Born: May 6, 1922, Bienville Parish, Louisiana. Died: November 23, 2008, Van Zandt County, Texas. Married: Louis Homer Wann, July 31, 1937. Children: Virginia Ann, Louis Homer, Jr., and Patsy. Father: Earnest Glen Whitaker. Mother: Rosa Pearl Edwards. Siblings: Earnest Gordon, Glenn L., Wade, Hormel, Ruth, Hazel, Janet, Helen, Harlon, and Maria. Comments: Ruby Wann lived most of her life in Travis County, Texas but moved back to Canton in 1996. She was an active member of the Eastern Star. Sources: *Tyler Morning Telegram*, November 28, 2008; Eubank Funeral Home records.

Ward, Henry Cozelle
(Photo page 154) Born: January 22, 1896, Van Zandt County, Texas. Died: October 26, 1918, England. Cause of death: Died in military service. Single. Father: William Henry Ward. Mother: Martha Arletha Samples. Siblings: Helen H. and William Harvey. Military: WWI, U. S. Army 361 Aero Squad. Comments: Henry Cozelle Ward was a young farmer who entered the U. S. Army in 1917. He was assigned to the fledgling WWI Air Unit of the Army and trained in New York and other stateside camps before being shipped overseas. He was assigned to the 361 Aero Squad based in England. He became ill and died before he could be shipped to the war zone. His body was buried in England, removed, and shipped home in April of 1920. He had a large and impressive military style funeral which was led by former servicemen in uniform. He was further honored when an American Legion Post was formed in Canton and named Cozelle Ward American Legion Post 300. The Post operated for many years before it was discontinued. Sources: WWI Draft Registration Records; *Canton Herald*, June 4, 1920; Ancestry.com, Find A Grave.

Ward, Martha Arletha "Letha"
Born: May 6, 1876, Van Zandt County, Texas. Died: March 4, 1967, Dallas County, Texas. Married: William Henry Ward, October 21, 1891. Children: Henry Cozelle, Helen and William Harvey. Father: Jessie F. Samples. Mother: Nancy Jane Jackson. Siblings: Caroline, Georgia A., Araminta, Alice Victoria, Nancy Arrena, Jettie, Jesse H. S, Mary Lou, and Rosa Dell. Comments: Martha Ward's parents were longtime residents of Canton. Her father was an early businessman on the Canton Courthouse Square. Sources: Eubank Funeral Home records, Find A Grave.

Ward, William Henry
Born: January 12, 1863, Missouri. Died: October 20, 1926, Dallas County, Texas. Cause of death: Kidney cancer. Married: Martha Arletha Samples, October 21, 1891. Children: Henry Cozelle, William Harvey, and Helen. Father: R. Ward. Mother: Helen Harris. Occupation: House carpenter. Source: Death Certificate, Find A Grave.

Warren, Joseph W.
Born: December 17, 1841, Indiana. Died: November 22, 1884. Married: Josephine Jones. Father: John Warren. Mother: Ann Newton. Occupation: House carpenter. Military: Union Army, Private, 9th Ill Infantry Co. H Comments: Joseph Warren joined the Union Army and later deserted at a camp near Fredericksburg, Virginia on December 20, 1862. He rejoined his company near Petersburg, Virginia on March 10, 1863. He was held in the brigade guardhouse for a time. He was captured April 1, 1865 and released June 20, 1865. He moved to Texas in 1869. Sources: 1880 U. S. Census, Union Civil War Records.

Warren, Josephine Jones
Born: September 6, 1845, Tennessee. Died: January 2, 1925, Kaufman County, Texas. Cause of death: Heart disease. Married: Joseph W. Warren, November 5, 1865, Tennessee. Children: J. G., Norman, three infant deaths. Father: Judd Jones. Mother: Unknown Lee. Comments: Joseph and Josephine Warren came to Texas in 1869. She had been a member of the Presbyterian Church since early childhood. Sources: Death Certificate; *Wills Point Chronicle*, January 22, 1925.

Warren, Watson Norman
Born: December 10, 1865. Died: June 19, 1881. Father: Joseph W. Warren. Mother: Josephine Jones. Source: Tombstone.

Weatherall, Charles L. "Charlie"
Born: December 14, 1861, Mississippi. Died: September 16, 1909, Van Zandt County, Texas. Married: Martha Jane Rogers, 1886. Children: Ernest Rushing, Dora N., Margaret, Alva, Thomas D., and Bailey. Father: Lafayette Weatherall, Mississippi. Mother: Margaret Jane Neely, South Carolina. Siblings: George, William, John, Henry, and Martha. Sources: 1870, 1900 U. S. Census, Ancestry.com.

Weatherall, Adis
Note: Adis Weatherall's name is on a double tombstone with Jack Chaney but she is actually buried in Haven of Memories Cemetery in Canton, Texas.

Weatherall, Ernest Rushing
Born: June 6, 1893, Collin County, Texas. Died: May 31, 1943, Kerr County, Texas. Cause of death: Tuberculosis.

Mary Elizabeth White, granddaughter Duskie Hilliard Kellam, great-granddaughter Kathryn Kellam Ashworth, and husband William Franklin White.

Ethel Lee Weaver

Leta Belle Wells

Married: Adis Cox, October 7, 1923. Father: Charles L. Weatherall. Mother: Martha Jane Rogers. Occupation: Farming. Military: WWI, Pvt. 1C1 309 Infantry, 78th Division. Comments: Ernest Weatherall's family moved to Van Zandt County in 1896. He was on the French battle line when the WWI Armistice was signed. He came back to Van Zandt County after the war. He was seeking treatment in the Legion Tuberculosis Hospital in Kerrville when he died. His wife is buried in Haven of Memories Cemetery in Canton, Texas. Sources: Death Certificate; *Canton Herald*, June 10, 1943.

WEATHERALL, MARTHA JANE "JENNIE"
Born: October 18, 1868, Mississippi. Died: June 16, 1924. Married: Charles L. Weatherall, 1886. Children: Dora N., Margaret, Ernest R., Alva, Thomas D., and Bailey. Father: Unknown Rogers. Mother: Martha J. Sword. Sources: 1900 U. S. Census, Find A Grave.

WEATHERALL, THOMAS DEWEY
Born: April 28, 1898, Lavon County,Texas. Died: November 12, 1955, Dallas County, Texas. Married: Tula Ann Reid, January 28, 1923. Father: Charles L. Weatherall. Mother: Martha Jane Rogers. Occupation: Farmer. Source: Hilliard Funeral Home records.

WEATHERALL, TULA ANN
Born: February 22, 1898, Texas. Died: May 6, 1975, Van Zandt County, Texas. Cause of death: Heart disease. Married: Thomas D. Weatherall, January 28, 1923. Father: George Reid. Mother: Etta McWilliams. Source: Death Certificate.

WEAVER, ARTHUR WILSON
Born: April 7, 1898, Van Zandt County, Texas. Died: December 10, 1951, Smith County, Texas. Cause of death: Lung cancer. Married: Ethel Lee Chaney, July 22, 1915. Children: D. C., Calvin, G. L., Garland Monroe, Marvin Arthur, Gladys Lorene, and Evelyn. Father: Wilson Weaver. Mother: Nora Etta Moore. Occupation: Produce merchant. Sources: Death Certificate, Find A Grave.

WEAVER, CALVIN FRANKLIN
Born: July 23, 1917, Van Zandt County, Texas. Died: August 17, 1966, Kaufman County, Texas. Cause of death: Heart disease. Married: Minnie Lee Whaley. Children: Joanne, Shirley Ann, and Mrs. W. E. Dobbs. Father: Arthur Wilson Weaver. Mother: Ethel Lee Chaney. Siblings: D. C., Garland Monroe, Marvin Arthur, G. L., Gladys Lorene, and Evelyn. Occupation: Produce Company owner, trucker. Military: WWII, U. S. Army TX Pvt. Sources: Death Certificate; *Canton Herald*, August 25, 1966.

WEAVER, ETHEL LEE
Born: August 13, 1900, Smith County, Texas. Died: September 1, 1973, Smith County, Texas. Married: Arthur Wilson Weaver, July 22, 1915. Children: D. C., Garland Monroe, Marvin Arthur, G. L., Gladys Lorene, and Evelyn. Father: Robert Lee Chaney. Mother: Margaret Ann Hinkle. Siblings: Thomas Monroe, Adie, Clyde, Claude, Fred Warren, Farris, Herron, Sam Houston, Randa Mae, and Octavia. Sources: *Canton Herald*, August 25, 1966; Eubank Funeral Home records.

WELDON, JOYCE JUANITA
Born: September 29, 1919, Van Zandt County, Texas. Died: August 3, 1952, Van Zandt County, Texas. Cause

of death: Heart disease. Single. Father: Wilson William Weldon. Mother: Nannie Eliza Paul. Siblings: Mrs. Terrell Ogletree. Occupation: Stenographer. Comments: Joyce Weldon graduated from Canton High School, attended North Texas College, Denton, Texas; Draughon's Business College, Dallas; and graduated from The Radio School of Engineering, Dallas, Texas. She worked at Sears Roebuck, Travelers Insurance Company, and Neiman-Marcus Company—all in Dallas. She died at the home of her sister, Mrs. Terrell Ogletree in Canton. Sources: *Canton Herald*, August 7, 1952; Hilliard Funeral Home records.

WELDON, NANNIE ELIZA

Born: July 23, 1888, Lamar County, Texas. Died: November 26, 1981, Van Zandt County, Texas. Cause of death: Heart disease. Married: Wilson William Weldon, December 12, 1909. Children: Evelyn and Joyce Juanita. Father: James Winston Paul, Kentucky. Mother: Mary Jane Scott, Kentucky. Comments: Eliza Paul came to Canton when she was 13 years old, married Wilson Weldon in 1909, and lived the rest of her life in this area. She was a member of the First Baptist Church in Canton and Chapter No. 667 Order of the Eastern Star of which she was a fifty-year member. Sources: Death Certificate; *Canton Herald*, December 3, 1981.

WELDON, WILSON WILLIAM

Born: January 3, 1888, Van Zandt County, Texas. Died: August 23, 1975, Van Zandt County, Texas. (Headstone has August 22, 1975. Death Certificate and newspaper has August 23, 1975.) Cause of death: Pneumonia. Married: Nannie Eliza Paul, December 12, 1909. Children: Evelyn and Joyce Juanita. Father: Wilson William Weldon. Mother: M. M. Martin. Occupation: Farmer. Sources: Death Certificate; Canton Herald, August 28, 1973.

WELLS, LETA BELLE

Born: February 22, 1902. Died: January 31, 1961. Cause of death: Heart disease. Married: Ray Wells. Father: Walter Smith. Mother: Lannie Belle Wynne. Siblings: Henry Hawthorne and Zeffie Telasca. Sources: Death Certificate, Find A Grave.

WHITAKER, EARNEST GLEN

Born: September 22, 1894, Alabama. Died: February 3, 1948, Cherokee County, Texas. Cause of death: Heart disease. Married: Rosa Edwards, May 13, 1917, Claiborne Parish, Louisiana. Children: Gordon, Glen, Wade, Harmel, Ruby, Ruth, Hazel, and Janet. Father: William Jasper Whitaker, Alabama. Mother: Amanda Julia Blunt, Alabama. Occupation: Oil company owner. Military: WWI. Comments: Earnest Whitaker moved to Texas in 1934 and founded G. W. Oil Company in Canton, Texas in 1936. He operated it until his death. The business passed to Gordon Whitaker and other family members. The business was operational for over fifty years. Sources: Death Certificate; *Canton Herald*, February 12, 1948.

WHITAKER, ROSA PEARL

Born: December 10, 1901, Bienville Parish, Louisiana. Died: January 26, 2000, Van Zandt County, Texas. Married: Ernest Glen Whitaker, May 13, 1917, Claiborne Parish, Louisiana. Children: Gordon, Glen, Ruth, Wanda, Harmel, Ruby, Hazel, and Janet. Father: Henry Titus Edwards. Mother: Fanny Lee Van Hooser. Comments: Rosa Whitaker moved from Louisiana to Texas in 1934 with her family. Her husband, Glen Whitaker, owned the G. W. Oil Company in Canton, Texas from 1936 until his death in 1948. The company was family owned for over fifty years. Rosa lived in Canton most of her adult life and was a member of the First Baptist Church in Canton. She was in charge of the church nursery for more than twenty years. Sources: *Canton Herald*, February 3, 2000; Ancestry.com.

WHITE, DANIEL COLUMBUS "D.C."

Born: November 15, 1847, Talladega County, Alabama. Died: February 3, 1882, Van Zandt County, Texas. Father: Timothy White. Mother: Eliza White. Comments: There were two legal hangings in Canton. One was a black man named Frank Wiley Dink who was convicted and hanged July 6, 1866, for killing a man named Frank McElvy. The murder was committed February 24, 1866 near Jordan Saline. Dink hit the sleeping McElvy in the head with an ax killing him. It is not known where Dink is buried; but in all probability, it was in Hillcrest Cemetery. This cemetery was near the courthouse where he would have been convicted. The other hanging was D. C. White. There are many accounts of the hanging of D. C. White. The following story is taken from the *Wills Point Local-Chronicle* of February 1882 right after the hanging and is presented in its entirety: "The *Wills Point Local-Chronicle* gives a short account of the life and crimes of White, the murderer executed in Van Zandt county a few days since: Daniel Columbus White was born in the town of Talladega, Alabama on the 15th day of November, 1847; was the son of Timothy White, a respectable citizen, and a tanner by trade. In 1849 the senior White moved with his family to Texas, and settled in Nacogdoches County. From there he moved to Harrison County, Texas, and lived near Jefferson until 1855, when he moved to Webster Parish, Louisiana, where he still lives. Dan White, as he was commonly called, was only eighteen years old when his father settled in Louisiana, and nothing is known of his conduct during his boy days. He served in the Confederate Army,* and after his return home, after the war, he had the reputation of being a bad man. Soon after his return from the army he shot and killed a doctor who lived near his father, in Louisiana. The best information we have in relation to the killing is that he shot the doctor in the back with a rifle as he was riding the road. For this crime

Daniel Columbus "D.C." White *was one of only two men in Canton to commit a crime, go through the justice system, and receive a sentence of execution by hanging. As a young man, he shot and killed a doctor who lived near White's father in Louisiana. He was tried, found guilty, given a lifetime sentence, and then pardoned by the governor after having served a portion of his sentence. He then moved to Van Zandt County and back to Louisiana again. In 1881, he was arrested in Louisiana and brought back to Canton where he was tried and convicted of having murdered a peddler named George Conquest. He was hanged February 3, 1882. Although all the other graves in the cemetery are aligned east-west as is Christian tradition, White's is aligned north-south.*

he was tried, found guilty, and received a lifetime sentence to the penitentiary, but was pardoned out by Governor Warmoth, after he had served some time. After this he traveled in Texas considerable, and spoke of having lived at several different places. He lived a short time at Wills Point, and worked at the shoemaker's trade. He also lived in the neighborhood eight or ten miles east of Canton, some time. He then returned to Louisiana, and the next we hear of him he was in company with George Conquest, a peddler, and was traveling on in the direction of the neighborhood of where he had lived. Conquest was an Englishman; had been in this country a few years; had lived in Chattanooga, Tenn, and Missouri, where he stood high. In the month of January, 1877, White and Conquest passed by Mr. Jackson's and after going about one mile they left the road and drove out to the woods about one hundred yards from an old unfrequented road. Here Mr. Geddie found the body of Conquest, sometime in February, in an advanced state of decomposition. An inquest was held, at which time the facts were brought out. After the murder, White had told that his partner had gone west and he was going to sell out the stock of goods, and he was selling them at any price. White went to Longview and sold his stock of goods for $20, and traded the wagon and team for a horse and left. Governor Roberts offered a reward for the arrest of White, and in May of 1880, Deputy Sheriff Tanner and Deputy Marshall Manning, armed with a requisition for his arrest, arrested White in Louisiana, and lodged him in jail at Canton. At the spring term, 1881, he came to trial and was convicted of murder in the first degree, with the death penalty. His case was appealed, and the Court of Appeals affirmed the judgement below in October. At the fall term of the court White was sentenced to be hung, suffered accordingly. He charged others with being accomplices in the crime." D. C. White was hanged February 3, 1882; and by all accounts the event was attended by a very large crowd of people. A heavy deluge of rain had Mill Creek on a rampage that day, and water was from "hill to hill." The county buried White, like the criminal he was found to be, north and south instead of east and west as is traditional. White had spent considerable time in Van Zandt County before and after the killing of Conquest. Court minutes reflect that D. C. White worked on the road crews of the county in February of 1878 and February of 1879. In June of 1876 an African-American Methodist elder was murdered in Wills Point, Texas; and White was a suspect in that killing. Wentworth Manning, who assisted in capturing D. C. White, was probably a private citizen and not a Deputy Marshall. He had been a Commander of a Company of State Police and a Militia Unit during Reconstruction, but there was no indication that he was in law enforcement when he assisted in the capture of White. J. I. Douglas, Postmaster at Wills Point, persuaded the Governor of Texas to post a $300.00 private reward, and it is possible that Manning assisted in the capture of White for the reward. Manning later became a successful businessman in Canton. In 1919 he wrote *Some History of Van Zandt County*, in which he detailed the capture and hanging of D. C. White. He died in 1921 in Wills Point, Texas and is buried in the White Rose Cemetery. A. D. Tanner, the deputy who assisted Manning in the capture of White, moved to Oklahoma shortly after its statehood. He became a pioneer newspaper man and lawyer. He was the editor of the *Star–Democrat* at Ada, and served two terms as County Court Clerk. Later he became publisher of the *Cleveland Democrat* and served as Municipal Judge and Justice of the Peace while residing in Britton, Oklahoma. He died in January of 1935 and is buried in Britton, Oklahoma. *Note: The news article indicates that White was born in 1837. He went to the gallows at the age of 34 in 1882, so the birth date could not have been 1837. The article also indicates that he was in the Civil War. He was only 12 in the 1860 census and would have been only 17 at the end of the War. Although it is possible that he served at a young age, his service in the war has not been confirmed. Sources: *Van Zandt County Texas Court Minutes, Vol C, 1872-1881*; 1860 U. S. Census; *Dallas Weekly Herald*, June 23, 1866; *Wills Point Local-Chronicle*, February 1882; *Canton Herald*, February 7, 1930 and January 29, 1932; *Britton Oklahoma Progress*, January 10, 1935.

WHITE, JESSIE G. JOHNSON

Born: June 21, 1892, West Virginia. Died: September 26, 1935, Dallas County, Texas. Married: Junius Eugene White. Father: Albert Johnson. Mother: Clara Pettit. Occupation: Billing clerk. Comments: Jessie White worked for a telegraph company. She fell from the Medical Arts Building in Dallas, Texas and died from a fractured skull. Source: Death Certificate.

WHITE, JUNIUS EUGENE "JUNE"

Born: February 27, 1878, Texas. Died: May 15, 1962, Harris County, Texas. Married: Jessie G. Johnson. Father: William Franklin White. Mother: Mary Elizabeth Guy. Occupation: Telegraph operator. Comments: June E. White's nephew was Homer Hilliard; and his niece, Ida P. White, was the wife of G. M. Hilliard. He had been living in Houston for thirty years and worked for the Shell Corporation. His wife, Jessie, died in 1935 after falling from the Medical Arts Building in Dallas, Texas. Sources: Death Certificate; *Canton Herald*, May 17, 1962; Ancestry.com.

WHITE, MARY ELIZABETH

(Photo page 158) Born: October 23, 1845, Georgia. Died: February 16, 1903. Married: William Franklin White. Children: Ida P., Robert, Lula, and Jimmy. Father: William R. Guy. Mother: Phoebe Guy. Siblings: Elizabeth R., Eliza, Melissa, Emaetta, and Virginia. Sources: 1850, 1860, and 1880 U. S. Census.

WHITE, WILLIAM FRANKLIN

(Photo page 158) Born: April 26, 1846, Macon County, Georgia. Died: November 25, 1908, Tarrant County, Texas. Married: Mary Elizabeth Guy. Children: Ida P., Robert, Lula, and Jimmy. Father: Samuel W. White. Mother: Penina Cain. Military: CSA, Co. B, 22nd Battalion, Georgia Heavy Artillery. Comments: William White was captured during the Civil War. He was paroled at Greensboro, North Carolina, April 26, 1865. His daughter, Ida, married G. M. Hilliard. Sources: *Grand Saline Sun*, December 3, 1908; Find A Grave.

WILBURN, NEPPIE A.

Born: March 17, 1888. Died: October 6, 1972. Married: William H. Wilburn, May 27, 1906. Father: Robert M. Burns. Mother: Martha Ann Redding. Siblings: Walker, Annie, Beulah, Robert Duncan, Joseph Mitchell, and James Jefferson. Source: Find A Grave.

WILBURN, WILLIAM HARDY "BILL"

Born: January 12, 1882, Texas. Died: April 21, 1963, Dallas County, Texas. Cause of death: Heart disease, diabetes. Married: Neppie A. Burns, May 27, 1906. Father: William Henry Wilburn. Mother: Mary Williams. Source: Death Certificate.

WILHITE, JOHN HARDEN

(Photo page 162) Born: March 13, 1839, Mississippi. Died: January 19, 1900, Van Zandt County, Texas. Married: (1) Jeff Nix, June 11, 1865. Child: Earnest. (2) Mrs. Annie Williams, August 6, 1874. Children: Charlie, Porter, Riley, and Walter. Father: Matthew Herbert Wilhite (Oldest marked grave in Hillcrest Cemetery). Mother: Nancy Hannah Burns. Occupation: Saloon owner, merchant, county official. Military: CSA, 1st Sgt. Co. E. 22 TX Cavalry. Comments: John H. Wilhite came to Van Zandt County with his family about 1855. By 1860 he had applied for and received a license to sell liquor from the old James Moore Grocery Store located on the west side of the Canton square. During his lifetime, he became a very well respected member of the Canton community. For over thirty years, he owned and operated such businesses as saloons, billiard parlors, general merchandise, and grocery stores. The *Free State Enterprise* reported at his death Resolutions of Respect from Castilian Lodge 141 in which he was a member. "He was a man endowed with more than ordinary intellect and a good education and his honesty and integrity was never questioned; and these attributes fitted and qualified him for the various public and official positions he was called upon to fill." He served as a Constable, County Bailiff, Deputy Sheriff, Justice of the Peace and as District Clerk for over ten years ending in 1894. He was the District Clerk through the year of 1877, when the so-called "Van Zandt County War" took place. The county records were taken to Wills Point before being returned to Canton. T. J. McCord who served over twelve years as District Judge once reported that John H. Wilhite was the best District Clerk that he ever saw. Sources: *Wills Point Chronicle*, January 25, 1900; *Free State Enterprise*, January 25, 1900 and February 15, 1900; Find A Grave.

WILHITE, LOUISA ANNA

Born: June 26, 1841, Breckenridge County, Kentucky. Died: February 19, 1933, Van Zandt County, Texas. Married: (1) C. Williams, August 1861. (2) John H. Wilhite, August 6, 1874. Children: Charlie, Porter, Riley, and Walter. Father: Ranson Norton. Mother: Elizabeth Norton. Comments: Anna Wilhite's husband was an early settler and long-time office holder in Van Zandt County. She stood four feet, five inches tall and weighed just seventy-four pounds. She told the story of her life on her 90th birthday. The following is her article published in the *Canton Herald*: "She was formerly Anna Norton, who was born in Breckenridge County, Kentucky, coming to Texas with her parents in the winter of 1850. They took

Louisa Anna Wilhite *moved from Kentucky with her parents in the winter of 1850. Her uncle transported the family in his oxcart to his home in Prairieville, Texas, with her father carrying the women on his back across the streams when necessary. In Prairieville, they farmed with oxen and principally lived off game in the woods. In 1861, she married a young man who joined the Confederate Army and died in Arkansas. After twelve years of widowhood, she married* **John Harden Wilhite.** *Soon after, they moved to Canton, where they raised John's son from a previous marriage and their own four boys. For more than thirty years, he owned and operated a variety of businesses in Canton. He served his community as a Constable, County Bailiff, Deputy Sheriff, Justice of the Peace and as District Clerk. He held that latter position during the so-called "Van Zandt County War" in 1977, when the county records were taken to Wills Point before being returned to Canton. At his death in 1900, he was eulogized as "a man endowed with more than ordinary intellect and a good education and his honesty and integrity was never questioned; and these attributes fitted and qualified him for the various public and official positions he was called upon to fill."*

the boat at Breckenridge, Kentucky, coming via New Orleans and up to Shreveport, Louisiana, where her uncle, who lived near Prairieville, met them in an ox wagon and conveyed them to his home. There were no railroads then. This drive required two weeks and it rained every day but one while they were on the road. There being no bridges, and all streams being swollen, it was a long, hazardous trip, and although being in the winter, landing at her uncle's between Christmas and New Year's Day, her father would wade and carry the women across the dangerous streams while his brother drove the ox teams across. Grandma Wilhite says she well remembers passing Jordin Saline and seeing a site she had never seen before--making salt by boiling water in big open kettles, which is very unlike the modern method of mining and preparing the product by electricity. Soon after arriving at their new home near Prairieville, Texas, her father went into the woods, cut and hewed cedar logs 20 feet long and erected them a home in this new and wild country, living mostly on game out of the woods. The meat consisted of deer, bear, turkey, prairie chicken and some squirrels, paying no attention to the small birds, such as wild pigeons, partridges, etc. In that day there were millions and millions of wild pigeons, lots of prairie chickens, ducks and geese. Groceries and a few dry goods they got had to be brought from Shreveport in the community ox wagon, which made three trips at intervals for the entire community. On one occasion Grandma said her mother sent a whole barrel of butter which, together with tallow and hides, were exchanged for groceries, when brought home, were all cooked on the open fire place, there being very few, if any, cook stoves. The beds were straw or grass, which was raked up from the open prairie where it was very plentiful. Their beds were placed on homemade steads, which were made out of poles from the woods and no springs were used. Still we frequently speak of 'hard times.' The first year, trying to farm with ox team and very little improved land, raising no cotton; but corn and potatoes, living principally from game in the woods, it was a very hard go. During these days they had very little preaching, and they would often walk to Elmo, where they had preaching once every three months. Later they moved to what is now Turner's Point, where Anna Norton (now Gran Wilhite) met and married a young man by the name of Williams. This marriage took place in August 1861. Williams was soon off to the Army as a Southern soldier. He visited home one time to get some home-made clothing for the soldiers, sickening soon after and dying in Fort Smith, Arkansas. Mrs. Anna Williams lived a widow for about twelve years, when she met and married John H. Wilhite, August 20, 1874, while living with her sister in the Tundra community in Van Zandt County." Shortly after she married John H. Wilhite, they moved to Canton and lived there until he died in 1900. In addition to their boys, Anna and John reared Ernest, John's son from a previous marriage. In 1932, Anna celebrated her 91st birthday at a large gathering; and at this gathering, there were also five African-American people from Terrell, Texas. One of this group was A. L. W. Wilhite, a colored Methodist minister. He was born a slave owned by John H. Wilhite's father and was about 15 years of age when he received his freedom. The *Canton Herald* of June 24, 1932, explained the relationship. "He has remained in close touch with the Wilhite family ever since his freedom was granted. His master gave him and his brothers to two of his sons, John H. and Columbus, or Bud, as he was called, just before that emancipation proclamation was issued by President Lincoln. Uncle A. L. W. Wilhite has so much love and respect for the old family that he made it possible to be present and help in his humble way to make the day pleasant for Grandmother Wilhite." Anna died February 19, 1933. Sources: Death Certificate; *Canton Herald*, July 3, 1931 and June 24, 1932 and March 3, 1933.

Wilhite, Matthew Herbert
Born: August 25, 1797, Greene County, Tennessee. Died: January 2, 1858, Van Zandt County, Texas (Oldest marked grave in Hillcrest Cemetery). Married: (1) Rachael Holley, 1819, Tennessee. Died ca. 1827. Children: Margaret and George. (2) Nancy Hanna Burns, September 5, 1833, Hardeman County, Tennessee. Children: Matthew, William Lane, Elizabeth, Nancy Jane, John Harden, Mary Ann, Eliza Angeline, Americus Columbus, Sarah Jane, and Martha Catherine. Father: Julius Wilhite (Wilhoit). Mother: Margaret "Peggy" Hise. Comments: Born in the eighteenth century, Matthew Wilhite is the oldest known person buried with a headstone in Hillcrest Cemetery. He brought his family to Van Zandt County, Texas about 1855 from Tippah County, Mississippi. He was elected County Commissioner August 4, 1856 and died while in office. A list of Van Zandt County officers published in the *Wills Point Chronicle* February 18, 1909 shows he died and was succeeded by J. R. C. Henderson on November13, 1857. His wife survived him by twenty-two years. Sources: *Wills Point Chronicle* February 18, 1909; Ancestry.com.

Wilhite, Nancy Hanna
Born: June 25, 1809, Tennessee. Died: February 21, 1880, Van Zandt County, Texas. Married: Matthew Herbert Wilhite, September 5, 1833, Hardeman County, Tennessee. Children: Matthew, William Lane, Elizabeth, Nancy Jane, John Harden, Mary Ann, Eliza Angeline, Americus Columbus, Sarah Jane, and Martha Catherine. Father: John William Burns. Mother: Margaret McFadden. Comments: Nancy Wilhite came with her family to Van Zandt County, Texas about 1855. She survived her husband by twenty-two years. Source: Ancestry.com.

Wilhite, William Walter
Born: May 11, 1875, Van Zandt County, Texas. Died: October 29, 1921, Van Zandt County, Texas. Cause of death: Pellagra. Single. Father: John H. Wilhite. Mother: Louisa Anna Norton Williams. Occupation: Office work, Justice of the Peace. Sources: Death Certificate; *Canton Herald*, November 4, 1921.

Williams, Isaac Frank
Born: April 15, 1869, Tennessee. Died: July 19, 1908, Van Zandt County, Texas. Father: Henry Williams, Mississippi. Mother: Ella Williams, Mississippi. Siblings: Maggie, John W, Robert, and Charles. Source: 1880 U. S. Census.

Williams, James G. "Jim"
Born: September 15, 1876, Van Zandt County, Texas. Died: July 10, 1946, Van Zandt County, Texas. Married: Terah Pearl Batts, January 22, 1901. Children: Merle, Lopez, Willard, Lois, and Audie. Father: Richard "Dick" Williams. Mother: Rebecca Christman. Occupation: Postal employee. Comments: Jim Williams had been a life-long Van Zandt County resident. Source: *Canton Herald*, July 18, 1946.

Williams, Laura
Born: February 27, 1860, Van Zandt County, Texas. Died: February 7, 1902, Van Zandt County, Texas. Father: Richard Williams. Mother: Rebecca Christman. Source: Tombstone.

Williams, Louvennie "Vena"
Born: ca 1853 (slave). Died: December 2, 1916. Father: Unknown Williams. Mother: Unknown. Comments: Vena Williams was born a slave, and her parents are not

known. She lived near Canton most of her life. She was well and favorably known. Source: *Canton Herald*, December 29, 1916.

Williams, Merle

Born: 1901. Died: 1904. Father: James G. "Jim" Williams. Mother: Terah Pearl Batts. Source: *Wills Point Chronicle*, August 25, 1904.

Williams, Millard

Born: 1907. Died: 1921. Father: James G. Williams. Mother: Terah Pearl Batts. Sources: *Canton Herald*, March 18, 1921; Ancestry.com.

Williams, Minnie Maud

(Photo page 166) Born: June 26, 1876. Died: October 21, 1903. Single. Father: Dr. William O. Williams. Mother: Minnie R. Stuart. Source: *Wills Point Chronicle*, October 22, 1903.

Williams, Minnie R.

Born: June 26, 1858. Died: December 4, 1906. Married: Dr. William O. Williams, September 19, 1875. Children: Maud, Jewell, Cecile, S., and Oscar. Father: Unknown Stuart. Mother: Unknown. Source: *Wills Point Chronicle*, December 6, 1906.

Williams, Nora

Born: June 7, 1882. Died: May 10, 1904. Father: Richard Williams. Mother: Rebecca Christman. Source: Tombstone.

Williams, R. Lee

Born: May 3, 1871, Van Zandt County, Texas. Died: November 22, 1901, Van Zandt County, Texas. Married: Dicie Inez Bateman, January 23, 1900. Father: Richard Williams. Mother: Rebecca Christman. Comments: Lee Williams' death was reported in the Free State Enterprise as follows: "Last Friday evening about sun-down Lee Williams and wife, who live about seven miles north of town, got in their wagon and went down in the field to get the wash pot and tubs. They put them in and in crossing a branch at a very rough crossing the pot and tubs jolted into the front, frightening the team and causing it to run away. Mrs. Williams was thrown out after they ran a short distance and both wheels ran over her body, rendering her unconscious. Pretty soon the breast yoke struck a tree. This threw Mr. Williams out and he was caught between one of the front wheels and the tree and crushed to death. His neck was broken and his body badly bruised. When Mrs. Williams became conscious and was able to get up she went to where the team was standing and found her husband in the awful condition before described. She gave the alarm and Messers John Bateman, W. S. Foster, and Will Johnson were soon present. Drs. T. P. Davis and C. P. Smith were sent for but arrived too late to do Mr. Williams any good. He was dead. However, they ministered to Mrs. Williams who was very much in need of the attention. The remains of Mr. Williams were placed in the Canton cemetery Saturday afternoon. Mrs. Williams is not expected to recover.* Truly, it was a deplorable affair and the Enterprise deeply sympathizes with the grief-stricken relatives." *Dicie Inez Williams survived and married Henry Clay Martin, February 18, 1906. She died in 1952 and is buried in Highland Cemetery, Van Zandt County, Texas. Sources: *Wills Point Chronicle*, November 28, 1901; *Free State Enterprise*, November 28, 1901.

Matthew Herbert Wilhite, *born in 1797 is the oldest known person buried with a headstone in Hillcrest Cemetery. He brought his family to Van Zandt County in about 1855 and was elected County Commissioner August 4, 1856 . He died while in office.*

Williams, Rebecca Christman

Born: November 14, 1838, Louisiana. Died: December 19, 1891. Married: Richard Williams, May 9, 1858, Van Zandt County, Texas. Children: Laura A., Nancy Alice, Joel, Frank, R. Lee, Francis Eugenia, James G. "Jim," and Nora L. Comments: Rebecca Williams' husband was a farmer who joined the Confederate Army in Canton, Texas. He was engaged as a teamster in Western Louisiana until his discharge in 1865. He married Julia E. Chappell on February 26, 1899. Sources: 1860, 1870, 1880 U. S. Census; Ancestry.com.

Williams, Richard "Dick"

Born: February 24, 1834, Mississippi. Died: July 13, 1915, Van Zandt County, Texas. Married: (1) Rebecca Christman, May 9, 1858. Died: December 19, 1991. Children: Laura A., Nancy Alice, Joel, Frank, R. Lee, Francis Eugenia, James G. "Jim," and Nora. (2) Mrs. Julia Ellen Landrum Chappell, February 26, 1899. Father: Joel Williams. Mother: Unknown Williams. Military: CSA, 11th TX Infantry Co. I. Comments: Dick Williams was a teamster in the in the Trans Mississippi Civil War De-

Historical Marker
Edmond A. Wynne

The Texas Historical Commission dedicated a Historical Marker in honor of Edmond A. Wynne on June 25, 2016. Located in Hillcrest Cemetery, the Marker reads as follows:

The Wynne community of Canton is one of the oldest African American communities in Texas. Its namesake, Edmond Arnold Wynne, was born June 18, 1850, in Cherokee County to a family of slaves. His family moved to the Big Rock area of Van Zandt County in 1866. By 1869, just four years after Emancipation, his father, Henry Wynne, managed to buy 100 acres of land. In July 1871, Edmond married Martha Shaw, and joined the state militia to stop the general lawlessness that had developed in opposition to Reconstruction. Edmond purchased his own land in 1876 and in 1879, he sold for one dollar an acre of this land to the Colored Methodist Church of Clear Springs, the name for the African American community which had formed in the Big Rock area. He and his father also established Clear Springs School for African American children. By 1882, Edmond sold his land at Big Rock and moved to Canton where he purchased another farm. After Martha died in 1883, Edmond married Ella Lawley.

As Edmond Wynne became more successful in farming, he supported what would be known as the Wynne community, aiding neighbors in becoming self-sufficient and even in raising money to build a mill. His own success and involvement also attracted other former slaves and struggling families to move to the area. In 1888 he sold for one dollar land for the site of the Promise Land Colored Methodist Church, used for church and school. He actively participated in the education of the black community, helping keep the respected educator Rufus Hardin as a teacher at one of the schools until 1896. One of the schools that Edmond sold land to in 1902 eventually became renamed Wynne School. In 1896, Ella died and Edmond married Ann Preisley Matthews that year. After a lifetime of community involvement, Edmond Wynne died on April 1, 1931. (2015)

partment. Sources: 1850, 1870 U. S. Census; Ancestry.com, Find A Grave.

Williams, Terah Pearl

Born: November 22, 1879, Alabama. Died: June 30, 1926, Van Zandt County, Texas. Cause of death: Tuberculosis. Married: James G. Williams, January 22, 1901. Children: Merle, Lopez, Williard, Lois, and Audie. Father: G. W. Batts. Mother: Manervia A. Greenhaw. Siblings: George W., Eula Oden, and Fannie M. Source: Death Certificate.

Williams, William Oscar

Born: February 20, 1879. Died: April 20, 1893. Father: Dr. William O. Williams. Mother: Minnie R. Stuart. Comments: William Oscar Williams' death was reported in the Canton Telephone as follows: "He (Oscar) has been a sufferer all his days with spine affliction, but for the past four and a half months had been confined to his bed. During his illness he talked a great deal about dying. He made his will—divided his little things among the family; told his parents not to grieve for him but to look well to the other children." Oscar died at the age of 14. Sources: *Canton Telephone*, April 28, 1893 and June 16, 1893.

Williams, Dr. William Oscar

Born: September 30, 1839, Alabama. Died: August 18, 1930, Cameron County, Texas. Cause of death: Senility. Married: Minnie R. Stuart, September 19, 1875. Children: Jewell, Cecile, S., Maude, and Oscar. Father: Warner Williams, Alabama. Mother: S. R. McCullers, Georgia. Occupation: Physician. Military: CSA, Pvt. Co. I, Texas Heavy Artillery. Comments: William Williams came to Van Zandt County in 1873. After his marriage, he began his study of medicine. He graduated from the Missouri Medical College in 1880. He first lived in Edom, Texas, then moved to Canton where he practiced medicine until after 1900. He then moved his practice to Henderson County. After his wife's death in 1906, he moved to Houston to live with his daughter, Jewell Valentine. In 1911 he moved to San Benito, Texas to live with another daughter, Cecile Goolsby. He died shortly before his 91st birthday in 1930. William helped organize and was a Charter Member of the Van Zandt County Medical Society. He had been a Master Mason for sixty-five years, a 32nd Degree Mason, a Knights Templar, and he was active in the Blue Lodge. Sources: Death Certificate; 1880 U. S. Census; *The Southland, 1903*; *Free State Enterprise*, November 7, 1901; *Special to the Herald San Benito*, August 19, 1930; *Canton Herald*, August 22, 1930.

Wilson, Drayton William

Born: May 23, 1900, Van Zandt County, Texas. Died: February 7, 1973, Tarrant County, Texas. Married: Gladys R. Poteet. Children: Wanda, Frances, and Harold Kenneth. Father: Frank Henry Wilson. Mother: Mary Isabell McCarty. Occupation: Postal employee. Comments: Drayton Williams found employment in Dallas in 1923. After retiring from the Dallas Post Office, he moved back to Canton in 1960. He then moved to Arlington in 1968. Sources: *The Dallas Morning News*, February 8, 1973. Eubank Funeral Home records.

Jesse Chapman "Bud" Wynne

Jessie Captain Wynne

Minnie Maud Williams

Joseph E. "Uncle Bud" Wynne

Wilson, Emma Lou

Born: May 6, 1947, Texas. Died: September 18, 1966, Van Zandt County, Texas. Cause of death: Burns. Single. Father: J. D. Wilson. Mother: Morine Thompson. Comments: Emma Wilson fell into a surface heater and had third degree burns over 70 percent of her body. These burns contributed to cardiac failure and her death. Sources: Death Certificate, Eubank Funeral Home Records.

Wilson, Eunice E.
Born: December 11, 1901. Died: September 24, 1904. Father: Frank Henry Wilson. Mother: Mary Isabelle McCarty. Source: Tombstone.

Wilson, Francis Henry "Frank"
Born: November 19, 1866. Died: June 9, 1928. Married: Mary Isabell McCarty, December 18, 1898. Children: Drayton William, Eunice, Vivian, and Orville. Father: Drayton M. Wilson. Mother: Emmaline Lutrick. Source: Ancestry.com.

Wilson, Gladys Ruth
Born: July 7, 1898, Johnson County, Texas. Died: December 22, 1987, Tarrant County, Texas. Married: Drayton W. Wilson. Children: Wanda, Frances, Harold Kenneth. Father: Hiram Poteet, Alabama. Mother: Mamie Poteet, Georgia. Comments: Gladys Wilson's family operated the telephone switchboard in Myrtle Springs, Texas from 1912 to 1915. She lived in Dallas most of her married life while her husband worked at the Dallas Post Office. He retired in 1958 and they moved to Canton in 1960. In 1968 they moved to Arlington. Sources: 1920, 1930 U. S. Census; *United States Social Security Death Index*; *Van Zandt News*, December 27, 1897.

Wilson, Mamie Wanda
Born: August 10, 1927, Dallas County, Texas. Died: August 19, 1930, Dallas County, Texas. Cause of death: Diphtheria. Father: Drayton W. Wilson. Mother: Gladys R. Poteet. Source: Death Certificate.

Wilson, Mary Isabell
Born: November 4, 1875, Van Zandt County, Texas. Died: April 4, 1950, Van Zandt County, Texas. Cause of death: Natural causes. Married: Francis Henry Wilson, December 18, 1898. Children: Drayton William, Eunice, Vivian, and Orville Rice. Father: Benjamin Franklin McCarty. Mother: Mary Elizabeth Plumlee. Siblings: Robert Thompson, Elizabeth A., William N., and Andrew Jackson. Sources: Death Certificate, Eubank Funeral Home records, Find A Grave.

Wilson, Vivian
Born: April 15, 1904. Died: June 19, 1910. Father: Frank H. Wilson. Mother: Mary I. McCarty. Source: Tombstone.

Winn, Columbus
Born: April 29, 1892. Died: July 1, 1894. Father: H. C. Winn. Mother: M. D. Winn. Source: Tombstone.

Wisdom, Gloria Ann
Born: May 14, 1933, Dallas County, Texas. Died: February 27, 1998, Harris County, Texas. Married: Wendell Wisdom. Divorced. Children: David, Gary, and Karen. Father: Lewis Lamar Sides. Mother: Kate Harris. Comments: Gloria Wisdom grew up in Canton and graduated from Canton High School in 1951. She married Wendell Wisdom from the 1950 Class of Canton High School; and they later divorced. She lived in the Dallas area for a number of years and then moved to Harris County. Source: *Canton Herald*, March 19, 1998.

Wisenteiner, Betty Louise Nolen
Born: October 6, 1902, Van Zandt County, Texas. Died: February 3, 1992, McClellan County, Texas. Married: Herman Francis Wisenteiner. Child: Herman. Father: George Tate Nolan. Mother: Mattie A. Clark. Occupation: Drug Store, civil service. Comments: Betty Wisenteiner attended Miss Hockady's School for Girls in Dallas and Baylor University in Waco. She was co-owner of Nolan Bros. Drug Store in Canton until it closed. She later worked in civil service. Source: *Canton Herald*, February 6, 1992.

Wisenteiner, Herman Francis
Born: February 3, 1901, McKinley County, New Mexico. Died: March 18, 1936, El Paso County, Texas. Cause of death: Bronchial congestion. Married: Betty Louise Nolan. Child: Herman. Father: August F. Wisenteiner, Austria. Mother: Josephine Gallagher, Belmont County, Ohio. Occupation: Drug store employee. Military: WWI, New Mexico Corp. Co. F. 7th Cavalry. Comments: Herman Wisenteiner was a resident of Canton since 1936 and worked for Nolan Bros. Drug Store. His wife was the daughter of Tate Nolan who was a partner in the store. Tate died just three weeks prior to the death of Herman. Betty later become co-owner of the firm. Sources: Death Certificate; *Canton Herald*, March 20, 1936.

Wood, J. White
Born: September 1, 1827, Alabama. Died: September 14, 1871, Van Zandt County, Texas. Married: (1) Delia J. Boyd, Alabama. Children: Sally, M. R., William P., and Willie. (2) Mrs. Louisa Posey Mathis, December 24, 1868. Occupation: Sheriff, merchant. Comments: J. White Wood came to Van Zandt County with his family about 1860 and settled in the Edom area. After his wife Delia died, he moved to Canton and was elected Sheriff of Van Zandt County on June 25, 1866. He served until November 1, 1867. He then entered the mercantile business in Canton. He married Louisa Mathis in 1968. After his death, she married David Tumlinson on December 17, 1879. She died December 21, 1916 and is buried in Hillcrest Cemetery. Sources: 1860, 1870 U. S. Census; *Van Zandt County Court Minutes Volume A&B, 1848-1871*; *Texas County Sheriffs.*

Wood, Dr. W. P. "Billie"
Born: October 29, 1861, Van Zandt County, Texas. Died: October 25, 1885, Van Zandt County, Texas. Cause: Typho-malaria. Father: J. White Wood. Mother: Delia J.

Isabelle "Belle" Yantis

Thomas Rusk Yantis

Boyd. Occupation: Medical doctor. Comments: Dr. W. P. Wood died at the home of his step-parents, Louisa and David K. Tumlinson. He had been practicing medicine in partnership with Dr. J. F. McCarty in Canton for a few years. The doctor's father had been a Van Zandt County Sheriff and a Canton businessman. Source: *Canton Telephone*, October 31, 1885.

Woods, Martha Ann "Mattie"

Born: July 31, 1867, Henderson County, Texas. Died: March 20, 1955, Van Zandt County, Texas. Cause of death: Heart disease. Married: (1) Levi Robin Lawler. Children: Katie Alba, Levi Henry, Nettie Pearl, and Effie May. (2) William Forest Woods, March 11, 1903. Children: Ray and William Edwin. Father: Louis Henry Townley. Mother: Margaret Dorsey Brakefield. Sources: Death Certificate, Eubank Funeral Home records, Find A Grave.

Woods, Mittie Ann

Born: June 9, 1876, Van Zandt County, Texas. Died: October 24, 1943, Van Zandt County, Texas. Cause of death: Heart disease. Married: Willian Jasper Woods, 1908. Father: Benjamin Webb. Mother: Mary C. "Polly" Burleson. Comments: Mittie Woods lived in Van Zandt County all of her life. Although William and Mittie had no children, they adopted Betty Lou and reared her as their own child. Sources: Death Certificate; *Canton Herald*, October 28, 1943; Hilliard Funeral Home records.

Woods, William Forest

Born: September 8, 1868, Jefferson County, Texas. Died: January 16, 1949, Van Zandt County, Texas. Cause of death: Heart disease. Married: Martha Ann "Mattie" Townley. Father: William Odom Woods. Mother: Alicia Allison. Sources: Death Certificate, Eubank Funeral Home records, Ancestry.com.

Woods, William Jasper

Born: August 16, 1876, Marion County, Texas. Died: January 10, 1946, Kaufman County, Texas. Cause of death: Heart disease. Married: Mittie Ann Webb, 1908. Father: William Jasper Woods. Mother: Martha Anderson. Occupation: Maintenance. Source: Death Certificate, Hilliard Funeral Home records.

Wyatt, Charles W. "Charley"

Born: March 17, 1864. Died: January 31, 1896. Married: Beulah M. Todd, November 22, 1883. Father: Riley B. Wyatt. Mother: Sarah Jane Jones. Siblings: Nancy Deliah, Henry, Cora Isabella, James E., and Claud Harrison. Comments: Charley Wyatt's father died in the Civil War, and his mother married Jefferson H. Sanders. Source: Kevin Todd, Todd Family historian; Find A Grave.

Wynne, Edmond Arnold

(Photo page 165) Born: June 18, 1850, Cherokee County, Texas (slave). Died: April 1, 1931, Van Zandt County, Texas. Cause of death: Influenza. Married: (1) Martha Shaw, July 29, 1871. Children: James "Jim" Henry, Lannie Belle, Hannah, and Jessie Captain. (2) Ella Lawley, March 23, 1884. Children: Naomi H., and Joseph E. "Uncle Bud." (3) Mrs. Ann Mathes Preisley May 10, 1896. Father: Henry Winn (Wynne), Tennessee. Mother: Eliza Polk, Tennessee. Siblings: Mary, Caroline, Elaney Belle, Margaret, Elizabeth, and Melvina I. Occupation: Farmer. Comments: Edmond A. Wynne was born into slavery. He and his family moved to Van Zandt County about 1866 during the turbulent Reconstruction Period. The family first settled in the Big Rock area, bought land, and farmed. On August 16, 1882, Edmond and Martha sold their fifty acres at Big Rock and moved about two miles north from Canton. They settled in what later became the Wynne Community. On November 4, 1882, they bought a 100-acre farm and established their permanent home. They reared their children and helped develop a community. The story of Edmond Wynne and the Wynne family reflects the struggle of African-Americans in their movement from slavery through their adjustments to living as a free people, a story that shaped the American nation after the Civil War. Wynne encountered many hardships from his emancipation at age 15 until his death in 1931. He persevered to establish a definite role for himself, not only in the Black community, but also in the larger society. He acquired some education, served in the State Militia during Reconstruction, bought land, and helped to establish churches and schools. The Wynne Community which evolved from slaves and their decedents is still in existence today. Sources: Death Certificate; Texas State Historical Marker, application, "Edmond A. Wynne," researched, prepared and submitted June 22, 2015 by Lawrence Greer.

Wynne, Ella

Born: October 7, 1867. Died: February 8, 1896. Father: Unknown Lawley. Mother: Unknown. Married: Edmond A. Wynne, March 23, 1884. Children: Naomi H., and Joseph "Bud." Comments: Ella Wynne was the second wife of Edmond Wynne, the namesake of the Wynne Community near Canton, Texas. Source: Vanessa Scott, Wynne Community historian.

Wynne, James Henry "Jim"

Born: May 7, 1872, Texas. Died: February 26, 1962, Van Zandt County, Texas. Cause of death: Heart disease. Single. Father: Edmond A. Wynne. Mother: Martha Shaw. Military: WWI. Occupation: Farm work. Sources: Death Certificate, Find A Grave.

Wynne, Jesse Chapman "Bud"

(Photo page 166) Born: July 12, 1916, Texas. Died: May 20, 1985, Dallas County, Texas. Married: (1) Geneva Shaw, August 30, 1935. Divorced. Child: Jesse Roberta. (2) Emily Odell Love Kennedy. Children: Charles Edward and Marsha Rae. Father: Jessie Captain Wynne. Mother: Bessie Lee Mauldin. Siblings: Carion Elizabeth, Vada, Opal, George Howard, Charles Jerry, Willie D., Elmer J., Carrie Louellen, and Elaine Margaret. Occupation: Worker at the Blue Bonnet Hotel and Sigel's Company in Dallas, Texas. Sources: *Canton Herald*, May 30, 1985; Vanessa Scott, Wynne Community historian; Ancestry.com.

Wynne, Jessie Captain

(Photo page 166) Born: September 13, 1879. Died: February 11, 1933. (Tombstone shows birth date 1877 and death date 1932.) Cause of death: Paralysis. Married: Bessie Lee Mauldin, January 14, 1911. Children: Carion Elizabeth, Mary Louise, Vada O., Jesse Chapman, Opal Laura, George Howard, Willie Duncan, Elmer Johnson, Carrie, Elaine Margaret, and Charles Jerry. Father: Edmond A. Wynne. Mother: Martha Shaw. Source: Death Certificate.

Wynne, Joseph E. "Uncle Bud"

(Photo page 166) Born: January 7, 1889, Van Zandt County, Texas. Died: June 1, 1982, Van Zandt County, Texas. Single. Father: Edmond A. Wynne. Mother: Ella Lawley. Military: WWI, US Army. Sources: Death Certificate; *Van Zandt News*, June 13, 1982.

Wynne, Martha

Born: 1853 (slave). Died: October 27, 1883. Married: Edmond A. Wynne, July 29, 1871. Children: James "Jim" Henry, Lannie Bell, Jessie Captain, and Hannah. Father: Major Shaw. Mother: Eviline Shaw. Comments: Martha Wynne was the first wife of Edmond Wynne, the namesake of the Wynne Community in Canton, Texas. Her parents were early settlers and land owners in a Black community at Big Rock, located on the southern border of Van Zandt and Henderson Counties. In 1882 Edmond and Martha moved to the Canton area and bought a farm. Martha's father was shot and killed December 18, 1891 in Kaufman County, Texas. Linzy Ellis was convicted of murder for the crime and sentenced to hang. The Governor of Texas reduced the sentence to life. He was pardoned in 1905 and released from prison. Source: Vanessa Scott, Wynne Community historian.

Wynne, Martha Louise

Born: March 27, 1915. Died: December 23, 1919. Cause of death: Burns. Father: Jessie Captain Wynne. Mother: Bessie Lee Mauldin. Comments: Martha Wynne's clothing caught fire from a stove, and she received severe burns. She lived twenty-four hours before she died. Sources: Death Certificate, Ancestry.com.

Y

Yantis, Isabelle California "Belle"

Born: February 16, 1868, Van Zandt County, Texas. Died: October 2, 1917, Van Zandt County, Texas. Married: Thomas Rusk Yantis, October 16, 1890. Children: David Love, Ruth, Albert Lapsey, Robert Hobbs, Mary, Ralph, and Baby. Father: David Love Riley, Jr. Mother: Mary C. Hobbs. Siblings: James T., Claude F., Lydia Colon, Jessie Riley, Mary Daisy, David Thompson, and

Jay Holt. Comments: Belle Yantis was one of the more popular young women In Canton. She graduated from Baylor University in 1885. Source: *Canton Herald*, October 12, 1917.

Yantis, Robert Hobbs

Born: February 18, 1900, Van Zandt County, Texas. Died: January 30, 1966, Taylor County, Texas. Father: Thomas Rusk Yantis. Mother: Isabelle California (Belle) Riley. Military: WWI, Texas CFR Air Service. Source: Tom McKinnon, Yantis Family historian.

Yantis, Thomas Rusk

(Photo page 168) Born: April 9, 1857, Rusk County, Texas. Died: February 8, 1932, Van Zandt County, Texas. Married: Isabelle Cloy (California) "Belle" Riley, October 16, 1890. Children: David Love, Albert Lapsey, Robert Hobbs, Mary, Ralph, Ruth, and Baby. Father: James Lapsley Yantis, Russell County, Kentucky. Mother: Amanda Catherine Suddeth. Occupation: Lawyer, County Judge. Comments: Thomas Yantis was named after Thomas Jefferson Rusk, Texas hero, and namesake of that county. His father was a tanner and came to Texas in 1852. Thomas lived in Rusk, Hopkins and Gregg counties before moving to Van Zandt County in 1879. He was educated at the Alexander Institute, Kilgore, Texas. This school was established in 1873 by Professor Isaac Alexander, a prominent educator. The school later became affiliated with the Methodist Church, moved to Jacksonville, Texas and became Lon Morris Junior College. For two years after moving to Van Zandt County, he was a school teacher at Canton and studied law on the side. He was admitted to the Van Zandt County Bar, May 9, 1881 and practiced law until his death. For years he was considered to be one of the more prominent attorneys in Van Zandt County. He was the senior partner in the law firm of Yantis and Hubbard with Attorney Charles L. Hubbard. He married a daughter of David Love Riley, Jr. and Mary C. Hobbs. Riley was one of Canton's pioneer merchants and leading citizens and known throughout the county and state. To this union, eight children were born, five surviving to adulthood. His wife died in 1917. Thomas was a staunch Democrat, a Mason, Woodman of The World, Knight of Labor and Knight of Honor, a member of the Baptist church and a Sunday School Superintendent. He was elected County Judge in 1892 and served from 1893-94. He was involved in the planning and later controversy over the building of the large brick court house finished in 1896. Thomas had many accomplishments and was connected through his wife to one of the more prominent families in Van Zandt County. However, he was also known to be very disagreeable with people who did not harbor his personal or political views. On several occasions he tried to settle these arguments with the use of pistols. The first such occasion occurred about a year and a half after he had begun his law practice and was reported by the *Dallas Weekly Herald* on October 5, 1882 as follows: "B. H. Kilgore and T. R. Yantis, two lawyers of Canton, exchanged several shots last night at that place, though none of them took effect. The trouble arose regarding an item printed in the *Dallas Herald* about the shooting affair of last Saturday at Canton. Both gave bond to await the action of the grand jury." There are no available local newspapers from that time period so what the Saturday shooting affair was about or the outcome of the grand jury is not known. The next notice regarding Thomas was from the *Canton Telephone* of April 24, 1886 which reported that during District Court proceedings in the case, State vs T. R. Yantis, assault to murder, the result was verdict not guilty. This verdict could have been from the 1882 case or it could have been a new event, records are not available. On 16 February 1895, Thomas became involved in a fatal shooting at the railroad station at Wills Point, Texas where he was trying to shoot the Populist County Attorney, W. W. Berzett. He missed and killed his friend, Clarence W. Swank. This is the account of the shooting from the *Wills Point Chronicle* of February 21, 1895: "As to the facts of the case, we simply give the statement of City Marshall Marable who was on the scene of the disturbance. Mr. Marable says, I was inside the office of the Texas & Pacific railroad as the east bound passenger train No. 2 came in, about 11:35 o'clock. The train had been in but a few seconds when I went to the door and discovered W. W. Berzett and T. R. Yantis engaged in a fist fight. Immediately attempted to stop them by getting between. I saw Berzett draw his pistol and in an instant, and before I could prevent it, Yantis had drawn his and fired, his hand just in front of me. Just as the first and only shot was fired, Berzett turned to run and sliping fell and I think the ball passed over him striking Mr. Swank. I am of the opinion that Berzett was between Yantis and Mr. Swank. At first I did not know who was shot as I took charge of Yantis and carried him inside the depot. Physicians were summoned immediately but to no purpose, for the leaden missile had done its deadly work and Capt. C. W. Swank was beyond all human aid. The ball passed entirely through his body, striking the lower point of the heart and causing instant death. Judge Yantis was taken in charge of by Marshall Marable and as Justice Riley was disqualified from hearing the trial, by reason of his kinship with Mr. Yantis, was carried to Canton on a charge of negligent homicide and was admitted to bail in the sum of $1,000. Mr. Yantis and Capt. Swank were the warmest personal friends and no one regrets the unfortunate affair more than he." On November 7, 1895, the case of Ex-County Judge Yantis, for the accidental death of Capt. C. W. Swank here on the 16th of February last, was tried in District Court at Canton with the jury returning a verdict of "not guilty." In addition, an article in the *Wills Point Chronicle* of December 2, 1897, reported that on December 1, 1897, T. R. Yantis, Ex-County Judge, shot and killed Justice of the Peace Calloway Dean. Yantis was placed under $750 bond. The following is what the *Dallas Dispatch* had to say about the shooting: "Justice of the Peace Calloway Dean was shot in court late yesterday afternoon at Canton, the county seat of Van Zandt County. During the trial of a case he

MARY JANE "MOLLIE" YOUNGBLOOD *and her husband,* **JAMES MARION YOUNGBLOOD,** *lived in Edom, Texas until 1882 when they moved to Canton. She assisted her husband in his saddle and harness shop and was known to be adept at driving oxen, whether hitched to a wagon or to a plow. Youngblood lived in the same house in Canton for fifty-three years before she died at the age of 95.*

became involved in a quarrel with a lawyer named T. R. Yantis and the latter used a pistol and shot Dean through the breast, inflicting a mortal wound. The shooting is said to be due to troubles between Populists and Democrats, growing out of a county courthouse contract. Five years ago a Populist county administration undertook to undo the work of the latter, and this is the second shooting the quarrel has caused. Yantis also killed a commercial traveler at the railway station about three years ago while shooting at the Populist County Attorney." The case was delayed and transferred to Henderson County where in January 1901, T. R. Yantis was found "not guilty" by a jury. Thomas was never convicted of any of these crimes. He was apparently a well-respected lawyer; and his father-in-law, David Love Riley, Jr. was a prominent Canton merchant and former Sheriff of Van Zandt County. He was also supported by his brother, Robert E. Yantis, a newspaper man, who founded the *Wills Point Chronicle* and later the Van Zandter. In 1900 Robert acquired the *Athens Review* and also served two terms as a member of the Texas State Legislature. Thomas lived in Canton for more than fifty years. Sources: Death Certificate; *The Southland 1903*; *Dallas Weekly Herald*, October 5, 1882; *Canton Telephone*, April 24, 1886; *Wills Point Chronicle*, February 21, 1895 and December 2, 1897; *Canton Herald*, October 10, 1919 and February 12, 1932.

YOUNGBLOOD, JAMES MARION

Born: July 10, 1837, Pike County, Alabama. Died: February 18, 1908, Van Zandt County, Texas. Married: Mary Jane Callahan, September 4, 1865. Children: Minnie, Cora, James Albert, Della, and Virdie. Father: Jacob Joel Youngblood. Mother: Sarah Stell. Occupation: Saddle, harness maker, Sheriff. Military: CSA, 33rd TX Calvary, Co. D. Comments: James Youngblood moved with his family to Dallas County, Arkansas about 1845 and then on to Texas about 1850. The family was living in Van Zandt County by 1856. James assisted his father on the family farm and then went to work as a mill hand by 1860. He worked as a Deputy Clerk for the District Court, and newspaper reports indicate that he sawed the lumber for the first courthouse in Dallas, Texas. James was elected Sheriff on August 4, 1862 and served until he entered the Confederate Army in 1864. After the War, he made saddles and harnesses for horses and set his shop up in Edom. In 1882 he moved to Canton and established his leather business on the south side of the public square. In addition to harness and saddles, he sold furniture, wagon and buggy materials, iron queenesware, and tin goods. In February of 1885, James and his brother, Elijah, purchased the hardware stock of A. N. Alford and added this line to their business. At his death, James had lived in Van Zandt County for more than fifty years. Source:s *Van Zandt County Court Minutes Volumes A & B*; *A History of Edom, Texas*; *Grand Saline Sun*, February 8, 1908; *Wills Point Chronicle*, February 20, 1908; *Texas Telephone*, February 14, 1885 and June 5, 1886; Ancestry.com.

YOUNGBLOOD, MARY JANE "MOLLIE"

Born: November 10, 1845, Cass County, Georgia. Died: December 10, 1940, Van Zandt County, Texas. Married: James Marion Youngblood, September 4, 1865. Children: Minnie, Cora, James Albert, Della, and Virdie. Father: Rev. Humphrey Edward Callahan. Mother: Rebecca Caroline Scott. Comments: When Mollie Youngblood died at the age of 95, she had lived in the same house in Canton for fifty-three years. She had moved to Texas with her family in early childhood. Her father was a pioneer Baptist minister who first settled in Collin County. He then moved to Dallas and organized one of the first Baptist churches there. Later he moved to Terrell, Texas and established the town's first Baptist Church. In addition to his ministering to the general public, he served as a Chaplain in the Confederate Army. Mollie and James lived in Edom, Texas until 1882 when they moved to Canton. Her husband was a saddle and harness maker by profession, and Mollie assisted him in his shop in Edom and Canton. And, when required, Mollie was adept at driving oxen when they were either hitched to a wagon or to a plow. On her death, in 1940, the *Canton Herald* noted her passing and marveled at her experiences from before the Civil War to modern times. Sources: *The Dallas Morning News*, December 12, 1940; *Canton Herald*, December 19, 1940; Eubank Funeral Home records; Ancestry.com.

UNMARKED GRAVES

Unmarked Graves

There is a certain sadness regarding the existence of unmarked graves in a cemetery. People lived, married, had children, worked, made a place for themselves in a community, and then died and left their loved ones behind. Over time, as their markers were destroyed—if they initially had them—the memories of these people were brushed aside as if they had never existed, and the graves were never to be visited by anyone who ever knew them.

There are various reasons why the graves are unmarked. Early settlers, for lack of other materials, used wood for their grave markers. None of these wooden markers in the Hillcrest Cemetery has survived. Some of the first commercial tombstones were made of native sandstone and other soft materials. The ever-changing Texas weather slowly destroyed these soft markers until only a mass of unrecognizable crumbled stone is left. Vandals and improper care also did their part in destroying the stones. While all these factors contributed to the loss of markers that were originally placed by caring family members, most of those buried in unmarked graves in Hillcrest Cemetery were ordinary people who simply could not afford a tombstone.

It is almost impossible to determine exactly how many unmarked graves are located in the Hillcrest Cemetery, and it is even more difficult to identify the names of the individuals buried in them. But as a matter of conscience, we would not allow ourselves to pass over these unfortunate souls without at least attempting to rescue as many of those who had been consigned to eternal anonymity as possible. Thankfully, we had access to death notices published in local newspapers, dating to 1884, funeral home records from 1937 until the current date, and cemetery surveys. Through diligent research in these sources, we were able to identify 169 individuals who were buried in this cemetery but have no current marker.

We respectfully present their information here and wish them peaceful eternal rest.

A

Alexander, Wiley Percy

Born: December 25, 1841, Georgia. Died: March 15, 1906, Van Zandt County, Texas. Married: (1) Mrs. Lucinda Matilda Trammel, October 12, 1865, Van Zandt County, Texas. Children: Matty W, Annie O., Zula E, Oscar W.,and Ephraim A. (2) Mrs. Mildred E. Malone, June 4, 1882. Father: Ephraim Ashley (E. A.) Alexander. Mother: M. A. Alexander, Georgia. Military: CSA, Private, Company I 15th Texas Cavalry, 2nd Regiment, Johnson's Brigade. Comments: Wiley Alexander was captured at Fort Hindman, Arkansas Post, Arkansas, on January 11, 1863. He was taken to the infamous Camp Douglas, Ill. and then paroled April 3, 1863. He returned to his old regiment and served until the end of the War. Wiley came to Van Zandt County, Texas with his parents before 1860. After serving in the Confederate Army, he married Lou Trammel. Her son, John Trammel, lived with the family. Lucinda died in 1881; and later, Wiley married the widow of a town barber, Thomas D. Malone. His son, Matty, is buried in Hillcrest Cemetery; and it is possible that Wiley's grave is next to his. Sources: 1860, 1880, 1900, 1910 U. S. Census; *Confederate Army Records*; *Van Zandt County Marriage Records*; *Van Zandt County Court Minutes, Volumes A & B*; *Wills Point Chronicle*, March 22, 1906 and March 29, 1906; Ancestry.com.

Allen, A Little Boy

Born: Unknown. Died: August 17, 1891. Cause of death: Congestion. Father: D.C. Allen. Mother: Unknown. Comments: The Allen family was living in the Crème Level Community of Van Zandt County, Texas when their son died. The Rev. Sam Allen delivered the funeral discourse. Source: *Canton Telephone*, September 4, 1891.

Easter Bell

B

Ballard, Elizabeth

Born: ca 1845, Blount County, Alabama. Died: April, 1890, Van Zandt County, Texas. Married: Wesley H. Ballard, March 10, 1865. Children: Fannie, John, Mary Ellen, Willie, and James. Father: David Cowen. Mother: Elizabeth Anderson. Comments: The Ballards came to Texas from Alabama about 1870. They first settled in Henderson County before moving to the Big Rock Community of Van Zandt County. Elizabeth's husband owned a blacksmith and wagon shop at Big Rock before moving his business to the southwest corner of the courthouse square in Canton. He sold his business to J. A. Peace in November of 1885. After Elizabeth's death, Wesley married Mary J. James. Sources: *The Telephone*, March 30, 1883; *Texan-Telephone*, November 1885; *Canton Telephone*, April 11, 1890; Ancestry.com.

Ballard, John "Johnie"

Born: 1871. Died: May, 1889. Father: Wesley H. Ballard. Mother: Elizabeth Cowen. Siblings: Ellen, Fannie, Mary Ellen, Willie, and James. Comments: The Ballards came to Texas about 1870. John's father owned a blacksmith and wagon shop in Canton until he sold it in 1885. Johnie died from an undisclosed illness. The *Canton Telephone* reported his death as follows: "Johnie was laying almost at the point of death over one hundred days. Rev. J. C. Calhoun conducted the service. He professed a hope in Christ during his siege of illness." Sources: *Canton Telephone*, May 24, 1889 and April 11, 1890.

Beasley, Payton

Born: Unknown date. Died: April 3, 1942, Henderson County, Texas. Cause of death: Burns. Father: Unknown Beasley. Mother: Unknown. Comments: Payton Beasley was living in Henderson County when he was burned to death from an unknown cause. He had a county burial. Source: Eubank Funeral Home records.

Bell, Easter M.

Born: May 10, 1893, Smith County, Texas. Died: June 2, 1969, Dallas County, Texas. Cause of death: Cancer. Married: Joseph W. Bell. Children: John, Jack, R. D., Bennie P, and Lela. Father: Unknown. Mother: Unknown. Sources: Death Certificate, Eubank Funeral Home records.

Bell, Green

Born: August 15, 1902, Van Zandt County, Texas. Died: January 5, 1977, Kaufman County, Texas. Father: Ed Fitzgerald. Mother: Fannie Toles (Towles). Source: Eubank Funeral Home records.

Bowers, George Henry

Born: February 3, 1893, Hunt County Texas. Died: August 5, 1946, Dallas County, Texas. Cause of death: Meningitis. Single. Father: John A. Bowers, Tennessee. Mother: Sallie Lou Fuller, Tennessee. Occupation: Machinist. Comments: George Bowers moved to Dallas in 1944. He was employed by the Dallas Engineering Company. Sources: Death Certificate; *Canton Herald*, August 15, 1946; Hilliard Funeral Home records.

Bowers, Robie

Born: September 10, 1901, Texas. Died: September 25,

Simpson P. Compton *lived in Paulding and Cobb Counties, Georgia prior to the beginning of the Civil War. He joined the Georgia Volunteers on May 31, 1861 and served for less than six months before resigning. The following year, he joined the 46th Volunteers of the Army of Tennessee; but on May 4, 1964, he deserted the Confederate Army and took the Oath of Allegiance to the U. S. Government at Chattanooga, Tennessee. In 1873, he moved with his family to Van Zandt County. Later he moved to Canton and opened a business. He lived into his early seventies, dying suddenly in a store in 1897.*

1952, Dallas County, Texas. Cause of death: Tuberculosis. Father: John A. Bowers, Tennessee. Mother: Sallie Lou Fuller, Tennessee. Siblings: John, Frank, Angie, and George Henry. Occupation: Ice company employee. Comments: Robie Bowers was employed by the Southern Ice Company in Dallas, Texas. Sources: Death Certificate, Hilliard Funeral Home records.

Bowers, Sallie Lou
Born: October 12, 1865, Tennessee. Died: November 14, 1936, Van Zandt County, Texas. Cause of death: Nephritis. Married: John A. Bowers. Children: Henry, Robie, John, and Angie. Father: Mitchell Fuller, Tennessee. Mother: Mary Fuller, Alabama. Comments: Sallie Lou Bowers lived with her family on a farm outside the Canton city limits for a number of years. Sources: Death Certificate; 1920 U. S. Census; *Canton Herald*, November 19, 1936; Eubank Funeral Home records.

Bowles (Boles), Abe J.
Born: 1854, Louisiana (slave). Died: April, 1915, Van Zandt County, Texas. Married: Rachel Johnson. Children: Wesley, Roy L., Minnie L., Willie C., Uyless, and Sallie. Father: Unknown Bowles. Mother: Unknown. Comments: The *Canton Herald* reported Abe Bowles' death as follows: "One by one the old-time darkies of Canton are being gathered up into the clouds. Last Monday afternoon the people of his race lowered Abe Bowles into a cold and silent tomb. He also has lived here since the memory of man runneth not to the contrary, though at last withered away to let others take his place." Sources: 1900 U. S. Census; *Canton Herald*, April 8, 1915.

Bowman, Charlie Percy
Born: April 4, 1912, Smith County, Texas. Died: February 15, 1970, Dade County, Illinois. Married: Lela Frances Bell. Father: Issac Bowman. Mother: Ethel Bowman. Sources: 1920 U. S. Census, Cook County Illinois Death Index, Eubank Funeral Home records.

Brazelton, William L.
Born: ca 1858, Tennessee. Died: January 11, 1885, Van Zandt County, Texas. Cause of death: Consumption (T. B.). Married: Susan May Dickson, October 9, 1883, Gregg County, Texas. Father: Unknown Brazelton. Mother: Unknown. Occupation: Sheriff. Comments: William Brazelton was elected Sheriff of Van Zandt County, Texas November 1884 and died less than two months after he was elected. He was buried with Masonic Rites. His wife and brother-in-law moved back to Gregg County, Texas, after his death. Susan later married S. E. Jones, March 24, 1888, in Rockwall County, Texas. Sources: *Texas Marriage Collection 1814-1909*; *Canton Telephone*, January 17, 1885; Ancestry.com.

Brown, Ethel
Born: ca 1871, Texas. Died: October 1898, Bexar County, Texas. Cause of death: Tuberculosis. Married: Charles L. Brown. Father: Arch B. Downing. Mother: M. Clementine Robison. Comments: Ethel Brown's father was in the mercantile business in Wills Point, Texas. Sources: *Wills Point Chronicle*, October13, 1898; Ancestry.com.

Brown, Nelce
Born: October 18, 1895, Van Zandt County, Texas. Died: June 24, 1953, Van Zandt County, Texas. Cause of death: Heart disease. Married: Marietta Stephens, February 6, 1910. Occupation: Farming. Father: Riley Brown, Alabama. Mother: Mary Hubbard, Van Zandt County, Texas. Sources: Death Certificate, Eubank Funeral Home records.

Brown, R.L.
Born: Unknown. Died: December, 1889. Cause of death: Bronchitis. Father: Unknown Brown. Mother Unknown. Comments: The *Canton Telephone* reported R. L. Brown's death as follows: "R. L. Brown, formerly of Bethel, Anderson County, Texas, died of bronchitis in Canton Wednesday noon, leaving four little orphan girls, ages ranging from two to fourteen years, thrown upon the cold charities of the world. The poor little girls have the sympathy of the entire community." Source: *Canton Telephone*, December 20, 1889.

William Conyer "Will" Dearing

BRUMMETT, INFANT
Born: December 1913. Died: January 1914. Father: Jim Brummett. Mother: Unknown. Source: *Wills Point Chronicle*, January 22, 1914.

BRUNSON, BERTHA
Born: May 1896, Van Zandt County, Texas. Died: June 19, 1928, Van Zandt County, Texas. Cause of death: Childbirth complications. Married: Eli Carroll Brunson, August 17, 1920. Children: Earnest (Bogue) Buyher, Jr., Leonard Wilson, Connie Lorene, and Christine. Father: James B. Branson, Kentucky. Mother: Dora Alice Bell, Texas. Siblings: William, Jim, Nettie, Josie, Wesley, Hattie May, and Ida. Comments: Bertha Brunson died from the effects of childbirth two months after the birth of Christine. Christine was reared by her aunt and uncle, William and Hattie Cross. It is believed that Bertha is buried next to her parents and sister, Josie Penny. Source: *Van Zandt County Texas Histories and Biographies 1848-1991, Volume II.*

BUNN, ALBERTA
Born: August 19, 1910. Died: March 25, 1976, Kaufman County, Texas. Cause of death: Uterine cancer. Married: William Bunn. Father: Unknown. Mother: Unknown. Sources: 1930 U. S. Census, Death Certificate, Eubank Funeral Home records.

BURNS, JOHN M.
Born: July 23, 1820, Tennessee. Died: March 24, 1883, Van Zandt County, Texas. Married: (1) Elizabeth A., unknown, Tennessee. Children: E. Jane, Susan E., Martha C., Laura M., James H., M. E., and Monroe L. (2) Nora J. Parrott, July 22, 1879, South Carolina. Occupation: Farmer, county official. Comments: There is a partial tombstone for John M. Burns which has been moved from his gravesite. The actual burial site is unknown. John Burns came to Van Zandt County in 1854; and although a farmer, he managed to serve in more county offices than anyone in the county history: Tax Assessor 1856-1858; Constable Pct. 1, 1860; Deputy Sheriff 1861; County Commissioner 1866-1868; Justice of the Peace 1870; Chief Justice (County Judge) 1871-1875; County Treasurer 1877. Sources: 1860, 1870, 1880 U. S. Census; *Van Zandt County Court Minutes Volume A, B, C*; *History of Van Zandt County by Mills*; *The Texan*, March 30, 1883.

BURRUS, CARL THOMAS JR.
Born: April 20, 1946. Died: April 21, 1946. Cause of death: Prematurity. Father: Carl Thomas Burrus, Sr. Mother: Helen Knowles. Sources: Death Certificate, Eubank Funeral Home records.

C

CARR, SALLIE
Born: ca 1854, Georgia (slave). Died: January 14, 1904, Van Zandt County, Texas. Father: Unknown. Mother: Unknown. Occupation: Laundress. Comments: In 1880 Sallie Carr and her 2-year-old son, Walter, were living in Fulton County, Georgia in the home of her sister and brother-in-law, James and Josephine Watts. She moved to Van Zandt County, Texas with the Watts before 1900. Sources: 1880 U. S. Census, *Wills Point Chronicle*, February 18, 1904

CHANEY, SARAH ELIZABETH "SACKY"
Born: April 10, 1858, Van Zandt County, Texas. Died: February 24, 1886, Van Zandt County, Texas. Married: Zacharia Taylor Chaney, December 22, 1874. Children: Charles Columbus, Minnie Drucilla, Eva May, Arthur A., and Albert B. Father: Joshua Ballard. Mother: Louisa Boulton (Bolton). Sources: R. J. Heddings, Chaney Family historian; Find A. Grave.

CHANEY, ZACHARIA TAYLOR "ZACK"
Born: April 21, 1848, Alabama. Died: July 31, 1939, Van Zandt County, Texas. Cause of death: Senility. Married:

Sarah Elizabeth Ballard, December 22, 1874. Children: Charles Columbus, Minnie Drucilla, Eva May, Arthur A, and Albert B. Father: Benjamin Burgess Chaney. Mother: Mellissa McClellan. Occupation: Farmer. Comments: Zach Chaney came from Talladega County, Alabama to Van Zandt County, Texas early in 1874. He spent the remainder of his life in the county. Sources: Death Certificate, Eubank Funeral Home records

CLARK, LUTHER JAMES

Born: May 16, 1917, Missouri. Died: December 26, 1932, Van Zandt County, Texas. Cause of death: Burns. Father: Ira Elmer Clark. Mother: Polly Bangher. Comments: The *Canton Herald* reported Luther Clark's death as follows: "Luther James Clark, 14 years, 7 months and 10 days old, died Monday morning at 12:55 o'clock as a result of burns received on Christmas Eve morning when he attempted to start a fire in a cook stove with kerosene oil, the gallon can falling in the stove and exploding. The boy's clothing caught fire instantly and he was burned fatally. Funeral services were held at the Canton cemetery where interment followed. The boy's people lived in Missouri and were unable to attend the last rites of their loved one. The deceased was making his home with his brother–in-law, O. E. Miller, who lived on the Ab Sides farm and went to school here. Mr. Miller attempted to save the boy from his fate and received some bad burns, also Luther James was burned all over his body with the exception of his face. The death was a very sad one and the people of Canton and community feel a sympathy which cannot be expressed for the bereaved." Sources: Death Certificate; *Canton Herald*, December 30, 1932.

COMPTON, JAMES M.

Born: 1866, Kentucky. Died: December 5, 1889, Van Zandt County, Texas. Father: Simpson P. Compton. Mother: Mariah A. Austin. Sources: *Canton Telephone*, December 13, 1889; Ancestry.com.

COMPTON, JOSEPHUS GREGORY "SEATH"

Born: July 1855, Paulding County, Georgia. Died: February 25, 1901, Van Zandt County, Texas. Cause of death: Black jaundice. Married: (1) Mary Jane Parsons, March 9, 1873, Georgia. (2) Nancy Elizabeth Carroll, May 22, 1881, Van Zandt County, Texas. Father: Simpson P. Compton. Mother Mariah A. "Lizzie" Austin. Sources: 1880 U. S. Census; *Wills Point Chronicle*, February 28, 1901; Ancestry.com.

COMPTON, MARIAH ALCEY AUSTIN "LIZZIE"

Born: ca 1826, Georgia. Died: January 18, 1890, Van Zandt County, Texas. Cause of death: Pneumonia. Married: Simpson P. Compton, ca 1852, Georgia. Children: Parker M., Narcissa L., Josephus, Martha J., Mary D., James M., William J., Josiah Ella, Allen, and Jessie. Father: Michael Austin. Mother: Narcissa Austin. Comments: Mariah Compton came to Texas from Georgia to Van Zandt County with her family about 1873 and settled near Grand Saline. Later the family moved to Canton where her husband was in business. She had numerous relatives in Van Zandt County. One of her relatives, Mary A. "Polly" Austin Strickland, is buried in Hillcrest Cemetery in a marked grave. It is believed that she, her husband and two sons are buried next to Polly. Mariah's daughter, Josiah Ella, married Nat Crawford, an attorney from Grand Saline, Texas. The Crawford's daughter, Lula Mae, married Paul H. Stanford of Canton. (Mae Stanford, in a contest sponsored by the Garden Club of Canton, in 1935, selected "Hillcrest" as the permanent name for the Canton City Cemetery.) Sources: 1880 U. S. Census; *Canton Telephone*, January 24, 1890.

COMPTON, SIMPSON P.

Born: ca 1824, Gwinnett County, Georgia. Died: February 3, 1897, Van Zandt County, Texas. Cause of death: Stroke. Married: Mariah Alcey "Lizzy" Austin, ca 1852, Georgia. Children: Parker M., Narcisa L., Josephus, Martha J., Mary D., James M., William J., Josiah Ella, Allen, and Jessie. Father: Joel D. Compton. Mother: Lamenta Fields. Occupation: Carpenter, mercantile store owner. Military: Mexican War, CSA, 2nd Lt. Co. C, 7th Regiment Georgia Volunteer Infantry, Private 46th Regiment, Volunteer Infantry, Army of Tennessee. Simpson Compton joined the Georgia Volunteers on May 31, 1861 as a 2nd Lt. before resigning his commission on November 22, 1861. Then on August 27, 1862, he joined the 46th Volunteers of the Army of Tennessee as a substitute for Nathaniel Hutchinson. He deserted on May 4, 1864 and took the Oath of Allegiance to the U. S. Government at Chattanooga, Tennessee on November 26, 1864. Comments: Simpson P. Compton lived in Paulding and Cobb Counties, Georgia prior to moving to Van Zandt County, Texas with his family about 1873. He later moved to Canton where he owned a business. The *Wills Point Chronicle* reported his death as follows: "S. P. Compton, a well-known citizen of this county, living at Canton, was taken very suddenly Monday with paralysis and died yesterday morning at 8 o'clock. He was sitting in a store apparently in good health when he complained of his head hurting him and in an instant fell over unconscious and never revived." Sources: 1880 U. S. Census; Civil War Records; Mexican War Pension Records; *Canton Telephone*, January 6, 1888; *Wills Point Chronicle*, February 4, 1897; *The Dallas Morning News*, February, 5, 1897; Ancestry.com; Find A Grave.

COOPER, LARRY LADELL

Born: July 10, 1954, Smith County, Texas. Died: May 30, 1955, Smith County, Texas. Father: Finnis Cooper. Mother: Ruby Lee O'Neal. Source: Eubank Funeral Home records.

COOPER, LOLA

Born: ca 1908. Died: August 15, 1943, Michigan. Father:

ELIZABETH EXONIA ENGLEDOW "BETTIE", *her husband, and son are all buried in unmarked graves in Hillcrest Cemetery. Bettie's father, George Rosinbaum, Sr., was a lawyer who practiced law in Virginia before moving to Van Zandt County in the 1850s. He was serving as District Attorney of the 9th Judicial District of Texas, when Texas voted to secede from the Union. George did not agree with this decision. He was placed on a Black List of Union sympathizers in Van Zandt County in 1863. He was arrested for conspiring to release Union prisoners at Camp Ford near Tyler, Texas. There is no record of his fate after the arrest.*

Unknown. Mother: Unknown. Source: Eubank Funeral Home Records.

COVERT, PATRICIA

Born: ca April 1917. Died: October 28, 1917. Cause of death: Erysipelas. Father: Frederick W. Covert. Mother: May Virginia Mills. Siblings: Mary Ruth, Frederick B., Howell Mills, and James Grady. Comments: Patricia Covert's death was reported in the *Canton Herald* as follows: 'Little Patricia, age six months, daughter of Mr. and Mrs. F. W. Covert, died at their home Sunday after an illness of two weeks of erysipelas. She was laid to rest in the Canton Cemetery Monday at 3 p.m. Rev. M. A. Quinlen conducted the services. Suffer little children to come unto me for of such is the Kingdom of Heaven." Source: *Canton Herald*, November 2, 1917.

COX, BABY

Born: November 1891. Died: November 1891. Cause of death: Stillborn. Father: J. W. Cox. Mother: Mrs. J. W. Cox. Source: Canton Telephone, December 4, 1891.

COX, J.R.

Born: December 31, 1908, Van Zandt County, Texas. Died: February 10, 1951, Kern County, California. Father: Issac Newton "Ike" Cox, Illinois. Mother: Altha Lee Moore, Texas. Siblings: Chester Boone, Alton Dewey, Jewel Dean, and Georgia Mae. Comments: J. R. Cox was living in Wheeler Ridge, California when he died. His body was shipped back to Canton for burial. Sources: 1910 U. S. Census, Eubank Funeral Home records, Ancestry.com.

CULLEN, ELIZABETH D.

Born: ca 1833, Tennessee. Died: November 8, 1891, Van Zandt County, Texas. Cause of death: Pneumonia. Married: Rev. D. P. Cullen, July 17, 1871, Anderson County, Texas. Father: Unknown Conaway. Mother: Unknown. Comments: D. P. and Elizabeth Cullen were living in Gregg County prior to moving to Van Zandt County, Texas. He was in charge of the Canton Methodist circuit. Elizabeth developed pneumonia and lived about a week before dying at the Methodist Parsonage in Canton. Rev. Hardy, the former pastor in charge of the circuit, conducted the funeral. Sources: *Texas Select Marriage Index, 1837-1937*; *Canton Telephone*, November 13, 1891; Ancestry.com.

D

DARDEN, CHARLIE

Born: November 12, 1871. Died: May 17, 1892, Van Zandt County, Texas. Cause of death: Congestion. Comments: Charlie Darden has a tombstone, but it has no first name listed. The *Canton Telephone* reported his death as follows: "Darden had come to town with some pork to sell Monday morning, and soon after making the sale, he was found by J. R. Kennedy in an unconscious state at an old house unoccupied, having spasms." Source: *Canton Telephone*, May 20, 1892.

DEARING, CARRIE FRANCES

Born: October 12, 1871, New York, New York. Died: March 20, 1945, Van Zandt County, Texas. Married: William C. Dearing, November 4, 1888. Children: Infant daughter, Marvin, Minnie, Henry, Etta, and Lillie May. Father: John Henry Tyson. Mother: Phebe Jane Sanger. Siblings: Spencer, Annie, and Mamie L. Comments: Will and Carrie Dearing were a highly respected farming family in the Wentworth Community. She belonged to the Methodist Church. She survived her husband by fourteen years. Sources: Death Certificate; *Canton Herald*, March 25, 1945; Eubank Funeral Home records.

Dearing, Marvin L.

Born: July 16, 1908. Died: August 23, 1933. Cause of death: Knee infection. Single. Father: William C. Dearing. Mother: Carrie Frances Tyson. Siblings: Minnie, Henry, Etta and Lillie May. Comments: Marvin Dearing had rheumatic fever early in his life. He was unable to walk until he was about 6 years old. In December of 1931, he had surgery at Baylor Hospital in Dallas, Texas to try to bring enough relief so that he could at least walk. The *Canton Herald* published an article titled "Wentworth Community Shows A Fine Spirit." The article reads as follows: "It is fitting and proper to mention what the good people of the community have done in the young man's behalf, who, being handicapped as he has been so long, is poor in the world's goods. The paper learns from W. S. (Bud) Mills, principal of the school at Wentworth, that the citizens generally of that locality made a free-will offering of various kinds of products grown on the farms, orchards, and gardens, consisting of potatoes, syrup, all kinds of home-canned vegetables, preserves, jellies, etc., which was taken in a truck to the hospital mentioned by Mr. Claude Fincher, a citizen of the Wentworth community, and applied the whole to the hospital account of young Dearing, the total being figured as $81.10. That is a fine spirit, and a fine answer to the old, old question, 'Am I my brother's keeper.'" Marvin lived until August 23, 1933, when he died from infection in his knee. Sources: Death Certificate; *Canton Herald*, December 11, 1931 and December 25, 1931.

Dearing, William Conyer "Will"

(Photo page 178) Born: ca 1866, Washington County, Arkansas. Died: March 24, 1931, Dallas County, Texas. Cause of death: Blood poisoning. Married: Caroline "Carrie" Frances Tyson, November 4, 1888, Washington County, Arkansas. Children: Infant daughter, Marvin, Minnie, Henry, Etta, and Lillie May. Father: Elihu Roger Dearing. Mother: Elizabeth Dearing. Occupation: Farming. Comments: Will Dearing came with his wife's family, the Tysons, from Arkansas, and settled in Van Zandt County. He was a highly respected farmer in the Wentworth Community for many years. He had an ingrown toenail which developed into blood-poisoning. His leg was amputated, and he died from the complication of this surgery. A contributing cause of death was diabetes. Sources: Death Certificate; *Canton Herald*, March 27, 1931; J. Hadley, Dearing Family historian; Find A. Grave.

Denton, Baby

Born: September 1911, Van Zandt County, Texas. Died: October 1911, Van Zandt County, Texas. Father: Will Denton. Mother: Unknown. Source: *Grand Saline Sun*, October 12, 1911.

Dubose, Glendora "Glenn"

Born: ca 1897, Texas. Died: March 15, 1932, Van Zandt County, Texas. Cause of Death: Pellagra. Married: Horace C. Dubose, November 22, 1914. Father: Munro P. Long. Mother: Unknown. Source: *Canton Herald*, March 18, 1932.

E

Engledow, Elizabeth Exonia "Bettie"

Born: ca 1848, Floyd County, Virginia. Died: April 2, 1897, Galveston County, Texas. Cause of death: Heart disease. Married: John Henry Engledow, June 7, 1868, Van Zandt County, Texas. Children: Creed, Bruce, Eugenia, Enia, Giles, and Arthur. Father: George Rosenbaum, Sr., Wythe County, Virginia. Mother: Mariah Foster, Virginia. Comments: Bettie Engledow had gone to live with her son, Creed, and daughter-in-law in Galveston, Texas but then decided to return to her old home near Canton. She planned to return on a Monday, but died from heart trouble in her sleep the Friday before. She was buried in the Canton Cemetery beside her husband and a son. All three are in unmarked graves. Bettie's father was a lawyer. He practiced law in Floyd County, Virginia, and then he moved to Van Zandt County by the 1850's. He took the Oath of Office for District Attorney of the 9th Judicial District of Texas on November 8, 1858. He did not agree with the Texas vote to secede from the Union. George was placed on a Black List of Union sympathizers in Van Zandt County in 1863 and was soon arrested along with two companions for conspiring to release Union prisoners at Camp Ford near Tyler, Texas. The two companions were released, but there is no record of George's fate. Mariah later married Richard Wells, an old friend from Virginia. She died in childbirth in 1873, and Richard raised her minor children. Sources: *Wills Point Chronicle*, April 8, 1897; Lisa Pierce Rosenbaum Family historian.

Engledow, John Henry

Born: ca 1837. Died: November 12, 1879, Van Zandt County, Texas. Married: Elizabeth Rosenbaum "Bettie," June 7, 1868, Van Zandt County, Texas. Children: Creed, Bruce, Eugenia, Enia, Giles, and Arthur. Father: Creed S. Engledow. Mother: Elvira Elizabeth Randolph. Comments: John Henry and Bettie Engledow left Tennessee and settled in Nacogdoches County, Texas in 1835. John Henry's father fought in the Texas Revolution in 1836 and later moved to Van Zandt, County, Texas. Betty's obituary in the *Wills Point Chronicle* stated that she was buried beside her husband and son in the Canton Cemetery. Source: *Wills Point Chronicle*, April 8, 1897.

Everett, A Little Child

Born: Unknown. Died: December 1893. Father: George

__Mastin M. Henderson__ was born in Tennessee in 1804 and had moved to Van Zandt County by 1856. The following year he rented space from the County in the old courthouse for $2.00 per month, where he developed a business selling groceries and liquor. He served his community as a Constable and County Judge before the Civil War and as Country Treasurer and Justice of the Peace after the War. During the War, however, he supported the Union and was placed on the Confederate Black List. It is believed Mastin Henderson is buried next to his third wife, Susan.

W. Everett. Mother: Elizabeth Gillispie. Source: *Canton Telephone*, December 15, 1893.

Evine, Fannie
Born: Unknown. Died: March 1889. Cause of death: Leg amputation. Father: Unknown. Mother: Unknown. Comments: Fannie Evine was ill with an undisclosed disease and had one of her legs amputated about a month prior to her death. The *Canton Telephone* reported her death as follows: "The citizens of Canton are to be complimented for their kindness and charitableness toward this unfortunate young lady; they did all in their power to restore her health-but God knew best, and called her from this mode of existence. The physicians and young ladies deserve special credit and praise for their treatment and attention. They will be rewarded in heaven for their good deeds. And Mrs. Hamilton, the lady who had her in charge, and was a mother to her in her illness deserves a greater reward, and more praise, perhaps, than all." Source: *Canton Telephone*, March 29, 1889.

F

Fitzgerald, Albert
Born: ca 1879. Died: December 1918. Cause of death: Gunshot wounds. Married: (1) Clara Shaw, December 21, 1898. (2) Mamie Fitzgerald, November 21, 1910. Father: Unknown Fitzgerald. Mother: Unknown. Comments: Albert Fitzgerald's death was reported in the *Canton Herald* as follows: “"Dixie" Potts, a Negro, was brought to Canton Tuesday and lodged in jail on a charge of murder. Monday afternoon on the Slaughter farm he plugged Albert Fitzgerald, another Negro, in the stomach, using a shotgun, and the victim died Monday night. It was reported here that the Negroes quarreled over an ordinary bridle, but Pott's statement of the deadly affair is that Fitzgerald broke into his house some nights previous and attempted to assault his wife. Potts claims further that he was out hunting Monday afternoon and met Fitzgerald on the Slaughter farm. Words passed between them and Potts claims the other kept trying to advance on him with a Negro woman intervening. Potts had the gun pointed at Fitzgerald and finally told the woman if she did not get from between them he would shoot her. The woman got out of the way and Potts fired on Fitzgerald, the wounds causing death a few hours after the shooting. Sheriff Carpenter went over Tuesday morning and brought Potts to jail. He did not ask for an examining trial and in view of the early approach of District court and the assembling of the grand jury, he will likely remain in jail. The Fitzgerald Negro formerly resided in Canton and the body was brought here Tuesday afternoon and buried." Potts later went to trial, but the jury could not reach a verdict. Albert's wife, Mamie, later married Earnest Riggs. She died January 3, 1957. Source: *Canton Herald*, December 13, 1918.

Fitzgerald, Cordy Mae
Born: October 14, 1937. Died: December 19, 1940. Father: Willis Fitzgerald. Mother: Easter Brown. Sources: Death Certificate, Eubank Funeral Home records.

Fitzgerald, Earnest
Born: 1900, Van Zandt County, Texas. Died: April 18, 1928, Van Zandt County, Texas. Cause of death: Tuberculosis. Single. Father: Jerry Fitzgerald, Alabama. Mother: Lena Ladd, Mississippi. Occupation: Farmer. Source: Death Certificate.

Fitzgerald, Eddie Dean
Born: June 1, 1946. Died: September 30, 1946. Father: Willie Fitzgerald. Mother: Easter Brown. Sources: Eubank Funeral Home records; Vanessa Scott, Wynne Community historian.

Jessie "Red" Fitzgerald

Victory Fitzgerald

FITZGERALD, JESSIE "RED"
Born: 1894. Died: Unknown. Married: Lottie Fitzgerald. Father: Jerry Fitzgerald. Mother: Lena Ladd. Siblings: Perry, Earnest, and Mamie. Source: Vanessa Scott, Wynne Community historian.

FITZGERALD, LOTTIE
Born: 1894, Van Zandt County, Texas. Died: June 15, 1946, Kaufman County, Texas. Cause of death: Stroke. Married: Jessie "Red" Fitzgerald. Father: Will Overstreet. Mother: Unknown. Sources: Death Certificate, Eubank Funeral Home records.

FITZGERALD, LUM
Born: January 1, 1875, Smith County, Texas. Died: March 28, 1950, Van Zandt County, Texas. Married: Victory Johnson, June 5, 1905. Father: Jerry Fitzgerald, Alabama. Mother: Leah Williams. Occupation: Farmer. Sources: 1920 U. S. Census, *Marriage Records Van Zandt County, Texas, 1948-1909*, Eubank Funeral Home records.

FITZGERALD, MAY F.
Born: May 10, 1933, Van Zandt County, Texas. Died: November 15, 1937, Van Zandt County, Texas. Father: Willis Fitzgerald. Mother: Easter Brown. Source: Eubank Funeral Home records.

FITZGERALD, TINY
Born: 1909. Died: August 1917. Cause of death: Fall from horse. Father: Ike Fitzgerald. Mother: Lizzie Payne. Comments: The *Canton Herald* reported Tiny Fitzgerald's death as follows: "Tiny Fitzgerald, a Negro girl about 8 years old, living with her parents, Ike Fitzgerald and wife, on Henry Side's place north of Canton, died Sunday from injuries received by falling from a horse last Friday evening. It is reported that the child was on the horse when it was frightened by her little brother. The horse ran away throwing the child against a stump, bursting her skull in several places causing several pieces of the skull to fall out." Source: *Canton Herald*, August 31, 1917.

FITZGERALD, VICTORY
Born: February 1, 1883. Died: January 4, 1966. Cause of death: Injuries from a fall. Married: Lum Fitzgerald, June 5, 1905. Father: J. T. Johnson. Mother: Luvena Jackson. Source: Death Certificate.

FLOYD, DE
Born: Unknown. Died: February 1902. Father: Unknown Floyd. Mother: Unknown. Comments: De Floyd cut his foot with an axe on a Thursday and died from the bleeding on Friday. Source: *Free State Enterprise*, February 13, 1902.

FORD, A LITTLE GIRL
Born: Unknown. Died: October 1888. Father: Duck Ford. Mother: Unknown. Source: *Canton Telephone*, October 19, 1888.

FORD, DUCK
Born: ca 1857, Mississippi. Died: November 1885, Van Zandt County, Texas. Cause of death: Typho-malarial fever. Married: Unknown. Father: Howell E. Ford. Mother: Fredonia C. Hubbard. Siblings: Isabella, James, Howell, and Grant. Occupation: Farmer. Comments: Duck Ford came with his parents to Van Zandt County before 1860. At his death, he left a wife and several young children. Sources: 1860 U. S. Census; *Texan-Telephone*, November 14, 1885.

FRANKLIN, IRENE
Born: June 6, 1905, Van Zandt County, Texas. Died: April 23, 1986, Van Zandt County, Texas. Married: Unknown Franklin. Father: Frank Hardman. Mother: Sallie Hardman. Siblings: Albert, Jesse Lee, Zella Mae, and May Ella. Comments: Irene Franklin was a lifelong resident of Canton, Texas and a member of the New Hope Baptist Church in the Wynne Community. Sources: 1920 U. S. Census; *Canton Herald*, May 1, 1986.

FULLER, EDWARD C. "UNCLE ED"
Born: October 7, 1852, Arkansas. Died: January 8, 1921, Van Zandt County, Texas. Cause of death: Fall. Single. Father: Unknown Fuller. Mother: Unknown. Occupation: Janitor. Comments: Edward C. Fuller fell on the Canton courthouse stairway and died from a fracture at the base of his skull. He was found on a Wednesday, died Saturday at 7: 15, and funeral services were held in the County Court room Sunday afternoon at 3 o'clock. The *Wills Point Chronicle* reported his death as follows: "Deceased was born October 7, 1852, in the state of Arkansas. He came to Texas at the age of 21 and lived for a long time at Sherman. He moved to Martin's Mill about 15 years ago,

Edward C. "Uncle Ed" Fuller *was born in Arkansas and moved to Texas at the age of 21. At the time of his death at age 68 he worked as janitor at the Van Zandt County Courthouse. His reputation was that of a devout Christian, and although Uncle Ed never married, he was known to have supported his widowed mother. It was said in the community that "If anyone has ever gone to Heaven, Uncle Ed will go."*

where he resided until three years ago, when he was appointed as janitor at the courthouse. He joined the Missionary Baptist church 11 years ago and from that time until his death came he lived a very consecrated Christian life. So much was he devoted to his Lord that his light was seen by others and it was remarked of him by one who was daily in company with him at the courthouse: 'If anyone has ever gone to Heaven, Uncle Ed will go.' Uncle Ed was never married but gave his love and support to a widowed mother who died only a few years ago, leaving only this one child. During the last three years, Uncle Ed served as janitor at the court house and there never was a more faithful servant of the people than he was. He worked diligently every hour of the day and often he was found working at his job in the 'small' hours of the morning and at night. He was a favorite of the county officials who often 'tipped' him for special favors he did for them. Not all of them were so good to him, however, and he did not fail to note the difference." Sources: Death Certificate; *Wills Point Chronicle*, January 20, 1921.

Fulton, Mrs. Eugene
Born: Unknown. Died: October 1899, Van Zandt County, Texas. Married: Eugene Fulton. Father: Unknown. Mother: Unknown. Source: *Free State Enterprise*, October 19, 1899.

G

Goins, Allie Fay
Born: August 3, 1910, Van Zandt County, Texas. Died: August 30, 1946, Kerr County, Texas. Cause of death: Tuberculosis. Married: L. E. Goins. Children: Betty June and Dick. Father: Willis E. Weaver, Alabama. Mother: Millie Head, Van Zandt County, Texas. Sources: Death Certificate, Eubank Funeral Home records.

Gray, L.B.
Born: February 26, 1900. Died: February 17, 1920, Arkansas. Cause of death: Gunshot wounds. Father: Unknown Gray. Mother: Unknown. Comments: L. B. Gray moved from Canton to Arkansas and within two weeks, he was shot to death. There was no information about the shooting. His parents requested that his body be shipped back to Canton for burial. Source: *Canton Herald*, February 20, 1920.

H

Hambrick, Trim
Born: April 14, 1900, Van Zandt County, Texas. Died: February 22, 1972, Smith County, Texas. Cause of death: Heart disease. Father: Will Hambrick. Mother: Katherine Farmer. Sources: Death Certificate, Eubank Funeral Home records.

Hashert, Mary Elizabeth
Born: April 18, 1878, Arkansas. Died: July 25, 1952, Van Zandt County, Texas. Cause of death: Heart disease. Married: Albert G. Hashert. Father: Robert W. Warner, Ohio. Mother: Laura Warner, Mississippi. Siblings: Deede, J.C., Buster, Dick, Albert, J. E., Mrs. Lesley Porter, Ethel (Bell), and Gladys. Sources: Death Certificate; 1880 U. S. Census; *Grand Saline Sun*, July 31, 1952; Bartley Funeral Home records.

Haynes, Baby
Born: August 1910. Died: September 1910. Father: Andrew H. Haynes. Mother: Annie Lee Griser. Source: *Grand Saline Sun*, September 14, 1910.

Heard, Mary Matilda Ellen
Born: 1871. Died: March 2, 1904. Cause of death: Pneu-

monia. Married: James Richard (Dick) Heard, 1889. Father: Unknown Turner. Mother: Unknown. Children: Johnny L., Oliver C., Onie C., Bertha, Willey, Richard Lee, and Arlie F. Comments: Mary Heard's husband's family were early settlers in Van Zandt County. Dick and Mary Heard had seven children, three of whom died as infants. After Mary's death, Richard married Cordelia Clementine Isom, August 7, 1905. They had five children. Dick died in Dalhart, Texas on March 20, 1930. He was buried in the Spring Creek Cemetery, Beckham County, Oklahoma. Sources: *Wills Point Chronicle*, March 3, 1904; Martha Heard, Heard Family historian.

Henderson, Mastin M.

Born: 1804, Tennessee. Died: November 28, 1882, Van Zandt County, Texas. Married: (1) Elizabeth Coldthorp, June 9, 1824, Jefferson County, Tennessee. Child: J. R. C., (2) Mary Elizabeth (Mrs. Scates) Blair, August 5, 1851, Rusk County, Texas. Divorced January 1, 1861, Van Zandt County, Texas. (3) Susan A. Thompson, Van Zandt County, Texas. Children: Anne E., Mastin Green, and Allen Thompson. Father: Andrew L. Henderson, Tennessee. Mother: Margaret McSpadden, Tennessee. Occupation: Farmer, business owner, county official. Comments: Mastin Henderson was in Van Zandt County by April of 1856 when he acquired a license to sell liquor on the Eye Tooth lot on the northwest corner of Canton courthouse square. In 1857 he rented the old courthouse for $2.00 a month from the county and expanded his business to sell groceries. By 1859 he was a constable, and by 1860 he was Chief Justice (County Judge). During the Civil War, he supported the Union and was on the Confederate Black List. His son, John R. C. Henderson, an attorney, was murdered on January 28, 1865 because of his Union support. Mastin was elected County Treasurer and served one term 1875-76. In 1877 he was appointed Justice of the Peace of Precinct 1. His will dated October 31, 1881 bequeathed all of his assets to his sons, Mastin Green and Allen Thompson Henderson. It is believed that Mastin is buried next to his wife, Susan. Sources: *Van Zandt County, Texas Court Minutes 1848-1871, 1872-1881, Vol. A. B. C*; Ancestry.com.

Highsmith, Louis C.

Born: ca 1852, Alabama. Died: October 1898, Van Zandt County, Texas. Married: Cyntha P. Copeland, November 15, 1876. Children: Brucie, Auby, Sebastian N., and Sebby. Father: Isaac Highsmith. Mother: Elizabeth Purdom. Siblings: Amanda, Wade H., Catherine M., Susan M., and Rhoda F. Occupation: Farmer. Comments: The *Wills Point Chronicle* reported Louis Highsmith's death as follows: "L. C. Highsmith, living near this place was taken sick Monday evening and died Wednesday afternoon at 4:30 o'clock. Remains were entombed in the Canton cemetery this afternoon. A short while previous to his death he traded his 120 acre farm near town for a 320 acre farm in Archer County and was intending to move out there next week." It is believed that Louis is buried next to his son, Brucie. Sources: 1880 U. S. Census; *Wills Point Chronicle*, October 13, 1898; Ancestry.com.

Huggard, N.

Born: Unknown. Died: September 13, 1900. Comments: The *Free State Enterprise* reported N. Huggard's death as follows: "An unmarried man about thirty years of age, died of congestion of the lungs at Will Darden's place about 1 ½ miles from Canton, Texas." Source: *Free State Enterprise*, September 13, 1900.

J

Johnson, Pauline

Born: February 21, 1913, Smith County, Texas. Died: January 14, 1942, Van Zandt County, Texas. Cause of death: Tuberculosis. Married: Luther Johnson. Father: Elige Williams, Smith County, Texas. Mother: Margrette Taylor. Sources: Death Certificate, Eubank Funeral Home records.

Jones, Lucy

Born: July 3, 1879. Died: March 24, 1949, Dallas County, Texas. Cause of death: Kidney disease. Father: Unknown. Mother: Belle Summers, Oklahoma. Sources: Death Certificate, Eubank Funeral Home records.

K

Kellam, James Legitus

Born: ca 1879. Died: October 3, 1947, Smith County, Texas. Cause of death: Paralysis. Single. Father: John Kellam. Mother: Cynthia P. Kellam. Siblings: Henry H., William F., George, and Jack. Comments: James Kellam was living at the Christian Home of Charity, Tyler, Texas as a pensioner when he died. Sources: Death Certificate, 1880 U. S. Census, Eubank Funeral Home records.

Kennedy, Infant

Born: February 1892. Died: February 1892. Father: J. R. Kennedy. Mother: Fannie Farrer. Source: *Canton Telephone*, March 5, 1892.

__Randal Lowry__ is believed to be one of the oldest people buried in Hillcrest Cemetery. He was born into slavery in approximately 1790. According to the 1880 U.S. Census, he was 90 years old. His death notice reported his age as 114. He probably was 94 when he died.

Keoun, J.B.
Born: Unknown. Died: July 1893, Van Zandt County, Texas. Father: Unknown Keoun. Mother: Unknown. Sources: *Canton Telephone,* July 7, 1893 and July 14, 1893.

Kidd, John H.
Born: Unknown. Died: April 1893. Cause of Death: Tuberculosis. Married: Francis Harris, May 11, 1890. Father: Unknown Kidd. Mother: Unknown. Sources: *Marriage Records Van Zandt County, Texas, 1848-1909*; *Canton Telephone*, April 14, 1893.

Kitchins, Palestine "Grandma"
Born: 1853, Mississippi. Died: September 1920, Van Zandt County, Texas. Married: William J. Kitchens, 1876. Children: Marion, Mittie, Albert, Mary Etta, plus seven with names unknown. Father: T. M. Holland. Mother: Martha Holland. Siblings: Mary J., Elizabeth, Vilona M., Martha, Azaleen S., Castine, Nathan, David L., and Lucy C. Comments: The *Wills Point Chronicle* reported Palestine Kitchins' death as follows: "Grandma Kitchins died Tuesday night at the home of her daughter, Mrs. Buck Brunson, south of Canton, and the remains were placed at rest in Canton cemetery Wednesday afternoon with appropriate religious services. The husband died last year of smallpox in Arkansas and afterward she returned to Van Zandt and was making her home with Mr. and Mrs. Brunson. The Kitchins were old citizens of the County and friends will learn with sorrow of the death of this good woman. Mr. and Mrs. Roy Downing were here from Arkansas to attend the funeral, Mrs. Downing being another daughter of deceased." Sources: 1860, 1900 U. S. Census; *Wills Point Chronicle*, September 9, 1920.

Knox, A Girl
Born: ca 1899. Died: September 1904, Van Zandt County, Texas. Cause of death: Carbolic acid. Father: Sam W. Knox. Mother: Dora E. Perry. Comments: The Knox family was living in Grand Saline when their five-year-old girl accidentally drank about an ounce of carbolic acid and died about an hour later. Sources: *Marriage Records 1849-1909, Van Zandt County, Texas*; *Wills Point Chronicle*, September 8, 1904.

Knox, Blanche
Born: ca 1858. Died: June, 1915. Married: (1) J. C. Davis, December 2, 1877. (2) Robert M Knox, January 31, 1884. Children: Jefferson Davis and Robert Vasco. Father: James J. Monroe. Mother: Blanche Narcissa Kelley. Siblings: Barney A., Caroline, James P., Jefferson Davis, John M., Juliette D., Monroe Hale, Napoleon B., Robert B., Joseph S., William S., and Sarah J. Source: *Wills Point Chronicle*, June 10, 1915.

Knox, Jefferson Davis "Jeff"
Born: March 30, 1893. Died: March 1918. Cause of death: Gunshot wound. Single. Father: Robert M. Knox. Mother: Blanche Monroe Davis Knox. Comments: The *Canton Herald* reported the death of Jeff Knox as follows: "Jeff Knox shot himself in the head at the home of his father, R. M. Knox, in the western part of town Tuesday evening about 7 o'clock. A 22-caliber target rifle was used and the bullet entered just behind the right ear, piercing the brain and lodging just under the skin in the forehead. Physicians were hurriedly summoned and soon found that he was to die, though he lingered for several hours after the tragedy. Funeral services were held Wednesday, internment taking place in the Canton Cemetery. The deceased was reared in Canton and was 24 years of age. He was a hard-working young man and held in high esteem by all who knew him. He had been called for physical examination at Wills Point on Wednesday of this week under the selective draft and it is understood that worry about army service is responsible for his tragic death. However, in filling out his questionnaire he placed himself in class one and at one time expressed himself as being willing and ready to go to the army. The tragedy was a great shock to this community and the bereaved relatives have the sympathy of the entire citizenship in their sorrow." Source: *Canton Herald*, March 22, 1918

Knox, Robert M. "Uncle Bob"
Born: ca 1853 Alabama. Died: December 1, 1925. Married: Blanche Monroe Davis, January 31, 1884. Children: Jefferson Davis and Robert Vasco. Father: Montgomery Knox, Alabama. Mother: Unknown. Occupation: Farmer. Comments: Uncle Bob Knox hauled freight into Canton for many years before trucks came to replace wagons and teams. He had one surviving son, Drew, living in Kansas City, Kansas. The *Canton Telephone* described an incident as: "A difficulty between Messrs. W. C. Gilmore and R. M. Knox near town last Friday has not been determined to be as serious as was at first suspected. The combat took place in the woods near town; in the meantime Mr. Gilmore received a painful gash under the shoulder blade

from the blade of an axe; also a painful wound on the hand from the blade of a knife. The wounded man is not considered to be in a dangerous condition. Mr. Knox is at home. They are brothers-in-law—and it is said that the fight is the result of an old feud. No one saw the contest—therefore we can't give the exact particulars." Sources: Death Certificate; *Canton Telephone*, January 6, 1888; *Wills Point Chronicle*, December 10, 1925.

KNOX, ROBERT VASCO
Born: ca 1886. Died: December 25, 1907, Van Zandt County, Texas. Cause of death: Pneumonia. Married: Eura Grumbles, November 10, 1907. Father: Robert M. Knox. Mother: Blanche Monroe. Comments: Robert Knox died at his parents' home. He had been married only six weeks. Source: *Grand Saline Sun*, January 2, 1908.

KOUNE, JOHNIE
Born: Unknown. Died: September 1885, Van Zandt County, Texas. Cause of death: Congestion. Father: Unknown Koune. Mother: Unknown. Source: *Texan-Telephone*, September 26, 1885.

L

LADD, MRS. LENA
Born: ca 1859, Mississippi (a slave). Died: August 25, 1920. Cause of death: Infection. Married: (1) H. Ladd, June 5, 1890. (2) Jerry Fitzgerald. Child: Earnest Fitzgerald. Father: Unknown Andrews. Mother: Unknown. Occupation: Cook. Source: Death Certificate.

LADD (LAD), ROBERT
Born: ca 1893. Died: April 1899. Cause of death: Gunshot wound. Father: Unknown Ladd. Mother: Unknown. Comments: The *Free State Enterprise* reported Robert Ladd's death as follows: "Yesterday morning Albert Fitzgerald (col) aged about 20 years, shot and killed Robert Lad (col) aged about 5 or 6 years. Fitzgerald was at the home of the boy's mother and he and she were practicing shooting a pistol. A stray bullet passed into Robert Lad's head and death resulted instantaneously. Fitzgerald was arrested by Deputy Sheriff Gentry and placed in jail to wait a fuller development of the facts." Source: *Free State Enterprise*, April 6, 1899.

LANDRUM, JOHN W.
Born: December 25, 1887, Texas. Died: December 19, 1946, Kaufman County, Texas. Cause of death: Kidney disease. Father: John W. Landrum. Mother: Mattie I. Kimbriel. Sources: Death Certificate, Eubank Funeral Home records.

LEE, KISSIAH ANN
Born: June 21, 1825, South Carolina. Died: 1881, Van Zandt County, Texas. Married: David Crockett Lee, October 18, 1843, Alabama. Children: John W., Anna Jane, James C., Infant daughter, Puss, David, Sweet, William, Pink, General, Luia, Robert David, and Robert G. Father: Francis E. Sanders. Mother: Barbara Oswalt. Source: Beth Gordon, Lee Family historian.

LOUGHMILLER, REBA FRANCINE
Born: November 23, 1950, Smith County, Texas. Died: September 11, 1951, Tarrant County, Texas. Cause of death: Pneumonia. Father: Richard Loughmiller. Mother: Francine Turner. Sources: Death Certificate, Eubank Funeral Home records.

LOWRY, RANDAL
Born: ca 1790 (slave). Died: November 7, 1884, Van Zandt County, Texas. Father: Unknown Lowry. Mother: Unknown. Comments: The 1880 U. S. Census listed Randal Lowry's age as 90. Newspaper notice listed Randal Lowry as 114 years old. He probably died at 94 years of age. Sources: 1880 U. S. Census; *Texan-Telephone*, November 19, 1884.

LUMMUS, EUGENE
Born: January 22, 1928. Died: November 2, 1931, Dallas County, Texas. Cause of death: Spinal meningitis. Father: William E. Lummus. Mother: Minnie Petty. Sources: Death Certificate; *Canton Herald*, November 6, 1931.

M

MANSFIELD, CHILD
Born: ca 1901. Died: August 23, 1903. Father: H. H. Mansfield. Mother: Lela Neely. Comments: The Mansfield family was living in the Willow Springs Community at the time of the child's death. Source: *Wills Point Chronicle*, September 3, 1903.

MANSFIELD, ELZY
Born: ca 1903. Died: June 1906. Father: H. H. Mansfield. Mother: Lela Neely. Comments: The Mansfield family was

living in the Elmo Community of Kaufman County, Texas when Elzy died. Source: *Wills Point Chronicle*, June 1906.

Marshall, Georgia

Born: March 8, 1861, Van Zandt County, Texas. Died: June 6, 1941, Van Zandt County, Texas. Married: James Monroe Marshall. Children: Ed, Bruce, and Louise. Occupation: School teacher. Father: George E. Rosinbaum, Sr., Virginia. Mother: Miriah Foster, Virginia. Comments: There is a large Marshall marker in Hillcrest Cemetery but no individual names to identify the graves. The Rosinbaums were among the early settlers in Canton and Van Zandt County. Georgia's father was a District Attorney for the 9th Judicial District of Texas and a Union supporter. He among others were placed on the Confederate Black List of 1863 and was subject to continued harassment. Sources say that George Rosinbaum and two other individuals made plans to set Union soldiers free who were being held as prisoners by the Confederates at Camp Ford in Tyler, Texas. The three were discovered and taken into custody by the Confederates. George's two partners were released, but George never appeared again in Van Zandt County records. Georgia's brother, Ed Rosinbaum, was killed in a saloon in Lawndale, Texas, in 1889; and he is buried in Hillcrest Cemetery. Sources: *Canton Herald*, June 1941, Eubank Funeral Home records.

Marshall, James Monroe

Born: May 9, 1861, Newton County, Mississippi. Died: March 17, 1940, Van Zandt County, Texas. Married: (1) Elizabeth M. Moore, April 10, 1884. Children: Two children died as infants. (2) Georgia Rosenbaum, February 12, 1892. Children: Ed, Bruce, and Louise. Father: Reading Marshall, North Carolina. Mother: Francis Beavers, North Carolina. Occupation: Farmer. Comments: There is a large Marshall marker in the Hillcrest Cemetery with no individual names. James Marshall came to Van Zandt County, Texas about 1880 and was a highly regarded farmer. Sources: *Canton Herald*, May 1940; Eubank Funeral Home records.

Mathis, Tom Jr.

Born: April 10, 1870, Van Zandt County, Texas. Died: August 22, 1942, Van Zandt County, Texas. Cause of death: Heart disease. Father: Thomas M. Mathes, Sr., Georgia. Mother: Easter Thompson. Occupation: Farmer. Comments: Tom Mathes, Sr., was a slave from Georgia and one of the first settlers in what is now the Wynne Community. He was a major land owner. Tom, Jr., helped his father on that land. Sources: Death Certificate, Eubank Funeral Home records.

Maume, Alice R.

Born: February 21, 1861, Missouri. Died: August 16, 1923 Van Zandt County, Texas. Married: Edward W. Maume. Children: Mrs. J. B. Baker, Mamie, Edward, Mrs. F. A. Tyson, and Thelma. Father: George Nash. Mother: Miranda J. Tacey. Siblings: Mrs. W. P. Smith and Floyd. Occupation: School teacher. Comments: When Alice Maume's husband died in 1922, she moved back to Canton, Texas, to live with her daughter, Mamie Maume. Mamie owned the noted Dixie Hotel in Canton. The *Canton Herald* reported Alice's death as follows: "Mrs. Alice R. Maume, aged 62 years, died at the home of her daughter, Miss Mamie Maume, on August 16, 1923. Mrs. Maume, who was the daughter of Mr. and Mrs. George Nash, was a pioneer resident of Van Zandt County, having been born in the state of Missouri February 21, 1861, and coming to Texas with her parents at the age of 17 years. The family

Alice R. Maume

first settled in Johnson County and she taught school for a number of years before her marriage to the late Edward W. Maume. They came to Van Zandt County and resided in Canton until 1919 moving to Arkansas where Mr. Maume passed to his reward in 1922. She is survived by two daughters, Mrs. J.B. Baker and Miss Mamie of Canton, one son, Edward Maume, of Ranger, Texas, Mrs. F.A. Tyson, Lincoln, Arkansas, and little Miss Thelma Lee Carter Maume, Canton, a sister, Mrs. W.P. Smith, Harriston, Ore., one brother, Floyd Nash, Tonopah, Nev. Burial was at Canton cemetery." Sources: *Canton Herald*, August 31, 1923; *Wills Point Chronicle*, September 6, 1923.

McClellen, Jimmie
Born: Unknown. Died: March 15, 1887. Cause of death: Typhoid fever. Father: T. M. McClellen. Mother: Unknown. Source: *Canton Telephone*, March 25, 1887.

McClellen, Sudie
Born: ca 1872. Died: April 13, 1904, Van Zandt County, Texas. Father: Unknown. Mother: Unknown. Source: *Wills Point Chronicle*, May 12, 1904.

McCord, Baby
Born: ca April 1906. Died: April 25, 1906. Father: Unknown McCord. Mother: Unknown. Source: *Wills Point Chronicle*, May 3, 1906.

McCoy, David Earl
Born: August 31, 1940, Mobile County, Alabama. Died: December 19, 1979, Dallas County, Texas. Cause of death: Seizure disorder. Father: Charles McCoy, Alabama. Mother: Emma B. Unknown, Alabama. Occupation: Landscaper. Comments: The Dallas County Medical Examiner ruled that David McCoy's death was the result of a seizure disorder. Sources: Death Certificate; 1930, 1940 U. S. Census; Find A Grave.

McCoy, Earlie Omega
Born: November 4, 1899. Died: September 28, 1900. Father: Elbert Milton McCoy. Mother: Pricilla Ann Bullard. Comments: The *Free State Enterprise* reported Earlie McCoy's death as follows: "One of E. M. McCoy's small children was buried in the Canton Cemetery Saturday." He is possibly buried beside his father who died February 5, 1901. Sources: *Free State Enterprise*, October 4, 1900; Find A Grave.

McCoy, Elbert Milton "E. M."
Born: May 12, 1850, Butler County, Alabama. Died: February 5, 1901, Van Zandt County, Texas. Cause of death: Paralysis. Married: Pricilla Ann Elizabeth Bullard, November 3, 1869. Children: Ezra Lee, Walter T., and Earlie. Father: John Robinson McCoy, Jr. Mother: Catherine Derinda Tillery. Siblings: Thomas Richard, Washington, William Joseph, Francis Mourning, Herbert M., John

Elbert Milton "E.M." McCoy

Earlie Omega McCoy sitting in the lap of her mother Pricilla Ann Bullard McCoy

Presley, Hesicah, and James C. Comments: Elbert McCoy and his family migrated to Cass County, Texas in the mid 1870's. They later moved to Van Zandt County. Elbert died from paralysis while living near the Tundra Community in Van Zandt County. All of his family, except Earlie, left Van Zandt County and are buried in different cemeteries. Earlie is thought to be buried next to his father. Elbert's wife died in 1924 and is buried in the Black Hills Cemetery in Navarro County, Texas. Sources: *Free State Enterprise*, February 7, 1901; Find A. Grave; Tim J. McCoy, McCoy Family historian.

McDougal, Mrs. Walter
Born: Unknown. Died: May 1912. Cause of death: Bright's disease. Married: Walter McDougal. Father: Unknown. Mother: Unknown. Comments: At her death, Mrs. Walter McDougal left a husband and a four-week old baby. Source: *Grand Saline Sun*, May 16, 1912.

McGuire, Alexander H.
Born: April 29, 1932, Kaufman County, Texas. Died: May 10, 1932, Van Zandt County, Texas. Cause of death: Premature birth. Father: J. L. McGuire. Mother: Fay Ogle. Comments: The McGuire family was living in the Starr/Wentworth Community when their baby died. Sources: Death Certificate; *Canton Herald*, May 20, 1932.

McKee, Infant
Born: Unknown. Died: December 1891. Father: J. M. McKee. Mother: Unknown. Source: *Canton Telephone*, December 4, 1891.

McKee, Maud
Born: Unknown. Died: June 1888. Father: Johnie McK-

***Susan Darlene Phillips** was living in Tyler, Texas when she disappeared December 31, 1976, nine months pregnant. Three years later, her remains were found in a locked car submerged in the Trinity River. The primary suspect was also murdered before the Van Zandt County officers were able to question him. According to one of Susan Phillips' children, no one was ever tried and convicted of these two murders.*

ee. Mother: Unknown. Comments: The *Canton Telephone* reported the death of Maud McKee as follows: "Sweet little Maud, daughter of Mr. and Mrs. Johnie McKee, died Monday night after several days of painful suffering. Its remains were interred in the Canton Cemetery, Tuesday evening at 4 o'clock. Rev. J. C. Calhoun conducted the burial service in great sublimity and in an impressive manner." Source: *Canton Telephone*, June 29, 1888.

McMillan, Dorothy
Born: February 13, 1924, Wood County, Texas. Died: July 4, 1940, Van Zandt County, Texas. Cause of death: Kidney disease. Single. Father: Lorenza McMillan. Mother: Adesa Smith. Sources: Death Certificate, Eubank Funeral Home records.

Meadors, Grandma
Born: Unknown. Died: November 1910. Married: Unknown Meadors. Father: Unknown. Mother: Unknown. Source: *Grand Saline Sun*, December 1, 1910.

Melton, Mrs. John H.
Born: Unknown. Died: September 6, 1900. Cause of death: Heart disease. Married: John H. Melton. Father: Unknown. Mother: Unknown. Comments: The *Free State Enterprise* reported Mrs. John Melton's death as follows: "Mrs. J. H. Melton of this city died very suddenly last Thursday night between 11 and 12 o'clock 6h inst., of heart failure. She was apparently in the best of health Thursday and retired that night without any complaint whatever. During the night, her husband was awakened by her struggles but by the time he could reach her bedside she had expired. The remains were carried to Canton Thursday for interment, that being the old home of Mrs. Melton. The *Chronicle* tenders sympathy to the family and relatives in their sudden bereavement." Sources: *Free State Enterprise*, September 13, 1900; *Wills Point Chronicle*, September 13, 1900.

Miller, Infant Daughter
Born: Unknown. Died: May 1931. Father: O. E. Miller. Mother: Unknown. Source: *Canton Herald*, May 29, 1931.

Morris, Baby Girl
Born: March 17, 1973, Smith County, Texas. Died: March 17, 1973, Smith County, Texas. Cause of death: Stillborn. Father: Fred Morris. Mother: Bertha Scates. Source: Eubank Funeral Home records.

Mullins, John Loftin "Uncle John"
Born: November 4, 1837, Pike County, Alabama. Died: February 6, 1906, Van Zandt County, Texas. Married: Mary Elizabeth Perdue, November 23, 1853, Alabama. Children: Alverado, Eugenia Augusta "Gussie", Samuel, Dora, and Laura W. Father: Thomas K. Mullins. Mother: Permelia H. Brockman. Sources: *Wills Point Chronicle*, February 15, 1906; Ancestry.com.

Mullins, Mary Elizabeth
Born: January 4, 1835, Alabama. Died: July 28, 1917, Van Zandt County, Texas. Cause of death: Tuberculosis. Married: John Loftin Mullins, November 23, 1853, Alabama. Children: Alverado, Eugenia Augusta "Gussie", Samuel, Dora, and Laura W. Father: William W. Perdue, Georgia. Mother: Sarah Ann Lyles, Georgia. Comments: After an illness of several months, Mary Elizabeth Mullins died at the home of her daughter, Gussie Griser. Sources: Death Certificate, *Canton Herald*, August 3, 1917; Ancestry.com.

N

Nolen, Walter Andrew Webster
Born: January 12, 1856, Smith County, Texas. Died: February 1890, Van Zandt County, Texas. Married: Ellen Adams, November 22, 1885. Father: Robert W. "Whit" Nolen, Alabama. Mother: Sarah Catherine Darden. Sources: 1880 U. S. Census; *Canton Telephone*, February 7, 1890; Ancestry.com.

P

Peace, Baby
Born: Unknown. Died: December 1890. Father: J. A. Peace. Mother: Ada Higginbotham. Source: *Canton Telephone*, December 19, 1890.

Peace, Baby
Born: Unknown. Died: May 25, 1888. Cause of death: Whooping cough. Father: J. A. Peace. Mother: Ada Higginbotham. Source: *Canton Telephone*, May 25, 1888.

Pennington, Baby
Born: Unknown. Died: March 1885. Father: Cap Pennington. Mother: Unknown. Source: *Texan-Telephone*, March 7, 1885.

Perry, Mrs. J.N.
Born: Unknown. Died: March 1900. Cause of death: Congestion. Married: J. N. Perry. Father: Unknown. Mother: Unknown. Source: *Free State Enterprise*, March 29, 1900.

Phelps, Charles
Born: Unknown. Died: June 1915. Cause of death: Gunshot wounds. Father: John Phelps. Mother: Unknown. Comments: The *Wills Point Chronicle* reported Charles Phelps' death as follows: "The boy, Charlie by name, about 10 or 12 years old, had been out with a small rifle and upon returning to the house endeavored to hang the weapon on a nail near the door. The gun was loaded and in some way was discharged, the ball striking him in the left breast and ranging downward." The family was living in the Starr Community at the time of Charlie's death. Source: *Wills Point Chronicle*, June 24, 1915.

Phillips, Rosa
Born: ca 1893. Died: December 12, 1900. Cause of death: Paralysis. Father: John Walter Phillips. Mother: Alice Chaney Bateman. Siblings: Bertha Lee, Dora, Ida Estelle, William Walter, John Henry, Lovie, Orville, James Edward, and J. B. Comments: John and Alice Phillips were living in the Willow Spring Community when their daughter died. Source: *Free State Enterprise*, December 20, 1900.

Phillips, Susan Darlene
Born: December 5, 1950. Died: January 1, 1977. Cause of death: Homicide, body found May 7, 1980. Married: (1) Michael Royce Whitlock. Child: Michael Royce. (2) Unknown Hendricks. Child: Donny Paul. (3) Billy Ray Phillips. Child: Russell Maurice. Father: Edwin T. Barnes. Mother: Lavada Gregg. Comments: The death of Susan Darlene Phillips is a story of tragic proportions. The trouble started when she disappeared on New Year's Eve night, December 31, 1976. At that time she was living on Rt. 8, Tyler, Texas, and was nine months pregnant. Susan had been missing for over three years when her remains and the remains of her unborn child were found May 7, 1980. They were discovered in a locked car trunk submerged in the Trinity River. She had been shot at the base of her skull. There was a prime suspect being held on unrelated charges in the Van Zandt County Jail, and he had notified officers of the location of her body. Billy Ray Phillips was initially a suspect; but when the police went to interview him, he was missing from his home. About two weeks after Susan's body was found, it was determined that he had been murdered and his body dumped in "Fisher's Pond" on a farm in Gregg County. One of Susan's children reported that no one was ever tried and convicted of these murders because of insufficient evidence. Van Zandt County authorities made arrangements for Susan to be buried in Hillcrest Cemetery. Billy Ray Phillips was buried in the Meredith Camp Ground Cemetery in Henderson County, Texas. The children were reared by family members. Sources: *The Gladewater Mirror*, February 3, 1977; *Canton Herald*, May 15, 1980 and May 22, 1980; Eubank Funeral Home Records; Interview with Russell M. Phillips, son of Billy Ray and Susan Phillips; February 26, 2016.

Pompey, Martin
Born: Unknown. Died: November 1920. Cause of death: Tree fell on him. Father: Unknown Pompey. Mother: Unknown. Comments: Martin Pompey was a Mexican national who had been living in Van Zandt County for a number of years. He supervised a crew of wood cutters. He was killed at a wood camp on W. P. Wallace's farm when a tree fell on him. Martin worked on the Sanger Bros. farm, a large commercial operation near Canton, Texas, before he was engaged as a wood cutter for Wallace. Source: *Canton Herald*, December 3, 1920.

R

Red, Minnie L.
Born: ca 1890. Died: June 21, 1922, Van Zandt County, Texas. Cause of death: Heart disease. Married: Rev. James Lafayette Red. Children: Artie May, Alma Louise, Minnie Ellen and four stepchildren. Father: Homer Long, Smith County, Texas. Mother: Sarah Artillssa Murl. Comments: Minnie Red's husband was the pastor

of the Methodist Church in Canton at the time of her death. Sources: Death Certificate; *Canton Herald*, June 30, 1922.

Reese, J.C.
Born: ca 1915. Died: September 1920. Cause of death: Bright's disease. Father: Dolphus Reese. Mother: Unknown. Source: *Canton Herald*, October 1, 1920.

Riggs, Mamie
Born: March 4, 1882, Mississippi. Died: January 3, 1957. Married: (1) Albert Fitzgerald. (2) Earnest Riggs. Father: Jerry Fitzgerald. Mother: Lena Ladd. Occupation: Hotel cook. Comments: Mamie Riggs had one son and one daughter. Sources: 1930 U.S. Census; Eubank Funeral Home records; Vanessa Scott, Wynne Community historian.

Robertson, "Old Man"
Born: Unknown. Died: June 1891. Cause of death: Old age. Father: Unknown Robertson. Mother: Unknown. Source: *Canton Telephone*, June 19, 1891.

Roe, Mrs. Harry
Born: Unknown. Died: September 1900. Married: Harry Roe. Father: Unknown. Mother: Unknown. Comments: Mrs. Roe left a husband and an infant girl. Source: *Free State Enterprise*, September 13, 1900.

Ross, Jim
Born: October 18, 1812, Tennessee (slave). Died: January 1916, Van Zandt County, Texas. Married: Priscilla Ross. Children: Jobe, Ula, Maura, Willie, Robert, and Frank. Father: Unknown Ross. Mother: Unknown. Occupation: Farmer. Comments: Jim Ross came to Texas in 1865. He settled at Myrtle Springs in 1871 and became well known all over the county. He had been a member of the Baptist Church for about sixty years. Jim and Priscilla had thirteen children—five boys and eight girls. Sources: 1910 U. S. Census; *Canton Herald*, January 14, 1916.

Ross, Richard
Born: January 2, 1883, Smith County, Texas. Died: January 4, 1943, Van Zandt County, Texas. Cause of death: Pneumonia. Married: Annie Belle Vernor, May 20, 1922. Father: Bato Ross, Smith County, Texas. Mother: Unknown. Occupation: Farmer. Sources: Death Certificate, 1940 U. S. Census, Eubank Funeral Home records.

Rowland, Lanis Leslie
Born: November 30, 1888, Lamar County, Texas. Died: May 12, 1953, Van Zandt County, Texas. Cause of death: Heart disease. Married: Margaret Rowland. Father: Willis D. Rowland, Kentucky. Mother: Victoria Page, Missouri. Children: Mrs. Leonard Harris, Mrs. L. J. Felty, Mrs. C. A. Groves, Mrs. Joe Coffer, and Rex. Occupation: Manager, Southern Ice Company, Dallas, Texas. Sources: Death Certificate, Hilliard and Sons Funeral Home record.

Russell, Ben F.
Born: 1860, Van Zandt County, Texas. Died: September 1892, Van Zandt County, Texas. Married: Fannie White. Father: David Russell. Mother: Phoeby Russell. Occupation: Farmer. Comments: Ben Russell's family was in Van Zandt County by 1854. His parents, wife, and two children survived him. Sources: *Texas Select County Marriages Index, 1837-1977*; *Canton Telephone*, September 9, 1892; Ancestry.com.

Russell, David
Born: ca 1819. Died: September 4, 1893. Cause of death: Apoplexy. Married: Phoeby Unknown. Father: Unknown Russell. Mother: Unknown. Occupation: Farmer. Comments: David Russell was living in Texas by 1850 and was in Van Zandt County by 1854. He was involved in the early development of the county. During the Civil War, David was responsible for acquiring Confederate uniforms for the volunteers of Whetstone's Company when it was formed in Van Zandt County. In 1863, the County Commissioners entrusted him to handle part of the Court's appropriations to provide for Confederate soldier's wives and children In 1864-65 he served as a County Commissioner. In 1887 he helped establish the Primitive Baptist Church in Canton. Sources: *Van Zandt County Court Minutes, Volumes A, B, & C*; *Canton Telephone*, September 8, 1893.

Russell, Phoeby
Born: ca 1819, Tennessee. Died: August 1901, Van Zandt County, Texas. Married: David Russell. Father: Unknown. Mother: Unknown. Comments: The Russell family lived in Van Zandt County for more than fifty years and had at least six children. Source: *Wills Point Chronicle*, August 29, 1901.

S

Scates, Alford
Born: August 20, 1900. Died: September 24, 1938. Married: Lucille Williams. Father: Henry Scates. Mother: Martha Gray. Comments: Alford Scates' wife died October 9, 1982 and is buried in Haven of Memories Memorial Park, Canton, Texas. Source: Eubank Funeral Home records.

ANGELINA JOHNSON SCATES *was born into slavery in Jackson County, Alabama in 1853. Sometime after the Civil War, she moved into a settlement of Freedmen near Canton, married Sam S. Scates, and they raised six children. Angelina became one of the first Black teachers in Van Zandt County and taught at one of the first Black schools in the county, established by her husband.*

Martha Jane Stanford

SCATES, ANGELINA
Born: August 27, 1853 (52), Jackson County, Alabama (slave). Died: June 6, 1919, Van Zandt County, Texas. Cause of death: Heart failure. Married: Sam S. Scates, 1873. Children: Prena, Martin, Bob, Riley S., and Jerry. Father: Isaac Johnson, North Carolina. Mother: unknown. Occupation: Teacher, farm worker. Comments: Angelina Scates was born a slave in Alabama and moved into a settlement of Freedmen near Canton sometime after the Civil War. The *Canton Herald* reported her death as follows: "Death of Respected Negro Woman" Friends, white and colored, were grieved Saturday morning, on learning that 'Aunt' Angelina Scates, in the negro settlement just north of Canton, had died suddenly Friday night. Her Children were in town rather late that night and when they got home found their mother had passed away during their absence. She had gone to bed and they found some simple remedies near, indicating that she was feeling badly and had put the medicine near for relief, without avail. Funeral services were conducted Saturday afternoon by a preacher of her race, burial being in the negro division of Canton cemetery. There was a large attendance of negroes, and a number of white people. 'Aunt' Angelina was an eccentric character. A good many years ago she built in her yard a mud railroad, and delighted to talk about it to white visitors. She was one of the first black teachers in Van Zandt County and talked intelligently upon various subjects, speaking often in rhymes of herself and what she had done. Her brother, J. W. Johnson, at Wills Point furnishes the following information in regard to her life: Her maiden name was Johnson and she was born in Jackson County, Alabama on August 27, 1852, passing away June 6, 1919. She is survived by six children, three daughters and three sons, and the brother mentioned. She joined the Methodist church when she was very young and lived as a consistent Christian until called from the walls of the living." Angelina's husband Sam established one of the first Black schools in the county. She was a teacher in that school. Sources: Death Certificate; 1880, 1900, 1910 U. S. Census; *Canton Herald*, June 13, 1919.

SCATES, HENRY
Born: Unknown. Died: January 24, 1917. Married: Martha Gray. Father: Unknown Scates. Mother: Unknown. Source: *Canton Herald*, February 2, 1917.

SCATES, MINNIE BELL
(Photo page 194) Born: March 4, 1899. Died: September 9, 1969. Married: Jerry Scates, December 6, 1922. Father: Zee Bell. Mother: Polly Williams. Comments: Minnie Scates was found dead. Cause of death was listed as "Unknown" on the Death Certificate. Oscar Bell was the informant on the Death Certificate. Source: Death Certificate.

SCATES, WILLIE RUTH
Born: January 22, 1943. Died: April 1945. Father: Unknown. Mother: Lucille Williams. Source: Texas Birth Index, 1903-1997; Eubank Funeral Home records.

SMITH, PAUL L.
Born: September 22, 1920, Tarrant County, Texas. Died: June 18, 1937, Van Zandt County, Texas. Cause of death: Influenza. Father: Unknown Smith. Mother: Eva Mathis, Wood County, Texas. Sources: Death Certificate, Eubank Funeral Home records.

Stanford, Martha Jane
(Photo page 193) Born: March 13, 1836, Quitman County, Georgia. Died: September 25, 1886. Married: Dr. William Johnathan Stanford, May 26, 1858. Children: Ada, Dorothy Ann, Mary C., Ross, Paul, John W., Claud Leonidas, Roxie Victoria, Thomas F., Homer Guilford, Mattie E., and Albert. Father: Colson Guilford. Mother: Cycie Mann. Source: Find A Grave.

Starkey, Fannie
Born: ca 1908. Died; July 1912. Father: W. H. Starkey. Mother: Unknown. Source: *Wills Point Chronicle*, July 18, 1912.

Stewart, Mrs.
Born: Unknown. Died: November 1884. Married: Unknown Stewart. Father: Unknown. Mother: Unknown. Source: *Texan-Telephone*, November 15, 1884.

Stoudenmire, Fannie K.
Born: August 13, 1872, Mississippi. Died: December 16, 1951, Van Zandt County, Texas. Cause of death: Heart disease. Married: (1) Unknown Layton. (2) Jessie Smith, March 26, 1925. (3) W. J. N. Stoudenmire, November 15, 1931. Father: Joe Mency, Georgia. Mother: Matilda Mills, Mississippi. Comments: Fannie K. Stoudenmire's second husband, Jesse Smith, died in 1929 and was buried in Hillcrest Cemetery. She later married, W J. N Stoudenmire, a cotton buyer from Wills Point. He died in 1942 and is buried in White Rose Cemetery in Wills Point. Fannie is believed to be buried next to Jessie Smith in Hillcrest Cemetery. Sources: Death Certificate; *Marriage Records, Van Zandt County Texas 1909-1931*; *Canton Herald*, November 20, 1931; Hilliard & Sons Funeral Home records.

Minnie Bell Scates

Strickland, Cynthia
Born: ca 1854, Van Zandt County, Texas. Died: December 1, 1884, Van Zandt County, Texas. Married: Michael J. "Doc" Strickland, November 13, 1873. Child: Lula Lee. Father: Curtis B. Moore. Mother: Francis (Sarah J.) Robertson. Comments: Cynthia Moore was born in the Moore community of Van Zandt County which was named after her grandfather, James Moore. In the 1860 Census at the age of 6 she was living with her aunt and uncle, Sol and Susan Carter. Cynthia's marriage to Michael was very contentious. The couple separated from time to time, and Cynthia filed for divorce March 4, 1884 charging extreme cruelty. She died before the divorce was final; and the case was dismissed April 7, 1885 because of her death. It is not known what became of Cynthia's daughter, Lula Lee. Michael married and divorced three more times. He died in 1928 and is buried in Smith County, Texas. Sources: *Van Zandt County History Book*; *Divorce Records of Van Zandt County*; *Texan-Telephone,* December 6, 1884.

Sudduth, Debbie Sophronia
Born: August 11, 1851, Smith County, Texas. Died: August 29, 1940, Van Zandt County, Texas. Cause of death: Colitis. Married: D. D. Sudduth. Divorced: April 18, 1906. Father: William Woods. Mother: Unknown. Comments: Debbie Sudduth's husband D. D. was involved in a shooting in Van Zandt County on April 15, 1901. He shot and killed J. C. Stewart at the latter's home in south Canton. The weapon used was a 41 Colt six shooter. The *Free State Enterprise* reported the following: "The facts in the case are about like this. It seems that Sudduth, and an advanced agent for the Hagg's show by the name of Charles Fanora, went up to the home of the deceased to kidnap Annett, the deceased's daughter, for purposes better known to Sudduth and Fanora. The sheriff, Cicero Rusk, and a deputy, Will Gentry, ran Sudduth and Fanora off. Sudduth returned later and in a confrontation the deceased shot at Sudduth and missed, where upon

Monroe Lafayette "Fate" Sumner *came to Van Zandt County in 1857 with his three children after the death of his first wife. He opened a retail liquor business on the west side of the Canton Town Square and married Martha Jane Burns, the younger sister of his first wife. Sumner was a staunch Unionist; and when the Civil War started, he refused to join the Confederate cause. He enlisted at Little Rock, Arkansas on July 12, 1864 and served in the Union Army until June 25, 1865. After the War, he returned to Van Zandt County and opened a mercantile store and saloon in Jordan's Saline, the first county seat of Van Zandt County. Radical elements of ex-Confederates and outlaws from other areas of the state came to the settlement, creating trouble with the Unionists and newly freed Blacks, and terrorizing the citizens. They robbed and plundered Sumner's store, beat his clerk, and burned his establishment to the ground. The town's doctor was killed, and his head was cut off and hung up as a warning to other Union supporters. Sumner then moved to Canton and was appointed County Treasurer by the Reconstruction Government and served from 1866 until 1870. He later become a Constable, District Court Bailiff, Deputy Sheriff, and Jailer. He died in 1909.*

Sudduth fired and struck Stewart in the right breast killing him. D. D. was arrested for murder and taken to jail." Debbie filed for divorce, and it was granted April 18, 1906. D. D. left Canton and moved to Arkansas to live with relatives. He died in 1919 in Arkansas. Sources: Death Certificate; *Free State Enterprise*, April 18, 1901; *The Canton Herald*, June 20, 1919; Hilliard & Sons Funeral Home records.

Sumner, Monroe Lafayette "Fate"

Born: December 1824, Hardin County, Tennessee. Died: May 22, 1909, Van Zandt County, Texas. Married: (1) Lurana Burns ca 1850. Children: William M. and Martha Amanda. (2) Martha Jane Burns, May 22, 1859. Children: Canzady L., Sarah C., James Monroe, Benjamin Franklin, and Fannie. (3) Martha (Mattie) Ann Davis Eads, December 9, 1897. Divorced: Mattie Sumner listed on the 1900 census as divorced. Father: Moses N. Sumner. Mother: Lucinda F. Caviness. Occupation: Farmer, merchant, politician. Military: Union, Pvt. Co. I, 4th Reg't. Arkansas Calvary. Comments: Fate Sumner came to Van Zandt County in 1857 with his three children after the death of his first wife. In May of 1857 he received a license to retail liquor from the county government. He established his business in a house in Canton on Lot 10 on the west side of the town square. In May 1859 he married Martha Jane Burns, the younger sister of his first wife, Lurana. Sumner was staunch Unionist; and when the Civil War started, he refused to join the Confederate cause. At the beginning of the War, the age limit for the Confederate draft was from 18 to 35. In 1864 the age limit was extended to 42 which meant that he was no longer exempt. He enlisted at Little Rock, Arkansas on July 12, 1864 and served in the Union Army until June 25, 1865. At the time of enlistment the Army records show that he was 40 years old, 5'5' inches in height, dark complexion, blue eyes and brown hair. After returning to Van Zandt County, he opened a mercantile store and saloon in Jordan's Saline, the first county seat of Van Zandt County. Radical elements of ex-Confederates and outlaws from other areas of the state came to the settlement, created trouble with the Unionists and newly freed Blacks, and terrorized the citizens. They robbed and plundered Sumner's store, beat his clerk senseless, and burned his establishment to the ground. The town's doctor was killed, and his head was cut off and hung up as a warning to other Union supporters. Sumner moved to Canton and was appointed County Treasurer by the Reconstruction Government and served from 1866 until 1870. He later become a Constable, District Court Bailiff, Deputy Sheriff, and Jailer. After his county service, he owned a grist mill and a saw mill in Canton. The only record of his death was reported by the Grand Saline Sun as follows: "Messrs W.J. and Tom Staton of Grand Saline, stopped in our community Sunday, on their way to attend the funeral of Uncle Fate Sumner at Canton." Sources: 1900 Census; *Civil War Records of Van Zandt County*; *Union Soldiers Civil War Records*; *Grand Saline Sun*, May 27, 1909; Ancestry.com.

T

Terry, Daughter

Born: Unknown. Died: October 1915. Father: Milton Terry. Mother: Unknown Terry. Source: The *Canton Herald*, October 8, 1915.

Thames, Mrs. T.T.

Born: Unknown. Died: January 1887. Married: T. T. Thames. Father: Unknown. Mother: Unknown. Comments: T. T. Thames was a local businessman. Mrs. Thames was an invalid for several years. At her death, she was survived by her husband and six children. Source: *Canton Telephone*, January 21, 1887.

Thomas, Mr.

Born: Unknown. Died: April 1894, Van Zandt County. Father: Unknown Thomas. Mother: Unknown. Comments: Mr. Thomas had recently come from Alabama. His father arrived a day or two prior to his son's death. Source: *Wills Point Chronicle*, April 19, 1894.

Thompson, Allen Fletcher

Born: 1858. Died: March 1889. Cause of death: Slow fever. Father: Allen Thompson. Mother: Elvira Bickerstaff. Comments: Allen Thompson died at the home of his brother, Tull Thompson. Source: *Canton Telephone*, March 15, 1889.

Thompson, Child

Born: Unknown. Died: December 1887. Father: J. T. Thompson. Mother: A. E. McCauley. Source: *Canton Telephone*, December 2, 1887.

Thompson, Mollie

Born: Unknown. Died: March 26, 1886. Married: R. B. Thompson, December 28, 1884. Father: Unknown Bates. Mother: Unknown. Comments: Mollie Thompson and her 9-day-old child died the same day. R. B. Thompson subsequently married Rhoda Sherbert, October 8, 1905. Source: *Canton Telephone*, April 3, 1886.

Tumlinson, Cora Merles

Born: Unknown. Died: October 1894. Cause of death: Erysipelas. Father: David Kaufman Tumlinson. Mother: Laura Calhoun. Comments: The *Canton Telephone* reported Cora Tumlinson's death as follows: "The *Telephone* is pained to chronicle the death of Cora Merles, the sweet little daughter of Mr. and Mrs. D. K. Tumlinson, which sad event occurred Wednesday evening at 5 o'clock after several days of intense suffering from fever and erysipelas." Source: *Canton Telephone*, October 5, 1894.

V

Valentine, James E.

Born: Unknown. Died: October 1916. Married: Mary Burrow. Father: Unknown Valentine. Mother: Unknown. Comments: The *Canton Herald* reported the death of James E. Valentine as follows: "Mr. J. E. Valentine, an old resident of Canton, died very suddenly Monday Morning at about 7 o'clock at the home of his son, J. P. Valentine. He had been in feeble health for many days, but the news of his death was a great shock to the many friends of the town and surrounding country. The deceased has made his home with his son here for many years and is known throughout the county, and the many friends will be sad to learn of his death. He was a consistent member of the Baptist Church and a Masonic lodge. The funeral was held at Canton cemetery Tuesday morning at 10 o'clock, and services being conducted by the members of the Masonic lodge. Just one year ago, while the institute was in session, a grandson of the deceased, Murray Valentine was brought here from San Benito and buried in the Canton cemetery." Source: *Canton Herald*, October 13, 1916.

Valentine, Murray Lockhart

Born: September 27, 1895. Died: October 1915. Cause of death: Automobile accident. Father: James P. Valentine. Mother: Azilla House. Siblings: Timothy, Zilla, Clark, John Leslie, Hardy W., James, John, Mary, and Kathleen. Comments: The *Canton Herald* reported Murray Valentine's death as follows; "Murray Lockhart Valentine was twenty years old the 27th day of last month. He held the responsible position of bookkeeper for a well-known mercantile firm at San Benito, in South Texas, and at the time of the horrible accident which resulted in his death. He was in a local garage cranking a Ford car for a friend of his already in the machine, as they had planned to make a short visit into the country. As related to a *Herald* reporter, the party in the car did not clearly understand the manipulation of same and at the time the engine started his foot happened to be pressing the wrong object, the quick result being that the car plunged forward instantly pinning the unfortunate boy against the wall, with a shelf attached to it with such force that injuries were sustained from which he could never recover. His father and step-mother, Mr. and Mrs. J. P. Valentine, and one sister, Miss Kathleen, reside in Canton, while three brothers also

MURRAY LOCKHART VALENTINE *was a 20-year-old bookkeeper for a mercantile firm in San Benito when he was killed in an automobile accident. He and a friend were planning to take a short drive out into the countryside. His friend was "already in the machine," as the newspaper reported, and Valentine was working the crank in the front. But the friend's knowledge of the car was limited. When the car started, the friend inadvertently pressed on the gas pedal instead of the brake. The car plunged forward and pinned Mr. Valentine to the wall, resulting in fatal injuries.*

survive him. Roger Valentine living in the town of Benito where the tragedy occurred. Leslie Valentine being a salesman for Swift & Co., in San Antonio and Tim Valentine being a valued employee of the Ford Motor Co., in Houston." Source: *Canton Herald*, October 15, 1915.

W

WALDRON, ELIZABETH
Born: Unknown. Died: January 1886. Married: William Samuel Waldron, August 7, 1870. Father: Unknown Clay. Mother: Unknown. Source: *Texan-Telephone*, January 23, 1886.

WALDRON, MARY ELIZABETH "BETTIE"
Born: November 1844. Died: February 11, 1916. Married: (1) John Marion Heald, ca 1864. (2) William Samuel Waldron, August 8, 1886. Father: Robert Hughes. Mother: Lavinia Whitehead. Comments: Mary Waldron lived in Van Zandt County for over thirty years. Her first husband was a Confederate soldier. He died about 1884 and is buried in the Palestine City Cemetery, Palestine, Anderson County. Texas. Mary and John Heald had ten children. Source: Canton Herald, February 18, 1916.

WALKER, HANNA CATHERN
Born: June 1843, Warren County, Tennessee, Died: November 23, 1924, Van Zandt County, Texas. Married: Francis Marion Walker, February 8, 1866. Children: Georgia Ann and Margaret Jane. Father: George William Martin. Mother: Mary Elizabeth Forest. Comments: Hanna Walker's husband had served in the Confederate Army. He died October 1, 1892, and was buried in the Canton Cemetery (Hillcrest Cemetery). She applied for a Widow's Pension on August 3, 1911 while living in Canton, Texas. She was 68 years old at the time and had lived in Texas 57 years. Hanna is believed to be buried beside her husband. Sources: *Civil War Veterans of Van Zandt County*, Find A Grave.

WARD, JAMES
Born: Unknown. Died: March 16, 1889. Cause of death: Pneumonia. Father: Unknown Ward. Mother: Unknown. Source: *Canton Telephone*, March 22, 1889.

WEATHERALL, BABY BOY
Born: ca December 1905. Died: August 1906. Father: Charles L. Weatherall. Mother: Martha Jane Rogers. Siblings: Earnest, Dora N., Margaret, Alva, Thomas D., and Bailey. Source: *Wills Point Chronicle*, August 9, 1906.

WILSON, J.D. JR.
Born: May 31, 1945. Died: February 2, 1946. Father: J. D. Wilson, Sr., Rusk County, Texas. Mother: Morine Thompson, Smith County, Texas. Source: Eubank Funeral Home records.

WINN, EMMA
Born: Unknown. Died: November 1901. Cause of Death: Murdered. Father: Unknown. Mother: Unknown. Comments: The *Wills Point Chronicle* reported Emma Winn's death as follows: "Last Monday between 11 and 12 o'clock at Canton, Emma Winn was shot and instantly killed by Tom Hubbard, both parties being colored. After the shooting Hubbard left in haste but Sheriff Rusk and several others went in pursuit and about 1 o'clock captured him two miles north of town and placed him in jail. The grand jury, then in session, found a bill against him and his case is set for trial today, Thursday. The court appointed M. G. Sanders and Alex Collins to defend him and Lively & Stanford and J. A. Germany to assist them. If the case goes to trial and Hubbard gets his dues it will be a shining example to such characters. The particulars of

the killing obtained from the deceased's mother, who was an eye witness, were about as follows: "We were washing at the wash place north of town when Hubbard came up. He told Emma that when he was sick she had wished that he would go blind. She denied this. He then demanded that she return the money and clothing he claimed to have given her. She told him she could not return the money, but would give back the clothes. One word brought on another till he pulled his pistol and began firing. Five shots were fired, three taking effect, two in the breast and one in the neck. She ran when he began shooting and he followed continuing to shoot after she had fallen. She was killed instantly." Hubbard was convicted and sentenced to ninety-nine years in the Texas State Penitentiary at Huntsville, Texas. He was pardoned by the Governor of Texas and released in 1922. Sources: *Huntsville State Prison Records*; *Wills Point Chronicle*, November 7, 1901.

Elizabeth "Betty" Wortham

The Wortham Hotel owned by Betty Wortham

WOMACK, B.S.
Born: Ca 1869. Died: July 17, 1900. Father: Unknown Womack. Mother: Unknown. Comments: The following article was published in The Van Zandt County Genealogy Society's quarterly, *Our Heritage*: "Tuesday evening, some travelers came through our town. Just as they were passing Dr. W.O. William's residence, Mr. Womack, a young man about 25 years of age, died suddenly of hernia. His remains were buried that night in the Canton Cemetery. The unfortunate young man had been sick about three weeks and was being carried from Harris County to his home in Grayson County." An article in *The Dallas Morning News*, reported that Mr. B. S. Womack, age 31, died in a wagon. The article also noted that Womack had been living with a sister, Mrs. John McWalters at Huffman, Harris County, and they were moving to Grayson, County, where he had another sister. Sources: *Our Heritage*, November 2000; *The Dallas Morning News*, July, 19. 1900.

WORTHAM, ELIZABETH "BETTY"
Born: Unknown. Died: August 1899. Cause of death: Stomach congestion. Married: C. A. Wortham. Father: Unknown. Mother: Unknown. Comments: Elizabeth Wortham was the owner of the Wortham Hotel on the square in Canton, Texas. Source: *Free State Enterprise*, August 10, 1899.

WORTHAM, INFANT
Born: Unknown. Died: August 1899. Father: C. A. Wortham. Mother: Elizabeth Wortham. Source: *Free State Enterprise*, August 10, 1899.

WRIGHT, JEFF DAVIS
Born: March 28, 1863, Texas. Died: August 12, 1881, Van Zandt County, Texas. Father: Dr. James Durham Wright, Kentucky. Mother: Delilah Manning, Ohio. Comments: Dr. James D. Wright came to what would become Van Zandt County in 1846. He helped establish the county, being the first District Clerk. When Canton was laid out in 1850, he moved there and was the first doctor. In 1861 he moved to Erath County and later to Comanche County. He died there in 1890. Jeff Wright, his son, was visiting his grandmother, Martha Manning, in Van Zandt County. He became ill and died. It is believed that he was buried close to his grandfather, Milo Manning. Jeff's parents are buried in the Oakwood Cemetery in Comanche, Texas. Sources: Obituary in an unnamed newspaper; Shirley Barrall, Wright Family historian.

WYNNE, ANNIE M.
Born: February 10, 1856 (slave). Died: June 24, 1930. Married: (1) J. S. Priesley, March 4, 1877. (2) Edmond A. Wynne, May 10, 1896. Father: Thomas M. Mathes, Sr. Mother: Unknown. Comments: Annie Wynne's father was a Freedman. He was one of the original settlers who became a large land owner in what became the Wynne Community near Canton, Texas. Annie was the third wife of Edmond A. Wynne, the namesake of the Wynne Community. Source: Death Certificate.

Y

YANTIS, BABY
Born: Unknown. Died: September 1895. Father: T.R. Yantis. Mother: Belle Riley. Source: *Wills Point Chronicle*, September 19, 1895.

YANTIS, RALPH
Born: 1904. Died: July 1912. Father: T. R. Yantis. Mother: Belle Riley. Comments: Ralph Yantis' father was a lawyer and a former County Judge. Source: *Grand Saline Sun*, August 1, 1912.

REMEMBERING MILITARY SERVICE

'Tis Sweet to be Remembered

Military Veterans of Canton's Hillcrest Cemetery

To everything there is a season,
and a time to every purpose under the heaven:

A time to be born, and a time to die;
A time to plant, and a time to pluck up that which is planted.

A time to kill, and a time to heal;
A time to break down, and a time to build up.

A time to weep, and a time to laugh;
A time to mourn, and a time to dance.

A time to cast away stones, and a time to gather stones together;
A time to embrace, and a time to refrain from embracing.

A time to get, and a time to lose;
A time to keep, and a time to cast away.

A time to rend, and a time to sew;
A time to keep silence, and a time to speak.

A time to love, and a time to hate;
A time of war, and a time of peace.

Ecclesiastes 3:1–8

U.S. Veterans

Mexican-American War
Compton, Simpson Patrick

Spanish-American War
Hale, Walter L.
Mills, Edward Hughes

World War I
Castle, Sam
Cornelius, Owen C.
Cornelius, Thomas G.
Dawson, Frank Albert
Dodson, James Frank
Fitzgerald, Perry
Flatt, James Arthur
Gabbert, Wesson B.
Haynes, William Francis "Bill"
Hilliard, George Homer, Sr.
Hilliard, Dr. Horace Hampton
Jones, Charlie Lee
Lewis, Frank McCoy
Moore, Dee Otis
Perry, Howard Carnelus
Prestley, Rufus
Riley, Charles Pendleton "Charlie"
Ross, Clinton "Clint"
Scates, Jerry
Shannon, Buck
Todd, Henry Grady "Buck"
Ward, Henry Cozelle
Weatherall, Ernest R.
Whitaker, Ernest Glen
Wisenteiner, Herman Francis
Wynne, James Henry "Jim"
Wynne, Joseph E. "Uncle Bud"
Yantis, Robert Hobbs

World War II
Bateman, Norman V.
Bowles, John Wesley
Brewer, John Harold (KIA)
Brown, Ed
Cox, Lee
Galloway, Francis Orman "Shorty"
Gamel, Melvin Lawrence
Griser, Jesse Daryl
Haynes, William Francis "Bill"
Heddins, Lettrial
Hilliard, Dr. George Homer, Jr.
Hilliard, Samuel Foster, Jr. "Sam"
Jones, Bonteel
Knox, Wallace Austin
Loughmiller, Richard Leon
Manasco, Sam
Moore, James Elmer
Morris, Maston Alford "Buster"
Nichols, D. W.
Redmon, Harold
Roberts, Theodore E.
Robertson, John Porter
Sambel, Walter William
Shaw, Dave
Shaw, Douglas, Jr.
Sides, Billy Gene
Slaughter, John W.
Slaughter, Dr. Manuel Owen "Jim"
Smith, Dr. Edgar Eugene
Stanford, Claud Leonidas "C. L."
Sumner, Laymon Lewis
Weaver, Calvin Franklin

Korean War
Branson, Jimmy Wilson
Moore, James Elmer
Phillips, William Robert "Billy"
Stanford, Claud Leonidas "C.L."
Starnes, Weldon F.

Vietnam War
Gamel, Johnny Lyman

Peacetime Veterans
Fitzgerald, Curtis "Tinker"
Fitzgerald, Jessie Henry
Galloway, Francis Orman, Jr.
Harris, Johnnie Ray
Shaw, Donnel
Walker, Scott

National Guard
Cox, Casey Lee

Civil War Soldiers

Union Army
Cox, Richard
Sumner, Monroe Lafayette "Fate"
Tyson, John Henry
Utts, Jacob J. "Major"
Warren, Joseph W.

Confederate Army
Alexander, Wiley Percy
Arendell, Jesse H.
Branson, James B.
Chaney, Thomas Washington
Chappell, Mastin
Clark, William Thomas
Compton, Simpson Patrick
Davidson, Leaston "Lete"
Eads, William Alexander
Ford, Howell Elmore
Foster, Thomas Jones, Sr. "Judge"
Gill, John T.
Gilmore, Wiley Coleman
Gossett, James P. "J. P."
Graham, Calvin B., Sr. (Enrolling Officer)
Hale, Willis Jarrell
Hall, John H.
Hurst, Joel Evans
Knox, W. M.
Matthews, Dr. James
McCarty, Benjamin F.
McClellen, Robert J.
Mills, James Harvey
Patterson, James Duncan
Prier, William Cats
Riley, David Love, Jr.
Samples, J. F.
Sanders, Jefferson H.
Spears, Lucius Mack
Stanford, Dr. William J.
Thompson, Allen
Thompson, Capt. William D.
Towles, Capt. Thomas Jefferson
Tull, George Washington, Sr.
Valentine, J. E.
Walker, Francis Marion
White, William Franklin
Wilhite, John Harden
Williams, Richard "Dick"
Williams, Dr. William Oscar
Youngblood, James Marion

RESEARCH & SOURCES

Our Research

When we were selected to be historians for The Hillcrest Cemetery Restoration project because of our affiliation with the Van Zandt County Historical Commission and our long-time membership with the Van Zandt County Genealogical Society, our initial intent was to develop a basic history of the Cemetery. But when we started looking for records of burials in the cemetery, we found none, other than the Cemetery survey books compiled by the local genealogical society. These books provided only names and birth and death dates. We could find no histories of these individuals. And sadly, most were far removed from the collective memories of even the most aged of Canton citizens.

But because we became so curious about these people and their stories, we got busy. With decades of genealogical research between the two of us, we initially thought it would be fairly easy to find the information we were looking for. We were wrong. Over 500 of these unfortunate souls had died before 1930; and out of that number, 280 had died before 1900. Working only with the name and dates on these old tombstones and using traditional methods of research looking for information on someone that died over one hundred years ago would have been fruitless much of the time. We used the traditional sources and the Internet; but we also had to rely heavily on the less used methods of research through newspapers, funeral home records, county court minutes, and death certificates.

The local newspapers became our major source of information for individuals who died after1884. From these newspapers we extracted death notices, obituaries, biographical sketches, wedding announcements, business ownerships, political announcements, and stories written every day regarding the activities of citizens of the city and the county. We also researched the Galveston News and the Dallas Weekly Times for coverage of local happenings that occurred in the 1860's and 1870's. At that time, these newspapers had statewide coverage.

We relied heavily on researching the County Court Minutes for individuals who migrated to Van Zandt County prior to 1880. The local road law mandated that all able-bodied males work on road-maintenance crews; and the names of these crews were entered into the Court Minutes. Normally, individuals were placed on these list within six months of entering the county, so we could pinpoint fairly accurately the date of entry. By using these same minutes, we could also determine when an individual was elected to public office, selected for a special committee, or was paid for work performed for the county.

In 1867-69 the federal government mandated that all eligible voters be registered. This list was used in determining age, state of birth, how long an individual had lived in Texas and how long in Van Zandt County. In the early 1870s, each county assessed an occupation tax on individuals who were in business and on practicing professionals. These tax rolls were extremely helpful in determining the specific type of business or work an individual was involved in during that time period.

We knew there were many individuals buried in Hillcrest Cemetery who never had a grave marker, or whose marker had worn away with time. We were determined to bring their stories to light, to bring them the respect they deserved. We identified 169 individuals buried in unmarked graves within Hillcrest Cemetery.

But we also knew there were many individuals buried in Hillcrest Cemetery who never had a grave marker, or whose marker had worn away with time. To us, these individuals were both anonymous and in need of the greatest research and care. We were determined to bring their stories to light, to bring them the respect they deserved, although we knew it would be almost impossible to determine exactly how many unmarked graves were within the Cemetery boundary.

First we searched early Van Zandt County newspapers dating from1884 to 1926 for published death notices. If the death notice mentioned the person was buried in the Canton Cemetery or even in the town of Canton, we noted these. We then searched all complied Van Zandt County funeral home records from 1937 until the present and listed all individuals who were buried in Hillcrest.

By cross checking the marked names against cemetery surveys, we were able to identify about 200 individuals who potentially did not have a tombstone. As a process of elimination, we identified all individuals whose given names were unclear on the death notices and compared death dates with tombstones that had the same last names and eliminated the ones that matched. We then compared death dates on tombstones with the names broken off against dates on the death notices and further eliminated names from the list.

We also searched for death certificates on individuals who had died between 1920 and 1976 and checked for burial place. As a further precaution, we used the website, Find A Grave, to see if the individuals were buried elsewhere in the county. As a final source, we researched the newer Canton cemetery, Haven of Memories Memorial Park, to make certain that the person had not been moved to that. location. Using those methods, we identified 169 individuals buried in unmarked graves within Hillcrest Cemetery

Sources

Adams, Frank Clark. *Texas Democracy, Volume 1. A Centennial History of Politics and Personalities of the Democratic Party, 1836-1936.* Austin, Texas: Democratic Historical Association, 1937.

Allen, Elvis N. *Van Zandt County Court Minutes, Volumes A & B, 1848-1871.* Fruitvale, Texas: Allen Publishing, 2005.

Allen, Elvis N. *Van Zandt County, Texas Court Minutes Volume C, January 30, 1872-January 1, 1881.* Fruitvale, Texas: Allen Publishing, 2002.

Ancestry.com.

Assumed Names Register. County Clerk's Records: Van Zandt County, Texas County Clerk's Office.

Barber, Quana. Sides Family historian.

Barber, Quana, et.al. *Marriage Records Van Zandt County Texas 1848-1908.* Canton, Texas: Van Zandt County Genealogical Society, 1989.

Barber, Quana, et.al. *Marriage Records Van Zandt County Texas 1909-1931.* Canton, Texas: Van Zandt County Genealogical Society, 1993.

Barber, Quana, et.al. *Marriage Records, Van Zandt County Texas 1932-1950.* Canton, Texas: Van Zandt County Genealogical Society, 2002.

Barber, Quana. *Divorce Records of Van Zandt County, Texas, 1848-1920.* Canton, Texas: Van Zandt County Genealogical Society, 2004.

Bartley Funeral Home Records.

Beall, John Bryant Sr. *A History of Edom, Texas*, 1998.

"Britton Progress."

"Canton Herald."

"Canton Telephone."

Carmack, Sharon Debartolo. *Your Guide To Cemetery Research.* Cincinnati, Ohio: Betterway Books, 2002.

Confederate Army Records.

Cook County, Illinois Death Index.

Cook, Mable. *Marriage Records 1848-1909 Van Zandt County, Texas.* Canton, Texas: Van Zandt County Genealogical Society, 1989.

Corbin, Barbara. McCarty Family historian.

Cravy, Dr. Betty Jean Dozier. *Capt. Thomas Smith, CSA, 11th Texas Infantry Company, 1862-1864 and 1854-1856 Diaries.* Hot Springs, Arkansas: Cravy Publishing Company.

Creasey, Sibyl. *1890 in Van Zandt County.* Canton, Texas: Van Zandt County Genealogical Society, 1997.

Creasey, Sibyl. *Civil War Veterans in Van Zandt County, Texas.* Canton, Texas: Van Zandt County Genealogical Society, 2005.

Crouch, Barry and Brice, Donaly E. *Governor's Hounds—The Texas State Police 1870-1873.* Albuquerque, New Mexico: Oakwood Printing, 1989.

Crow, Jan Hinsley. *Ministers of Van Zandt County, Texas, Pastors, Preachers, and Officiants of Weddings and Funerals, Volume 1, A-L.* Canton, Texas: Van Zandt County Genealogical Society, 2015.

"The Dallas Morning News."

"Dallas Weekly Times."

Death Certificates.

"Edgewood Enterprise."

Engledow, Joe. Blackwell Family historian.

Erwin, James and Ivolue Lantrip. Lantrip Family historians.

Eubank Funeral Home Records.

Find A Grave.

Fold 3.

Foster, Dr. Billy Glenn. Dowdle Family historian and Foster Family historian.

"Free State Enterprise."

"Galveston News."

"Gladewater Mirror."

"Grand Saline Sun."

The Handbook of Texas Online.

Hadley, J.M. Tyson Family historian.

Heard, Martha. Heard Family historian.

Heddins, R.J. Heddins Family historian and Helms Family historian.

Hilliard and Son Funeral Home Records.

Hilliard, Cary. Hilliard Family historian.

Hilliard Funeral Home Records.

Hoot, Margaret Scott. Hilliard Family historian.

Hunter, Jane. Ashworth Family historian.

Huntsville State Prison Records.

Johnson, Sid S. *Texans Who Wore The Gray*, 1907.

Manning, Wentworth. *Some History of Van Zandt County*. Winston-Salem, North Carolina: Hunter Publishing Company, 1919.

Mays, Linda. *Reconstruction Records of Van Zandt County, Texas (1867-1874)*. Canton, Texas: The Van Zandt County Genealogical Society, 2008.

McGee, Ruth Mara. *Van Zandt County Pictorial History, 1848-1994*. Canton, Texas: The Van Zandt County Historical Commission, 1994.

McGee, Ruth Mara. *Van Zandt County Texas Histories and Biographies-Volume II*. Wills Point, Texas: Van Zandt County Genealogical Society, 1991.

McKinnon, Tom. Yantis Family historian.

Mills, W. S. *History of Van Zandt County*, 1950.

Mize, Benja Pittman. *Sacred Harp, Minutes of the Central Texas Musical Conventions 1892-1930 plus (1981-1982)*. Canton, Texas: Van Zandt County Genealogical Society, 2014.

Newman Brothers Funeral Home Records.

Phillips, Elizabeth Rasco. Rasco Family historian.

Pierce, Lisa. Pierce Family historian and Rosinbaum Family historian.

Pippin, Ernestine Dove. *Van Zandt County Pensioners and Civil War Veterans*. Canton, Texas: Van Zandt County Genealogical Society, 2005.

Probate Records. County Clerk's Office: Van Zandt County, Texas County Clerk's Office.

Poulan, Shirley Estes. Couth Family historian.

Riley, Foy. Riley Family historian.

Rodriquez, Sylvia. Peace Family historian.

Scott, Vanessa Fitzgerald. Wynne Community historian.

Select Marriage Index, 1837-1865.

The Southland, Volume XII. Waco, Texas 1903.

Tatum, Carol Baskin. Allen Family historian.

"The Texan."

"Texan Telephone."

Texas General Land Office.

Texas Select Marriage Index.

"Texas-Telephone."

Todd, Kevin. Todd Family historian.

"Tyler Morning Telegraph."

Untiedt, Kenneth L., Editor. *Death Lore: Texas Rituals, Superstitions, and Legends Of The Hereafter*. Publications of the Texas Folklore Society LXV. Denton, Texas: University of North Texas Press, 2008.

U. S. Census: 1850, 1860, 1970, 1880, 1900, 1910, 1920, 1930, 1940.

U. S. Social Security Death Index, 1936-2007.

Union Civil War Records.

Van Zandt County History Book Committee. *The History of Van Zandt County, Texas. Wills Point, Texas*. Van Zandt County Genealogical Society, 1984.

Walker, Nell Deets. Sumner Family historian and Walker Family historian.

Wheeler, Kitty. Chaney Family historian.

Wills Point, Texas: Van Zandt County Genealogical Society, 1984.

Vaughn, Cheryl D. *Desperate Characters of Van Zandt County*. Canton, Texas: Cheryl D. Vaughn Publishing, 2004.

Veterans' Affairs Headstone Application.

Wharton, Clarence. *Texas Under Many Flags*. Chicago, Illinois: American Historical Society, 1930.

"Wills Point Chronicle."

"Wills Point Local Chronicle."

Yalon, Marilyn. *The American Resting Place*. Boston, Massachusetts: Houghton Mifflin Company.